LONGMAN LINGUISTICS LIBRARY
Title no 12
PHONETICS IN LINGUISTICS
A BOOK OF READINGS

LONGMAN LINGUISTICS LIBRARY

Title no:

THE LINGUISTIC SCIENCES AND LANGUAGE TEACHING 1
M. A. K. Halliday, Angus McIntosh and Peter Strevens

GENERAL LINGUISTICS 2
AN INTRODUCTORY SURVEY
R. H. Robins

A LINGUISTIC STUDY OF THE ENGLISH VERB 3
F. R. Palmer

IN MEMORY OF J. R. FIRTH 4
Editors: *C. E. Bazell, J. C. Catford, M. A. K. Halliday and R. H. Robins*

PATTERNS OF LANGUAGE 5
PAPERS IN GENERAL
DESCRIPTIVE AND APPLIED LINGUISTICS
Angus McIntosh and M. A. K. Halliday

A SHORT HISTORY OF LINGUISTICS 6
R. H. Robins

SELECTED PAPERS OF J. R. FIRTH 1952-59 7
Editor: *F. R. Palmer*

ESSAYS ON THE ENGLISH LANGUAGE 8
MEDIEVAL AND MODERN
Randolph Quirk

STUDIES IN ENGLISH ADVERBIAL USAGE 9
Sidney Greenbaum

TOWARDS A SEMANTIC DESCRIPTION OF ENGLISH 10
Geoffrey N. Leech

ELICITATION EXPERIMENTS IN ENGLISH 11
LINGUISTIC STUDIES IN USE AND ATTITUDE
Sidney Greenbaum and Randolph Quirk

PHONETICS IN LINGUISTICS 12
A BOOK OF READINGS
W. E. Jones and J. Laver

STRUCTURAL ASPECTS OF LANGUAGE CHANGE 13
James M. Anderson

PHILOSOPHY AND THE NATURE OF LANGUAGE 14
David E. Cooper

SEMANTICO-SYNTAX 15
F. M. P. Liefrink

Phonetics in Linguistics

A book of readings

EDITED BY

W. E. Jones
J. Laver

LONGMAN

LONGMAN GROUP LIMITED LONDON

Associated companies, branches and representatives throughout the world

This Edition © Longman Group Ltd 1973

First published 1973
ISBN 0 582 52451 2

Made and printed in Great Britain by
William Clowes & Sons, Limited, London, Beccles and Colchester

Preface

In selecting the articles in this book of readings in phonetics, we have had chiefly in mind the needs of postgraduate students. We make the assumption that a major part of the teaching effort at the postgraduate level is directed towards communicating the basic attitudes and current philosophy underlying the professional phonetician's approach to his data. In trying to demonstrate and explain these attitudes to our students in Edinburgh, we have found that we make continual reference to a particular body of representative articles, published in a fairly wide range of academic journals.

We thought it would be convenient and interesting to make some of these articles more readily accessible to students, in a book such as this. While a consideration of the needs of postgraduate students in phonetics and linguistics has been foremost in making the collection, we hope that undergraduates might also benefit from it, and that it will be not without interest to phoneticians and linguists themselves, as well as to those more generally interested in language study.

Several criteria were applied: we decided to restrict the choice of authors to those who could be thought of as members of the British school of phonetics; each article had to be seen to have initiated, or to illustrate, a current attitude in an area lying legitimately within the field of phonetics; and lastly, since it was not our intention to offer a historical perspective of the subject, each article had to be of relatively recent date.

There are a number of other collections concerned with more specific areas within the field, such as F. R. Palmer's *Prosodic Analysis* (O.U.P., 1969) and Ilse Lehiste's *Readings in Acoustic Phonetics* (M.I.T. Press, Cambridge, Mass, 1967). The present book is intended to complement such specialized collections, though occasional duplications of certain seminal articles have been unavoidable.

The bringing together of these articles may give some impression of the range and character of British phonetics over the last forty years. We believe that the articles show a homogeneity of attitude and interest that makes it possible to speak meaningfully of a 'British' school of phonetics. The emergence of phonetics as an established academic subject in Britain goes back at least to Henry Sweet, in the late nineteenth century; by 1900 the subject had a widely-accepted name, had its practitioners, and could already provide a set of procedures and techniques for the examination and description of a broad area of linguistic activity.

Sweet, who was Reader in Phonetics at Oxford, published a series of books – *A Handbook of Phonetics* (1877), *A Primer of Phonetics* (1890) and *The Sounds of English* (1907) – in which he demonstrated techniques of analysis which continue to arouse admiration. Sweet is generally regarded as the father of British phonetics, but he himself generously acknowledged his debt to some of his contemporaries. He described A. J. Ellis (who published *The Essentials of Phonetics* in 1848, and his magnum opus *On Early English Pronunciation* between 1869 and 1889) as 'the pioneer of scientific phonetics in England', and said that A. M. Bell, the author of *Visible Speech* (1867), had done 'more for phonetics than all his predecessors put together'.

Sweet died in 1912. As early as 1907 Daniel Jones gave his first lectures on phonetics at University College London (Jones 1948), and it is from the Department of Phonetics he established there that the traditions and growth of the subject as a university discipline have taken their major impetus. From this single-department beginning other departments have grown, and there are professional phoneticians teaching their subject in many British universities.

The definition of a subject's legitimate field is never a simple matter, especially when other disciplines bring specialized interests to bear on particular sections of that field. Phonetics concerns itself with speech; but anthropology, sociology, psychology, psychiatry, speech therapy, neurology, anatomy, physiology and physics are all examples of disciplines that may examine *some* aspect of speech. The fact that phonetics is the study of *all* aspects of speech effectively defines its domain; the field is wide, but specific. Phonetics is above all a synthesizing subject, taking part of its conceptual stock from each of the many disciplines with which it shares an interest in speech. It is clear from this that to be a competent phonetician one must be in some degree familiar with relevant areas of a wide range of subjects.

Phonetics both learns from and contributes to all these other subjects, but inevitably a more immediate and fluent dialogue is maintained with those subjects to which it considers itself more intimately related. In Britain, phonetics (together with linguistics) is seen as essentially one of the social sciences, having its strongest links with anthropology, sociology and psychology. The articles in this collection reflect this relationship: they are concerned with language, and show the underlying assumption that language is above all a social phenomenon.

These articles show how wide the range of the subject has become. For example, although a major interest has always been the description of English and the teaching of its pronunciation, the following languages are also exemplified: Arabic, Chaga, Danish, French, Gaelic, Georgian, German, Hindustani, Hunanese, Italian, Japanese, Korean, Malayalam, Punjabi, Portuguese, Russian, Sechuana, Siamese, Sinhalese, Spanish, Swahili, Sundanese, Szechuanese, Tamil and Turkish. Many of these papers describe linguistic material in terms of some particular theory of analysis and description; others are discussions of problems of theory, illustrated by language examples. This thread of 'linguistic relevance' runs through all the work presented here. It has governed the making of our selection, and is the reason for our title.

N. C. Scott, in his inaugural lecture at the School of Oriental and African Studies, London, in 1961, discussing the role of the phonetician, said: 'It is . . . not easy to say of any one person where the phonetician ends and the linguist begins.' We would take his point further: we would say – and offer these papers as evidence – that the phonetician, and the linguist in his capacity as a phonologist, are one.

The articles are printed here as nearly as possible in their original form, and without editorial comment or exposition. Some printer's errors have been corrected, and minor changes have been made for consistency of presentation; there are a few additions to footnotes and bibliographies; and articles by Arnold (1966), Catford (1959) and Jones (1931), originally in transcription, are printed in normal orthography. Reading the collection, one becomes quickly aware of a number of interests and points of view which seem to characterize the British school, over and above the development of the basic skills of perception and performance that one takes for granted in a phonetician. It may be useful, however, if we draw attention to five particular areas, as they are exemplified here.

1. The development and presentation of a general phonetic theory is of course a central concern of all phoneticians; the papers by Abercrombie (1964b), Arnold (1966), Catford (1939) and Ladefoged (1958, 1960) show how the general theory has been subjected to continual rescrutiny.

2. General phonological theory is discussed by Jones (1944a, 1946b, 1957), Lyons (1962) and Robins (1957). The articles by Scott (1948, 1956) illustrate the characteristic attitude that alternative phonological solutions of a given set of data are possible.

3. Transcription theory has important implications for both phonology and general phonetics; examples of the continuing interest shown by

phoneticians in transcription problems are seen in particular in Abercrombie (1954) and Jones (1957).

4. Many areas of phonology are covered by the articles in this collection, but one area in particular has attracted attention: suprasegmental phonology and its phonetic exponents. Stress is discussed by Gimson (1956) and Ladefoged (1958); juncture by Jones (1931); rhythm by Abercrombie (1964a); intonation and tone by Gimson (1945–49), Halliday (1963), Jones (1944a), Sharp (1954), Trim (1959) and Uldall (1960).

5. Instrumental techniques have always played an important part in phonetic research; this is reflected in Fry (1960) and Ladefoged (1958).

There are a number of papers which we have been unable to include. The collection is therefore more representative than ideal: we hope it will nonetheless serve to show the central linguistic orientation of British phonetics and the range of interests which it covers. Phonetics is a means to an end, and the end is the study of all aspects of speech; ultimately it is, as Sweet wrote in the preface to his *Handbook*, 'the indispensable foundation of all study of language'.

Department of Linguistics
University of Edinburgh

WEJ/JL

Contents

Acknowledgements

We have been fortunate in having help and advice from a number of colleagues and friends. We offer our thanks to all of them, and in particular acknowledge our debt to Professors D. Abercrombie, A. C. Gimson and E. J. A. Henderson.

Acknowledgements and thanks for permission to reproduce copyright material are due to the individual authors, and to the following: *Acta Linguistica*, for Gimson 1945–49, Jones 1944a; *Archivum Linguisticum*, for Albrow 1963, Halliday 1963; *Asia Minor*, and Lund Humphries, for Henderson 1949; *Bulletin of the School of Oriental and African Studies*, for Butlin 1936, Scott 1947 and 1956, Sharp 1954; *Clinics in Developmental Medicine*, and the Medical Education and Information Unit of the National Spastics Society, for Abercrombie 1964b; *International Journal of American Linguistics*, for Lyons 1962; the International Phonetic Association, for Arnold 1966, Catford 1939, Jones 1931 and 1957, Ladefoged 1958, Trim 1959; *Language and Speech*, for Uldall 1960; the Linguistic Circle of New York, and the Johnson Reprint Corporation, for O'Connor and Trim 1953; The Linguistic Society of America, for Ladefoged 1960; *Linguistics*, and Mouton and Co., for Abercrombie 1964a; *Orbis*, for Abercrombie 1954; Oxford University Press, and Miss J. M. Wheeler, for Firth 1948; the Philological Society, for Firth 1948, Fry 1960, Jones 1944b; the University of Durham Philosophical Society, for Robins 1957; and *Zeitschrift für Phonetik, Sprachwissenschaft und Kommunikationsforschung*, for Gimson 1956, Jones 1948.

David Abercrombie

The recording of dialect material

I want to discuss, in this paper,[1] not the *mechanical* recording of dialect material by machines, but its recording in writing by the field-worker; and my subject would have been indicated more precisely, perhaps, if I had called the paper 'the recording *and presentation* of dialect material.' I want to deal, in other words, with problems of notation.

What I have to say applies equally whether the field-worker himself, in the field, takes down the material; or whether he makes tape or disk recordings, brings them home, and he or someone else puts them into writing there. The procedure is the same, merely displaced and deferred in the latter case (and not done so well, probably, since we transcribe by eye to some extent as well as by ear). (What I have to say does not concern dialect investigations carried out by the postal or 'indirect' method, such as used for example by André Martinet in his study of the pronunciation of contemporary French.)

What the field-worker puts down in writing will normally be in phonetic transcription. The theory, and the practical use, of phonetic transcription has always been one of the strong points of the English (or British) school of phonetics. It has not always been used to best advantage in dialect work, however, and now that there is a revival of practical interest in British dialect studies, I want to make a special plea for more attention to notation.

There are various misunderstandings to be met with about phonetic transcription. For instance there is the commonly stated half-truth that it does not really matter what symbols are used, as long as they are

First published in *Orbis* Vol III, No 1: 232–235, 1954, and subsequently as Ch 10 of D. Abercrombie, *Studies in Phonetics and Linguistics*, Oxford University Press, London, 1965.

properly defined. It often *does* matter; but I am here mainly concerned with how symbols are put together, with *transcription* as such, and not with symbol shapes.

I regard as another misunderstanding the feeling that in dialect work the field-worker's notes, as originally taken down on the spot, are in some way sacred: that they are the *basic facts* of the study, which must on no account be tampered with. Edmond Edmont, of the Linguistic Atlas of France, sent his notes back to Gilliéron as soon as he had finished the investigation of each locality, one reason being that he would thus be prevented from yielding to the temptation to 'edit' what he had taken down.

Briefly, my point in this paper is that the field-worker's original notes are *not* the basic facts that they might appear to be; and that, as a consequence of this, they are probably not the best form for presenting results of dialect investigation to the public (I mean of course the academic public).

First, the question of the field-worker's transcriptions. The feeling which I regard as mistaken is that his notes are the raw material of the investigation in the same way as the actual utterances are, so that to tamper with them would be like faking the utterances. It is felt that they *are* the utterances, captured and transfixed for examination and analysis. The ideal trained phonetician is thus looked on as being in some way like a recording machine – his hearing of sounds automatically produces a transcription in the same way as the cutting head makes a groove in the wax. But the fact is that a transcription is not a *simple record* of an utterance; it is a *generalization about* an utterance. The utterances are the original basic facts. The field-worker's transcriptions are the first processing, the first analysis, of these facts. The transcriptions embody the initial classification of, and even theorizing about, the raw material; they are not the facts themselves.

The real raw material, the utterances, cannot of course be handled directly, because they are unique events and they are complex events. Before we can say anything about them, we must be able to treat them as made up of constituent elements, each element being the representative of a class.

ᵀThis analysis, and systematization, is what all alphabetic writing does – sometimes well, sometimes badly. It represents by a linear succession of symbols in *space* something which in *time*, as normally apprehended by the listener and as felt by the speaker, is not a linear succession (the artificiality of this procedure of splitting the utterance up into small elements is much more obvious to, say, a Chinese than to us who are literate in an alphabetic system). Furthermore, it represents these elements, which are infinite in their variety, by a finite number of symbols.

The very fact, then, of putting spoken utterances into writing produces out of them a *system* with a known number of elements. Every new utterance which has to be written down is done so by being referred to this system. Phonetic transcription is a specialization of alphabetic writing, from which, in this respect, it is no different. Through it the utterances of spoken language are made tractable for linguistic investigation.

When a phonetician is listening to, and transcribing, *uninvestigated* speech, what is the system to which he refers utterances in order to write them? Whence are derived the classes to which the elements are assigned?

Whether or not it is clear to the transcriber himself what he is doing (it may not be clear), the system is a *general phonetic* one, that is to say the classes are general human categories of sound. A transcription of this kind is called *impressionistic*.

An impressionistic transcription is distinguished from what is called a *systematic* one. These are the two basic classes into which the many different types of phonetic transcription all fall. (This is not the familiar division into 'broad' and 'narrow', which are both varieties of systematic transcriptions.) In a systematic transcription, the symbols do not symbolize with reference to the general human ability to produce speech sounds, that is to say with reference to general human sound-types, but with reference to a particular language or form of speech only. The symbols are thus used more economically, and the classes of sound they represent are established on more complex grounds than phonetic similarity – on *phonemic* grounds, those who like to use that term could say.

So anything recorded in phonetic notation is not raw material but processed material, processed according to known and easily-formulated principles if it is a systematic transcription, but processed in a very individual, personal, way if it is an impressionistic one. This must necessarily be so: the categories on which an impressionistic transcription is based are *personal* categories. Since they are established on purely phonetic grounds the boundaries between them are inevitably vague and fluctuating, and each transcriber will make them where his experience, and the degree and nature of his training, dictate.

A dialect field-worker's transcriptions must be impressionistic, when he is investigating pronunciation. The utterances he is dealing with must be treated as part of unknown language whether they are in fact or not, in so far as he must at least not assume anything about the points he is looking for. Hence his transcriptions will be personal, idiosyncratic. Gilliéron for this reason was quite right to insist on a single field-worker doing all the work. The American field-workers on the New England Atlas went to considerable trouble to make their impressionistic transcriptions as alike as possible. But even when this can be done, a transcriber's mother tongue, and the philological tradition in which he is brought up, have their effect. Thus English field-workers might be likely in their transcriptions to pay great attention to variations of vowel sounds in stressed syllables; and to pay no attention at all, for example, to varieties of *s*.

It is because of this personal, idiosyncratic character of impressionistic transcriptions that I believe they are not suitable for publication of dialect material (also because they are likely to be encumbered with diacritics). I believe the New England survey was mistaken in presenting much of its material in this form.

Dialect material, it seems to me, should always be presented in a systematic transcription. There are several varieties of systematic transcription, and the same material, I believe, can be most advantageously presented on different occasions in different ways.

It is misleading to say that types of systematic transcription vary in exactness or accuracy. A systematic transcription really consists of two parts: the symbols in the *text*, on the one hand, and the *conventions* governing their interpretation, on the other. Taken together, these two always give the same total amount of information; but it is sometimes more convenient to have a given item of information in the conventions, sometimes to have it in the text. What you put into the one you take out of the other. 'Broad' and 'narrow' are not very precise terms, but they refer to this kind of difference.

Let us consider three typical situations in which dialect material may appear in phonetic transcription: 1. in a connected text; 2. in isolated words and phrases in a monograph upon a particular dialect; 3. in isolated words and phrases involved in comparison of related dialects – on a map, for example.

1. A basic principle in making phonetic transcriptions is that whenever possible they should be readable. The philosopher Thomas Hobbes once said of a work by John Wallis, Professor of Geometry at Oxford, that it was 'so covered over with the scab of symbols' that he had not the patience to see if it said anything worth while. People have felt the same about linguistic works, and especially about connected phonetic texts. This is the hardest situation in which to make phonetic transcription readable. Connected texts should have the maximum possible of information in the conventions, and the bare minimum in the symbols, thus gaining great typographical simplicity by using the fewest possible different symbols of the simplest possible shapes. I can think of many instances of dialect texts where this is not done.

2. When isolated words and phrases are under discussion in a dialect monograph, it is an advantage to have distinctions made explicit in the symbols which, in a connected text, would be better confined to the conventions. Here I would like to suggest the adoption of a practice of which recent works of descriptive linguistics from the London school, and also from Americanists, have demonstrated the usefulness in different ways. This is the use of two types of transcription simultaneously. A word is transcribed first, for instance, in a way which re-

veals its sound-structure; secondly, immediately after, in a way which reveals details germane to the discussion but whose presence in the symbols obscures the structure. The first might make clear the phonemes, the second the allophones. The method makes for remarkable clarity of presentation.

3. When dialects are being compared, a transcription is needed which brings out, not 'internal' distinctions, those *within* a given form of speech, but 'external' ones, between two or more forms of speech. These distinctions equally are usually stated in the conventions; but on a map, for instance, they are better explicit in the symbols. A transcription of this kind is called a *comparative* one.

I said I was not mainly concerned in this paper with symbol shapes, but I would like to add a word or two about them. They are often, in all kinds of linguistic works, hideous. The presence in the same transcription of capitals, italics, tiny letters, raised letters, diacritics, and letters from assorted founts, is nearly always unnecessary, but distressingly common. One almost suspects the existence of a feeling that the more ungraceful and untidy a transcription is the more scholarly it is – a belief that devotion to the spoken word is best expressed by neglect of the appearance of the printed page. What a pity that a new periodical like *Orbis*, mainly interested in the study of dialects, should not yet, apparently, be equipped typographically to deal pleasantly with phonetic notation! Why is it so rare to find a periodical like *English Language Teaching*, in which it is clearly demonstrated that elegance is not incompatible with sound phonetic transcriptions?

May I conclude by quoting a famous mathematician, Hyman Levy: 'Notation is indeed the very life-blood of science.'

Note

1 Read, on 25 August 1953, at the Second International Conference of University Professors of English, Paris.

David Abercrombie

A phonetician's view of verse structure

May I say, right away, that my interest in prosody, in the study of verse structure, is not an *amateur's* interest. I would like to claim prosody as part of my own subject, phonetics; and I would therefore assert that my interest in prosody is a professional one.

It is true that, in fact, most phoneticians have paid little attention to verse structure. Most writers on prosody, moreover, have paid little attention to phonetics, which is possibly why they have never reached any agreement on a common body of knowledge.

I claim prosody as part of my subject, because verse *is* verse as a result of the way certain aspects of the sound, or rather perhaps the sound-producing movements, of speech have been exploited or organized. The study of the sound of speech, in all its aspects, and of the bodily move-ments which produce the sound, is the province of phonetics. Phonetic techniques of observation and analysis can be applied to verse structure as successfully as they can to any other aspect of language where the sound is important. I would like to start, therefore, with that part of elementary phonetic theory which is relevant to our present purpose.

Speech, as is well known, depends on breathing: the sounds of speech are produced by an *air-stream* from the lungs. This air-stream does not issue from the lungs in a continuous flow, as might be thought at first. The flow is 'pulse-like': there is a continuous and rapid fluctuation in the air-pressure, which results from alternate contractions and relaxa-tions of the breathing muscles. Each muscular contraction, and conse-quent rise in air-pressure, is a *chest-pulse* (so called because it is the

First published in *Linguistics* 6: 5–13, June 1964, and subsequently as Ch 3 of D. Abercrombie, *Studies in Phonetics and Linguistics*, Oxford University Press, London, 1965.

intercostal muscles in the chest that are responsible); and each chest-pulse constitutes a syllable. This syllable-producing process, the system of chest-pulses, is the basis of human speech.[1]

This, however, is not the whole story of the production of the air-stream which we use for talking; there is in addition a second system of pulse-like muscular movements on which in part it depends. This system consists of a series of less frequent, more powerful contractions of the breathing muscles which every now and then coincide with, and reinforce, a chest-pulse, and cause a more considerable and more sudden rise in air-pressure. These reinforcing movements constitute the system of *stress-pulses*, and this system is combined in speech with the system of chest-pulses.

The rhythm of speech is a rhythm of these two systems of pulses: it is a product of the way they are combined in producing an air-stream for talking. The rhythm is already *in* the air-stream, in fact, before the actual vowels and consonants which make up words are superimposed on it.

The two pulse systems are, as far as we know, present when all languages are being spoken, but languages coordinate them in different ways. Two different kinds of periodicity can result from their organization: the pulses in either the one, or the other, of the two systems can be made to recur at equal intervals of time. *Either* the stress-producing pulses *or* the syllable-producing pulses can be in isochronous sequence, and in the former case we have a *stress-timed* rhythm, in the latter a *syllable-timed* rhythm (to use terms which have recently become widely current).[2] The languages of the world fall into two classes, depending on whether the rhythm with which they are spoken is stress-timed or syllable-timed. English is a typical example of a language with a stress-timed rhythm. French is a typical example of a language with a syllable-timed one.

It may not be immediately obvious that a necessary consequence of having one series of pulses in isochronous sequence is that the other series can *not* be in isochronous sequence; but it is so. Thus if, as in English, the isochronous pulses are the stress-pulses, it follows that the chest-pulses will come at unequal intervals of time. An illustration may help to make clear why this must be the case.

Let us consider the utterance:

This is the house that Jack built.

It contained, as I spoke it then, four stress-pulses, and they occurred on the syllables *This, house, Jack* and *built*. Now if I say the sentence again, and while I do so tap with a pencil on the table every time there is a stress-pulse, the taps will be unmistakably isochronous, showing that the stressed syllables are too. But there are seven syllables in all in the sentence. Suppose I now tap on *every* syllable: it is at once plain that *they* are *not* isochronous – they are unevenly spaced in time. A moment's thought shows why: the unstressed syllables are unequally distributed between the stressed ones, and must therefore be spoken at varying speeds to fill the spaces between the latter, being sometimes compressed and sometimes expanded and therefore constantly varying in rate of succession. (We recognize, incidentally, as a typical French mispronunciation the use of isochronous chest-pulses in this sentence.)

The stress-timed rhythm of English is the basis of the structure of English verse, and syllable-timed rhythm need claim our attention no further.

The rhythmic basis of verse is thus the same as that of prose (and, it should be added, of conversation too) – as far, at any rate, as English is concerned. I shall say later what I consider to be the crucial difference between prose and verse; but I do not believe their rhythmic features to be different *in kind* from each other. In fact any smallish sequence of words taken out of verse *could* be a bit of conversation, and any smallish excerpt from conversation *could* be a bit of verse. This explains why poets have no need of prosodic theory in order to compose verse, and why listeners and readers, equally, have no need of special knowledge in order to appreciate verse: all that they need is already there, in their normal experience of the language.

I said, at the beginning, that it was rather the *sound-producing movements*, than the sound of speech itself, of which the organization in a special way results in verse. All rhythm, it seems likely, is ultimately rhythm of bodily movement. Language rhythm is thus something which belongs primarily to the *speaker*, rather than the hearer; something which arises out of the speaker's movements, and especially out of the muscular movements which produce the air-stream. It is natural to ask, therefore, how it is that rhythm can exist for the *hearer*.

The explanation, briefly, is that our perception of speech – not only its rhythmic side, but other features of it too – depends to a considerable extent on the hearer identifying himself with the speaker. As we listen to the sounds of speech, we perceive them not simply as sounds, but as clues to movements. It is an intuitive reaction of the hearer to be aware of the movements of the various organs of speech which the speaker is making. We perceive speech in muscular terms. This is perhaps part of what I. A. Richards meant when he said that metre 'is not *in* the stimulation, it is in our response'.[3]

It has been pointed out that a somewhat analogous situation may obtain in listening to music. As P. E. Vernon has written, 'rhythm is an aspect of music that is more of a bodily than an auditory nature', and he points out that many people perceive music in terms of their hands at the piano or other instruments.[4] This is probably to some extent true of every musical performer when listening to others; but we are all, when it comes to language, performers.

Speech rhythm, and therefore the rhythm of verse, is *in* the speaker, and it is in the hearer in so far as he identifies himself with the speaker. We might coin the term 'phonetic empathy' for the process by which he does so. In order to be able to 'empathize', of course, the hearer must know a language intimately; probably it is necessary for it to be his mother-tongue, in most cases.

The rhythm of speech, therefore, is primarily muscular rhythm, a rhythm of bodily movement, rather than a rhythm of sound. This is why verse can be immediately recognized and felt as verse in *silent* reading, which otherwise would not be easy to explain.

I must next make an important point: that a stress-pulse can occur without sound accompanying it. There is one famous and often quoted example of this; attention was drawn to it first, I think, by Daniel Jones.[5] The phrase *thank you*, when spoken in a perfunctory way, is often pronounced in England in a way that can be represented in phonetic transcription as ['ḳkju]. As far as the ear is concerned, the first syllable has disappeared; as most people say the phrase, however, it is still present in the speaker's movements – and present, moreover, as a stressed syllable.

In this instance, although there is silence in the place of the initial stressed syllable, the speaker makes a movement of the articulators as well as of the breathing muscles: he actually says a long [k] at the beginning of the word. But a stress-pulse may also occur in English at a point during an utterance where there is a gap in the sequence of words, and there is no articulatory movement. This is what happens when I say something like the following: 'A funny thing happened to me, on my way here this evening.' Between 'me' and 'on', as I said the sentence then, there is what may be called a *silent stress-pulse*, as distinct from an actual *stressed syllable* (which would be a stress with some articulatory movements superimposed on it). We can say, therefore, that that utterance contained six stress-pulses, one of which was silent and the other five were stressed syllables (*fun*ny, *hap*pened, *me*, *way*, *eve*ning).

Such silent stresses are not a matter of chance, nor of the speaker's whim, and they merit more linguistic investigation than they have received so far. When one starts listening for them they turn out to be surprisingly frequent in conversation, and even more frequent in prose read aloud. Moreover, as we shall see, they are an integral part of the structure of English verse.

From now on, therefore, I shall use the word 'stress', by itself, to mean simply the rhythmical recurrence of the reinforced chest pulse; it may coincide with an articulated syllable, which will then be a stressed syllable; or it may be a silent stress.

One must not suppose that because a silent stress *is* silent, it therefore does not exist for the hearer. There is a *stress*, even if not a stressed syllable; and this stress is felt by the speaker and (because he would do the same if he were speaking) 'empathized' by the hearer.

I should now like to be historical for a moment. The strongest influence on prosodic speculation in England has, of course, been classical prosody, the theory of the structure of Latin verse and, originally, of Greek verse. Most writers on the subject until the end of the eighteenth century believed that the principles and categories of analysis of Latin verse could be applied to English verse; or at least that they could be adapted so that they would apply. It was even believed by some that if they couldn't be adapted, then English verse should be written in such a way that they *would* fit. Latin verse was based on syllable quantity. All attempts to apply this basis to English failed. Since the appearance of Coleridge's preface to *Christabel*, however, in 1816, theories of prosody have been largely transformed.[6]

What Coleridge said in his preface was, 'The metre of "Christabel" is . . . founded on a new principle: namely, that of counting in each line the accents, not the syllables'; and he goes on to say, 'In each line the accents will be found to be only four.'

This has often been taken to mean, both by Coleridge's followers and by his opponents, that English verse is regulated by the number of stressed (or accented) syllables in the line. However, if the 'new principle' is formulated in this way, it will not really work. *Christabel* itself, it is true, usually has four stressed syllables in the line:

'Tis the 'middle of 'night by the 'castle 'clock

(I show the stressed syllables in the usual manner by the stress-mark ' at the beginning of the syllable.) Sometimes, however, there seem to be only three stressed syllables:

My 'sire is of a 'noble 'line.

The formulation of the 'new principle' should, of course, be to the effect that a line such as one of *Christabel* contains four *stress-pulses*, not stressed *syllables* (and it is perhaps possible to interpret Coleridge in this sense). In other words, we must be prepared for some of the stresses to be silent. In the line quoted immediately above, for instance, a silent stress comes between 'sire' and 'is': the line contains three stressed syllables, but four stress-pulses, one of which, though silent, is nevertheless as much sensuously present as the others.

If we look for five stressed syllables in English blank verse, we will often fail to find them. But nearly always, when we so fail, we *can* find – usually we cannot avoid finding – five *stresses*, some of which may fall on silence. To quote two famous instances (the caret, ₐ, may be conveniently used to indicate any silence or pause which forms an integral part of the structure of a line; 'ₐ therefore indicates a silent stress):

To 'be or 'not to be, '$_\wedge$ 'that is the 'question

Of 'man's 'first diso'bedience '$_\wedge$ and the 'fruit.

The recurrent stress-pulses in a line of English verse give rise to units which we may call (following many others) *feet*. A foot, in this usage, may be defined as the space in time from the incidence of one stress-pulse up to, but not including, the next stress-pulse. Thus, with this definition, it is the same thing to say that a given line consists of a certain number of feet as that it contains a certain number of stresses, and I shall prefer to put it in the former way from now on. If we use the conventional vertical line to indicate the limits of the foot we can dispense with the stress mark:

'Tis the | middle of | night by the | castle | clock |

My | sire | $_\wedge$ is of a | noble | line |

To | be or | not to be | $_\wedge$ | that is the | question |

Of | man's | first diso|bedience | $_\wedge$ and the | fruit |

English verse, it is clear, like classical verse, depends on a rhythm which is temporarily organized – it depends on the division of time into temporal units. English verse must be therefore in some sense quantitative. As in Latin verse, all the feet within a piece of English verse are of equal length or quantity.

(It is of interest that the foot, defined as above, turns out to be of importance in several other ways in the study of English.)

There remain three points to be dealt with in order to complete this very brief phonetician's outline of the structure of English verse.

The first point is that silent stresses are much more frequent than one at first would suppose. Several writers have at different times put forward the theory that all lines of English verse contain an *even* number of feet. Where it seems at first that a line contains an odd number, there is always a silent final stress at the end of the line which brings the number of feet up to an even one. Thus lines which are commonly supposed to have, for instance, three, or five, feet really have four, or six. The so-called 'iambic pentameter', therefore, goes like this:

| Know then thy|self, pre|sume not | God to | scan | $_\wedge$ |

– the silent final stress forming the beginning of the sixth foot must be inserted before the next line can be started. And the limerick, which is a verse-form reputed to begin with two three-foot lines, really goes like this:

There | was an old | man in a | tree | $_\wedge$
Who was |horribly | bored by a | bee |$_\wedge$
    When they | said, does it | buzz,
    He rep|lied, yes it | does,
It's a | regular | brute of a | bee. | $_\wedge$ |

(The unstressed syllables which begin each line are attached to the silent stress concluding the preceding line, forming with it a 'line-divided' foot – except for the anacrusis which begins the stanza.) This theory is, then, to the effect that the *double* foot, or 'dipode', is the measure of verse in English. It certainly seems to be true in a very large number of cases, whether or not it applies without exception to the whole corpus of English verse.

The second point concerns the variety of the feet themselves, which is considerable: we find in English verse many more kinds of feet than in Latin verse, for example. This variety is of two kinds: it lies both in the number of syllables, and in the relative length or quantity of the syllables, which are in the foot. The number of syllables may vary from none (if it is a completely silent foot) to four or even occasionally more. In

| Know then thy|self, pre|sume not | God to | scan |

there is one three-syllable foot, three of two syllables, and one one-syllable foot. The relative length of syllables is a further source of variety, even between feet containing the same number of syllables. Syllable-quantity, in other words, is a factor which cannot really be left out of account (though it usually is) in examining the structure of English verse. When a foot consists of two syllables, for example, it does not necessarily follow that these syllables, will divide the time of the foot into two equal halves. They may do so; but they may divide it into (approximately) one-third and two-thirds respectively, or conversely into two-thirds and one-third. Take the line from Milton's *L'Allegro*:

| Meadows | trim with | daisies | pide

It contains three two-syllable feet, but they are manifestly different from each other in their syllable quantities. In |*meadows*| the first syllable is shorter than the second; in |*trim with*| the first syllable is longer than the second; and in |*daisies*| the two syllables are of equal length (this is true, at least, of my pronunciation). These quantities, it must be emphasized, are not haphazard, but follow strict rules, which, however, there is no time on this occasion to expound.[7] Three-syllable and four-syllable feet offer even greater possibilities of variation. (It should be remembered that syllable-quantity in English is entirely distinct from stress: the two factors are quite independent of each other. Syllable quantity must not, moreover, be confused with vowel quantity; a so-called 'short' vowel often occurs in a long syllable (as in *trim* above).

The third point concerns the line itself. The foot, and the syllable quantities within the foot, are phonological categories which are just as much needed to describe English prose or conversation as they are to describe verse; but the line is a unit of rhythm which occurs in verse only. Prose is rhythmic but not metrical (as Aristotle said), but verse is both rhythmic and metrical. The rhythmic unit of both prose and verse is the foot; the metrical unit of verse is the line. This is the crucial difference between the two modes: in prose the feet are not organized into a higher metrical unit.

A line of verse, if it is to function as a unit, must of course be recognizable to the ear as such – it must be delimited. This is done by various devices which may be called *line-end markers*, and there seem to be three of these in use in modern English verse. All three may be used together, or any two, or any one alone. They are:

1. rhyme, or assonance,
2. a silent final stress,
3. a monosyllabic foot, not used anywhere else, concluding the words of the line.

All three of these line-end markers can be seen operating in Gray's *Elegy*:

The | curfew | tolls the | knell of | parting | day | ∧
The | lowing | herd wind | slowly | o'er the | lea | ∧
The | plowman | homeward | plods his | weary | way, | ∧
And | leaves the | world to | darkness | ∧ and to | me. | ∧ |

English verse thus turns out, as Hopkins suggested it would, to be really rather simple in its structure. The complicated thing that has sometimes been made of it is due partly, I think, to the lingering influence of classical prosody; and partly to lack of knowledge of the elementary phonetic facts that lie behind all speech rhythm.

Notes

[1] For further details see R. H. Stetson, *Motor Phonetics*, Amsterdam, 1951.
[2] They were put forward by K. L. Pike, *The Intonation of American English*, Ann Arbor, 1946.
[3] *Principles of Literary Criticism*, London, 1924, *p* 139.
[4] In *The Pleasures of Music*, ed Jacques Barzun, London, 1952, *p* 173.
[5] *Outline of English Phonetics*, Cambridge, 1932, *p* 227.
[6] T. S. Omond, *English Metrists*, Oxford, 1921, Ch 4.
[7] See my article 'Syllable quantity and enclitics in English' in the forthcoming Daniel Jones memorial volume. [Abercrombie, D., *et al*, eds, *In Honour of Daniel Jones*, Longman, 1964. (Eds)]

David Abercrombie

Parameters and phonemes

I have defined Phonetics elsewhere as 'the study of the medium of spoken language in all its aspects', and these aspects include, of course, the process of acquiring, in childhood, the skills needed for the production of the medium, and also the failure to acquire these skills. (The acquirement of *language* as such, and the acquirement of the ability to produce and to receive the *medium* which carries it, are, naturally, bound up together; but it is often useful to distinguish the two things, particularly since there may be failures or breakdowns in the one which do not involve the other.)

Phonetics provides two sets of techniques which are relevant to studies of the development and disorders of speech; techniques of observation, and techniques of description. There is a close connection between the two, of course – we tend to observe in terms of our categories of description. It is these latter that I want to talk about mostly.

Although phonetics is the study of *all* aspects of the medium, it has been dominated, in the past, as an academic subject, by one aspect – at any rate in this country, and this has left its mark on it. Phonetics has, until recently, been the handmaid of language teaching. Indeed this has more than just left its mark on the subject – it has deeply influenced it, particularly as concerns the categories used for analysing and describing the

Paper given, under the title 'The Contribution of Phonetics', to an International Study Group on the Development and the Disorders of Hearing, Language and Speech in Children, held in Durham in September 1963, under the auspices of the Medical Education and Information Unit of the National Spastics Society. First published, as 'The Contribution of Phonetics' in *The Child Who Does Not Talk*, Clinics in Developmental Medicine, No 13: 39–42, 1964, and subsequently as 'Parameters and Phonemes', Ch 12 of D. Abercrombie, *Studies in Phonetics and Linguistics*, Oxford University Press, London, 1965.

sound of speech. When people need the help of phonetics in other fields, they almost inevitably make use of the categories which have been worked out for language teaching – under the quite understandable impression that these are 'absolute' categories. But they are *not* 'absolute' categories. Phonetics today has emancipated itself from language teaching, and as an academic subject it is much wider than in the past. Its interests cover many fields. In our department at Edinburgh, language teaching occupies only a small place (possibly too small, in reaction from the past). Our main interest is in the use of phonetics in descriptive linguistics. But we co-operate closely on various research projects with departments such as physiology, physics, electrical engineering, with the College of Speech Therapists and the Dental Hospital, and with the various neurologists in different institutions in Edinburgh. And we have special interest in speech synthesis. We have learnt that the traditional categories of analysis and description nearly always will not do in these wider fields. The making of synthetic speech especially has brought this home to us.

The phoneme-dominated approach

What characterizes the traditional approach to the analysis of the sound of speech? Although it is an approach which goes back long before the term 'phoneme' was invented, one could nevertheless call it a 'phoneme-dominated' approach. Speech is looked at as consisting of *segments*, each one of which represents a phoneme, which are put together to build up speech. It could equally well be called a 'building-block' approach. Its categories of description are all in these terms; they are all (or almost all) designed to describe these phoneme-representing segments, or 'speech-sounds'. True, intonation is abstracted and dealt with separately; but the syllable is ignored, and so are voice quality and rhythm. In fact the aural medium is treated as if it were closely parallel to the visual medium: as if, just as letters are put together to form written words, so phoneme-representing segments are put together to form spoken ones.

Another way of describing the traditional approach would be to call it the 'posture and glide' view of speech. Each segment is envisaged as a *posture* of the vocal organs, and these postures are joined together by means of *glides*, which take us from one to the next.

However, we know – it is no new discovery – that there *are* no held postures in speech. Nothing brings this home more effectively than a slow-motion x-ray film of speech. The concept of the speech-sound as a stable (even if only momentarily stable) posture of the vocal organs is a fiction, albeit for many purposes quite a useful one.

The phoneme, which is based on this view of the sound of speech, is a construct devised to enable linguists to analyse their material *for certain purposes only*. It is not something which has a 'real existence'. The categories used for talking about speech in the 'phoneme-dominated' approach have worked very well in language teaching, and it is possible to get *some* way with them in any field. But people in all fields concerned with speech talk in term of phonemes nowadays. It has become a vogue-word. It has also become a status-symbol – to use it shows that you are 'with it' linguistically. I constantly see the word used in situations where it is quite inappropriate. I would not think, for instance, that any of the group of doctors, teachers and therapists who assembled at Durham need ever use the term.

I do not think that the phoneme, unlike some status symbols, is harm-less; I think it is apt to confuse people's thinking about speech if they are not aware of its fictional nature. I am sure it gives rise, for example, to mistaken ideas about the perception of speech, making people think that phoneme-representing segments are perceived separately and serially – which is most unlikely. But it is not only sometimes misleading; it is often not the most efficient means for thinking about and describing speech.

A parametric approach

Certainly we have found these traditional categories unsatisfactory for many of the fields in which we in Edinburgh are interested. The most striking of these, perhaps, is speech synthesis. If you try to synthesize speech on a 'building-block' basis, it just doesn't work, and we do not make the machine operate by making it add together synthetic speech sounds corresponding to phoneme-representing segments. The machine, by the way, is called PAT, which stands for Parametric Artificial Talker, and the first word gives the clue as to how the machine works. *Parametric* comes from *parameter*, and the machine operates by adding together parameters, not segments. A parameter is a variable, an ingredient which is continually present but changing in value. The division of speech into phoneme-representing segments represents a division at right-angles to the time axis, whereas the division into parameters is a division parallel to the time axis.

I believe that a parametric approach is more useful for many of the purposes that we are here to discuss than a segmental approach, and that it is always a valuable supplement to a segmental approach.

The parameters of PAT are *acoustic* parameters, and I need not here go into what they are. I would like to suggest the use for our purposes of *physiological* parameters, thought of in terms of the producing mechanisms of the medium. I feel sure that these give a more realistic view of what goes on than segments do. I simply don't believe that the child, in acquiring speech, learns a series of separate units or items, which are the phoneme-representing segments, and strings them together, with varying degrees of success, at the same time superimposing on the string the rhythm of syllable-succession and the melodies of intonation. I suggest that what the child learns are patterns of movement which are quite large in time, and it learns them at first sketchily and roughly, filling them in, in more detail, as it improves. The learning of these patterns is best thought of as being in parametric terms. This is certainly better than saying, as one authority has, that the average baby under two months of age has mastered seven and a half phonemes!

What might such physiological parameters in the producing-process of the medium be? Here is a suggested list – not complete, since some of the parameters could be subdivided, and certainly some more could be added:

In the respiratory system (*a*) the syllable-pulse process
                          (*b*) the pulse-reinforcing, or stress process
In the phonatory system (*c*) phonation-type control
                       (*d*) on/off switching of voicing
                       (*e*) voice-pitch variation
In the articulatory system (*f*) velic valve-action
                      (*g*) tongue-body movements
                      (*h*) tongue-tip movements
                      (*i*) lip movements
                      (*j*) jaw movements.

These parameters have, of course, to be exactly coordinated for the production of the medium to be correctly learnt.

I am not suggesting that we normally listen to these parameters. We *hear* the medium as a single unanalysed continuing noise, fluctuating in quality. We *listen*, perhaps, in terms of three parameters representing three expressive systems:

1. articulatory patterns,
2. intonation patterns,
3. register ('voice quality') variations.

The three systems operate in speech quite independently of each other, and they are listened to *as language*, plus indications of mood, character, and so on.

But we can *learn* to listen in terms of the physiological parameters enumerated above, or even subdivisions of them, so that failures to master the medium can be described in their terms, and so can the development of speech in the child. It is almost impossible to describe babbling in terms of phoneme-representing segments (though attempts have been made to do so), but it can be done parametrically.

This is put forward very tentatively. What we badly need is research at the post-graduate level, in a phonetics department, into the problems of the learning of speech and of speech pathology. I have in mind, in this connection, not only the contribution which phonetics can make to such research, but also the contribution which such research can make to the development of phonetics, for it has been found that the study of speech in one set of circumstances and for one set of purposes is always illuminating for the study of it in all others.

K. H. Albrow

The phonology of the personal forms of the verb in Russian

The present statement exemplifies the following aspects of a theory based on the work of linguists at the School of Oriental and African Studies, London, under J. R. Firth:

1. The concept of phonology as a level of analysis relating grammar and lexicon to phonetic exponence, with differentiation where advantageous of the phonology of grammar from that of lexicon. In the present case the link is between a grammatical category (the word-class verb) and the phonetic exponents.
2. Necessarily therefore the concept that all linguistic statement should by the nature of language be polysystemic.
3. Further, the concept that statement in terms of prosodies and phonematic units will yield simpler and more comprehensive results than statement in terms of phonemes. An elaboration of these points will be introduced under *Phonology* below.

The following analysis is an attempt to apply this theory to part of a major European language. So far it has mainly been exercised in the field of Oriental and African Studies where it had its origin. The object of this statement is to handle a problem of the phonic data of the verb in Russian in what, as just stated, I feel to be a more explanatory and at the same time more comprehensive way than is possible, *eg*, in terms of phonemes. I feel that more is accounted for in general (and in respect of certain of the data more certainly is accounted for) in this way than would otherwise be the case. The particular problem, as one which must present itself to any who teach the language to foreign learners, has usually of course (in

First published in *Archivum Linguisticum*, Vol XIV, Fasc 2: 146–156, 1963.

teaching-grammars) been approached with the learner in mind. Two statements (apart from those in teaching-grammars) which have so far appeared in articles, are however equally made with the learner in mind. These are Roman Jakobson, 'Russian Conjugation', *Word*, iv (1948), *p* 155, and R. Hingley, 'The Present Tense of the Russian Verb', *The Slavonic and East European Review*, xxxiii (1955), *p* 486.[1] Hingley's statement is in terms of orthography and bases itself, as do most statements elsewhere, on the learning of certain forms from the verb scatter (in this case the infinitive and the 3rd person singular), and derivation according to certain rules of the remaining forms from them. As is common the rules prove fairly complex and there are a number of exceptions owing in great part to the interpretations imposed by the orthography. Jakobson's statement is made in terms of linguistic abstractions (stated as stems and endings), the bringing together of which with the application of certain rules is designed to account for the phonetic data and ultimately therefore the phonic. In the nature of things (the things being phonemes) more is kept apart, in the way of forms, than one would perhaps wish if it seemed possible to bring them together. It is the claim of the present statement that they can in fact be so brought together and to show in what way, using a prosodic approach, this can be done.

It is part of the advantage of the prosodies to make it possible to set up forms whose basic **CV** structure shall be invariable, at the same time having as wide an application as possible. This is the case here with the verbal roots set up, the phonological formulae for which, together with the prosodies, will account not only in fact for a particular verb, but in some cases for another related verb or verbs (perfective or imperfective, etc).

What follows here is not a teaching statement but a linguistic description, from which I think an adaptation for teaching purposes can be made, but which is expressly made without deference at this point to such a need.[2]

Grammar

The occurrence of 'verb' in the title implies a grammar of Russian in which *words* have been delimited and placed in *classes* – if verb, then also noun, adjective and so on. No justification of this grammar is attempted here. It is in a sense simply assumed that there can be such things as verbs in a grammar of Russian which is sufficiently established to be taken as 'given' for my present purposes. (This is not to say that there may not be many details in the grammar of Russian as at present formulated which could not be better handled. I do not think that the class verb (as a required word-class) would be one of them.)

The discussion therefore concerns:

unit – word
class – verb

The verb can be said to have the following three moods:

infinitive, imperative, indicative;

three tenses:

past, present and future;

and two aspects:

perfective and imperfective.

The latter combine with all moods and all tenses, except that in the indicative mood only imperfective combines with present.[3] This article is concerned with the present (imperfective) and future perfective only, more specifically with the junction of verbal root or stem and personal ending. (The infinitive has its own grammatical and phonological structure, and the imperative its own systems with different exponents from the indicative. A statement of these is intended in a subsequent article. The roots set up here for personal forms have been set up with infinitive and imperative in mind, and the analysis is in fact based on a consideration of all parts of the verb.)

The elements of structure of these two tenses (the endings of which are identical) may be stated for the present purpose as a maximum of three which will be represented formulaically as

structure – $R(S)P$

where R = verbal root, P = personal ending, and S = a stem ordered between these in the case of some verbs. Actual structures are therefore:

RP or *RSP*

(A more detailed statement of verbal structure in Russian would have to include mention of further elements, *eg* prefix (preceding R) and infix (following R but preceding either S, or P if no S). It would also have to include a reflexive element for many verbs, following P. Since, however, the occurrence of these elements does not affect the phonology of the junction of P with R or S (whichever it is ordered with), prefix and infix have been subsumed under R and the reflexive element under P for the purpose of this statement. No reflexive verbs are in fact instanced here.)

Phonology

The units of phonology are:

Units – foot, syllable, prosody, phonematic unit.
Classes of foot – major, minor (*ie* with strong syllable, without strong syllable)
Classes of syllable – accented, non-accented
Classes of phonematic unit – **C, V**
Structures of foot – $S(W_n)$, W_n. (S = strong (syllable), W = weak (syllable))
Structures of syllable – **CV(C)**, *ie* either **CV** or **CVC**

Though the foot is involved, since accent is involved, it is not referred to again.

Prosodies and phonematic units

(*a*) *prosodies of the foot* – Accent, non-accent, symbolized by ' and zero respectively.
(*b*) *prosodies of the syllable* – There are three of these, to be symbolized $\bar{y}/y_1/y_2$. The part of the verbal structure with which this article is concerned includes part of two syllables, *ie* is phonologically:

-**VCV**- (*ie* the **C** may be said to be medial)

The prosodies are 'focused' at **C**. These prosodies may be described as articulatory.

Exponents of these prosodic systems are:

Accent prosodies

' – strong stress.
Zero symbol – weak stress.

Articulatory prosodies

$\bar{y}$ – secondary articulation of velarization or non-palatalization (see consonant exponents below).
y_1 – secondary articulation of palatalization or velarization, depending on **C** (see below).
y_2 – either secondary articulation of palatalization or velarization, depending on **C**, or
primary articulation of alveolar laterality with secondary articulation of palatalization (see under the labials in consonant exponents below). (An overlap occurs with the labial exponents of **C**.)

Terms of the **C** *system*

C is the final segment of R in each case. (R may end in more than one **C** – see examples below.) Terms comprise:

P	T	K
B	D	G
M	N	
	R	
	L	
(F)[4]	S	X
V	Z	

For exponents of these see below.

Terms of the **V** *system*

V is the first segment of all Ps. The system comprises three terms over all, *viz*

ι, ϵ, α[5]

Exponents of these are:

ι – in general terms closeness [i, ɪ, ɨ, ɯ, u, ʉ] according to the context in which it is stated to occur.

ϵ – in general terms half-openness [ǫ, ɪ, ɨ] according to the context in which it is stated to occur.

α – in general terms openness [a, ə] according to the context in which it is stated to occur.

Relation of these to the grammatical categories of person and number

In the personal forms of the Russian verb there are three persons (1st, 2nd, 3rd) and two numbers (singular, plural). The Ps which are exponents of these categories fall into two sets, distinguished phonologically by the pattern of **V**s with which the Ps begin and the pattern of prosodies occurring with them. (Each P has **C** following the **V** referred to here, except 2nd pl which has **CV**, and 1st sing which has only the **V** referred to here. The exponents of these endings are not discussed.) The patterns are:

1. ι	ϵ	2. ι	ι
ϵ	ϵ	ι	ι
ϵ	ι	ι	α

These are traditionally referred to as 1st and 2nd conjugation and will be so called here.

Alternation in exponents of C preceding P and prosodic nature of Russian syllable

The problem here dealt with concerns most obviously the alternation at the phonetic level in the verbal paradigm in Russian of the (phonetic) consonant types preceding P, *eg*:

[mʲɪˈt̪u]	'sweep'	[lʲɪˈtʃu]	'be flying'
[mʲɪˈt̪oʃ]		[lʲɪˈtʲiʃ]	
[mʲɪˈt̪ot̪]		[lʲɪˈtʲit̪]	
[mʲɪˈt̪om]		[lʲɪˈtʲim]	
[mʲɪˈt̪öt̪ɪ]		[lʲɪˈtʲitʲɪ]	
[mʲɪˈt̪ut̪]		[lʲɪˈtʲat̪]	
[t̪] alternates with [t̪]		[tʃ] alternates with [t̪]	

One also finds [tʃ] in all cases. (Compare, for example, the verb [ˈprat̪ət̪] – 'hide'; 'sweep' is 1st conj, 'be flying' 2nd.) This is the main and most immediately striking feature of verb forms with P and is a feature of all Russian verbs. However, it is noticed that not only do the consonants alternate, but the quality of adjacent vowels varies in a general way consistently and in a parallel manner according to whether there is palatality (frontness) or non-palatality/velarity (centrality/backness) present at a particular syllable junction. Most if not all writers on the phonetics of Russian have remarked on this fact. Phonemically this feature has usually been assigned to the consonant, although it has been remarked at the same time that very frequently the presence or absence of this feature of C is more obvious in the quality of the adjacent vowel(s) than in the C itself.[6] In fact therefore it would certainly seem preferable to regard these features as characteristic of the syllable (beginning, ending, junction) rather than of phonematic C or V units, and there is clearly place for at least a two-term prosodic system, frontness/non-frontness $(y/ȳ)$. This factor of Russian pronunciation is the excuse (if any is needed) for the analysis proposed here.

However it turns out that application of prosodic analysis to the verb, having in mind a grammatico-phonological statement which shall make it possible to state a single form for R having as wide an application as possible (as noted earlier) calls for a three-term system such as has been set up here. The distribution of these terms in relation to the two conjugations is as set out below.

Distribution of the prosodies in relation to the two conjugations

Prosodies are distributed as under:

1. (1st conj)   2. (2nd conj)

Either (*a*)   or (*b*)

ȳ	y_1	y_2	y_2	y_2	y_1
y_1	y_1	y_2	y_2	y_1	y_1
y_1	ȳ	y_2	y_2	y_1	y_1

That is, there are two prosodic patterns for the 1st conj but only one for the 2nd. If these patterns are applied to the statement of all verbs in terms of *RP* or *RSP* as prosodies of the junction of **V** of *P* with the final phonematic unit of *R* or *S* (**C** or **V** respectively – *S* is always phonologically **V**, except for one small group of verbs), the phonetic facts of all verbs except three[7] can be accounted for, with the final **C** or *R* stated as the appropriate term of **C** listed above, the exponents being as given below. 1(*a*) occurs with junction -**C**(of *R*)**V**- only (*ie* never with *S*). The exponent of all y's in junction -**VV**- (of -*SP*) is [j]. This is treated as exponent of a prosody only. (See below among examples.)

As an aid to the understanding of the examples which follow, below are listed the exponents of -**C**s of *R* with each of the three prosodies. The hyphen on either side of the symbol for the prosody is intended as a reminder that the prosody does not in fact apply to **C** only (by definition) but has extent.

	-ȳ-	-y_1-	-y_2-	
P	p	p̣	pḷ	
B	b	ḅ	bḷ	
M	m	ṃ	mḷ	
F	f	f̣	fḷ	←(included for one verb only – [grʌˈfiṭ])
V	v	ỵ	vḷ	
T	ṭ	ṭ	tʃ[8]	
D	ḍ	ḍ	ʒ	
N	ṇ	ṇ̣	ṇ̣	
R	r	ṛ	ṛ	
L	—[9]	ḷ	ḷ	
S	ṣ	ṣ	ʃ	
Z	z̧	z̧	ʒ	
K	k	tʃ	tʃ	
G	g	ʒ	ʒ	
X	x	ʃ	ʃ	

The occurrence of velarization as an exponent of y_1 and y_2 prosody (*viz* with G and x) and of [ḷ] with y_2 prosody and labial consonants alluded to in the notes on the exponents of the prosodies is perhaps made clearer by this chart. The following points may be noted:

1. The occurrence of the *same phonetic* consonant as exponent of a particular phonological consonant with different prosodies, and also of

different consonants – *eg* [ʧ] as exponent of K with y_1 and y_2 and also of T (with y_2). Similarly with [ʃ] and [ʒ] as exponents with these two prosodies of X and S, and G and D respectively. Similarly also with [ɳ], [ɽ] and [ḷ] as exponents of N, R and L with both y_1 and y_2 prosody. Only by seeing this as permissible can a clear interpretation of the facts be arrived at. The view that one phonetic item must always be accounted for by reference to one and the same phonological item, regardless of its relationship to items at the corresponding place in other terms of the paradigmatic scatter, would seem to make a clear and linguistically intuitively 'right' statement impossible; certainly in the case of Russian and in all comparable cases. The data must be interpreted as seems best from the widest possible phonetico-grammatical or -lexical point of view.

2. The occurrence of [ḷ] in addition to a bilabial (*ie* two consonants) as exponents of the *single* phonological units P, B, M, etc. Any attempt to regard this [ḷ] as exponent of a phonological lateral consonant and consequently as linked with either (or worse still both) [ḷ] exponents of L would introduce confusion and destroy the parallelism between the labials and other consonants which must be maintained if simplicity is to be achieved. The [ḷ] of [pḷ] [bḷ] etc has nothing to do phonologically with these other [ḷ]'s according to this interpretation, and there is in my view no reason why it should have (in fact every reason why it should not).

3. Further connected with the subject of labials, is the fact that F is certainly a 'foreign' consonant in the verb (and in general in Russian in fact) and need not therefore be included in the main Russian system. If excluded, this would leave V no longer a pair with F. This raises the question of whether [v], etc, is to be regarded as exponent of a consonant at all, or whether in fact it would not also be better regarded as exponent of another prosody (say ᵛ). Phonetic [v], etc, might be seen as pairing in this case with [j]. The occurrence of [v] in the infinitive of such verbs as ['ʈɽɛbəvəʈ] as against [u̯] in the indicative ['ʈɽɛbu̯ju̯], etc, would be an additional inducement to this interpretation. The [u̯] and [v] could be regarded as prosodically similar. If such an interpretation were adopted forms such as ['s̱ţavḻu̯, 's̱ţavi̯ʃ], etc ('put') would be stated as ['s̱ţa]$^{vy_2}_i$, ['s̱ţa]$^{vy_1}_i$ [ʃ], etc, with juxtaposition of two prosodies. This is however very much a speculation and no decision has been taken concerning the possibility yet.

Below follow some examples of Russian verbs, the phonology of which is stated in accordance with the system outlined here. No phonological statement of the verb is attempted other than at the point referred to here. Only the final **C** of *R* appears in phonological transcription.[10]

Examples of RP verbs

1(*a*)   -ȳ-   -y$_1$-
[ɪ'du, ɪ'doʃ], etc   -'Dι, -'Dє-, etc, 'be going'
[mɪ'tu, mɪ'toʃ], etc   -'Tι, -'Tє-, etc, 'sweep'

                      -ȳ-   -y$_1$-
[mʌ'gu, 'moʒɪʃ], etc   -'Gι, '-Gє-, etc, 'be able'

                      -ȳ-   -y$_1$-
['ḷagu, 'ḷaʒɪʃ], etc   '-Gι, '-Gє- etc, 'lie down'

                      -ȳ-   -y$_1$-
['ʒṇu, 'ʒṇoʃ], etc   -'Nι, -'Nє-, etc, 'reap'

                      -ȳ-   -y$_1$-
['ʒmu, 'ʒṃoʃ], etc   -'Mι, -'Mє-, etc, 'press'

                      -ȳ-   -y$_1$-
[ʒɪ'vu, ʒɪ'voʃ], etc   -'Vι, -'Vє-, etc, 'live'
    (regarding [v, y] as exponents of a consonant v)

(*b*)   -y$_2$-   -y$_2$-
[drɪm'ḷu, 'drεmḷɪʃ], etc   -'Mι, '-Mє-, etc, 'slumber'

                      -y$_2$-   -y$_2$-
[pɪ'ʃu, 'pɪʃɪʃ], etc   -'Sι, '-Sє-, etc, 'write'

                      -y$_2$-   -y$_2$-
[mʌ'ʃu, 'maʃɪʃ], etc   -'Xι, '-Xє-, etc, 'wave'

                      -y$_2$-   -y$_2$-
['ʃḷu, 'ʃḷoʃ], etc   'SLι 'SLє-, etc, 'send'

                      -y$_2$-   -y$_1$-
2. [xʌ'ʒu, 'xodɪʃ], etc   -'Dι, -'Dι-, etc, 'go'

                      -y$_2$-   -y$_1$-
[ḷɪ'tʃu, ḷɪ'tiʃ], etc   -'Tι, -'Tι-, etc, 'be flying'

                      -y$_2$-   -y$_1$-
[ḷɪ'ʒu, ḷɪ'ʒɪʃ], etc   -'Gι, -'Gι-, etc, 'be lying'
    (*cf* ['ḷagu] above which also has G; also exponents of previous two
      verbs)

                      -y$_2$-   -y$_1$-
['kontʃu, 'kontʃɪʃ], etc   '-Kι, '-Kι-, etc, 'finish'
    (again *cf* first two verbs under 2)

                      -y$_2$-   -y$_1$-
[prʌʃ'ʃu, prʌṣ'tiʃ], etc   -s'Tι, -s'Tι-, etc, 'forgive'

Examples of RSP

                      -y$_2$-   -y$_2$-
[tʃɪ'taju, tʃɪ'tajɪʃ], etc   '- ι, '- є-, etc, 'read'

                      -y$_2$-   -y$_2$-
['tṛεbuju, 'tṛεbujɪʃ], etc   '- ι, '- є-, etc, 'demand'

                      -y$_2$-   -y$_2$-
['ṇju, 'ṇjoʃ], etc   -' ι, -' є-, etc, 'drink'

This last verb has a prosody (statable as y_1) as S, but no vowel, R consisting of one consonant only. So for the other four similar verbs in the language as well. This takes one over to a consideration in these RSP verbs of the junction of RS, which will be undertaken in considering the infinitive and the phonological relation between the aspects. ['ɟjy̧, 'ɟjoɟ], etc, 'sew' is interesting here. If RS junction is interpreted in the same terms as the junction of SP, R emerges phonologically as x with y_1 prosody (cf 'drink'). Similarly [ʌt̪ɣɪ'tʃaj̧y̧], etc has an R ending т with y_2 prosody, the т being the same as in [ʌt̪'ɣetʃy̧], etc, the perfective aspect of this verb. (Translation 'reply'.) This aspect is comparable to 'be flying' in the list of examples in its phonetic alternations.

This concludes the outline of the phonology of these forms of the Russian verb. As already indicated, the roots set up here to account for part of the data are applicable to the other forms of the verb, such as infinitive, imperative, past tense, aspect. The prosodic and consonant and vowel systems involved in the phonology of these forms will be dealt with in a subsequent article.

Notes

[1] A further article by W. S. Cornyn, 'On the Classification of Russian Verbs,' *Language*, xxiv, 1948, 64 *ff*, is in comparable terms to Jakobson's.

[2] It is hoped to present a teaching statement subsequently in conjunction with D. Ward, of the Department of Russian, Edinburgh University.

[3] This is on the traditional view that *eg* [ɲəɲi'ʄu] etc is future (perfective).

[4] Occurrence in one verb only – see below.

[5] There were to have been four terms *viz* ɩ, υ, ε, α. I am indebted to J. Carnochan for pointing out that only one close vowel was necessary, since frontness and unrounding or backness and rounding etc are adequately accounted for by the prosodies. The four-term system was itself an 'interpretation imposed by the orthography'.

[6] It is noteworthy that Russian orthography assigns the features referred to to the vowels broadly speaking – in all ways a more satisfactory solution alphabetically. (See D. Ward, 'A Critique of Russian Orthography', to appear in the forthcoming commemorative volume for Daniel Jones.) [Abercrombie, D., *et al*, eds, *In Honour of Daniel Jones*, Longman, 1964. Eds.]

[7] These are 'weave', [t̪ku, t̪koɟ, etc . . .], the only verb having [k̪], not [tʃ], as (by definition) exponent of y_1 with к; and 'give', [d̪am, d̪aɟ etc] and 'eat' [jɛm, jɛɟ etc] in the singular. These have their own phonology, which will be dealt with under the infinitive.

[8] [ʃʃ] with some verbs. This is usually described as South Slavonic in origin. It is not part of the Russian system.

[9] L does not occur with ȳ prosody.

[10] One grammar of Russian known to me states verbal roots comparable to those set up here. This is *Colloquial Russian* by Mark Sieff, in the 'Colloquial' series. [Published by Kegan Paul. Eds.]

G. F. Arnold

Concerning the theory of plosives

In the past it has been the practice of most writers on English phonetics to consider pulmonic egressive plosives, from the articulatory/auditory standpoint at any rate, as consisting of three sequential stages. These three stages have been variously designated. Ward (*Phonetics of English*, *p* 113) for instance, labels them stop, release, and some sound following the release; whereas, more recently, Gimson (*Introduction to the Pronunciation of English*, *p* 145) has closing stage, hold or compression stage, and release or explosion stage.

In the present writer's view the features in question, which have hitherto been subsumed under three heads however designated, are more logically treated under four. These are

1. *Closure*
One or more articulatory movements leading to the complete sealing off of the vowel tract, thereby making possible

2. *Stop period*
A period of time during which the closure is maintained, the pulmonic compression is achieved (and, in the case of a final, unexploded plosive, the necessary decompression is brought about) and the vocal cords are made to vibrate for all, part or none of its duration. This is followed by

3. *Release*
The converse of the closure, one or more articulatory movements which,

First published in *Le Maître Phonétique*, 3rd series, No 125: 2–5, January–June 1966.

if the pulmonic compression is maintained, allow the compressed air to escape and give rise to

4. *Plosion*

An auditory feature, namely the noise made by the escaping compressed air. Now it is true that these four stages are for the most part implicit in previous descriptions, particularly Gimson's. There is nonetheless more than simple logic to be gained by their explicit recognition. Generally the tendency has been to telescope the third and fourth stages listed above; but if, in view of their widely differing nature, a clear distinction is made between release and plosion, it then becomes possible to make a more rigorous and a more comprehensive statement concerning those phenomena which are often to be observed in a Southern British English pronunciation of, for instance, /k/ in /æktə/ and /ʃɒk/, and /t/ in /bɒtl/ and /mʌtn/.

The gain with respect to the description of /k/ in /æktə/ is obvious. In this context /k/ would now be generally, though not universally, categorized as an incomplete *plosive*, its incompleteness lying in the fact that it lacks its fourth, plosion stage. Contrary to what Ward explicitly states, this /k/ does have its third, release stage, a median oral velar release in fact; but this release, owing to the prior formation of the first, closure stage for the following /t/ during the second, stop period stage of /k/, does not lead on to the fourth, plosion stage for /k/. Similarly /k/ in /ʃɒk/, if unexploded in an utterance-final or some other comparable prejuncture position, has a release stage – in addition to the median oral velar release, the soft palate may also be lowered – but, on account of prior pulmonic decompression during the stop period, no plosion ensues. Once release and plosion are clearly differentiated the undesirability of regarding, as some writers have done, two such occurrences of /k/ as examples of incomplete *plosion* becomes self-evident. In these and all similar cases it is the plosive, not the plosion, which is incomplete; the plosion is nonexistent.

The advantage to be derived from the rigid distinction between release and plosion is equally important, though perhaps less obvious, in the description of the phenomenon often present in a Southern British English pronunciation of /t/ in /bɒtl/. This phenomenon has sometimes been called lateral release, by Gimson for example, and sometimes lateral plosion, by Ward amongst others. With release and plosion now taken to be two completely separate stages of the plosive, it becomes possible to regard lateral release and lateral plosion no longer as vaguely synonymous terms, but rather as terms for two sharply differentiated articulatory/auditory phenomena. At the same time these two terms can be used to resolve the question discussed at length by Gimson (*p* 153): are the plosives in /æpl, bləʊ, kliːn, iːgl/, for example, to be considered as comparable with /t/ in /bɒtl/, at least in so far as their release and/or plosion are concerned?

The term *lateral release*, it is suggested, should be used solely to indicate that the third, release stage of the plosive is brought about simply by lowering the sides of the articulator which forms its oral closure. It therefore follows that, to conform to this definition of lateral release, the plosive and its following lateral must be homorganic. Since English has neither bilabial nor velar lateral to match its bilabial and velar plosives, only /t/ and /d/, homorganic with /l/, can in English have lateral release. The plosives in /æpl, bləʊ, kliːn, iːgl/ are consequently excluded; their release in these and all other words in which the sequences /pl, bl, kl, gl/ occur is in fact median oral. This is not to say that in general phonetics it is impossible for [p, b, k, g] to have lateral release; as Gimson explains (*p* 153), they can indeed be laterally released provided that their complete oral closure, bilabial or velar, is removed in such a way as to retain a bilabial or a velar median oral contact.

On the other hand, *lateral plosion* should be understood to mean the auditory effect of the outrush of pulmonically compressed air round a median oral obstruction and as such can be applied to all sequences of plosive plus lateral, in English to /pl, bl, gl, kl/ as well as to /tl, dl/, provided that, in the former sequences in which plosive and lateral are not homorganic, the median obstruction for the lateral is formed before the median oral release of the plosive takes place. If this proviso is not fulfilled, then the plosive has neither lateral release nor lateral plosion.

Very similar considerations apply to the phenomenon exemplified by a typical Southern British English pronunciation of /t/ in /mʌtn/. Here again an advantageous distinction can be drawn between the two terms often used more or less synonymously in this connection. *Nasal release* (Gimson) – perhaps following Pike, velic release might be a more appropriate term – can be restricted to those sequences of plosive plus nasal in which the consonants are homorganic; it therefore designates the one, single supraglottal movement necessary to bring about the plosion stage of the plosive, that is, the lowering of the soft palate. Thus in English the plosives in /əʊpm, rɪbm, mʌtn, sʌdn, θɪkŋ, ɔːgŋ/ all have nasal (or velic) release, whereas in /əʊpn, rɪbn, θɪkn, ɔːgn, əʊtmiːl, rəʊdmæp, əknɒlɪdʒ, frɒgmaːtʃ/ for example, they do not.

By contrast *nasal plosion* (Ward), like lateral plosion, can have a wider significance. This term is appropriately used to label an auditory feature, namely the outrush of pulmonically compressed air exclusively through the nasal cavity. In English therefore nasal plosion is exemplified by all the possible sequences of plosive plus nasal, provided that, when, as in the second list of words above, the plosive and nasal are not homorganic, the oral closure for the nasal precedes the median oral release of the plosive, thereby ensuring that none of the pulmonic compression achieved during the stop period of the plosive is lost through the oral cavity. If the plosive closure is released first, the plosion, as well as the release, of the plosive is oral, not nasal.

Raymond T. Butlin

On the alphabetic notation of certain phonetic features of Malayalam

To search for 'unity' and 'system' at the expense of truth is not, I take it, the proper business of philosophy, however universally it may have been the practice of philosophers.   G. E. MOORE

It is proposed here to offer some considerations on the representation of certain Malayalam[1] sounds. It is not the purpose of these notes to present a detailed laboratory account of the acoustic and physiological phenomena to be symbolized, but while characterizing these phenomena sufficiently for the reader to appreciate their general nature, rather to consider certain specific circumstances of their occurrence and the significance of these in the elaboration of a notational system.

[A brief indication is here given of the sound-values which the reader should attach to the symbols hereafter employed, in order to enable him to make some verbal response to the visual forms, and in the case of those familiar with the language, to assist in the identification of the words.

Vowels and diphthongs

The precise value to be given to the vowels and diphthongs is irrelevant to the present discussion. Twelve symbols will be used, *viz* a, aa, e, ee, i, ii, o, oo, u, uu, ə, ai. (A symbol is not a letter: aa and a are two distinct symbols.) It will be found sufficient for the present purposes to read these symbols in accordance with international phonetic usage, length being represented by double letters.

Consonants

The reader will find it sufficient to attach to the following symbols the

---

First published in *Bulletin of the School of Oriental Studies*, Vol VIII, No 2: 437–447, 1936.

values described in J. R. Firth's 'Short Outline of Tamil Pronunciation '[2]: p, pp, t, tt, ṭ, ṭṭ, c, cc, j, k, kk, m, mm, ṇ, ṇṇ, ɲ, ɲɲ, ŋ, ŋŋ,
l, ll, ḷ, ḷḷ, v, vv, y, yy. Those who are unfamiliar with this work may, without prejudice to the main considerations of this article, interpret these
symbols, together with b, ṭh, g, jj, s, ç, ʃ, and h, in accordance with
international phonetic usage, subject to the following modifications: c, cc,
j, jj are palato-alveolar affricates, ç is used for the International Phonetic
Association ɕ, ʃ is retroflex, y has its English value in *yes*.
      The following symbols require special explanation: ṭṭ, n, nn, ṇ, ṇṇ,
ŋ̇ŋ̇, r, ṛ, ṛ, ḳḳ.
ṭṭ. The primary articulation of the sound represented is alveolar and
      tense, with slight secondary palatalization.
n, nn. To be read respectively as short and long nasals with primary den-
      tal articulation and slight secondary velarization.
ṇ, ṇṇ. Short and long nasals respectively with primary alveolar articula-
      tion and slight secondary palatalization.
ŋ̇ŋ̇. Pre-velar articulation, intermediate between ɲ and ŋ.
r. A short alveolar trill with slight secondary velarization.
ṛ. A denti-alveolar or dental trill with secondary palatalization.
ṛ. The symbol should be given the value assigned by Firth (v.s.) to ɹ. A
      retroflex frictionless continuant.
ḳḳ. Should be interpreted as a tense voiceless palatal plosive.]

      Our observations are based upon an examination, on the phonetic level,
of the circumstances in which certain sounds occur in a number of selected
Malayalam words. These sounds will, as a result of our analysis, be
symbolized by (t, tt, ṭṭ, ṭ, ṭṭ), (m, mm, n, nn, ṇ, ṇṇ, ɲ, ɲɲ, ŋ̇ŋ̇, ŋ, ŋŋ), (l, ll,
ḷ, ḷḷ), (r, ṛ, ṛ), (k, kk, ḳḳ). Both from the point of view of orderliness of
exposition and of typographical convenience, we shall find it advantageous
to treat the material in groups, as indicated above by the use of brackets.
It should be stated that this methodological device has been so chosen as
in no way to affect our conclusions.
      We shall examine in detail the alternances occurring within these
groups in initial, intervocalic, medial and final positions. The material
will not, however, be presented in this schematic order, but in diminishing
sequence from the series presenting the maximum, to that presenting the
minimum number of alternative terms.[3]
      In certain cases it has been possible to establish a complete series on the
basis of a single-term alternance in complete words. Such series are pre-
fixed with an asterisk.
      Important as such cases are, it would, however, be impossible to devise
an adequate notational system exclusively on the basis of entire words,
since, of the theoretically possible number of single-term alternances in
complete words, only comparatively few are actual. No doubt further investigation will reveal such series which the writer has not yet had the
good fortune to discover. Nevertheless, it is certain that no amount of re-

search would reveal single-term alternances in all the contexts chosen for the present purpose.

In the majority of cases, therefore, it has been necessary to employ words exhibiting multiple alternance, by extracting from them appropriate isolates[4] in the form of particular phonetic sequences exhibiting single-term alternance. The specificity of the isolates selected for the present purpose is such as to enable us to devise a notation making the fullest use, compatible with unambiguity and practical convenience, of contextual conventions involving contiguous terms. By increasing the degree of specificity, such contextual conventions could be considerably reduced.

Table A

Series 1: Intervocalic

t		tt		ṭṭ		ṭ		ṭṭ	
*pati	husband	*patti	hood of snake	*paṭṭi	glued	*paṭi	a step	*paṭṭi	dog
*kuti	a jump	*kutti	stabbed	*kuṭṭi	tent-peg	*kuṭi	a drink	*kuṭṭi	boy
koti	greed	kotti	stung			koṭi	flag	koṭṭi	struck
paata	path			paaṭṭa	cockroach	paaṭa	scum		
						koṭa	umbrella	koṭṭa	basket

Series 2: Medially, preceded by homorganic nasal

t		ṭṭ		ṭ	
pantə	ball	taṇṭṭe	one's	kaṇṭu	saw
niintuka	to swim	makaṇṭṭe	son's	niiṇṭu	became long
		eṇṭṭe	my		

Series 3: Medial groups (other than those included in series 2 and 4)

t		ṭ	
vaastavam	truth	kaʃṭam	troublesome
paṇti	column	ʃaʃtipuurtti	60th birthday

Series 4: Medially, with r or y

tt	
ṛaattri	night
varttamaaṇam	news
sattyam	truth
marttyaṇ	man

Series 5: Initial (including initial groups)

t	
tanta	father
tekkə	south
tiircca	decision
tuṭal	a chain
tyaagam	a sacrifice
tyajiḳḳuka	to discard
staṇam	breast

It will be seen that in *Table* A the series exhibiting the maximum alternance occurs intervocalically and contains five terms, while medially with preceding homorganic nasal we have a three-term series, in other medial groups a series of two terms, and a single term initially and in medial groups with r or y.

It is evident that the number of symbols necessary and adequate for the representation of a series of alternative terms is in direct proportion to the number of such terms. The maximum number of symbols will be required in the series exhibiting the maximum alternance, the minimum in the minimum series.

Now it is important to realize that no useful purpose whatsoever can be served by seeking a chimerical unity between a term in a major series and one in a minor series, or even between the terms of two different series containing an equal number of terms, since to do so is to leave out of account the relevant context of their occurrence and so to invalidate any conclusion.

Strictly speaking each term might be distinctively symbolized, but for the practical purposes of notation it is desirable to practise some measure of symbol economy. This may best be effected if the choice of symbols in a minor series be determined by an empirical comparison of the sounds in question to similar sounds in a major series (subject, however, to a provision to be explained subsequently). Thus tt is used in medial consonant groups in the foregoing examples on the ground that empirical observation shows the sound to be almost identical with that symbolized by tt in the intervocalic series.

Absence of approximate acoustic identity does not necessarily preclude the use of identical symbols for two terms in different series. Thus, although there is a difference of tensity and voicing between the terms of the initial and intervocalic series symbolized by t, no ambiguity can arise if the appropriate convention be adopted. It would, nevertheless, have been equally legitimate to employ a distinctive symbol, say ð, for the term in the intervocalic series; and such a proceeding might, for certain pedagogical purposes, be advantageous. Since, however, Malayalam is a written language, and that in the orthography both terms are represented by identical symbols, for general purposes it is perhaps more convenient, without implying any relationship, to use similar symbols in both cases.

The nasal group presents a maximum series of ten terms intervocalically. The series with following homorganic stop presents six terms. It will be observed that for the second, fifth, and sixth terms of this series, symbols have been employed which do not occur in the notation of the maximum series, *viz* n, ɲ, ŋ.

Table B

Series 1 : Intervocalic

m
- aama — tortoise
- kamukə — areca palm
- roomam — hair

mm
- umma — kiss
- cemmaaṇ — cobbler
- tammil — between us

ṇ
- maṇi — bell, clock
- paṇam — money
- ṭeeṇu — dust
- piṇam — corpse

ṇṇ
- ciṇṇaṇṇi — crocodile
- kaṇṇə — eye
- kaṇṇaaṭi — glass
- maṇṇə — soil

ṇ
- gaaṇam — song
- aṇumaaṇam — a guess
- miṇiṇṇi — shone
- itiṇə — for this

ṇṇ
- kaṇṇi — month
- paṇṇaasə — rotten
- piṇṇal — a plait

nn
- raanni — (place name)
- pookunnu — is going
- cennu — went
- ninniṟunnu — waited

ṉṉ
- paṇṇi — cotton
- kuṇṇə — infant
- tikaṇṇu — became full
- ṇaaṇṇuul — earthworm

ñ
- naaraṅṅa — lemon
- mattaṅṅa — pumpkin
- ciṅṅam — name of a month

ññ
- maaṅṅa — mango
- mooṅṅuka — to moan
- viṅṅi — sobbed

Series 2: Medially, following homorganic stop

m
- kampə — stick
- kampi — wire
- tuumpa — spade
- panta — ball

n
- canta — market
- cantam — a sight, *eg* in 'What a sight'
- javanti — kind of flower

ṇ
- raṇṭə — two
- piṇṭam — a burnt offering
- kaṇṭham — neck
- paṇṭə — once

ṇ
- tanṭə — one's
- enṭə — my
- avanṭə — his
- panṭə — ball

ñ
- añjanam — lampblack
- mañcal — litter
- iñci — ginger

ŋ
- maṅka — virgin
- aṅkam — organ (of body)
- saṅgati — news
- paṅkə — a, share

Series 3: Other medial groups (excluding those in Series 4)

m	ṇ	ŋ
samsaaṛikkuka to talk	aṇyan stranger	paŋti column
	tiṇmaaṇ for eating	

Series 4: Initial

m	n	ɲ
maaṭṭuka to move	naaṛaṅṅa lemon	ɲaaṇ I
maṛam tree	ninnu stood	ɲaŋŋaḷ we
muḷa bamboo	niinti swam	ɲoṭi moment

Series 5: Medially, after r or ṛ

mm	nn
nirmmikkuka to appoint	tiirnnu finished
	taaṛnna lower

Series 6: Final

m	ṇ
maṇam smell	payyaṇ boy
ikkaalam this time	veeṭaṇ hunter
addeeham he	cemmaaṇ cobbler

Series 7: Initial group

ṇ
ṇyaayam justice

Now, although the sounds thus symbolized [n, ɲ, ŋ] do not occur intervocalically, it would be possible, by establishing a contextual convention as to length, to employ either nn, ɲɲ, ŋŋ, or n, ɲ, ŋ in both series. Such simplification nevertheless appears unnecessarily schematic and is of no practical convenience. It is gratuitous to assume that in all cases contextual conventions are necessarily preferable to additional symbols.

Table c

Series 1: Intervocalic

l		ll		ḷ		ḷḷ	
palaka	plank	pallakkə	a litter	kaḷa	weed	veḷḷam	water
baalika	girl	alli	bud	kaḍaḷi	kind of banana	paḷḷi	church
mula	breast	mulla	kind of plant	muḷa	bamboo	muḷḷə	thorn

Series 2: Final

l		ḷ	
pakal	daytime	avaḷ	she
mayil	peacock	kaviḷ	cheek
vaçaal	perhaps	aaḷukaḷ	persons

Series 3: Initial

l

laaṭam	horseshoe
lookam	world
lejja	shyness

Series 4: Medial groups

l

taalpparyam	meaning
kalppam	kind of tree

Similar arguments have been advanced for the use of either h or ŋ for both h initially and ŋ finally in English. It is interesting to note that by applying the method here described, such fruitless discussions are avoided. The intervocalic series in English contains both h and ŋ, while the initial (a minor series) contains h but not ŋ, and the final (also a minor series) contains ŋ but not h. Reference to the intervocalic (major) series will suggest the use of h for a similar sound in the initial series, while reference to the same series will suggest the use of ŋ for a similar sound in the final series.

Tables c and d are presented without comment, since they involve no new problem.

Table d

Series 1: Intervocalic

r		ṛ		ṭ	
*kara	sap	*kaṛa	coast	*kaṭa	punt-pole
kiiri	tore	kiiṛi	mongoose	kiṭi	bundle
coorə	cooked rice	cooṛa	blood	kooṭi	fowl
		puṛa	thatched hut	puṭa	a stream
mara	screen			maṭa	rain

Series 2: Medial groups

r		ṛ		ṭ	
iircca	uneasiness	suuṛyaṇ	sun	covvaaṭcca	Tuesday
yaattra	journey	kaaryam	fact		
tarkkam	dispute	viiṛyam	bravery	taaṭnna	lower

Series 3 : Initial

r   ṛ
raantal   lantern   ṛaattri   night
raaṇi   queen   ṛuci   sense of taste
ravukka   cotton or silk   ṛoomam   hair
          jacket (women's)

Series 4 : Final

r
payar   peas
kayar   rope
malabaar Malabar

Series 5 : Initial groups

r
kramam   gradual
çramiccu tried

There remain the velar and palatal unaspirated plosive alternances (*Table* E). It should be noticed that previous writers have failed to observe the alternance value of the third term of the intervocalic series, Aiyyar,[5] for instance, treating such cases as variants of kk 'in association with palatal vowels'. The following examples leave no doubt that ḳḳ is a discrete term.

Table E

Series 1 : Intervocalic

k		kk		ḳḳ	
akam	inside	akkam	a numeral		
pookə	go (imper.)	pookkə	gait		
makaḷ	daughter	makkaḷ	children		
		kakkuka	to guard	kaaḳḳuka	to ripen
		aṛakkə	sealing wax	aṛaḳḳə	grind (imper.)
		arakkuka	to saw	araḳḳuka	to disguise
		avan	he is	avaṇ	he is
		vikkaaṇ	going to	viḳḳaaṇ	going
		pookunnu	stammer	pookunnu	to sell

Series 2: Initial (including initial groups)
k
karam   tax
kariŋŋaali name of tree
kiiri   mongoose
kramam   gradual

Series 3: Medially, preceded by homorganic nasal
k
maŋka   virgin
vaŋkaṇ   fool
paŋkajam   lotus

Series 4: Other medial groups
kk
tarkkam   dispute
markkaṭam   monkey
karkkaṭakam name of a month

Conclusion

Avoiding that crude hypostatization of the visual symbol which vitiates so much contemporary research, it has been possible, by a methodical examination of certain sounds in their relevant contexts, to establish a systematic, unambiguous and manageable notation. Although not an end in itself, a notation is an indispensable instrument both in broader linguistic studies, whether descriptive or historical, and in pedagogical practice.

In itself a notation cannot be said to constitute a phonetic analysis of a language, nor can any mere enumeration of the symbols employed, however precise the accompanying definitions of their acoustic values, possibly be accounted as such. A true phonetic analysis is provided only by a systematic presentation of the material investigated on the basis of alternances established in specific contexts, together with precise definitions of the acoustic and physiological characteristics of the sounds symbolized.

Analyses of this type are particularly valuable both to the linguistic historian and to those engaged in the practical teaching of languages. To the former the historical study of phonetic phenomena in specific contexts can alone be profitable. Attempts to investigate data divorced from the relevant context have repeatedly led, and must inevitably lead, to bewildering confusion.

The value of systematic phonetic analysis in linguistic pedagogy needs no emphasis. The establishment of alternance tables such as those presented above is the first task of those who seek to give a truly linguistic basis to their practical phonetic teaching, since only by a consideration of the particular circumstances in which varying degrees of phonetic differentiation occur in the foreign language and in the mother tongue, is it possible to bring order and proportion into what is otherwise so apt to degenerate into a meaningless travesty of pedagogical method.

Notes

[1] Our informants were Travancore Brahmins.
[2] Appendix to Arden's *Grammar of Common Tamil* (new and revised edition), published by the Christian Literature Society of India, 1934.
[3] The expression 'alternative phonetic terms' is used by J. R. Firth in 'The Use and Distribution of Certain English Sounds' (*English Studies*, 1935).
[4] The term has been adopted from Professor H. Levy.
[5] L. Vishwanātha Rāmaswāmi Aiyyar, *A Brief Account of Malayalam Phonetics*.

J. C. Catford

On the classification of stop consonants

It is well known that phonetic terminology is in a rather chaotic state. In particular, there is a lack of system in the usual classification and naming of stop consonants. For example, most writers tend to keep what are usually called implosives, ejectives and clicks apart, as though they don't enter into a general classification scheme along with other stop consonants. There is no very good reason why this should be, and I believe that the practice is pedagogically unsound, in that it obscures the true relationships which exist between all stop-type consonants, and leads to vagueness in students' minds regarding the mechanism of these sounds.

Dr Beach, in his admirable work on the phonetics of Hottentot,[1] writes of three types of click – 'pulmonic', 'glottalic' and 'velaric'. I see no reason why this kind of classification shouldn't be extended to form a basis for describing all kinds of stop consonants (and even fricatives). It seems to me that something would be done towards clarifying people's ideas on the subject if writers, and lecturers, on general phonetics presented to their students some classification such as I outline here.

I should define a stop consonant as a speech-sound involving in its production the complete enclosure of a body of air.

This body of air may be 1. compressed or 2. rarefied. Stop consonants which involve air compression may be called pressure stops, those involving rarefaction, suction stops.

The air which is compressed or rarefied in producing a stop is bounded by an outer and an inner closure. The outer closure is always in the supraglottal region (except, of course, in the case of ʔ, when it is at the glottis). The inner closure is normally situated at one of the three following points: (a) the lungs, (b) the glottis, (c) the velum. Stops with inner closure at

First published in *Le Maître Phonétique*, 3rd series, No 65: 2–5, 1939.

these points may be called, as Beach suggests, (*a*) pulmonic, (*b*) glottalic and (*c*) velaric.

All stop consonants, then, may be described by reference to these two characteristics: air compression or rarefaction, and situation of the inner closure point, and their interrelationships may be clearly shown in tabular form thus:

inner closure point	*compression*	*rarefaction*
lungs	pulmonic pressure stops	pulmonic suction stops
glottis	glottalic pressure stops	glottalic suction stops
velum	velaric pressure stops	velaric suction stops

Pulmonic pressure stops (p. p. stops) are, of course, the ordinary plosives p t k ʔ, etc, or voiced, b d g, etc.

Pulmonic suction stops (p. s. stops) are simply inverse plosives, produced with expansion of the thoracic cage and consequent rarefaction of the imprisoned air, resulting in some sort of implosion[2] on the release of the outer closure.

   P. s. stops are what would be called 'pulmonic clicks' by those who use the term 'click' to denote any kind of suction stop. Voiced p. s. stops are difficult to produce, and almost certainly don't exist in any language.

Glottalic pressure stops (g. p. stops) have an outer closure in the supraglottal region, and an inner closure at the glottis. The larynx is elevated, so that the enclosed body of air is compressed, and some kind of explosion[2] occurs when the outer closure is released. These are the ordinary 'ejectives', p', t', k', etc.

   Voiced g. p. stops do not occur.

Glottalic suction stops (g. s. stops). As in the case of g. p. stops, the glottis is closed, a sudden depression of the larynx, by enlarging the supraglottal cavities, rarefies the imprisoned air, so that an implosion occurs when the outer closure is released. Voiceless g. s. stops are what Beach calls 'glottalic clicks'; they might also be called 'inverse ejectives'.

   It might be argued that voiced g. s. stops cannot exist, since voicing implies incomplete, or rather intermittent, glottal closure. What are usually called 'implosives' can, however, be legitimately called 'voiced glottalic suction stops'. In this case the inner closure is formed, not by the closed glottis, but by the vibrating vocal cords. In the production of voiced g. s. stops (ɓ, ɗ, etc) there is, naturally, an outer closure in the supraglottal area. At the same time the glottis is loosely closed (for 'voice'). The larynx is rapidly depressed. A small quantity of air is sufficient to enable the vocal cords to vibrate (producing 'voice'), but is insufficient to raise the air pressure in the expanding supraglottal cavities to the atmospheric level, so that when the outer closure is released there is an implosion.

The mechanism of voiced g. s. stops is closely analogous to the fault known to engineers as 'wire drawing', in which steam, entering the cylinder of an engine working at high speed, is 'strangled', and does not come in quickly enough to keep up with the fast receding piston, with a consequent drop in pressure in the cylinder, and loss of efficiency.

Velaric pressure stops (v.p. stops) have an outer closure in the front part of the mouth, and inner closure formed by bringing the back of the tongue against the velum. The enclosed body of air is compressed by a forward movement of the back part of the tongue, and an explosion occurs on the release of the outer closure. V. p. stops are sometimes called 'inverse (or inverted) clicks' by those who use the term 'click' in the sense of 'velaric suction stop'.

Velaric suction stops (v. s. stops) are formed with outer closure in the front of the mouth, and inner closure between the back of the tongue and the velum. The enclosed air is rarefied by a backward movement of the back part of the tongue, which is followed by an implosion on release of the outer closure.

V. s. stops are what are most commonly called 'clicks' (ʇ ʗ ʘ etc.). Velaric stops cannot be voiced, in the usual sense of the term, since the body of air which enters into the formation of the stop is cut off from the larynx by the inner (velar) closure. They can, however, be accompanied by voice. Such sounds are called 'voiced clicks' by some people, and consist of v. s. stops performed against a background of voice, in the form of a variety of g or ŋ ('nasal voiced clicks').

When glottalic pressure stops, voiceless glottalic suction stops, and the velaric stops occur in the chain of speech (followed, for instance, by a vowel sound) they inevitably involve two releases. In the case of g. p. stops (ejectives), there is a primary release (of the outer closure) producing some kind of explosion in the mouth, and a secondary release, with a more or less strong glottal explosion. Velaric pressure stops also have two explosive releases, the secondary being of a velar type.

Voiceless glottalic and all velaric suction stops have a primary implosive release, and a secondary explosive release. The secondary release of 'voiced' v. s. stops is of the g or ŋ type.

Voiced glottalic suction stops (implosives), owing to the nature of their inner closure, which is formed by the vibrating vocal cords, may be followed by vowels with no secondary release of the inner closure.

If desired, it is perfectly possible to extend this kind of classification to other sounds as well as stops.

The ordinary fricatives of the f, s, z, ʒ type are pulmonic pressure fricatives, and the sound produced with a sudden intake of breath, under the influence of pain, is a pulmonic suction fricative. Ejective fricatives (such as Hausa s') are glottalic pressure fricatives, and so forth.

The above is no more than a brief outline of the classification and terminology proposed, but I think it is at least possible to judge from it the convenience of some consistent system such as this.

Notes

[1] D. M. Beach, *The Phonetics of the Hottentot Language*, Heffer, Cambridge, 1938.

[2] I use the terms 'implosion' and 'explosion' with the recognized English meanings of a sudden inflow, and outflow, respectively, of air, into or out of the mouth. It seems a pity that French writers use the terms 'implosion' and 'explosion' in a totally different sense, referring to a function of any sound in a syllable.

J. R. Firth

Sounds and prosodies

The purpose of this paper is to present some of the main principles of a theory of the phonological structure of the word in the piece or sentence, and to illustrate them by noticing especially sounds and prosodies that are often described as laryngals and pharyngals. I shall not deal with tone and intonation explicitly.

Sweet himself bequeathed to the phoneticians coming after him the problems of synthesis which still continue to vex us. Most phoneticians and even the 'new' phonologists have continued to elaborate the analysis of words, some in general phonetic terms, others in phonological terms based on theories of opposition, alternances, and distinctive differentiations or substitutions. Such studies I should describe as paradigmatic and monosystemic in principle.

Since de Saussure's famous *Cours*, the majority of such studies seem also to have accepted the monosystemic principle so succinctly stated by Meillet: 'chaque langue forme un système où tout se tient.' I have in recent years taken up some of the neglected problems left to us by Sweet. I now suggest principles for a technique of statement which assumes first of all that the primary linguistic data are pieces, phrases, clauses, and sentences within which the word must be delimited and identified, and secondly that the facts of the phonological structure of such various languages as English, Hindustani, Telugu, Tamil,[1] Maltese,[2] and Nyanja[3] are most economically and most completely stated on a polysystemic hypothesis.

In presenting these views for your consideration, I am aware of the

First published in *Transactions of the Philological Society*, 127–152, 1948, and subsequently in J. R. Firth, *Papers in Linguistics 1935–1951*, Oxford University Press, 1957.

danger of idiosyncrasy on the one hand, and on the other of employing common words which may be current in linguistics but not conventionally scientific. Nevertheless, the dangers are unavoidable since linguistics is reflexive and introvert. That is to say, in linguistics language is turned back upon itself. We have to use language about language, words about words, letters about letters. The authors of a recent American report on education win our sympathetic attention when they say 'we realize that language is ill adapted for talking about itself'. There is no easy escape from the vicious circle, and 'yet', as the report points out, 'we cannot imagine that so many people would have attempted this work of analysis for themselves and others unless they believed that they could reach some measure of success in so difficult a task.' All I can hope for is your indulgence and some measure of success in the confused and difficult fields of phonetics and phonology.

For the purpose of distinguishing prosodic systems from phonematic systems, words will be my principal isolates. In examining these isolates, I shall not overlook the contexts from which they are taken and within which the analyses must be tested. Indeed, I propose to apply some of the principles of word structure to what I term *pieces* or combinations of words. I shall deal with words and pieces in English, Hindustani, Egyptian Arabic, and Maltese, and refer to word features in German and other languages. It is especially helpful that there *are* things called English words and Arabic words. They are so called by authoritative bodies; indeed, English words and Classical Arabic words are firmly institutionalized. To those undefined terms must be added the words *sound, syllable, letter, vowel, consonant, length, quantity, stress, tone, intonation*, and more of the related vocabulary.

In dealing with these matters, words and expressions have been taken from a variety of sources, even the most ancient, and most of them are familiar. That does not mean that the set of principles or the system of thought here presented are either ancient or familiar. To some they may seem revolutionary. Word analysis is as ancient as writing and as various. We ABC people, as some Chinese have described us, are used to the process of splitting up words into letters, consonants and vowels, and into syllables, and we have attributed to them such several qualities as length, quantity, tone, and stress.

I have purposely avoided the word *phoneme* in the title of my paper, because not one of the meanings in its present wide range of application suits my purpose and *sound* will do less harm. One after another, phonologists and phoneticians seem to have said to themselves ' *Your* phonemes are dead, long live *my* phoneme'. For my part, I would restrict the application of the term to certain features only of consonants and vowels systematically stated *ad hoc* for each language. By a further degree of abstraction we may speak of a five-vowel or seven-vowel phonematic system, or of the phonematic system of the concord prefixes of a Bantu language,[4] or of the monosyllable in English.[5]

By using the common symbols c and v instead of the specific symbols for phonematic consonant and vowel units, we generalize syllabic structure in a new order of abstraction eliminating the specific paradigmatic consonant and vowel systems as such, and enabling the syntagmatic word structure of syllables with all their attributes to be stated systematically. Similarly we may abstract those features which mark word or syllable initials and word or syllable finals or word junctions from the word, piece, or sentence, and regard them syntagmatically as prosodies, distinct from the phonematic constituents which are referred to as units of the consonant and vowel systems. The use of spaces between words duly delimited and identified is, like a punctuation mark or 'accent', a prosodic symbol. Compare the orthographic example 'Is she?' with the phonetic transcript iʒʃiy? in the matter of prosodic signs. The interword space of the orthography is replaced by the junction sequence symbolized in general phonetic terms by ʒʃ. Such a sequence is, in modern spoken English, a mark of junction which is here regarded as a prosody. If the symbol *i* is used for word initial and *f* for word final, ʒʃ is *fi*. As in the case of c and v, *i* and *f* generalize beyond the phonematic level.

We are accustomed to positional criteria in classifying phonematic variants or allophones as initial, medial, intervocalic, or final. Such procedure makes abstraction of certain postulated units, *phonemes*, comprising a scatter of distributed variants (allophones). Looking at language material from a syntagmatic point of view, any phonetic features characteristic of and peculiar to such positions or junctions can just as profitably and perhaps more profitably be stated as prosodies of the sentence or word. Penultimate stress or junctional geminations are also obvious prosodic features in syntagmatic junction. Thus the phonetic and phonological analysis of the word can be grouped under the two headings which form the title of this paper – sounds and prosodies. I am inclined to the classical view that the correct rendering of the syllabic accent or the syllabic prosodies of the word is *anima vocis*, the soul, the breath, the life of the word. The study of the prosodies in modern linguistics is in a primitive state compared with the techniques for the systematic study of sounds. The study of sounds and the theoretical justification of roman notation have led first to the apotheosis of the sound-letter in the phoneme and later to the extended use of such doubtful derivatives as 'phonemics' and 'phonemicist', especially in America, and the misapplication of the principles of vowel and consonant analysis to the prosodies. There is a tendency to use one magic phoneme principle within a monosystemic hypothesis. I am suggesting alternatives to such a 'monophysite' doctrine.

When first I considered giving this paper, it was to be called 'Further Studies in Semantics'. I had in mind the semantics of my own subject or a critical study of the language being used about language, of the symbols used for other symbols, and especially the new idioms that have grown up around the word 'phoneme'. Instead of a critical review of that kind, I am now submitting a system of ideas on word structure, especially emphasizing the convenience of stating word structure and its musical attributes as distinct orders of abstractions from the total phonological complex. Such abstractions I refer to as prosodies, and again emphasize the plurality of systems within any given language. I think the classical grammarians employed the right emphasis when they referred to the prosodies as *anima vocis*. Whitney, answering the question 'What is articulation?' said: 'Articulation consists not in the mode of production of individual sounds, but in the mode of their combination for the purposes of speech.'[6]

The Romans and the English managed to dispense with those written signs called 'accents' and avoided pepperbox spelling. Not so the more ingenious Greeks. The invention of the written signs for the prosodies of the ancient classical language were not required by a native for reading what was written in ordinary Greek. They were, in the main, the inventions of the great scholars of Alexandria, one of whom, Aristarchus, was described by Jebb as the greatest scholar and the best Homeric critic of antiquity. The final codification of traditional Greek accentuation had to wait nearly four hundred years – some would say much longer – so that we may expect to learn something from such endeavours.[7] It is interesting to notice that the signs used to mark the accents were themselves called προσῳδίαι, prosodies, and they included the marks for the rough and smooth breathings. It is also relevant to my purpose that what was a prosody to the Greeks was treated as a consonant by the Romans, hence the 'h' of hydra. On the relative merits of the Greek and Roman alphabets as the basis of an international phonetic system of notation, Prince Trubetzkoy favoured Greek and, when we talked on this subject, it was clear he was trying to imagine how much better phonetics might have been if it had started from Greek with the Greek alphabet. Phonetics and phonology have their ultimate roots in India. Very little of ancient Hindu theory has been adequately stated in European languages. When it is, we shall know how much was lost when such glimpses as we had were expressed as a theory of the Roman alphabet.

More detailed notice of 'h' and the *glottal stop* in a variety of languages will reveal the scientific convenience of regarding them as belonging to the prosodic systems of certain languages rather than to the sound systems. 'h' has been variously considered as a sort of vowel or a consonant in certain languages, and the glottal stop as a variety of things. Phonetically, the glottal stop, unreleased, is the negation of all sound whether vocalic or consonantal. Is it the perfect minimum or terminus of the syllable, the beginning and the end, the master or maximum consonant? We have a good illustration of that in the American or Tamil exclamation

PaPa! Or is it just a necessary metrical pause or rest, a sort of measure of time, a sort of mora or matra? Is it therefore a general syllable maker or marker, part of the syllabic structure? As we shall see later, it may be all or any of these things, or just a member of the consonant system according to the language.

We have noticed the influence of the Roman and Greek alphabets on notions of sounds and prosodies. The method of writing used for Sanskrit is syllabic, and the Devanagari syllabary as used for that language, and also other forms of it used for the modern Sanskritic dialects of India, are to this day models of phonetic and phonological excellence. The word analysis is syllabic and clearly expressive of the syllabic structure. Within that structure the pronunciation, even the phonetics of the consonants, can be fully discussed and represented in writing with the help of the prosodic sign for a consonant closing a syllable. For the Sanskritic languages an analysis of the word satisfying the demands of modern phonetics, phonology, and grammar could be presented on a syllabic basis using the Devanagari syllabic notation without the use of the phoneme concept, unless of course syllables and even words can be considered as 'phonemes'.

In our Japanese phonetics courses at the School of Oriental and African Studies during the war, directed to the specialized purposes of operational linguistics, we analysed the Japanese word and piece by a syllabic technique although we employed roman letters. The roomazi system, as a system, is based on the native Kana syllabary. The syllabic structure of the word – itself a prosody – was treated as the basis of other prosodies perhaps over-simplified, but kept distinct from the syllabary. The syllabary was, so to speak, a paradigmatic system, and the prosodies a syntagmatic system. We never met any unit or part which *had* to be called a phoneme, though a different analysis, in my opinion not so good, has been made on the phoneme principle.

Here may I quote a few of the wiser words of Samuel Haldeman (1856), first professor of Comparative Philology in the University of Pennsylvania, one of the earlier American phoneticians, contemporary with Ellis and Bell. 'Good phonetics must recognize the value for certain languages "of alphabets of a more or less syllabic character", in which "a consonant position and a vowel position of the organs" are regarded "as in a manner constituting a unitary element".'[8] Sir William Jones was the first to point out the excellence of what he called the Devanagari system, and also of the Arabic alphabet. The Arabic syllabary he found almost perfect for Arabic itself – 'Not a letter,' he comments, 'could be added or taken away without manifest inconvenience.' He adds the remark, 'Our English alphabet and orthography are disgracefully and almost ridiculously imperfect.' I shall later be using Arabic words in roman transcription to illustrate the nature of syllabic analysis in that language as the framework for the prosodies. Sir William Jones emphasized the importance as he put it of the 'Orthography of Asiatic Words in Roman Letters'. The development of comparative philology, and especially of phonology, also meant increased attention to transliteration and transcription in roman letters. Sir William Jones was not in any position to understand how all this might contribute to the tendency, both in historical and descriptive linguistics, to phonetic hypostatization of roman letters, and theories built on such hypostatization.

In introducing my subject I began with sounds and the Roman alphabet which has determined a good deal of our phonetic thinking in Western Europe – as a reminder that in the Latin word the letter was regarded as a sound, *vox articulata*. We moved east to Greek, and met the prosodies, *ie* smooth and rough breathings, and the accents. The accents are marks, but they are also musical properties of the word. In Sanskrit we meet a syllabary built on phonetic principles, and each character is əkṣərə, ultimate, permanent, and indestructible. Any work I have done in the romanization of Oriental languages has been in the spirit of Sir William Jones, and consequently I have not underestimated the grammatical, even phonetic, excellence of the characters and letters of the East where our own alphabet finds its origin. On the contrary, one of the purposes of my paper is to recall the principles of other systems of writing to redress the balance of the West.

And now let us notice the main features of the Arabic alphabet. I suppose it can claim the title 'alphabet' on etymological grounds, but it is really a syllabary.[9] First, each Arabic letter has a name of its own, Secondly, each one is capable of being realized as an art figure in itself. Thirdly, and most important of all, each one has syllabic value, the value or *potestas* in the most general terms being consonant plus vowel, including vowel zero, or zero vowel. The special mark, *sukuun*, for a letter without vowel possibilities, *ie* with zero vowel, or for a letter to end a syllable not begin it, is the key to the understanding of the syllabic value of the simple letter not so marked, and this is congruent with the essentials of Arabic grammar. Like the hələnt in Devanagari, sukuun is a prosodic sign. The framework of the language and the etymology of words, including their basic syllabic structure, consist in significant sequences of radicals usually in threes. Hence a letter has the potestas of one of these radicals plus one of the three possible vowels i, a, or u or zero. Each syllabic sign or letter has, in the most general terms, a trivocalic potentiality, or zero vowel, but in any given word placed in an adequate context, the possibilities are so narrowly determined by the grammar that in fact the syllable is, in the majority of words, fully determined and all possibilities except one are excluded. The prosodies of the Arabic word are indicated by the letters if the context is adequate. If the syllabic structure is known, we always know which syllable takes the main prominence. It is, of course, convenient to make the syllabic structure more precise by marking a letter specially, to show it has what is called zero vowel, or to show it is doubled. Such marks are prosodic. And it is even possible to maintain that in this system of writing the diacritics pointing out the vowels and consonants in detail are added prosodic marks rather than separate vowel signs or separate sounds in the roman sense; that is to say, generalizing beyond the phonematic level, fatħa, kasra, ðamma, sukuun, alif, waw, taʃdiid and hamza form a prosodic system.

In China the characters, their figures and arrangement, are designs in their own right. Words in calligraphy are artefacts in themselves of high aesthetic value, for which there is much more general respect than we have in England for the Etonian pronunciation of the King's English. For my purpose Chinese offered excellent material for the study of institutionalized words long since delimited and identified. With the help of Mr K. H. Hu, of Changsha, I studied the pronunciation and phonology of his dialect of Hunanese.[10] Eventually I sorted out into phonological classes and categories large numbers of characters in accordance with their distinguishing diacritica. Diacritica were of two main types, phonematic and prosodic. The prosodic diacritica included tone, voice quality, and other properties of the sonants, and also yotization and labiovelarization, symbolized by y and w. Such diacritica of the monosyllable are not considered as successive fractions or segments in any linear sense, or as distributed in separate measures of time.[11] They are stated as systematized abstractions from the primary sensory data, *ie* the uttered instances of monosyllables. We must distinguish between such a conceptual framework which is a set of relations between categories, and the serial signals we make and hear in any given instance.[12]

Before turning to suggest principles of analysis recognizing other systems of thought and systems of writing outside the Western European tradition, let me amplify what has already been said about the prosodies by quoting from a grammarian of the older tradition and by referring to the traditional theory of music.

Lindley Murray's English Grammar (1795) is divided in accordance with good European tradition,[13] into four parts, *viz* Orthography, Etymology, Syntax, and Prosody. Part IV, Prosody, begins as follows: 'Prosody consists of two parts: the former teaches the true PRONUNCIATION of words, comprising ACCENT, QUANTITY, EMPHASIS, PAUSE, and TONE; and the latter, the laws of versification. Notice the headings in the first part – ACCENT, QUANTITY, EMPHASIS, PAUSE, and TONE.'

In section I of ACCENT, he uses the expression the *stress of the voice* as distinguishing the accent of English. The stress of the voice on a particular syllable of the word enables the number of syllables of the word to be perceived as grouped in the utterance of that word. In other words, the accent is a function of the syllabic structure of the word. He recognizes principal and secondary accent in English. He recognizes two quantities of the syllable in English, long and short, and discusses the syllabic analysis and accentuation of English dissyllables, trisyllables, and polysyllables, and notices intonation and emphasis.

The syntagmatic system of the word-complex, that is to say the syllabic structure with properties such as initial, final and medial characteristics, number and nature of syllables, quantity, stress, and tone, invites comparison with theories of melody and rhythm in music. Writers on the theory of music often say that you cannot have melody without rhythm, also that if such a thing were conceivable as a continuous series of notes of equal value, of the same pitch and without accent, musical rhythm could not be found in it. Hence the musical description of rhythm would be 'the grouping of measures', and a measure 'the grouping of stress and non-stress'. Moreover, a measure or a bar-length is a grouping of pulses which have to each other definite interrelations as to their length, as well as interrelations of strength. Interrelations of pitch and quality also appear to correlate with the sense of stress and enter into the grouping of measures.

We can tentatively adapt this part of the theory of music for the purpose of framing a theory of the prosodies. Let us regard the syllable as a pulse or beat, and a word or piece as a sort of bar-length or grouping of pulses which bear to each other definite interrelations of length, stress, tone, quality – including voice quality and nasality. The principle to be emphasized is the *interrelation of the syllables*, what I have previously referred to as the *syntagmatic relations*, as opposed to the *paradigmatic or differential relations* of sounds in vowel and consonant systems, and to the paradigmatic aspect of the theory of phonemes, and to the analytic method of regarding contextual characteristics of sounds as allophones of phonematic units.

A good illustration of these principles of word-analysis is provided if we examine full words in the spoken Arabic of Cairo, for which there are corresponding forms in Classical Arabic. Such words (in the case of nouns the article is not included) have from one to five syllables. There are five types of syllable, represented by the formulae given below, and examples of each are given.

SYLLABIC STRUCTURE IN CAIRO COLLOQUIAL[14]

1. CV: open short. C+*i*, *a*, or *u*.
   (*a*) fíhim nízil
   (*b*) ҳálamu Ꜥitláxam ḍárabit
   (*c*) Ꜥindáhaʃu (*cvc–cv–cv–cv*)

2. CVV: open medium. C+*i*, *a*, or *u*, and the prosody of vowel length indicated by doubling the vowel, hence VV – the first V may be considered the symbol of one of the three members of the vowel system and the second the mark of the prosody of length.

Alternatively y and w may be used instead of the second i or u.

(*a*) fáahim fúulah nóobah*

(*b*) muṣíibah ginéenah* misóogar*

(*c*) ʕiʃtaddéenah* (*cvc–cvc–cvv–cvc*)

(*d*) ʕistafáad náahum

3. CVC: closed medium. C + *i*, *a*, or *u*.

(*a*) ʕáfham dúrguh

(*b*) yistáfhim duxúlhum

(*c*) mistalbáxha (*cvc–cvc–cvc–cv*)

4. CVVC: closed long. C + *i*, *a*, or *u* and the prosody of vowel length – see
under 2.

(*a*) naam ṣuum ziid
    baat ʃiil xoof*

(*b*) kitáab yiʃíil yiṣúum

(*c*) ʕistafáad yistafíid yifhamúuh

(*d*) ʕistalbaxnáah tistalbaxíih

5. CVCC: closed long. C + *i*, *a*, or *u* and the prosody of consonant length
in final position only, the occurrence of two consecutive consonants in final position.

(*a*) ʃadd bint

(*b*) ḍarábt yimúrr

(*c*) ʕistaɣádd yistaɣídd (*cvc–cv–cvcc*)

In the above words the prominent is marked by an accent. This is, however, not necessary since prominence can be stated in rules without exception, given the above analysis of syllabic structure.

Though there are five types of syllable, they divide into three quantities
short, medium, and long. When vowel length is referred to, it must be
differentiated from syllabic quantity – vowels can be short or long only.
The two prosodies for vowels contribute to the three prosodies for syllables.

The special case of ee and oo
In most cases Colloquial ee and oo correspond to Classical *ay* and *aw*,
often described as diphthongs. There are advantages, however, in regarding *y* and *w* as terms of a prosodic system, functioning as such in the
syllabic structure of the word. xawf and xoof are thus both closed long,
though *cvwc* is replaced by *cvvc*. Similarly in gináynah and ginéenah,
náy and née are both medium, one with *y*-prosody and one with vowel
length. Though the syllabic quantities are equivalent, the syllabic structure is different. Two more vowel qualities must be added to the vowel
system, e and o, different from the other three in that the vowel quality
is prosodically bound and is always long.

There are other interesting cases in which, quite similarly, colloquial
C + ee or oo with the prosody of length in the vowel in such words as
geet or ʃuum, correspond to equivalent classical monosyllables jiʕt,

ʃuʕm. The phonematic constituents of the pairs of corresponding words are different, but the prosody of equipollent quantity is maintained. Many such examples could be quoted including some in which the prosodic function of ʕ (glottal stop) and 'y' are equivalent.

classical		*Cairo colloquial*
ðiʕb		diib
qaraʕt	[Cyrenaican: garayt]	ʕareet
faʕs		faas
daaʕim		daayim
naaʕim		naayim
maaʕil		maayil
ḍaraaʕib		ḍaraayib

The prosodic features of the word in Cairo colloquial are the following: in any word there is usually such an interrelation of syllables that one of them is more prominent than the rest by nature of its prosodies of strength, quantity, and tone, and this prominent syllable may be regarded as the nucleus of the group of syllables forming the word. The prominent syllable is a function of the whole word or piece structure. Naturally therefore, the prosodic features of a word include:

1. The number of syllables.
2. The nature of the syllables – open or closed.
3. The syllabic quantities.
4. The sequence of syllables ⎫
5. The sequence of consonants ⎬ [radicals and flexional elements separately treated]
6. The sequence of vowels   ⎭
7. The position, nature, and quantity of the prominent.
8. The dark or clear qualities of the syllables.

There is a sort of vowel harmony and perhaps consonant harmony, also involving the so-called emphatic or dark consonants.

I think it will be found that word-analysis in Arabic can be more clearly stated if we emphasize the syntagmatic study of the word complex as it holds together, rather than the paradigmatic study of ranges of possible sound substitutions upon which a detailed phonematic study would be based. Not that such phonematic studies are to be neglected. On the contrary, they are the basis for the syntagmatic prosodic study I am here suggesting. In stating the structure of Arabic words, the prosodic systems will be found weightier than the phonematic. The same may be true of the Sino-Tibetan languages and the West African tone languages.

Such common phenomena as elision, liaison, anaptyxis, the use of so-called 'cushion' consonants or 'sounds for euphony', are involved in this study of prosodies. These devices of explanation begin to make sense when prosodic structure is approached as a system of syntagmatic relations.

Speaking quite generally of the relations of consonants and vowels to prosodic or syllabic structure, we must first be prepared to enumerate the consonants and vowels of any particular language for that language, and not rely on any general definitions of vowel and consonant universally applicable. Secondly, we must be prepared to find almost any sound having syllabic value. It is not implied that general categories such as vowel, consonant, liquid, are not valid. They are perhaps in general linguistics. But since syllabic structure must be studied in particular language systems, and within the words of these systems, the consonants and vowels of the systems must also be particular to that language and determined by its phonological structure.

Let us now turn to certain general categories or types of sound which appear to crop up repeatedly in syllabic analysis. These are the weak, neutral, or 'minimal' vowel, the glottal stop or 'maximum' consonant, aitch or the pulmonic onset – all of which deserve the general name of laryngals. Next there are such sounds as ħ and ʕ characteristic of the Semitic group of languages which may also be grouped with 'laryngals' and perhaps the back ɣ. Then the liquids and semi-vowels l, r, n (and other nasals), y and w.

Not that prosodic markers are limited to the above types of 'sound'. Almost any type of 'sound' may have prosodic function, and the same 'sound' may have to be noticed both as a consonant or vowel unit and as a prosody.

First, the neutral vowel in English. It must be remembered that the qualities of this vowel do not yield in distinctness to any other vowel quality. The term neutral suits it in English, since it is in fact neutral to the phonematic system of vowels in Southern English. It is closely bound up with the prosodies of English words and word junctions. Unlike the phonematic units, it does not bear any strong stress. Its occurrence marks a weak syllable including weak forms such as wəz, kən, ə.

Owing to the distribution of stress and length in Southern English words, it is often final in junction with a following consonant initial. Two of the commonest words in the language, *the* and *a*, require a number of prosodic realizations determined by junction and stress, ðə, ði, 'ðiy, ə, ən, 'ey, æn. In other positions, too, the neutral vowel often, though by no means always, marks an etymological junction or is required by the prosodies of word formation, especially the formation of derivatives. The distribution of the neutral vowel in English from this point of view would make an interesting study. The prosodic nature of ə is further illustrated by the necessity of considering it in connection with other prosodies such as the so-called 'intrusive' r, the 'linking' r, the glottal stop, aitch, and even *w* and *y*. Examples: *vanilla ice, law and order, cre'ation, behind, pa and ma, to earn, to ooze, secretary, behave, without money.* The occurrence of Southern English diphthongs in junctions is a good illustration of the value of prosodic treatment, *eg:*

1. The so-called 'centring' diphthongs, iə(r), eə(r), ɔə(r), uə(r).
2. What may be termed the 'y' diphthongs, iy,[15] ey, ay, oy.
3. The 'w' diphthongs uw, ow, aw.

It may be noted that e, æ, ɔ do not occur finally or in similar junctions, and that ɔː, aː, and əː all involve prosodic *r*.

Internal junctions are of great importance in this connection since the verb *bear* must take *-ing* and *-er*, and *run* leads to *runner up*. Can the r of *bearing* be said to be 'intrusive' in Southern English? As a prosodic feature along with *ə* and in other contexts with the glottal stop, aitch and prosodic *y* and *w*, it takes its place in the prosodic system of the language. In certain of its prosodic functions, the neutral vowel might be described temporarily as a pro-syllable. However obscure or neutral or unstressed, it is essential in *a bitter for me* to distinguish it from *a bit for me*. In contemporary Southern English many 'sounds'[16] may be pro-syllabic, *eg* tsn̩'apl, tstuw'mʌtʃ, sekr̩tri or sekətri, s'main, s'truw. Even if *'s true* and *strew* should happen to be homophonous, the two structures are different: c̣ cvw and 'cvw. 'Linking' and 'separating' are both phenomena of junction to be considered as prosodies. In such a German phrase as ʔin ʔeinem ʔalten 'Buch, the glottal stop is a junction prosody. I suppose Danish is the best European language in which to study the glottal stop from the prosodic point of view.[17] Unfortunately, I am not on phonetic speaking terms with Danish and can only report. The Danish glottal stop is in a sense parallel with tonal prosodies in other Scandinavian languages. It occurs chiefly with sounds said to be originally long, and in final position only in stressed syllables. If the word in question loses its stress for rhythmical or other reasons, it also loses the glottal stop. It is therefore best considered prosodically as a feature of syllabic structure and word formation. The glottal stop is a feature of monosyllables, but when such elements add flexions or enter compounds, the glottal stop may be lost. In studying the glottal stop in Danish, the phonematic systems are not directly relevant, but rather the syllabic structure of dissyllabic and polysyllabic words and compounds. In Yorkshire dialects interesting forms like 'fɔʔti occur. Note however 'fowər and 'fəwə'tiyn. A central vowel unit occurs in stressed positions in these dialects, *eg* 'θəʔti, 'θəʔ'tiyn.

There may even be traces of a prosodic glottal stop in such phrases as t 'θədʔ'dɛɛ, t 'θədʔ'taym. Junctions of the definite article with stressed words having initial t or d are of interest, *eg* əntʔ'tɛɛbl, itʔ'tram, tətʔ'tɛytʃə, fətʔ'dɔktə, witʔ'tawil. These are quite different junctions from those in 'gud 'dɛɛ or 'bad 'taym. Compare also Yorkshire trɛɛn (*cvvc*) t'rɛɛn (*c'cvvc*), tət'ʃɔp, tə 'tʃɔp, and especially witʔ'tak (*with the tack*) and wid

'tak (*we'd take*), also witə'tak (*wilt thou take*). In London one hears
'θɔːʔ'tsiyn and 'θɔːt'ʔiyn, where the two glottal stops have somewhat
different prosodic functions.

The glottal stop as a release for intervocalic plosives is common in
Cockney, and is a medial or internal prosody contrasting with aspiration,
affrication, or unreleased glottal stop in initial or final positions. Such
pronunciations as 'kɔpʔə, 'sapʔə, 'wintʔə, dʒampʔə are quite common. I
would like to submit the following note of an actual bit of conversation
between two Cockneys, for prosodic examination: i 'ʔɔːʔ ʔə 'ʔɛv iʔ 'ʔɔːf,
baʔ i ''waw̃ʔ ʔɛv iʔ ɔːf.

I have already suggested the *y* and *w* prosodies of English, including
their effect on the length prosody of the diphthongs and their function in
junctions when final. After all, human beings do not neglect the use of
broad simple contrasts when they can combine these with many other
differentiations and in that way multiply phonetic means of differentiation. In the Sino-Tibetan group of languages the *y* and *w* element is found
in a large number of syllables – there are many more *y* and *w* syllables
than, say, *b* or *d* or *a* syllables. In the many roman notations used for
Chinese, these two elements are variously represented and are sometimes
regarded as members of the paradigm of initials, but, generally, as members of the paradigm of finals. They can be classified with either, or can
be simply regarded as syllabic features. Sounds of the y or w type, known
as semi-vowels or consonantal vowels, often have the syllable-marking
function especially in initial and intervocalic position. In Sanskrit and the
modern languages affiliated to it, it is clear that prosodic *y* and *v* must be
kept distinct from similar 'sounds' in the phonematic systems. The verbal
forms aya, laya, bənaya in Hindustani are not phonematically irregular,
but with the *y* prosody are regular formations from a-na, la-na, and
bəna-na. In Tamil and other Dravidian languages *y* and *v* prosodies are
common, as markers of initials, for example, in such Tamil words as
(y)enna, (y)evan, (y)eetu, (v)oor, (v)oolai, (v)oottu. However, the prosodies of the Dravidian languages present complicated problems owing
to their mixed character.

Other sounds of this semi-vowel nature which lend themselves to prosodic function are r and l, and these often correspond or interchange with
y or *w* types of element both in Indo-European and Sino-Tibetan languages. Elements such as these have, in some languages, such pro-syllabic
or syllable-marking functions that I think they might be better classified
with the syntagmatic prosodies rather than with the overall paradigmatic
vowel and consonant systems. Studies of these problems in Indo-European and Sino-Tibetan languages are equally interesting.

The rough and smooth breathings are treated as prosodies or accentual
elements in the writing of Greek. It is true that, as with accents in other
languages, the rough breathing may imply the omission of a sound, often

s, or affect the quality and nature of the preceding final consonants in junction. 'h' in French is similarly connected with junction and elision. Even in English, though it has phonematic value in such paradigms as *eating, heating; eels, heels; ear, hear; ill, hill; owl, howl; art, heart; arming, harming; anchoring, hankering; airy, hairy; arrow, Harrow;* and many others, it is an *initial signal* in stressed syllables of full words having no weak forms. English h is a special study in weak forms, and in all these respects is perhaps also to be considered as one of the elements having special functions, which I have termed prosodic. In English dialects phonematic 'h' (if there is such a thing), disappears, but prosodic 'h' is sometimes introduced by mixing up its function with the glottal stop. I have long felt that the aitchiness, aitchification, or breathiness of sounds and syllables, and similarly their creakiness or 'glottalization' are more often than not features of the whole syllable or set of syllables. Indeed, in some of the Sino-Tibetan languages, breathiness or creakiness or 'glottalization' are characteristic of prosodic features called tones. In an article published in the *Bulletin* of the School of Oriental and African Studies, Mr J. Carnochan has a few examples of aspiration and nasalization in Igbo as syntagmatic features of a whole word, rather like vowel harmony, which is prosodic.

Apart from the fact that nasals such as m, n, ŋ are often sonants – that is to say, have syllabic function – they are also quite frequently initial or final signals, and in Bantu languages such signals have essentially a syntagmatic or syllable or word-grouping function. In a restricted prosodic sense, they can be compared with the glottal stop in German.

In bringing certain types of speech sound into consideration of the prosodies, I have so far noticed the neutral or weak vowel, the minimal vowel, which often becomes zero; the glottal stop, the maximal consonant which unreleased is zero sound; aitch, the pulmonic onset, and the liquids and nasals. The first two, I suggest, deserve the name of laryngals, and perhaps h. There remain such sounds as ħ, ʕ, ɣ, and χ, characteristic of the Semitic group of languages. These sounds are certainly phonematic in Classical Arabic. But in the dialects they are often replaced in cognate words by the prosody of length in change of vowel quality, generally more open than that of the measure of comparison.

When words containing these sounds are borrowed from Arabic by speakers of non-Semitic languages, they are usually similarly replaced by elements of a prosodic nature, often with changes of quality in the vowels of the corresponding syllable.

Hindustani and Panjabi provide interesting examples of phonematic units in one dialect or style being represented in another by prosodies. Instances of interchanges in cognates between phonematic units of the vowel system and units of the consonant system are common, and examples and suggestions have been offered of interchanges and correspondences between phonematic units of both kinds and prosodies. The following table provides broad transcriptions to illustrate these principles.

Table 1

h

Hindustani,	*Hindustani,*	*Panjabi,*
Eastern, careful	*Western, quick*	*(Gujranwala)*
pǝhyle	pǝyhle	pôylle
bǝhwt	bǝwht	bôwt
pǝhwŋcna	pǝwhŋcna	pôwŋc
bhǝi		ḅǝi
kǝr rǝha hǝy	kǝrrahǝyh	
rǝhta (ræhta)		rôynɗa

In pǝhyle we have a three-syllable word in which h is phonematic (*cvcvcv*). In pǝyhle there are two syllables by a sort of coalescence in which ǝyh indicates an open 'h'-coloured or breathy vowel of the æ-type (*cvhcv*). Similarly in the phrase bǝhwt‿ǝccha there are four syllables (*cvcvc‿vccv*), in bǝwht‿ǝccha three, the vowel in the first of which is *open* back and 'h'-coloured (*cvhcvccv*).

In Panjabi pôylle the open vowel carries a compound high falling tone and the structure is prosodically quite different (*ĉccv*) which, I think, is equipollent with *cvhcv* (pǝyhle). bôwt similarly is *ĉc*, reduced to a monosyllable with initial and final consonant and a tonal prosody. In Hindustani verbal forms like rǝhna, rǝhta; kǝhna, kǝhta; the ǝ vowel in the h-coloured syllable immediately followed by a consonant is open with a retracted æ-like quality. yɪh is realized as ye, vwh as vo, in both of which there is a similar lowering and potential lengthening in emphasis.

Table 2

Arabic ع in Urdu loan-words

spelling transliterated	transcription of realization in speech
mǝعlum	malum
bǝعd	bad
dǝfع	dǝfa
mǝnع	mǝna
mǝعni	mǝani, mani
ystعmal	ystemal

In all these cases the vowel realized is open and fairly long. In Maltese, words which in Arabic have h and which still retain h in the spelling are pronounced long with retracted quality, *eg* he, hi, ho, eh, ehe, as in

fehem, fehmu, sehem, sehmek, qalbhom. These long vowels may be unstressed. Similarly all the għ spellings (transliterated ɣ) are realized as
long slightly pharyngalized vowels which may also occur in unstressed
positions, which is not possible with vowels other than those with the
Semitic h and għ spellings. *Eg* ɣa, aɣ, aɣa, ɣo, oɣ, oɣo, ɣi (ɣey), ɣe, ɣu
(ɣəw) in such words as għidt, għúda magħmul, bálagħ. In the phrase
balagħ balgħa (*he swallowed a mouthful*) the two forms are pronounced
alike with final long a (for form, *cf* ħataf ħatfa, *he snatched*). h and għ are
often realized in spoken Maltese as a prosody of length.

In Turkish the Arabic ع in loan-words is often realized as a prosody of
length in such pronunciations as fiil (*verb, act*), saat (*hour*) and similarly
Arabic ɣ, in iblaa (*communicate*), and Turkish ğ in uultu (*tumult*). We are
reminded again of Arabic ع which is also realized as a prosody of length in
the colloquials, *eg* Classical jiʕt is paralleled by geet in Cairo, jɛɛt in
Iraqi, and ʒiit in Cyrenaican Saʕadi. In Cairo and Iraqi the prosody of
length is applied to an opener vowel than in Classical, but this is not always
the case.

The study of prosodic structures has bearing on all phonological studies
of loan-words, and also on the operation of grammatical processes on
basic material in any language. Taking the last-mentioned first, elision or
anaptyxis in modern Cairo colloquial are prosodically necessary in such
cases as the following: misíkt + ni = misiktíni, where the anaptyctic i is
required to avoid the junction of three consonants consecutively which is
an impossible pattern. The prominence then falls on the anaptyctic vowel
by rule. Pieces such as bint + fariid are realized as bintifaríid. With the
vowels i and u, elision is possible within required patterns, *eg:* yindíhiʃ +
u = yindihiʃu, titlíxim + i = titlíximi, but not with a, ʕitlaxam + it =
ʕitlaxamit.

Amusing illustrations of the effect of prosodic patterns on word-
borrowing are provided by loan-words from English in Indian and African
languages and in Japanese. Prosodic anaptyxis produces səkuul in Panjabi and prothesis iskuul in Hindi or Urdu. By similar processes səteʃən
and isteʃən are created for *station*. In Hausa *screw-driver* is naturalized as
sukuru direba. Treating skr and dr as initial phonematic units, English
screw-driver has the structure 'cvw-cvycə the prosodies of which Hausa
could not realize, hence cvcvcv-cvcvcv, a totally different structure which
I have carefully expressed in non-phonematic notation, to emphasize the
fallacy of saying Hausa speakers cannot pronounce the 'sounds', and to
point to the value of studying prosodic structure by a different set of abstractions from those appropriate to phonematic structure. It is not implied that there is one all-over prosodic system for any given language. A
loan-word may bring with it a new pattern suited to its class or type, as in
English borrowings from French, both nominals and verbals. When
completely naturalized the prosodic system of the type or class of word in

the borrowing language is dominant. In Japanese strange prosodic transformations take place, *eg* bisuketto (*biscuit*), kiromeetoru, kiroguramu, supittohwaia, messaasyumitto, arupen-suttoku, biheebiyarisuto, doriburusuru (*to dribble*).

Linguists have always realized the importance of the general attributes of stress, length, tone, and syllabic structure, and such considerations have frequently been epoch-making in the history of linguistics. Generally speaking, however, the general attributes have been closely associated with the traditional historical study of sound-change, which, in my terminology, has been chiefly phonematic. I suggest that the study of the prosodies by means of *ad hoc* categories and at a different level of abstraction from the systematic phonematic study of vowels and consonants, may enable us to take a big step forward in the understanding of synthesis. This approach has the great merit of building on the piece or sentence as the primary datum. The theory I have put forward may in the future throw light on the subject of Ablaut which, in spite of the scholarship expended on it in the nineteenth century from Grimm to Brugmann, still remains a vexed question and unrelated to spoken language. I venture to hope that some of the notions I have suggested may be of value to those who are discussing laryngals in Indo-European, and even to those engaged in field work on hitherto unwritten languages. The monosystemic analysis based on a paradigmatic technique of oppositions and phonemes with allophones has reached, even overstepped, its limits ! The time has come to try fresh hypotheses of a polysystemic character. The suggested approach will not make phonological problems appear easier or oversimplify them. It may make the highly complex patterns of language clearer both in descriptive and historical linguistics. The phonological structure of the sentence and the words which comprise it are to be expressed as a plurality of systems of interrelated phonematic and prosodic categories. Such systems and categories are not necessarily linear and certainly cannot bear direct relations to successive fractions or segments of the time-track of instances of speech. By their very nature they are abstractions from such time-track items. Their order and interrelations are not chronological.

An example is given overleaf of the new approach in sentence phonetics and phonology[18] in which the syntagmatic prosodies are indicated in the upper stave and the phonematic structure in the lower stave, with a combination text between. Stress is marked with the intonation indicated.

It is already clear that in cognate languages what is a phonematic constituent in one may be a prosody in another, and that in the history of any given language sounds and prosodies interchange with one another. In the main, however, the prosodies of the sentence and the word tend to be dominant.

To say the prosodies may be regarded as dominant is to emphasize the prosodies $\left\{ \dfrac{.\ \ ^{\shortmid}\diagdown.\underline{\quad}.\ \ \ .\ \ \ ^{\shortmid}\underline{\quad}\ \ ^{\shortmid}\diagdown.\ \ .\ \ \underline{\quad}}{cy\ \ vc\partial\ \ vc\partial\ \ c\partial z\,\underline{\,}mvt\!\int\underline{\,}bvc\partial\ \ vy\ \ cvcc} \right.$

ðy ʌðə⁽¹⁹⁾ ɔfə wəz mʌtʃ betə ay θiŋk

phonematic structure $\left\{ \text{ð—ʌð—ɔf—w–z mʌtʃ bet—a—θiŋk} \right.$

prosodies $\left\{ \dfrac{^{\shortmid}\underline{\quad}\ ^{\shortmid}\underline{\quad}\ \ ^{\shortmid}\underline{\quad}\ \ \ .^{\shortmid}\underline{\quad}..\ \ ^{\shortmid}\diagdown\ \underline{\quad}}{cvy\ \ hvz\,\underline{\,}\!\int vy\ \ \partial ccvccic\ \ cvc\ \ cvc} \right.$

way hæz ʃiy əkseptid ðis wʌn

phonematic structure $\left\{ \text{wa æz ʃi ksept d ðis wʌn} \right.$

phonetics and phonology of synthesis. It accords with the view that syntax is the dominant discipline in grammar and also with the findings of recent American research in acoustics. The interpenetration of consonants and vowels, the overlap of so-called segments, and of such layers as voice, nasalization and aspiration, in utterance, are commonplaces of phonetics. On the perception side, it is improbable that we listen to auditory fractions corresponding to uni-directional phonematic units in any linear sense.

Whatever units we may find in analysis must be closely related to the whole utterance, and that is achieved by systematic statement of the prosodies. In the perception of speech by the listener whatever units there may be are prosodically reintegrated. We speak prosodies and we listen to them.

Notes

[1] At one of the 1948 meetings of the Linguistic Society of America, Mr Kenneth Pike suggested that in certain Mexican Indian languages it would be convenient to hypothecate a second or phonemic sub-system to account for all the facts. Taking part in the discussion which followed, I pointed out my own findings in Tamil and Telugu for both of which languages it is necessary to assume at least three phonological systems: non-brahman Dravidian, Sanskrito-dravidian, and Sanskritic.

[2] See J. Aquilina: *The Structure of Maltese*, A Study in Mixed Grammar and Vocabulary. (Thesis for the PHD degree, 1940. University of London Library.)

[3] See T. Hill: *The Phonetics of a Nyanja Speaker*, With Particular Reference to the Phonological Structure of the Word. (Thesis for the MA degree, 1948. University of London Library.)

[4] See T. Hill: *The Phonetics of a Nyanja Speaker*.

[5] Miss Eileen M. Evans, Senior Lecturer in Phonetics, School of Oriental and African Studies, has work in preparation on this subject, as part of a wider study of the phonology of modern English.

[6] Amply illustrated by the patterns to be seen on the Visible Speech Translator produced by the Bell Telephone Laboratories.

[7] See 'A Short Guide to the accentuation of Ancient Greek', by Postgate.

[8] *Cf* 'The English School of Phonetics', *Trans. Phil. Soc.*, 1946.

[9] Or rather Arabic writing is syllabic in principle. Professor Edgar Sturtevant has stated this view and recently confirmed it personally in conversation.

[10] See my 'The Chinese Monosyllable in a Hunanese Dialect (Changsha)', *BSOS.*, Vol VIII, Pt 4, 1937 [with B. B. Rogers].

[11] In the sending of Japanese morse ak = ka, the first signal being the characteristic sonant. (Joos, *Acoustic Phonetics*, L.S.A., 1948, *pp* 116–126, and conclusions on segmentation.)

[12] See also N. C. Scott, 'A Study in the Phonetics of Fijian,' *BSOAS*, Vol XII, Pts 3–4, 1948, and J. Carnochan, 'A Study in the Phonology of an Igbo Speaker,' *BSOAS*, Vol XII, Pt 2, 1948. Eugénie Henderson, 'Prosodies in Siamese', in *Asia Minor*, N.S. Vol I, 1949.

[13] *Cf* 'Arte de Escribír', by Torquato Torío de la Riva, addressed to the Count of Trastamara, Madrid, 1802. The four parts of grammar are etimología ó analogía, syntaxis, prosódia, or ortografía. Prosódia teaches the quantity of syllables in order to pronounce words with their due accent. There are three degrees in Spanish, acute or long, grave or short, and what are termed *común* or *indiferentes*.

[14] See also Ibrahim Anis, *The Grammatical Characteristics of the Spoken Arabic of Egypt*. (Thesis for the PHD degree, 1941. University of London Library.) $t \underset{.}{d} \underset{.}{s} \underset{.}{z} = t \not{d} \underset{.}{s} \not{z}$ (IPA).

[15] It is, I think, an advantage from this point of view to regard English so-called long i: and u: as *y*-closing or *w*-closing diphthongs and emphasize the closing termination by writing with Sweet *ij* or *iy*, and *uw*.

[16] In the general phonetic sense, not in the phonematic sense.

[17] See Sweet, 'On Danish Pronunciation' (1873), in *Collected Papers*, *p* 345, in which he makes a prosodic comparison with Greek accents. (On *p* 348 he uses the term 'tonology'.)

[18] For a fuller illustration of the scope of sentence phonology and its possible applications, see Eugénie Henderson's 'Prosodies in Siamese'. [In this volume, *pp* 127–153. Eds.]

[19] The use of *ə* as a prosodic symbol in such final contexts implies potential r or ʔ according to the nature of the junction.

D. B. Fry

Linguistic theory and experimental research

Linguistics as a science

The claim that linguistics is and should be a science is of long standing but
it has been made with greater insistence in the last ten or twenty years than
ever before. To many linguists, indeed, it would seem surprising that the
word 'claim' should be used; it appears to them an indisputable fact that
linguistics is a science. The purpose of this paper is not to debate the just-
ness of the claim but rather to examine some of its implications.

Two things are necessary for any science: suitable material for study
and the adoption of the methods of science. The latter can be summarized
very briefly as observation, the devising of categories for the observed
facts, the construction of a theory, the testing of the theory by renewed
observation, and the revision of the theory. In some fields it is convenient
to shorten the process of theory testing by having recourse to experiment,
that is the setting up artificially of a chain of events in order to test predic-
tions based on the tentative theory. This method is naturally not an indispensable part of science, but there are undoubtedly some spheres in which
progress is very difficult without it.

If we accept linguists' own statements about the procedures of linguistics, we can have no doubt that they endorse without reservation the use
of scientific method and all that it implies. Not only are there papers and
books with such titles as 'The status of linguistics as a science' (Sapir) and
'Introduction to Linguistic Science' (Sturtevant) but there are quite cate-
gorical statements which show sometimes even a tinge of vehemence. It
will be enough to quote one such affirmation, by Trager (review of Pike's
Phonemics) who says: 'The analysis of these (behaviour) patterns is not a

First published in *Transactions of the Philological Society*, 13–39, 1960.

matter of personal preference or of belief, or of strenuous attempts to bolster established opinions; it is a matter of objective observation and classification', and further on 'Let us rather go about doing linguistic analysis vigorously and objectively, perfecting and refining our theory as we go along. As in any science, those procedures which do not stand up under test will be discarded'. The intention at least could not be expressed more clearly.

Linguists are equally explicit and generally in agreement about the material that they are studying. A handful of quotations will be enough to give the general view. Trager says (review of Pike's *Phonemics*) 'Linguistic behaviour is a set of physical events, like any other human behaviour. This set of events constitutes a pattern, or rather a pattern of patterns (cultural systems)'. It is these behaviour patterns, he goes on to say, that form the material for linguistic study and must be 'a matter of objective classification and observation'. Hockett (*Manual of Phonology*) too refers to 'what is directly observable: the behaviour of humans'. But since this behaviour takes specific physical forms, the linguist needs information about two spheres in particular. To quote Trager again (*The Field of Linguistics*) 'The linguist must have a body of knowledge about the physiological activities . . . he must be provided with descriptions of the articulatory movements of the organs of speech', and also Hockett who says that the object of analysis is 'to abstract the phonological pattern, as a system, from the articulatory and partly acoustic framework in which the observed events occurred'.

Thus the material for scientific study and the method are clear enough and there are some linguists at least who believe that the results achieved are of the highest order. This point of view is aptly summed up by Lees (review of Chomsky's *Syntactic Structures*) who says: 'Social scientists seeking greater precision in the formulation of their special theories look with envy upon the very exact grammatical statements and the impressive laboratory-phonetic descriptions which are to be found in the pages of linguistic journals, and the linguist himself has come to believe in some instances that he alone among social scientists points the way to a new scientific revolution in our understanding of human behaviour'.

It must be said at once that there are many linguists, as well as people outside the linguistic world, to whom such statements would come as a considerable shock. This is true most of all, perhaps, of those who are concerned with the use of experimental methods in the study of language and speech, for it appears to many of us that there are serious weaknesses in the methods of some present-day linguists. I shall try to specify some of these weaknesses and to show in what directions experimental research may reasonably be expected to make a contribution to linguistic knowledge.

In the earlier stages of any science, a multiplicity of theories is to be expected; that there are a number of co-existing linguistic theories is not therefore an unhealthy sign. The most disquieting feature of linguistics is that the feed-back from observation to theory is very weak indeed. In a healthy science, this process of continual reference of theory to observation is the most important factor; yet it is difficult to think of any major modification in a general linguistic theory that has been the outcome of renewed observation of human linguistic behaviour. The general tendency has been to begin operations with a modicum of phonetic observation, to construct a system of categories on the basis of such observations and thereafter to devise theories, to modify them, or to discard them because of inter-relations *within the theory* rather than because of relations between the theory and observations of behaviour.

One aspect of this tendency is to be found in the recurrent theme of 'distribution' which forms a part of many linguistic discussions, often connected with questions of the importance of phonetic data. Thus Garvin (review of *Preliminaries*) refers to 'the status of phonetic data in linguistics: are they linguistic in nature, to be used in the statement (or discovery) of phonemic patterns, or should phonemic analysis be based on distribution alone, with phonetic data considered mere irrelevant substance?' But a distribution is obviously a distribution of something – in this case usually of letters in a phonemic transcription. The choice of letters is based on observation of the phonetic data and hence the phonemic analysis is in no sense independent of the phonetic data.

The fact that such a question is formulated seems, however, to be symptomatic of a desire on the part of some structural linguists in particular to cut themselves off at the earliest possible stage from the material of their scientific study. The reason for this is not far to seek; the essential nature of this material, that is of linguistic behaviour, is at variance with the picture that these scholars have formed for themselves of scientific work and of its results. For them, self-consistency in the analytical system and logical rigour (and almost boundless ingenuity) in the formulation of a theory provide the illusion – for it is an illusion – of the scientific precision which they so much desire, forgetting that in science the pre-requisites are precision combined with ingenuity in observation and extreme rigour in inferring from the observed data.

These qualities are even more essential in dealing with linguistic behaviour than in some other fields, because all the relationships that are to be found here are statistical relationships. If we examine the relation between one level of analysis and another, we find no case of a one-to-one correlation; if we study relations within the same level, we soon discover that they are governed by statistical laws. Such material, as we have said, is at variance with the treatment that some linguists wish to impose upon it. They are trying, as it were, to construct a 'mathematics of constancy' to deal with material that in fact requires a 'mathematics of variation'. It is not surprising, therefore, that they should want to free themselves from many considerations that the material would in its turn impose.

The role of redundancy in language

It is a matter of some importance that the most striking feature of linguistic behaviour, the use that it makes of redundancy in the language system, was first clearly formulated by engineers and mathematicians, not by linguists. The word 'redundancy' has a technical meaning which can be exemplified quite easily in an operational way. In any system used for transmitting information, a message can be regarded as a sequence of events of a particular kind; a message in spoken English, as a sequence of phonemes, or of morphemes or words; a message in printed English as a succession of letters and spaces, or of words; a message in the morse code as a string of dots, dashes, and pauses. At any point in the message, the probability that any particular signal will occur, that is that a given phoneme, letter, word, dot, or dash will fill the next position, is dependent upon the whole of the sequence that precedes this position. A very commonly used method, which is due to Shannon, serves to demonstrate this fact. We can take anyone who uses a particular system, for example anyone who can read English, and ask him to guess successively the signals that make up the message, without his having any prior knowledge about the message itself. This would mean, in this particular case, asking him to guess, say, the letters occurring in a given printed English sentence which he has never seen. He begins with the letter in the first position, and his guesses are naturally restricted to choosing one out of the 26 letters of the alphabet. In the first position, he is quite likely to make a considerable number of wrong guesses before he hits on the right letter. Even if he guesses randomly, provided he has the sense not to repeat any letter, he cannot make more than 25 wrong guesses. But in fact he is not likely to guess randomly, since he knows English, and thus, without being aware of the fact, knows that certain letters are more likely to appear at the beginning of a sentence than other letters. When he says the right letter for position one, we tell him that it is the right one and get him to go on and guess the second letter, and so on through the whole sentence. If we keep a score of the number of wrong guesses he makes at each succeeding position, we shall find that it varies throughout the sequence, within the range of values 0–25. That is to say, sometimes he will supply the right letter with his first guess, and sometimes he will need many more. These numbers are an expression of the probability of a particular letter's occurring in a given position. Where there are no wrong guesses, it is quite certain what the next letter must be, so that the information conveyed by the letter itself is redundant, in the everyday sense of 'not needed'. In the technical sense, there is redundancy at each position in the sequence and a measure of the redundancy is given by the probability at each position. Where the letter has a high probability of occurrence the redundancy is great, and where it has a low probability of occurrence the redundancy is small. This variation in redundancy can be demonstrated in a gross way by omitting letters in a sequence. The vowel letters in English spelling have generally higher re-dundancy than the consonant letters. It is therefore very much more diffi-cult to read a text in which consonant letters are left out than one in which vowel letters are not specified. Compare, for example, these two se-quences:

M − R Y H − D − L − T T L − L − M B
O − E − − − E − I − − − A − − − A − A − A −

Every language exhibits this kind of fluctuation in sequential proba-bility; it is a fundamental quality of language systems. If we should have any doubt about this we can dispel it by trying to find material in which the probability of each succeeding unit is independent of that of the pre-ceding ones. This is to be found only in the random sampling number tables that are used for randomizing experimental sequences and the like. They give a completely random succession of digits. It is clear that they form the antithesis of a language, and could not be used for any linguistic purpose, nor subjected to anything akin to linguistic analysis. It is interest-ing to note that if we apply the guessing technique to random sampling numbers we shall discover no fluctuation in sequential probability. If the subject guesses randomly, then the number of wrong guesses at each posi-tion will simply form another random series of digits generated by the guessing process. The subject might, of course, try to instil some order in-to his guessing by counting serially, beginning with nought each time and going on until he reached the right number. In this case the number of wrong guesses would be a random series identical with the series being guessed. Thus if the digit sequence were for example 31074. . . ., he would make three wrong guesses at the first position, 1 at the second, 0 at the third, and so on.

It is evident that such sequences form the antithesis of linguistic sequences where sequential probability is a very powerful factor in deter-mining the occurrence of any unit. In the guessing experiment with English letters described earlier, the subject produces the result because he is familiar with the system, that is he knows the 'language', and further-more his guessing tells us something about the language. The variation in the number of wrong guesses shows a certain patterning. As he proceeds through the sentence there is a strong tendency for the general level of the number of guesses to decrease, showing that the force of the constraints increases as the sentence proceeds. Within this general tendency, how-ever, we find that there are peaks in the histogram at word and at mor-pheme boundaries. In other words, this probability curve is in itself an expression of structural features of the language. Indeed, there are grounds for supposing that it is here we should look for criteria that will enable us to make a linguistic analysis which is in keeping with the material we are treating.

All this is not meant to suggest that linguistics has entirely failed to take account of the statistical properties of language; at least by implication and in a rather disguised form it uses the notion of redundancy or sequential probability, for example in some aspects of the theory of immediate constituents where successive segmentations are in fact based on increasing values of sequential probability. In general, however, linguistic theory reduces sequential probability to a two-valued system, containing the terms possible–impossible; the probability is either 0 or 1, whereas in the functioning of language it may take many values between these limits.

Redundancy has so far been considered within its technical meaning – the statistical dependence of items in a sequence – and it is most important to realize that in this strict sense it is to be found at all levels and in every type of linguistic behaviour. Articulatory movements are not independent of each other, but one is more likely in a given sequence than another; one acoustic change is more probable than another, one letter, one phoneme, one morpheme, one word, one sentence more probable than another at a given point. This idea has usually been summarized in linguistics by referring to the effect of context, at many different levels. Statements about context are qualitative and very general in character, and it may be worth while, therefore, before leaving the subject of redundancy, to mention that by adopting an experimental method as an aid to observation we can begin to gain a more precise idea of context and begin to measure some of its effects. In the exchanges of everyday life, there is great interaction between various kinds of context and the effect is very diffuse. An experimental method consists in setting up artificially trains of events in which the important factors are better known to us than they are in everyday linguistic behaviour.

In one series of experiments reported by Bruce, the situation was designed to show the importance of what psychologists call 'mental set' in the reception of messages; in linguistic terms, the work can be viewed as exploring the effect of context at the word level. A sample of the results is given in *Fig* 1. It is not necessary to describe the conditions in detail. Listeners were asked to repeat back a large number of sentences which they heard in very difficult listening conditions. Before each sentence they heard clearly a single key-word, which was one of five shown on the graph: *travel, sport, weather, food, health*. The results shown are for the test sentence, 'You said it would rain, but the sun has come out now', and each curve shows the effect of preceding the sentence by a different key-word. The vertical axis shows the number of times the listeners

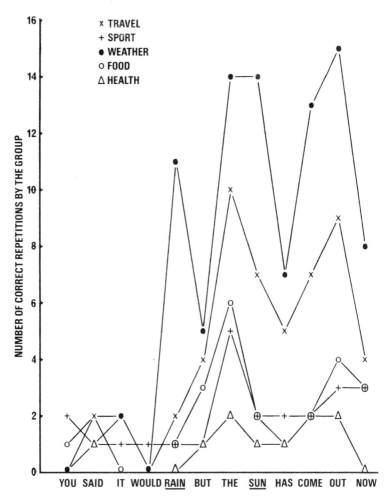

Fig 1: A typical result from an experiment by Bruce showing the effect of
context on the reception of words in a sentence.

heard the sentence correctly. It is clear that the listeners can interpret
the sentence more successfully when it is preceded by the most appropriate key-word, *weather*, than when the other key-words are given, but
the other words are also graded in their effect. Thus *travel* is second to
weather in its effect, and *health* has the least positive influence on the
reception of the sentence. The effect is differentiated not only with regard
to the key-words, but also with respect to the words in the test sentence.
The key-words have little or no influence on the reception of 'You said

it would', but a great deal, as one would expect, on 'rain', 'sun', and 'come out', the main content words of the sentence. One of the most interesting observations made in the experiment was that although subjects were given the same sentences repeatedly with different key-words, they had no idea that the same sentences re-appeared in the test. The effect of context was so strong that even after a subject had heard a sentence with its most appropriate key-word, he was unable to recognize it when it occurred again with a less appropriate one.

This is but one example of the work that is being done on context effects, but it seems to show the great influence that they have on linguistic be-haviour. If sequential factors are so powerful they certainly cannot be dis-regarded in linguistics nor can they be entirely omitted from linguistic theory if it is to bear any relation to linguistic behaviour.

The importance of the reception phase

The experiments just mentioned draw attention not only to redundancy but also to the importance of the listener in language behaviour. The second major weakness of current linguistic theory is that it disregards almost entirely the reception phase of communication. Though articula-tory events are freely admitted as the data on which the linguist must work, and although in more recent years the acoustic events too have been accorded some importance, there is very rarely any mention of the listener in the speech situation. The linguist is content to observe the behaviour of the speaker, his articulations and the sound-waves that he generates, but does not study the listener who receives these sound-waves. When dealing with a language unfamiliar to him, a linguist will, of course, make noises back to his informant, but this has little connection with the problem of reception. The behaviour of one native listener (the informant) faced with messages from a foreign speaker (the linguist) does not give much infor-mation about linguistic behaviour in a community, for here once more we encounter a basically statistical problem; we have to study variation and to discover limits by observing the behaviour of a number of listeners.

In the normal linguistic situation, the speaker plays an active role and the listener a passive one so that observation of the listener is not likely to be very rewarding. We can gain information only when the listener be-comes the speaker and gives a behavioural indication of what he has heard. This creates a complex situation in which it is not very easy to make reli-able observations and the adoption of an experimental method becomes a necessity. It is in this field that experimental research can make the greatest contribution to our knowledge of linguistic behaviour and in the rest of this paper we shall try to show by referring to a relatively small number of experiments that its results have a direct bearing on linguistic theory.

It will be necessary before describing the experiments to deal with a number of general considerations. The reason for adopting an experimental method is first that we can place the listener in a position to make some behavioural response other than speech. This does not mean that his judgment will be independent of his own speech habits – it will not and we should certainly not want it to be so; it means, however, that the *expression* of his judgment will not be complicated for the experimenter by the listener's own speech.

In the second place, the method enables us to send messages in controlled conditions so that we can repeat experiments and observe the reactions of a reasonable sample of listeners, often taking them in groups.

The third point concerns the basic experimental method to be used. The purpose of experimenting with the listener is to find out if we can what features of the sounds that he hears are most important to him and which are less important. We have therefore to begin with knowledge of the physical constitution of these sounds. This information has been gathered for a very long time now and has been added to more recently through the widespread use of the spectrograph so that we have available a certain capital of physical information about speech sounds. For example, it has been known since the time of Helmholtz that for each vowel sound there are usually two considerable concentrations of energy, two formants, in the spectrum below about 2,500 cps. Since these formants are to be found each time a vowel occurs, it has been assumed, quite justifiably, that a listener's recognition of a vowel depends in part upon the presence of these two formants. But let us suppose that we wish to know more about the function of these formants in recognition. Each vowel shows two formants, a lower one, F_1, and a higher, F_2. Does the listener depend more on hearing F_1 or F_2 for his recognition, or is it the frequency relation between the two that he depends on? Is the intensity relation of the formants important? and so on. In order to resolve such questions we need to supply to the listener vowels in which these factors have been modified. Broadly speaking, there are two methods by which this can be done. The first we might call the method of subtraction. We could take samples of all the English vowels, and subtract, by filtering, a part of the frequency range. For example, we might divide the frequency range below 2,500 cps into two parts and first suppress all frequencies above 1,250 cps. This would take away F_2 for some vowels and leave others still with two formants. Listener experiments with such sounds would begin to show whether the sounds with one formant were recognized less easily than those with two. A change to sounds in which frequencies below 1,250 cps were suppressed would add further information of a similar kind.

A great deal of work on these lines has been done in the past thirty years and it has certainly added greatly to our knowledge of the reception process. But the main result of such experiments has been to show that the listener continues to decode speech even in the face of the most extreme subtractions and distortions, in other words when we subtract from the speech sound-waves, we have little idea how much information is contained for the listener in what is left. This type of experiment has in fact served rather to underline the redundancy of speech at the physical level. It is clear that the listener in the normal situation gets far more physical information than he needs for recognition; he evidently has a multiplicity of cues for any one recognition and he will work with some selection from these cues as circumstances demand.

A much more fruitful approach to the problem has been provided by the use of speech synthesizers, of which there are now a considerable number in existence. The principle here is to produce artificial, speech-like sounds in which we know what has been put into the speech, rather than what has been taken out of it. It is not necessary for the present purpose to describe the machines or the method in detail and indeed many of the results of experiments with synthetic speech are so well known as to call for little discussion. What we shall do is to take several examples and show how they may help to clarify linguistic problems.

The problem of phonetic similarity

First, there is the problem of phonetic similarity, which has given rise to considerable difficulty in linguistic theory. Thus Bloch, and others, have defined a phoneme as a 'class of non-contrastive and phonetically similar phones'. They have become worried, quite justifiably, by the idea of similarity and the criteria for judging it, and so have advanced the notion of discarding 'similarity' as a criterion and relying on 'distribution'. This, as we have seen, is plain nonsense; the issue of similarity has been settled long before there is any question of 'distribution'. There can be no question but that the issue of phonetic similarity has to be settled. The whole operation of language depends upon judgments of likeness and difference, at every level, and therefore first and foremost at the phonetic level. But it is a cardinal error to assume that the judge of similarity should be the linguist himself; the only information of interest is what things are similar to the speakers and listeners in the language in question.

This can be discovered only by well-designed experiments since it is no use asking the speaker directly. The listener who decides that two events are similar will do so first on the basis of sequential probability; if sequential probability indicates that they are the same, he will judge them to be so. If sequential probability does not settle the issue, then he will use any one or any selection of dimensions that are appropriate in a particular case. Phonetic similarity, in other words, is multi-dimensional. The Haskins Laboratories experiments have shown how in judging English plosives, listeners may take notice of the frequency of a burst of noise, the extent

tion of a formant transition, the time of onset of a formant, the
of a particular part of the sound-wave.

t perhaps seem in these circumstances impossible to throw more
light on phonetic similarity by means of experimental methods than by
any others, but in this connection the greatest importance attaches to
some of the more recent experiments by the Haskins Laboratories, of
which some results are given in *Figs* 3 and 4. It was known from earlier experiments that the transition to Formant 2 of a vowel was a cue which
English listeners could use to distinguish between /b/, /d/, and /g/. The
series of patterns in *Fig* 2 shows how it was possible in a speech synthesizer

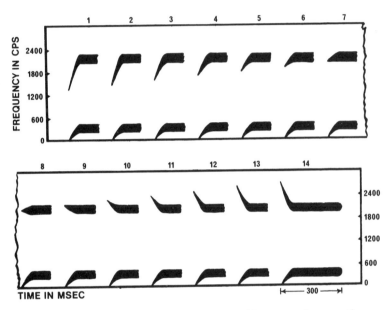

Fig 2: The range of synthetic speech patterns used in an experiment on the
discrimination of speech sounds within and across phoneme boundaries.

to generate a series of syllables in which there was a continuum of quality
change from /b/ through /d/ and /g/. Formant 1 has a minus transition
which is constant throughout and is used because it was found to be a cue
for the recognition of voiced as opposed to voiceless plosives. Formant 2
transition changes throughout the series from a large minus transition in
pattern number 1 through zero transition in pattern 8, to a large plus
transition in pattern 14. These transitions were used in formants appropriate to the vowel /e/ and recordings of all the stimuli were used in two
kinds of experiment. First, the subject was presented with the stimuli in

random order and asked to label each one as /b/, /d/, or /g/. The results are shown in *Fig* 3. Over the first part of the continuum, he consistently heard an initial /b/. Then at stimulus 4 the judgments became less consistent; for less than half the presentations he now heard /b/ and for more than half, he was already hearing /d/. The same pattern is repeated between /d/ and /g/.

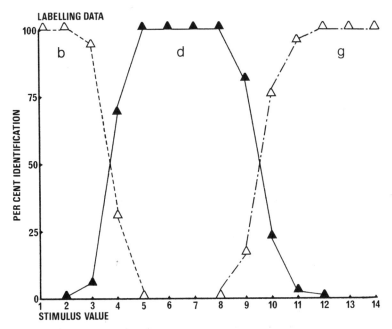

Fig 3: The results of a labelling experiment with the stimuli represented in *Fig* 2. The numbers on the horizontal axis correspond to the pattern numbers in *Fig* 2. The plotted points give the number of judgments (expressed as a percentage of the total) identifying each stimulus as /b/, /d/ or /g/.

In the next part of the experiment, the stimuli were arranged in such a way as to determine the subject's sensitivity to differences between the stimuli, by a commonly used experimental psychological technique. In this case there was no question of labelling the sounds as /b/, /d/, or /g/, but simply of trying to detect a difference between one stimulus in the series and another which differs from it by 1, 2, or 3 steps. A typical result from this experiment is shown in *Fig* 4, where the stimuli differed by two steps on the continuum. It should be noted that this figure gives the discrimination results for the same subject whose labelling data are given in *Fig* 3.

The first point is that the subject was not equally sensitive to differences throughout the range. At some points he was very sensitive – in the result shown here, he was 100 per cent correct in his judgment of the two-step stimuli at two places in the series. At others, he was much less sensitive, sometimes falling to the level of random guesses at 50 per cent. The most important feature is that the points of maximum sensitivity tend to fall at what we might call the 'phoneme boundaries' as established in the first part of the experiment. It seems therefore that in the language learning

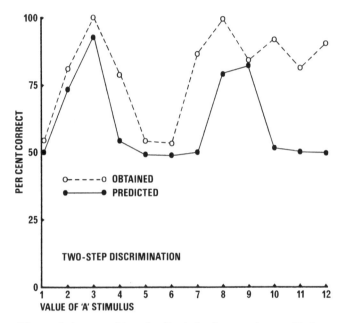

Fig 4: The result for one subject of a discrimination experiment with the stimuli represented in *Fig* 2. The subject was trying to discriminate between patterns separated by one pattern in the series, that is to distinguish between numbers 1 and 3, 2 and 4, 3 and 5, and so on. The dotted curve indicates how often he succeeded in this. The continuous curve refers to a predicted result based on the assumption that the subject can discriminate the stimuli only to the extent that he can identify them as different phonemes.

process, our perceptions are influenced in such a way that we remain relatively insensitive to differences which lie well within the boundaries of one phoneme and sensitive to those which lie on the boundaries.

This result is of the greatest importance for the problem of phonetic similarity. The perception of speech or speech-like sounds is dominated by the phonemic grouping to which the listener is accustomed. It is truer to say that sounds are similar if they belong to the same phoneme than to say that sounds belong to the same phoneme because they are similar. The relation between stimulus change and perception of similarity is not linear and in normal language behaviour, as we have seen, similarity is not a matter of a single stimulus dimension. The experiment just quoted shows, however, that it is possible experimentally to measure similarity with respect to one stimulus dimension at a time and that if we do so, we may expect to find well-defined patterns of linguistic behaviour. The results of the discrimination experiment with English-speaking subjects were highly consistent and it may be that we have here for the first time a method of establishing phonemic grouping in a language experimentally and without asking the subjects to do any labelling of sounds. Many further experiments of different kinds are needed to confirm the appropriateness of the method but preliminary results are already available which show that the increased sensitivity to change at certain places in the stimulus continuum does not appear when the subject is listening to non-speech-like sounds. In other words, the curve of *Fig* 4 may turn out to be typical of speech behaviour and the maxima of sensitivity may appear consistently at 'phoneme boundaries' when the stimulus dimensions are properly chosen. It would be necessary to explore a number of dimensions for any group of sounds and one would expect the maxima of sensitivity to be better defined in some dimensions than in others but this in itself would be valuable information about the grouping of the sounds.

One crucial experiment that has yet to be done, in this context, is a labelling experiment using one set of stimuli with two or more groups of listeners, each group having a different native language. If the effects that we have noted are truly indicative of phonemic grouping in a language, then we shall expect in the labelling experiment to find minima of agreement at different points in the continuum for different language groups, provided the stimulus dimension is operative in all the languages concerned. Discrimination experiments with the same stimuli and the same listeners would provide important evidence for or against the hypothesis that 'phoneme boundaries' are marked by maxima of sensitivity to change.

One thing that emerges from this type of experiment is that, as we have said, the linguist cannot be the arbiter of phonetic similarity. In the learning of our native language, our perceptions take on a pattern that is appropriate for the language. The linguist through his professional training is able to get rid of the areas of relative insensitivity but this of course makes it impossible for him to know what sounds are similar for the native speaker of some language other than his own.

A short note might be added to this section to the effect that linguists who are uneasy over the phonemic status of /h/ and /ŋ/ in English should perhaps begin experimenting with a continuum that covers both types of sound. It would no doubt be possible to synthesize such a continuum, though it might be difficult to do so with a single dimension of variation. With such material it would be possible to see whether phoneme boundaries are apparent as minima in the labelling data and maxima in the discrimination data and so solve the problem in the only reasonable way – by observation of the behaviour of those who use the language.

The problem of stress

A problem of another kind that is apt to cause difficulties in linguistic analysis is that of stress, not only the difficulty of deciding what kind of variation constitutes a difference of stress but also how many degrees of discrimination are appropriate to a given language. If questions of phonetic similarity can be settled only by reference to the users of a language, it is even more certain that questions of stress can be solved only in the same way. We use the term *stress* to summarize the total effort that a speaker puts into uttering some particular stretch of a speech sequence. The listener who perceives stress differences does so very largely by inferring, from what he hears, the amount of effort he himself would have put into the utterance. The sound-waves contain information on the basis of which he makes this inference and it can be shown experimentally that this information is again multi-dimensional.

Although in linguistics the multi-dimensional nature of stress has to some extent been recognized, there is often a tendency to assign the chief role to one dimension without the support of real evidence. References to languages as having a 'pitch accent' or a 'length accent' are no longer very common in the literature but on the other hand many American linguists refer to 'loud stress' in English, which certainly implies that the perceptual dimension of 'loudness' is the most important one. This is not justifiable unless we have reliable evidence that the users of the language are more influenced by variations in loudness than by other changes. We need in fact to be able to measure the relative 'weight' of the different kinds of information that the listener uses each time he makes a stress judgment, and we cannot do this in the conditions of everyday communication. Experimental research is required for this and once more the use of synthesized speech has proved very valuable.

An account of these experiments has been published and it will not therefore be necessary to devote much space to the experimental technique. As we said earlier, one advantage of an experimental method in dealing with the listener's linguistic behaviour is that we can set up the conditions in such a way that his behavioural response is clear-cut. In order to achieve this, however, we have to choose very carefully the task we set him and the questions we ask him. In the work on phonetic similarity, the questions were essentially simple, in one case 'Do you hear /ba/, /da/, or /ga/', and in the discrimination experiment, 'Does the sound X sound more like sound A or sound B?' It is more difficult to find a means of making the listener respond in a way that will reveal his stress judgments, but there are, in English, word pairs like OBject and obJECT, SUBject and subJECT, CONtract and conTRACT which can be differentiated by their stress patterns and it has proved possible to use these as material for experiments on stress. Listeners were asked to decide whether they heard the noun or the verb form, and their response was simply to underline one of two printed words of this kind: OBject : obJECT.

By using a speech synthesizer it was possible to control a number of dimensions independently. In the first series of experiments many versions of such test words as *object, subject, contract* were synthesized in which the relative duration and the relative intensity of the two vowels in each word were varied over a wide range. These items were recorded in random order and large groups of listeners judged with respect to each item whether it was the noun or the verb form. A summary of the results is given in *Fig 5*. The scale on the vertical axis gives the proportion of listeners (expressed as a percentage) who judged each item to be a noun. The horizontal axis shows the ratio of vowel one to vowel two in duration or in intensity. The continuous curve shows that when vowel one was short compared with vowel two, only 18 per cent of listeners judged the test items to be nouns (that is to say 82 per cent judged them to be verbs). As the duration ratio of vowel one to vowel two increased, the percentage of listeners who heard nouns also increased until eventually 90 per cent registered noun and only 10 per cent verb. The dotted curve shows the effect of intensity change. When vowel one was much less intense than vowel two, 43 per cent of the listeners heard nouns (that is a little less than half) and at the other end of the scale where vowel one was much more intense than vowel two, 77 per cent heard nouns. It is clear then that both differences of duration and of intensity will signal stress differences for English listeners but it seems that of the two, the duration differences have the greater weight since they swing a greater proportion of the listeners from verb to noun judgment.

The next experiment was an attempt to explore the dependence of stress judgments upon fundamental frequency. This would correspond in natural speech to the vocal cord frequency and thus would be related to the pitch heard by the listener. We should expect that if this factor is important in the perception of stress, a syllable on a higher frequency would tend to be judged stressed in comparison with a lower syllable. On this occasion only one word-pair was used, SUBject : subJECT, and the effect of change in fundamental frequency was balanced against the effect of duration change. The frequency patterns consisted simply of step changes of frequency between the first and second syllable of each test item, and the size of the step varied over a range of nearly one octave. The same range of duration ratio was used as in the previous experiment and the results are presented in a similar way in *Fig* 6. The effect of duration ratio is again apparent in all the curves. The one labelled *monotone* refers to the cases where no change of frequency was introduced; it differs from the

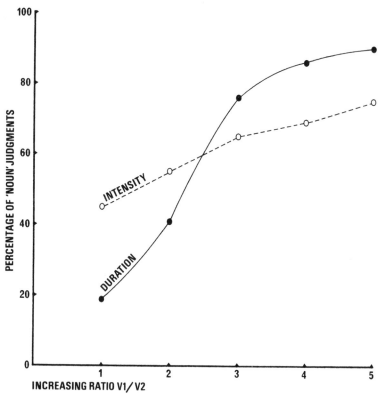

Fig 5: Curves summarizing the results of an experiment with word pairs of the type SUBject : subJECT, showing the influence on listeners' stress judgments of increasing the duration ratio and the intensity ratio of the first vowel to the second vowel.

curve of the previous figure only because it refers to a single word-pair, whilst the previous one summarizes the results for five word-pairs. In the step-down versions where the first syllable was always higher than the second, we should predict a tendency to more noun judgments and this is what the results show; the whole curve is transposed in the direction of a higher percentage of nouns. The step-up, where the second syllable is higher, transposes the curve in the opposite direction and we get an increase in verb judgments.

An interesting feature of the results in this experiment is shown in *Fig* 7. We might predict that the power of fundamental frequency change in influencing stress judgments would be partly dependent upon the size of the change – in this experiment the size of the frequency step between the two

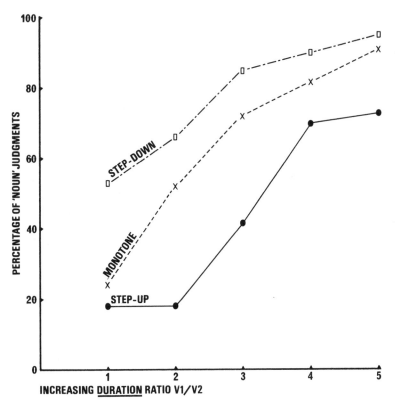

Fig 6: The effect of a step-change of fundamental frequency between the two syllables of a word on listeners' stress judgments.

syllables. This could be tested by taking all the cases in which the higher syllable was judged to be stressed and seeing how these were distributed amongst the intervals of different size. This distribution is shown in the figure. The frequency steps ranged from 5 cps to 90 cps but there are no significant differences between the scores. It seems therefore that this fundamental frequency effect in stress judgments is not a graded one but rather an all-or-none effect, suggesting that provided a syllable sounds higher than a neighbouring one it will tend to be judged stressed, regardless of how much higher it sounds.

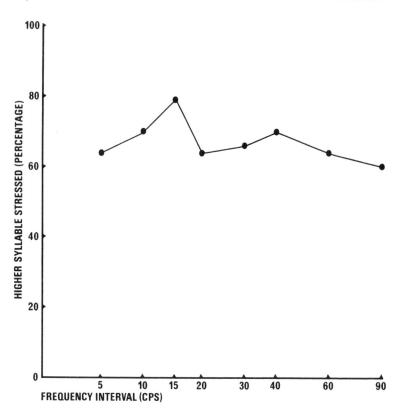

Fig 7: The number of higher syllables that are judged as being stressed does
not vary significantly with the size of the step-change in fundamental
frequency.

The last experiment is a preliminary attempt to explore the interaction
of intonation and stress judgments by imposing on the synthesized words
a fundamental frequency pattern that simulates sentence intonation. The
results for two sample patterns are shown in *Fig* 8. The same duration
ratios as before are combined with frequency patterns appropriate for a
sentence final noun (pattern A) and a sentence final verb (pattern B). The
effect is now more definite than before since for pattern A there is always a
majority of noun judgments (the lowest value is 57 per cent nouns) while
for pattern B there is always a majority of verb judgments (the lowest value
is 62 per cent verbs). Evidently the weight of the fundamental frequency
factor in stress judgments depends very much on whether the frequency
pattern forms an important part of a sentence intonation. If it does, then
this factor will tend to over-ride all others, even that of duration.

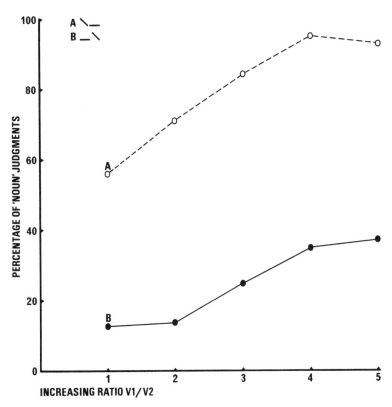

Fig 8: The effect on stress judgments of two fundamental frequency patterns
that simulate English intonation patterns. On the horizontal axis the
steps again indicate increasing duration ratio of vowel one to vowel two;
despite the duration effect, pattern A gives always a majority of 'noun'
judgments, and pattern B a majority of 'verb' judgments.

These experiments have been concerned with the general nature of
stress in English but they suggest methods of dealing with the question of
degrees of stress, and further much of what has been said about stress
applies equally to tone. In neither case is it much use adopting theories
which have never been put to experimental test. When Twaddell says (review of Stetson), for example, 'There is general agreement that there are
three degrees of lexical stress in American English' and again 'There is
general agreement that English syntax includes at least three and probably
four different relative pitch levels', he means that there is general agreement amongst linguists. But this is irrelevant for the science of linguistics;
what we need to know is what agreement there is among English speakers

and listeners as to degrees of stress, and levels of tone, and these things we cannot hope to discover except by experiment.

Conclusion

The experiments that have been referred to form only a small part of all the work that is being done in this field. They have been chosen largely in order to stress the fact that there is a very great deal of human linguistic behaviour which is not directly accessible to the ear and eye of the linguist. Almost all linguistic behaviour is organized at a brain level where the subject, speaker or listener, is unaware of what happens. We may say, indeed, that successful experiments are possible *because* the subject is unaware of the processes. If we devise the tasks and frame the questions carefully enough, the subject will supply information which is indispensable to an understanding of the way in which language works.

It must be made quite clear that such experimental work depends on the observations that the linguist and the phonetician can make directly; without these, there would be no basis for experiment. On the other hand, linguistic theory, if it is to have any validity as a summary of linguistic behaviour, cannot afford to ignore a whole area of the subject which is revealed only by experimental methods.

It is not easy to find things out in this way. Much of the work is laborious yet it calls for a great deal of ingenuity. Progress in our knowledge of the way in which language works would be much more rapid if some linguists would only devote the very high order of ingenuity that they now display in the building of logical theoretical structures to the business of observation and to the rigorous testing of theories. Let us by all means, as Trager says, 'go about doing linguistic analysis vigorously and objectively, perfecting and refining our theory as we go along'. But hypotheses must relate to linguistic behaviour, and they must be put to the test, where necessary to experimental test. In this way we may hope to build up a body of linguistic theory which is not incompatible with the results of experimental research.

Bibliography

BLOCH, B. 'Studies in Colloquial Japanese,' IV, *Language*, 26, 1950, 86.
BRUCE, D. 'The effect of listeners' anticipations on the intelligibility of heard speech,' *Language and Speech*, 1, 1958, 79.
FRY, D. B. 'Experiments in the perception of stress,' *Language and Speech*, 1, 1958, 126.
GARVIN, P. L. Review of *Preliminaries to Speech Analysis* (Jakobson, Fant, and Halle), *Language*, 29, 1953, 472.
HOCKETT, C. F. *A Manual of Phonology*, Baltimore, 1955.

LEES, R. B. Review of *Syntactic Structures* (Chomsky), *Language*, 33, 1957, 375.

LIBERMAN, A. M. 'Some results of research on speech perception,' *J. acoust. Soc. Amer.*, 29, 1957, 117.

LIBERMAN, A. M. *et al.* 'The discrimination of speech sounds within and across phoneme boundaries,' *J. exp. Psych.*, 54, 1957, 358.

SAPIR, E. 'The status of linguistics as a science,' *Language*, 5, 1929, 207.

SHANNON, C. E. and WEAVER, W. *The Mathematical Theory of Communication*, University of Illinois, 1949.

STURTEVANT, E. H. *Introduction to Linguistic Science*, New Haven, 1947.

TRAGER, G. L. Review of *Phonemics* (Pike), *Language*, 26, 1950, 152.

TRAGER, G. L. 'The field of linguistics,' *Studies in Linguistics, Occasional Papers*, 1, 1949.

TWADDELL, W. F. 'Stetson's model and the "supra-segmental phonemes",' *Language*, 29, 1953, 415.

A. C. Gimson

Implications of the phonemic/chronemic grouping of English vowels

A phonemic transcription is generally agreed to be the most convenient for practical teaching of English to foreigners and for many other purposes. As far as the representation of the English vowel system is concerned, such disagreement as there is appears to centre around the determining of the number of vowel phonemes. The matter has been complicated in English by the fact that certain pairs of vowels are said to differ through a complex of quality and quantity. In this way Professor Daniel Jones reduces a 21 vowel phoneme system to one of 11 simple vowel phonemes and 5 complex phonemic/chronemic groupings (also treated as 5 phonemes). An English vowel system is, therefore, established of 16 phonemes. Two questions seem to be raised by the introduction of these complex groupings:

1. While the chronemic distinction is certainly present, can it be said to be significant in the language? And, if it is significant, is it of greater or smaller importance than the purely qualitative distinction?
2. If complex chronemic/phonemic groupings are to be admitted as valid, can the present groupings be regarded as the most correct phonetically speaking, or even as the most acceptable from the point of view of usage?

In answer to the first question, one's immediate impression is that the quantity of a vowel in English has relatively little significance by comparison with that of its quality. The difficulty of obtaining confirmation one way or the other is that the normal individual is not analytically conscious of the more subtle speech distinctions that he makes, whereas the phonetically trained person can hardly give an opinion which is not influenced by his knowledgeable prejudices. Nevertheless, it did seem possible to

First published in *Acta Linguistica*, Vol v, Fasc 2: 94-100, 1945-49.

find out from a group of phonetically untrained persons just how far they would allow, while still interpreting the words correctly, qualitative and quantitative variations of vowel sounds; and to deduce from the results the relative importance of vowel quality and quantity.

The conditions of any such tests are, of course, extremely difficult to control – even a group of untrained subjects will individually have varying capacities of perception or linguistic acuteness; individuals will in varying degrees, consciously or unconsciously, tend to interpret unfamiliar sounds as approximately equivalent familiar sounds; and the person who carries out the test has to be sure that his own performance of the variations is constant, and that habitual interactions of quality and quantity should not be allowed unconsciously to affect his articulations.

The test was, therefore, carried out on some 26 English persons of little linguistic knowledge, all of London or near-London origin, and all familiar with my way of speaking. (The test was also attempted as a matter of interest with a mixed group of foreigners, speaking Latin, Germanic and Slav languages; but obviously the results obtained depended on their command of English, and the interpretations varied according to their own original linguistic habits.)

The experiment was concerned with varying length and quality of the vowels in parallel pairs of words containing the so-called chronemic/ phonemic pairs i, iː; a, aː; ɔ, ɔː; u, uː. (ə, əː were not included since it was felt that in this case there was little doubt that quantity was all important.) Thus *seat* and *sit* were said, the first word with the normal quality but shortened, and the second with the normal quality but lengthened. The same variations were made with these vowels closed by a voiced consonant in the words *lid* and *lead* (infinitive). The same changes were also applied to words containing the other three pairs of vowels. Each time the subjects were asked to write down the English word which first came to their mind. Words pronounced in a normal way were interspersed among the distorted examples. In this way there was some check on the subject's perception of sounds, though the test was not so much one of ear training as of normal linguistic interpretation.

As a supplementary test, a given word was pronounced with variants of quality and quantity in the vowel, and the subjects were asked to say which of the variants they most readily identified as the word. Thus *lid* was pronounced as [liːd] and as [lid], and the question was put 'Which is most like the normal [lɪd]?' The same method was applied to all the vowel pairs in voiced and voiceless contexts.

The following results were obtained (test words being shown in brackets):

1. *Pair* [iː], [ɪ]

The shortening of the long variety closed by a voiceless consonant (*seat*) does not seem to obscure the sense, whereas a lowered variety with correct length is less acceptable. With a voiced ending (*lead*), there is not quite the same readiness to understand the long variety when the vowel is shortened, but there is nevertheless a marked tendency to prefer a shortened close variety to a lengthened half-close (*meat*, *read*) in the case of both voiced and voiceless closure.

The lengthening of [ɪ] (*sit*, *lid*) provided much more confusion, very few subjects recognizing the words, but understanding the vowel either as [ɛ] or as an [ei] diphthong, in the case of both voiced and voiceless closure. A lengthened [ɪ] was on the whole better understood than a shortened [iː] (*fit*, *lid*).

It seems, therefore, that in this pair, the difference in quality is more marked and more significant than the difference of quantity. In the case of [iː], the quality of the sound is particularly important; as for [ɪ], while the qualitative distinction seemed to remain the essential one, any addition of length caused the vowel to be confused with another, though not with the so-called long member of the phoneme.

2. *Pair* [æ], [ɑː]

Here there was not the same likelihood of useful comparison, partly because the qualities are so dissimilar in Southern English, and partly because of the tendency to lengthen considerably the so-called short member of the phoneme.

But [ɑː] shortened with a voiceless closure (*part*) was regularly (90 per cent) mistaken for [ʌ], although, of course, there was no question of preferring a lengthened [æ]. With the voiced ending (*hard*) there was a greater tendency to understand [ɒ] for shortened [ɑː], and at the same time a greater readiness to understand [ɑː] correctly even when the vowel was shortened.

Such is the length of [æ] normally that abnormal length given to the sound (*pat*, *had*) did not render it any the less recognizable as [æ], not only by the English but also by the foreign subjects.

It would seem, therefore, that in the case of this pair, the quality is, as expected, all-important. From the point of view of English reactions, it is certainly more reasonable to pair [ɑː] with either [ʌ] or [ɒ], with a slight preference for [ʌ].

3. *Pair* [ɒ], [ɔː]

The long vowel [ɔː] closed by a voiceless consonant (*hawk*) was, when shortened, generally mistaken by English people for [ɶ]. The majority of the English preferred the lengthened [ɒ] (in *caught*) to a shortened [ɔː]. With the voiced ending (*cord*), the long vowel was again regularly taken for [ɶ], when shortened; all the subjects preferred a long [ɒ] to a shortened [ɔː] in this case.

The short member of the phoneme with a voiceless closure was regularly taken to be [ɑː] when lengthened (*hock*). This was true also with the voiced closure (*cod*), and the foreigners showed plain signs of the same confusion. However, all English subjects preferred a lengthened [ɒ] to a shortened [ɔː] to represent the [ɒ] vowel (*cot*, *nod*).

This pair revealed a somewhat unexpected relationship between [ɔː] and [ɒ]. Length appearing to be the main distinguishing feature between them. This indicates probably that my [ɔː] is very close and my [ɒ] rather open. In the comparative recognition of [ɔː], the quantitative difference seemed most significant.

The confusion of lengthened [ɒ] with [ɑː] was expected, and the fact that [ɒ] could be given the length of [ɔː] and still be accepted confirms the lengthening of these short vowels and, in this instance, underlines the importance of the qualitative difference.

4. *Pair* [ɷ], [uː]

This pair presents difficulties in the choice of specimen words. It was explained that it should be taken that I pronounce *suit* as [suːt] and *soot* as [sɷt].

Generally speaking, with both voiceless and voiced closure (*wooed*, *suit*), the shortened [uː] was not mistaken. It is thought that the confusion with [ɷ] which did occur may have been due to dialect translation on the part of the English subjects, as well as the comparative unfamiliarity of the word 'wooed'. All the English declared a shortened [uː] rather than lengthened [ɷ] to be nearer normal [uː] (*shoot*, *food*).

There was a great deal of confusion, however, when [ɷ] was lengthened (*soot*, *would*), though the sound was rarely mistaken for [uː]. The most striking confusion occurred when it was understood as [ɔː] (*cf* shortened [ɔː]=[ɷ]). It was also noticeable that the English, unanimously in the case of the voiceless closure and with a smaller majority in the case of the voiced ending, understood shortened [uː] for [ɷ] more easily than lengthened [ɷ].

It would seem, therefore, that [uː] was recognized whatever its length, and that in consequence quality is all-important in this sound; whereas in the case of [ɷ] an addition of length caused great confusion, and, when the correct length was given even to a closer sound, understanding (as [ɷ]) was made considerably easier. Quantity was, therefore, important in the examples of [ɷ].

5. *Short vowels* [ɛ] and [ʌ]

As a matter of interest abnormal length was also given to the short vowels in the words *bet*, *cut*. The change of quantity did not cause any of the English subjects to misunderstand the words, though one might have expected the second word to be mistaken for *cart* – (this error was made by nearly all the foreigners). The correct interpretation by the English may have been due to the fact that my [ʌ] is a very fronted variety.

Conclusions

It would seem, therefore, from this preliminary test, that, in answer to the first question as to the relative importance of quality and quantity in the four vowel pairs, there can be no doubt that the distinction of quality is to the average speaker of Southern English the more significant. Any transcription of English which sets out to express significant values should accordingly lay first emphasis on differences of quality, the number of vowel phonemes being probably 20 or 21. This last statement amounts to a criticism of the broad system of transcription which takes advantage of the quality/quantity complex of these pairs to express a difference of sound quality by means of a length mark. It is, of course, a convention which can be assimilated by the foreign learner, but it would appear that such conventions as have to exist should be based on sound quality rather than on quantity. And there seems no reason why, for practical purposes, such a purely phonemic broad transcription should not be slightly narrowed, and therefore made slightly more helpfully descriptive, to the extent of using length marks with the regularly long vowels. It is surely not valid to treat the English vowel system on the same terms as, for instance, the Serbo-Croat system, where quantitative distinctions in vowel sounds are supremely significant without important correlated differences of quality.

These considerations supply some answer to the second question as to whether the correct grouping of sound qualities into chroneme pairs has been made, if the chronemic/phonemic group is to be admitted as valid at all. It would appear, at the outset, that there must be considerable doubt whether, in a language such as English, these groupings are legitimate or useful in any practical sense. In any case, the present pairing seems highly artificial. From a phonetic point of view, there would have to be a different basis of grouping on grounds of pure qualitative proximity (*eg* [ʌ] with [ɑː], [ɒ] with [ɔː], as far as my own pronunciation is concerned); and from the standpoint of the Englishman's traditional conception of long and short vowels – a conception usually confused by the spelling – there are grounds for coupling [æ] with [ei].

Pursuing the reasoning of the present arbitrary coupling, and in the case of my own pronunciation (which has not the [ɔə] diphthong and which regularly uses an intrusive linking *r* for all [ɛə], [uə], [iə] groups final in a word, whatever their origin), I can conceive a phonemic/chronemic transcription which touches upon absurdity. I might, in fact, use a ten phoneme/two chroneme transcription in the following manner:

(present broad transcription shown in brackets)

		short chroneme		long chroneme	
	1.	i	(i)	iː	(iː)
	2.	e	(e)	eː	(ei)
	3.	a	(a)	aː	(ai)
phoneme	4.	ʌ	(ʌ)	ʌː	(aː)
	5.	o	(o)	oː	(oː)
	6.	u	(u)	uː	(uː)
	7.	ə	(ə)	əː	(əː)
	8.	–		oi	(oi)
	9.	–		ou	(ou)
	10.	–		au	(au)

My three centring diphthongs might be expressed by [ir], [er], [ur], with the convention that, when the [r] occurs in the same syllable and is preceded by [i] or [e] or [u], it must simply indicate a diphthongization of the previous vowel towards [ə], and that, when it occurs finally in a word followed by a vowel, the additional [r] glide must also be pronounced.

But it is obvious that such an arrangement would overstep the bounds of reason, and would demand of the foreign learner the assimilation of an absurd number of conventions before he could read the transcription. There must be a strict limit to the number of conventions; the number must, in fact, be rigidly governed by the phonemic structure of the language, and the issue should not be confused in a language such as English by chronemic considerations.

A. C. Gimson

The linguistic relevance of stress in English

To Professor Diedrich Westermann† on his eightieth birthday

It is customary to think of English as a language in which stress has a role
of supreme linguistic importance. The term 'stress', however, is one
which has come to be used with great laxity of definition. This lack of precision has, perhaps, been most marked among English writers on the subject, for whom stress and, for instance, 'prominence' have become words
of almost interchangeable significance. It would appear that the fundamental distinction between the levels of speech and language has not
always been kept in mind. It is time, therefore, to decide what we mean by
stress and whether, in fact, it has that linguistic significance which is commonly attributed to it.

We must, of course, be clear as to what we consider to be a matter of linguistic reality. As far as the spoken language is concerned, there is a mass
of observable material which we may investigate and measure in a variety
of ways. Whether this investigation deals with articulatory or acoustic
facts, we find ourselves on a purely phonetic level where linguistic meaning or relevance has no place. On this level of phonetic observation, there
may be considered to exist a first degree of linguistic reality, concerned
with the spoken word as a means of communication, which has constantly
to be borne in mind. At this stage, only those sound features are worthy of
consideration which are capable of being perceived by a listener. Those
observed facts which, as it soon may appear, have no significance in terms
of perception in the speaker-listener relationship can, even at this level, be
considered irrelevant. In other words, some speech phenomena which are

First published in *Zeitschrift für Phonetik und allgemeine Sprachwissenschaft*,
Vol IX, 2: 113–149, 1956.

capable of measurement may have, at an early stage, to be discarded as irrelevant to the function of speech as a means of communication. At a later
stage, we are concerned with pure linguistic realities of a second degree,
where the essence has been distilled from the gross phonetic material and
the signs organized in terms of a phonemic structure. The manifestations
on the purely phonetic level of these essential linguistic features of the first
and second degree repay further detailed investigation on the part of the
phonetician; though the phonetician's task is to study the observable facts
as a first step to linguistic analysis, he would do well in his further investigations, once the linguistic organization has been made apparent, to con-
centrate his efforts on those phonetic features which are relevant to the
language structure and to avoid confusion by leaving aside those which are
not.

As has been said, the term 'stress' has been linked with the prominent
or more perceptible segments of an utterance. It has, however, been
generally admitted that a listener's perception of a segment as being more
prominent than its surroundings is not entirely due to a matter of increased
energy of articulation on that particular segment on the part of the speaker.
Daniel Jones has said: 'Prominence of a syllable may be due to strong
stress, but it may also be due to other features of pronunciation, and particularly to the inherent quality of sounds, to the length of syllables . . . or
to intonation.'[1] The impact on an Englishman's ear and interpretative
powers of the continuous flow of acoustic signals which constitutes an
utterance may, in fact, be analysed in terms of an everchanging pattern of
sound qualities (consciously interpreted as a succession of discrete units
by reason of his past linguistic experience and prejudices), of a certain
significant melody in word and utterance, and of apparently varying degrees of length of the syllables. In addition, he will be conscious of the
emotive colouring which is superimposed upon the utterance by such
means as variations in voice quality. He would appear to perceive certain
segments as standing out from their neighbours on account of their having an apparent greater loudness, or a distinct change in pitch, or distinctive length. He will also have the impression that some sounds make
in themselves a greater auditory impact than others, are 'inherently more
sonorous'. Many of these phonetic prominences may be interpreted in his
mind as features of semantic significance and related to the prominence of
the important ideas of the utterance.

There is, in addition, a more elusive feature which characterizes the
whole utterance, a certain beat or rhythm, also related to what is known as
stress, which corresponds with the occurrence of at least some of the 'prominent' segments. At the outset, it is difficult to say whether it is the regular occurrence of prominences which produces an impression of a beat,
or whether it is the essential rhythm of English which determines the
choice of syllable to be rendered prominent. It can, however, be said that

in the long utterance there exists a certain periodicity which is indicated by landmarks (beats) and which produces an overall effect of regular rhythm. In short words, said by themselves, where there can be no question of a periodic beat, there is nevertheless a feeling of a rhythmic unit which is linked to a certain pattern of variations in perceptibility. The importance of the rhythmic unit in English has recently been emphasized by W. Jassem,[2] who points out the essential changes of sound length which are involved according to the composition of such rhythmic units and who believes that the juncture between rhythmic units is a feature which should be indicated in a phonetic or phonemic transcription of English. R. H. Stetson[3] has treated the matter in greater detail and has sought to prove that the stress (defined in terms of acoustic and physiological intensity) is the primary factor in the establishment of the rhythmic groupings of speech.

The term 'stress' is, therefore, customarily applied to two main categories of speech phenomena – the one which is concerned with making a sound or syllable stand out from its neighbours, and the other which refers to a beat which may characterize a whole utterance. Of the two categories, the first is the one which is most commonly correlated with a linguistically appreciated effect of stress. The confusion may have arisen from the gradual abandonment by English writers of the term 'accent', which included hitherto a variation of pitch or intensity as a means of rendering a syllable prominent. If accent was particularly one of intensity in the Indo-European parent language, it appears to have passed through stages of development from one of primarily pitch accent in Sanskrit and Greek to one of mainly intensity accent in later Greek and Latin. It would seem, then, that historically it is difficult to treat pitch and intensity accents as entirely separate phenomena, not to mention the relevance of syllabic quantity. It is evident that when the term 'stress' begins to replace that of 'accent', often by implication if not by definition, the same variety of manifestation may be applied to the former as to the latter. It is the more confusing when, as in the following examples, an attempt is made at a strict definition of the term: (Henry Sweet):[4] stress is 'organically, the result of the force with which the breath is expelled from the lungs; acoustically, dependent on the size of the sound vibrations, the bigger the waves, the louder the sound, the greater the stress'; (Gray and Wise):[5] 'intensity or loudness depends on the amount of breath expended, proper use of the resonators, effectiveness of vibration of the vocal cords'; (T. Chiba):[6] 'stress is defined as the degree of force in utterance . . . means both subjective force of the voice and force of breath'; (K. L. Pike):[7] 'a degree of intensity upon some syllable which makes it more prominent or louder than an unstressed syllable'; (Daniel Jones):[8] 'force of utterance, abstracted from the other attributes of speech sounds, is termed stress. Stresses are essentially subjective activities of the speaker'; (R. M. S.

Heffner):[9] 'stress is reflected in the quantum of muscular energy which goes into each articulatory movement . . . in the amount of sound a given speech articulation makes'. Even in this brief selection of definitions great weight is given to the effect of loudness produced by stress. If we are merely concerned with our first degree of linguistic relevance, the phenomenon might quite adequately be dealt with in terms of 'loudness'. On the other hand, if stress sometimes occurs as intensity on the speaker's part without any corresponding effect being communicated to the listener, except in a recollective habit stimulated by other accompanying phonetic features, then it is not in itself linguistically considerable.

It is to be noted that in the definition by Daniel Jones quoted above mention is made of stress as a subjective activity of the speaker, a matter of an intensive psychological stimulus. Of course, a speaker's linguistic stimuli are normally psychological, but the stimulus itself does not constitute a reality of communication, unless it is accompanied by an expression capable of being interpreted by a listener. Subjective stressing remains a reality for the speaker, as in the example given by Jones:[10] the phrase 'Thank you' is often pronounced 'kkju, where the stress is felt by the speaker on the first k, although from the auditory point of view this 'sound' consists merely of silence. There is no doubt that this kind of subjective stressing plays a large part in the actual delivery of such a rhythmic language as English. In verse based upon a regular rhythmic pattern, a shortened line will always have its missing feet compensated in the mind of an English reader by the appropriate rhythmic beat. It is significant that A. Classe in his study of English prose rhythm[11] deals with the question of stress and says that it may be 'signalized by any or all of a change of auditory intensity (loudness), change of quantity, change of pitch direction, change of the characteristics of vowel and consonant, and increased amplitude of physiological movements'; yet he defines stress as 'an impulse (primarily of a psychological nature) which expresses itself in the first place by an increase of pressure in the speech canal and approximately coincides with the point of greatest prominence'. Stress for him, then, is a speech phenomenon which 'approximately coincides' with a feature of linguistic relevance, prominence. His supporting experimental evidence is based on kymographic tracings, with his subjects indicating psychological stresses by pressing a switch. His syllable is initiated by a peak of pressure in the speech canal: thus, he differentiates the syllabification of the sk clusters in ə nais kʌlə skiːm by showing that the pressure peak occurs in the first instance on k and in the second case on the s. He maintains that the whole syllable following the pressure peak provides an objective impression of being stressed. In this way, he is able to amplify Jones's example of 'kkju, where Jones had assumed a subjective stress on the first k; for Classe, there is an actual pressure peak on the mute sound.

Thus we see that what arose, in the case of such a so-called stress language as English, from a conception of an accent of intensity by implicit opposition to an accent of pitch, has been defined by modern writers in terms of psychological impulses and extra expiratory effort or extra intensity of articulation, which result in an impression of loudness or prominence of the sound in question. It remains to be seen what is the linguistic function of stress conceived in this way. It is not difficult to show that stress, defined in terms of effort or loudness, is not an efficient means of rendering a syllable prominent. As we have said above, much more easily appreciated by a listener are variations in qualities, quantities and pitch. It has often been demonstrated that certain sounds are more sonorous than others; for instance, that, all other things being equal, open vowels are more easily perceived than close vowels. The well-known test carried out before the war by Lloyd James set out to illustrate this point. The word *mechanically* was said on a monotone or in a whisper with stresses on the first and third syllables, whereas, on account of the relatively greater sonority of the vowel æ, the second syllable was always perceived by English people as receiving the stress. This would appear to show that, if the usual manifestations of stress are not available, the subjective strong beat, even when accompanied by a greater articulatory effort, does not suffice to provide an objective impression of stress. But it is hardly a proper test to require English people to appreciate a shift of stress on a familiar English word, for the rhythmic structure of which each listener will be subject to linguistic constraints arising from his past experience. Much the same result has been obtained with such words as 'impact or 'brickbat. When these words are said on a monotone with the customary sound lengths retained, it is still quite difficult to produce an impression of stress on the second syllable merely by greater articulatory effort, despite the fact that the second vowel in each case is said to be much more sonorous than the first. A fairer test is made when a nonsense word, containing English sounds, is used. Such a sound group as iːvɔlimæ, said on a monotone or in a whisper, usually evokes from English listeners an impression of stress on the second syllable, or occasionally on the last. But once pitch change and lengthening are brought into operation, any syllable can be made to appear stressed to an English ear. Even the third syllable may be felt to have a strong stress if the group is said with the intonation - - ‾ - or - -‗-, or if the third vowel is lengthened. (In this last case, it is true that the English listener may no longer feel that he is hearing the quality of the vowel in *bit*, but may interpret the diphthong of *bate*, although no diphthongal glide is uttered.) It may, in fact, be said that the most significant means of expressing a psychological intensive pulse and of rendering a segment or group of segments prominent are, first, a change of pitch and, secondly, an extension of quantity, or a combination of the two. Length, by itself, is rarely used in English for this purpose. Perhaps the only case of its use (apart from musical recitative) is the intoning of prayers still to be heard in church, eg '. . . and the blessing of God be upon us . . .', where the rhythmic stressing of the short vowels in *bless*, *God*, and *upon* may be brought out by a slight lengthening of the vowels.

It will be seen that the so-called distinctions by means of stress are most usually realized by means of changes of pitch. The case of those words whose substantival or verbal form is said to be determined by the stress affords an illustration. Such a word as *insult* in normal speech distinguishes its forms for a hearer mainly by different pitch patterns. Thus, the word said in isolation may be realized as, for instance, $\searrow$ - for the noun, and - $\searrow$ for the verb. There is also a relative lengthening of the syllable which has the pitch-fall, as well as a change of rhythmic structure for each word form; but the main oppositional impact is that afforded by the pitch change. Certainly stress in terms of extra expiratory effort or extra loudness would not be sufficient to make the distinction. The inefficiency of stress as a sole means of achieving prominence has been well illustrated by N. C. Scott in his example[12] hiː sed wud impɔːts wud, spoken in such a way that both syllables of the word *imports* are pitched on a low level note. He found that English listeners who heard this phrase were most uncertain whether it meant *He said* (*Mr*) *Wood imports* (*vb*) *wood* or *He said wood imports* (*n*) *would*.

But although pitch is a factor of supreme importance in manifesting a subjective stress, there are certain qualifications to be made as to its use. There does not appear to be a clearcut correlation in English between the actual degree of loudness produced by the stress and the corresponding pitch curve, nor is the corresponding tune change merely one involving relatively higher pitch. The relationship of stress to pitch is usually that the stress is manifested in terms of a change of level of pitch or direction of pitch in the syllable to be stressed. And as far as loudness is concerned, the sentence 'Did you say "insult"?' said with the intonation ⁻ - ‿ · , such as might be used in an indignant question form, has a strong psychological stress on the first syllable of *insult* when the noun form is intended, but a greater loudness may well be heard on the second syllable. Moreover, the pitch in this case is very low on the stressed syllable and very high on the unstressed syllable – the equivalent of a rise spread over the two syllables. Here the effect of prominence is produced by the outstandingly low pitch reached on the first syllable of *insult* in relation to the general fall-rise curve of the whole utterance. If the verbal form of *insult* had been intended in the same kind of intonation context, the direction change would have had to take place on the second syllable, *ie* an intonation of the sort ⁻ -· ╱ or - · - · ╱ where the rise on *sult* would begin at a point lower than the pitch of the first syllable, or more rarely at about the same level. An intonation of the sort -·- ‿ ╱ , where the pitch interval between the two syllables leaves doubt as to whether the second syllable begins the pitch change of direction (the rise) or whether the first syllable stands out by reason of its low prominence, would be unnatural and confusing to the Southern English ear, and it would be correspondingly difficult to decide whether noun or verb were meant.

The so-called 'emphatic stress for contrast' need not be accompanied by any extra force of articulation or extra loudness. Such a sentence as 'We were *all* there', said with a high fall on *all*, sufficiently brings out the meaning of 'with no exceptions', merely by the high pitch change of the word in question. If there is in fact greater articulatory effort on *all* as well as the pitch change, it is as likely to be manifested by abnormal voice quality (often of a strongly glottalized nature) as by greater loudness. Indeed, emphatic stress in languages appears rarely, if ever, to be a matter of extra energy alone. In addition to pitch and length changes, devices such as the change of word order, addition of particles, etc, or reduplication, seem to be common.

And finally, the frequent 'lively' intonation of such sentences as 'The captain went on board his ship', with all the unstressed syllables (*the, tain, on, his*) on a high pitch and the stressed on a low pitch, demonstrates that sometimes intonation is not at all a good guide to the stresses. Many a foreign listener might readily appreciate the stresses as occurring on the high pitched syllables. Moreover, in verses which have this kind of rhythm, it is perfectly possible to articulate the unstressed syllables so that they give a clear impression of greater loudness. This often happens when children recite poems such as 'Goosey, goosey gander, whither shall you wander, Upstairs or downstairs, or in my lady's chamber'. They will say nearly all the unstressed syllables on a high prominent pitch and with loudness at least equal to that of the stressed syllables; yet they will keep the impression of rhythm and stress intact by means of the variation of length between the stressed and unstressed syllables.

Stress has often been referred to as a phoneme, which may distinguish meaning, and in this connection there is one other all-important adjunct to stress which we should consider in English. It is a characteristic of the language that vowel quality and stressing (quite apart from intonation) are intimately connected. Thus when we say that the position of the stress changes the meaning (as between noun and verb) in the case of words like *object* or *rebel*, we are not making a wholly true statement of the facts, since in the present state of the language at least, the variation of vowel quality has in these cases assumed a large part of the onus for distinguishing words. Moreover, it is doubtful whether stress, even accompanied by its various manifestations, is an effective means of showing syllable or word boundaries. Daniel Jones in an article on 'The Word as a Phonetic Entity'[13] gives several examples of words which are, in his opinion, distinguished primarily by the stress placement and only secondarily by a variation of quality or length. The well-known opposition *a name, an aim* might well appear to be an example of a case where stress may be considered all-important for indicating the syllabic division. It may, in fact, be so in very slow speech, where the stress manifestation (point of pitch change, length of n, etc) may be made very obvious; but in normal speech it is doubtful whether any difference at all is made or perceived. Various groups of English people were asked to write down phrases at my dictation, and the phrase *an aim*, very strongly stressed on the second word, was included in the list. It was, nevertheless, more common for the listeners to write down *a name* in response, no doubt because of the greater familiarity with the latter word. In other cases, where the phonetic distinctions as apart from stress were much greater, the confusion was considerably less. But there is a danger that we phoneticians should create fine distinctions for ourselves which constitute no kind of reality for ordinary speakers of the language. From an historical point of view, such confusion of syllabic and word boundaries must be postulated in order to explain the development of such forms as *an adder, an umpire, a nickname, an apron*, etc. The speech instinct as to the separation point of these syllables has always been most uncertain, despite the stress; and it can hardly be thought of as being any surer now, except as the result of the conditioning of our minds by the orthography. Normally, too many linguistic constraints are provided by the context of present or recollected situation for stress, even when manifested, to have as much essential phonemic importance as has often been claimed for it.

To sum up, we may say that stress certainly exists in English in terms of a mental pulse or beat, measurable perhaps in the nervous activity of the brain. This may well be the stimulus for the sensation of rhythm or the subjective feeling which enables us to tap out the beats of a sentence even when it is not completed. It must, however, be considered as non-linguistic, in the sense that it remains a speaker-activity, and becomes a communicated fact only when interpreted through a listener's 'kinaesthetic memory', in which case it is a reciprocal action of linguistic recollection rather than an exchange of meaningful signals. This mental beat may, nevertheless, be manifested in terms of extra articulatory effort or greater loudness, both of which may be measured instrumentally. But these manifestations are not linguistic in the sense that they are capable by themselves of conveying efficiently a signal to a listener. The only realizations of stress which are linguistic, in that they are capable of creating an impression of relative prominences, of accent, in a listener's mind, are those which are effected with the complex help of pitch, quantity and quality variations. It is important to keep this clear, from the theoretical point of view, so that, in any discussion of accent in the utterance, the confusion between stress and prominence may be avoided; and, from the practical point of view, especially that of the foreigner learning English, so that the phenomenon of stress may be treated in its proper and very important place, as a basis for rhythmic grouping in delivery.

Notes

[1] *The Phoneme: its Nature and Use*, 1950, para 435.

[2] 'Indication of Speech Rhythm in the Transcription of Educated Southern English', *Le Maître Phonétique*, No 92, Juillet-Décembre 1949.

[3] *Motor Phonetics*, 1951.

[4] *The Sounds of English*, 1908.

[5] *The Bases of Speech*, 1934.

[6] *A Study of Accent*, 1935.

[7] *Phonemics*, 1947.

[8] *The Phoneme*, 1950.

[9] *General Phonetics*, 1950.

[10] *Outline of English Phonetics*, 1949.

[11] *The Rhythm of English Prose*, 1939.

[12] 'An Experiment on Stress Perception', *Le Maître Phonétique*, No 67, Juillet-Septembre, 1939.

[13] *Le Maître Phonétique*, No 36, Octobre-Décembre, 1931. [In this volume, *pp* 154–158. Eds.]

M. A. K. Halliday

The tones of English

1

Natural conversation in 'British Standard' English[1] may be represented as involving continuous selection from a set of five tones. These five tones constitute a phonological system, at the primary degree of delicacy, that is both chain-exhausting and choice-exhausting. That is to say, connected speech can, it is suggested here, be analysed into an unbroken succession of tone groups each of which selects one or other of the five tones. For purposes of analysis, the selection can be regarded as discrete on both axes, both syntagmatically and paradigmatically: we can make a good description, that is, if we postulate that each tone group begins where the previous one ends, with no overlap and no hiatus, and that each tone group can be unambiguously assigned to one tone, this assignment thereby excluding all the other tones.

Descriptive statements in linguistics are best regarded as having 'more/less' validity, 'yes/no' being merely a special case of 'more/less'; it is thus *a priori* likely that a small number of utterances in this variety of English lies outside this system. I can myself construct examples which may not be accounted for by it. But in the samples examined for the purpose of this study (of which the main sample, that subjected to exhaustive textual analysis, contained just under 2,000 tone groups) there were no tone groups which did not select one or other of the five tones.

Each of the tones of course exhibits subdivisions, to be recognized when the analysis is carried beyond the primary degree of delicacy.

First published in *Archivum Linguisticum*, Vol XV, Fasc 1: 1–28, 1963, and subsequently in revised form, as part of M. A. K. Halliday, *Intonation and Grammar in British English*, Janua Linguarum Series Practica 48, Mouton, The Hague, 1967.

Delicacy is a variable to which no theoretical limit can be set; nor is there any valid and objective means of measuring it. But in a phonological statement it is possible to be guided, in the choice of an appropriate degree of delicacy, by certain formal considerations. In describing English intonation, we let the grammar decide how delicate we should be. This is made possible by the relation between phonology and linguistic form. One should perhaps apologize for raising once again this old problem of linguistic theory; but a minimum of discussion is perhaps needed to clarify the subsequent statement.

The reason for recognizing phonology as an independent level in descriptive linguistics is that this is the only way in which it can provide a bridge between form and substance. In phonology we make a separate abstraction from phonic substance, and represent this in statements which show how the given language organizes its phonic resources in such a way as to carry (or 'expound') its grammatical and lexical patterns. If we tie phonology directly to form, the result is likely to be either excessive complication or distortion. It is curious for example that although no linguist has ever suggested that all grammatical categories should be assigned direct phonological exponents – there is no language in which all *classes*, at every rank, are marked phonologically, though the linguist is naturally delighted when he finds a class that is so marked – it has been assumed by many that they must find direct exponents for the *units* of English grammar. But the idea that phonological criteria, such as pitch and juncture, serve as direct markers of grammatical units such as morpheme, word and sentence is surely untenable; it may lead either to weak phonology or to weak grammar, sometimes both. Of course there is always an *ultimate* phonological exponent of all formal categories and items: this is a requirement of linguistic theory. But the 'direct exponence' view, though greatly preferable to the notional (or 'no exponence at all') view which it superseded, must give way to a recognition that exponence is, or may be, 'indirect', involving a long chain of abstraction.[2] If we really did use pauses, or pitch movements, to mark boundaries of grammatical units in English, the relation between the grammar and the phonology would be very much simplified.

Whenever we describe a language we are concerned with meaning, and all *contrast* in meaning can be stated either in grammar or in lexis. If we regard intonation in English as meaningful – if, for example, the choice between two possible utterances which differ only in that one has tone 1 and the other has tone 4 is a true choice between different utterances – then we should seek to state the place which such choices occupy relative to the total set of formal patterns in the language; and there are only two kinds of formal pattern: grammatical and lexical. It is not enough to treat the intonation systems as if they merely carried a set of emotional nuances superimposed on the grammatical and lexical items and categories.

The contrasts made by intonation in English are clearly not lexical. In this respect English differs from, say, Vietnamese: Vietnamese is a 'tone language', given that we define 'tone language' as one in which intonation carries lexical meaning. English intonation contrasts are grammatical: they are exploited in the grammar of the language. The systems expounded by intonation are just as much grammatical as are those, such as tense, number and mood, expounded by other means. They are not even necessarily more delicate than the latter: some are and some are not. There is no difference *in the way they work in the grammar* between systems with direct phonological exponence, such as those carried by intonation, and those expounded indirectly through a long chain of grammatical abstraction.

Therefore, in a description of the grammar of spoken English, 'intonational' and 'non-intonational' systems figure side by side. They are not to be treated as systems of different types. Moreover since 'intonational' systems operate at many different places in the grammar, they will not be isolated in a chapter by themselves, but incorporated throughout the description wherever appropriate. The decision whether a given system that happens to be expounded by intonation is to figure in the grammar or not is a grammatical, not a phonological decision; thus it is the requirements of the grammar that set the limits of delicacy on the phonological statement. The latter is just so delicate that it includes those sub-systems of each tone which are required for the grammatical description. This of course is merely pushing the problem one stage further back: a decision still has to be taken regarding the degree of delicacy of the grammar. For the purpose of the present paper this has been defined as the requirement of a 'comprehensive' grammar; 'comprehensive' being in turn defined as complete, for all categories at all ranks, at the primary degree of (grammatical) delicacy.

The view that phonological statements represent an abstraction from phonic data that is independent of the abstraction made at the formal levels, and that this status enables the linguist to describe more powerfully the exponents of the formal items and categories, does not mean that the phonology cannot be 'polysystemic' in the sense that different phonological systems can be recognized to account for different sets of formal contrasts. One must however guard against neglecting likeness for the sake of, and in the course of, recognizing unlikeness. Since, for example, the contrast between tone 1 and tone 2 means one thing – that is, is doing one grammatical job – if the tone group coincides with a clause that is affirmative in mood, and another if with a clause that is interrogative, it might be asserted that we should here recognize two distinct *phonological* systems. But phonetically the exponents are indistinguishable in the two cases; and their identity would be obscured, or the statement of it complicated, if two distinct phonological systems were set up. A more serious objection, however, is that unless one specifies 'distinct phonological systems only where the *phonology* (as opposed to the formal levels) requires them' there is no telling where to stop. We will certainly be prepared to describe the 'phonology of the verbal group' and the 'phonology of the nominal group' in a given language if the phonological situation demands it; but not just because they are grammatically distinct – otherwise why not 'phonology of the active verbal group' and 'of the passive verbal group', and so on to the limits of delicacy? There would be no tone system in Mandarin Chinese: only as many systems as there were sets of lexical items distinguished by intonation. The rejection of the 'phoneme inventory' view in favour of a 'prepared-to-be-polysystemic' prosodic phonology rests on purely phonological grounds.

In English intonation we can, and I think should, set up a single independent phonological system irrespective of the very many different roles that are played by (different selections of) its terms in English grammar. Tone 1, for example, may be, and is, exponent of a number of terms each in a different grammatical system. But at the same time it is important to note that tone 1 is phonetically identical – that is, has the same range of phonetic variety – in all its uses. The concept of 'tone 1' rests on an abstraction from the phonic data in which one has asked simply 'is this distinction, which I can abstract from observations of the substance, *meaningful:* is it exploited *somewhere* in the grammar or lexis of the language?' A mass of noise, or rather of observations of noise, is thus reduced to a relatively simple set of contrastive exponents.

2

In the description of English phonology we need to recognize four units. These are, in descending order, tone group, foot, syllable and phoneme. They are related taxonomically as are the units of the grammatical rank scale: each one consists of one or more of the one below it. More accurately, an exponent of each unit consists of one, or of more than one, complete exponent of the unit next below it.[3] (In phonology, however, unlike grammar, there is no rankshift.) Thus each tone group consists of one, or of more than one, complete foot; and so on down the line.

The foot has been described by Abercrombie.[4] It is the unit of rhythm in English, and has a structure of two elements, 'ictus' and 'remiss', in that sequence: each ictus begins a new foot. The unit below the foot is the syllable, displaying a two-term system of 'strong' and 'weak': the strong syllable operates at 'ictus' and the weak syllable at 'remiss'. Every foot contains the element 'ictus', which may however be silent (have zero exponent) if the foot follows a pause or has initial position in the tone group. A foot with non-silent ictus is referred to below as a 'complete' foot. Not every foot contains the element 'remiss'. Thus each foot consists of one strong syllable, either alone or followed by one or more weak syllables (the maximum number in the sample was six); in addition a foot that is tone-group initial may consist of weak only. The structure of the foot can thus be symbolized as

I(R...n),

with each place (capital letter or dot) representing one syllable, including the possibility of silent beat at I; and elements in parentheses optional. The foot is characterized by *phonological* isochronicity: there is a tendency for strong syllables to occur at roughly regular intervals of time whatever the number of weak syllables, including zero, in between. In a small sample of loud-reading studied by Katherine Patch, the ratio of the average durations of one-, two- and three-syllable feet was shown instrumentally to be about 5:6:7. The fact that the foot and not the syllable is the unit of rhythm is referred to by Abercrombie, following Pike, as 'stress-timing'.

It is the foot which operates in the structure of the tone group. Like the foot, the tone group comprises two elements of structure: in the case of the tone group these are 'tonic' and 'pretonic'. The element 'tonic' is obligatory: it is present in every tone group; the element 'pretonic' is optional: it may or may not be present. If the pretonic is present, it always precedes the tonic. Moreover it is defined relative to the tonic: a tone group contains a pretonic if, always if and only if, there is at least one foot *with ictus not zero* (*ie* at least one strong syllable) before the beginning of the tonic. The reason for this definition of the pretonic will appear from what follows, but it may be summarized here: all primary tone contrasts are carried by the tonic, but some secondary contrasts are carried independently by an element preceding the tonic – these operate only, and always, if there is at least one strong syllable in this position.

Tonic and pretonic may each consist of one, or of more than one, complete foot. The reason for considering a tone group whose tonic consists of two or more feet as having *one* tonic (and not as many tonics as there are feet) is that selection of primary tone can be made once, and only once, in each tone group: except for tone groups with 'double tonic', in which it is made twice. There are thus two basic structures to be recognized for the tone group: one having single tonic and one, not necessarily less frequent but much more restricted in choice of tone, having double tonic. (In the latter, the first tonic can select only tone 1 or tone 5, and the second only tone 3.) In both structures a pretonic element may precede the tonic; there is never more than one pretonic, however, even in a 'double tonic' tone group.[5]

Each tone group therefore has a structure consisting of either one tonic or two tonics, with or without pretonic preceding the (first) tonic. Each element, tonic or pretonic, may consist of one foot or of more than one.

The structure of the tone group can thus be symbolized as

(P . . . n)T(. . . n) or (P . . . n)T(. . . n)T(. . . n),

with each place (capital letter or dot) representing one foot, and elements in parentheses optional.

Since each tonic can select only once for tone, and since the phonic exponent of the tone selected falls largely on the first syllable of the first foot of the tonic, this syllable being almost always by itself sufficient to permit the tone to be identified correctly, it is tempting to use the term 'tonic' to refer to all of three different things: a section of the tone group, a foot and a syllable. This may cause confusion, and it seems better to use distinct terms,

'tonic': element in structure of tone group comprising one or more complete foot

'tonic foot': first (complete) foot in tonic

'tonic syllable': first (strong) syllable in tonic foot.[6]

Note that weak syllables occurring *before* the tonic syllable, but not preceded by a strong syllable in the same tone group (*ie* in foot with silent ictus), do *not* constitute a pretonic; they carry no separate contrasts and are 'proclitic' in the tonic. In no case is a separate contrast carried by any feet *after* the tonic foot; the pitch movement is distributed over the whole tonic, and there is no 'post-tonic' element.[7]

What are often referred to as 'four degrees of stress' are rather, at least in British English, structurally identified syllable classes whose exponents are marked by contrast not only (if indeed at all) in intensity but also in pitch and duration. Primarily (in delicacy), there are two classes of syllable: strong and weak. Since in each tone group one (in 'double tonic' tone groups two) strong syllable is a 'tonic syllable', this gives a secondary distinction of strong syllables into 'strong tonic' and 'strong non-tonic'. In most examples cited by those who refer to four degrees of stress, primary stress seems to correspond to strong tonic and secondary to strong non-tonic – but these are *not* two sets of labels for 'the same thing', since the difference between strong tonic and strong non-tonic syllables is one of pitch first, duration second and intensity third or not at all.[8] Within the weak syllables there are a number of systems of secondary classes, involving not only 'reduced/non-reduced' but also differences in duration correlating with number of syllables in the foot; the relation of 'tertiary' and 'weak' 'stress' to these is difficult to discover and in any case not relevant to intonation.[9]

The following (textual) examples illustrate the various structures of the tone group. In these and all subsequent examples, conventional symbols are used as follows:

|| tone group boundary
| foot boundary
___ tonic syllable
ʌ silent ictus
. . . pause
† constructed example.

It follows from the relation among the units that each boundary subsumes boundaries of all units lower in rank: a tone group boundary, for example, must be also a foot, syllable and phoneme boundary. For the two units of lower rank, syllable and phoneme, orthography has been used instead of the complete phonological transcription, to avoid unnecessary complication and distraction from the main purpose. The underlining of the tonic syllable serves as the marker of the tonic, since everything following it (as well as any preceding weak syllables if no strong syllable precedes) falls within the tonic. A pause is defined as silence which effects a break in the rhythm. Arabic figures at the beginning of each tone group indicate the tone; for further exposition of these, see below.
With tonic only:

Single
	1 <u>no</u>	
	2 <u>is</u> that what you / mean	
	2 ʌ are you / <u>serious</u>	
	4 ʌ but the / <u>can</u>didates / don't get nine / grades	
Double
   ||53 <u>I</u> didn't / <u>think</u> so ||
   ||13 ʌ oh it / <u>does</u> level / out in the / <u>long</u> run ||

With tonic and pretonic:

Single tonic
   ||1 this of course de/pends on the / country where they / <u>live</u> ||
   ||1 + ʌ I / thought / <u>cats</u> always / ate them ||
Double tonic
   ||13 ʌ I / <u>think</u>   the / <u>rabbit</u>   was / <u>more</u> / <u>prominent</u>   than   they
          in/<u>tend</u>ed it to / be as a / <u>matter</u> of / fact||

To summarize

In any tone group, if there is only one complete foot this must always be an exponent of the tonic. If there are two or more complete feet, the tonic may start at the beginning of any one of them – that is, at any strong syllable; and if there are any complete feet preceding the one at which the tonic begins, the tone group has a pretonic as well as a tonic element. Syntagmatically there are only two places in the tone group where tone contrasts can be made, one obligatory (the tonic) and one optional (the pretonic); primary tone contrasts are carried by the tonic, and distinct sets of secondary contrasts both by the tonic and the pretonic. No further contrast can be made after the tonic syllable;[10] everything following this forms part of the tonic, and has its pitch movement determined entirely by the tonic.[11]

3

The primary tone system is as follows:

term in system:	visual symbol:	tonic movement:	terminal tendency:
1	\	falling	low
2	/	rising	high
	∨	falling-rising	high
3	⌐/	rising	mid
4	∼⌐	(rising-)falling-rising[12]	mid
5	⌐∼	(falling-)rising-falling[12]	low

Double tonics:

term in system:	visual symbol:	tonic movement:	terminal tendency:
13[13]	\⌐/	(as tone 1 plus tone 3)	mid
53[13]	∨∼⌐/	(as tone 5 plus tone 3)	mid

For the purposes of the present analysis the following secondary systems are recognized:

A: Secondary systems at tonic

term in primary system:	term in secondary system:	transcription symbol:	visual symbol:	tonic movement:
	1 wide	1+	\	high to low
1	1 (neutral)	1	\	mid to low
	1 narrow	1−	⌐	mid-low to low[14]
	2 (neutral)	2	/	rising to high
2	2 broken	2	∨	high falling-rising to high
4	4 (neutral)	4	∼⌐	falling to mid, rising
	4 low	4	∼⌐	falling to low, rising

B: Secondary systems at pretonic

term in primary system:	term in secondary system:	transcription symbol:	visual symbol:	pretonic movement:
1	1 (neutral)	1	− − − \	stepping towards point of onset of tonic[15]
	1 bouncing	−1	V V V \	each strong syllable low, foot movement rising
1	1 (neutral)	1	− − − \	stepping towards point of onset of tonic
	1 listing	...1	⌐⌐⌐ \	each strong syllable mid, foot movement rising
2	2 (neutral)	2	⁻/; ⁻V	high level (may step down with neutral tonic)
	2 low	−2	_/; _V	low level
3	3 (neutral)	3	− ⌐	mid level
	3 low	−3	_ ⌐	low level
4	4 (neutral)	4	⁻⁻⁻∿⁄	high stepping to mid
	4 low	4̱	∧∧ ∿⁄	each strong syllable mid, foot movement falling

The last of these, the pretonic secondary system at tone 4, is in fact not an independent system, since the choice of pretonic is entirely determined by the choice of tonic: hence the use of the same names 'neutral' and 'low'. It is included here, however, in order to show the two distinct pretonic pitch movements involved, without which the account of possible pretonics would not be complete.

It is clear that out of this fairly simple inventory of systems, which involve only one step beyond the primary degree of delicacy, very considerable possibilities already emerge in the choice of tone. The primary selection is among five (or, if the tone group has more than one complete foot, among seven); but the selection of tone 1 is in fact a decision to choose between three possible tonics each of which may combine with any of three possible pretonics. There are of course probability restrictions on the combination of tonic and pretonic: the 'bouncing' pretonic to tone 1, for example, exerts a strong pull towards the 'wide' tonic. (The case of tone 4, mentioned above, is merely a special case of this where the probability concerned is equal to certainty.) Similarly, there are probability restrictions on the combination of tone with other, non-intonational grammatical features: for example, the 'listing' pretonic to tone 1 is largely confined to the occurrence of two or more items of the same *unit* (usually word, group or clause) and the same *class* operating (except in the case of the clause) as exponent of *one* element in the structure of the unit above (*eg* three nominal groups as subject). But the choice of tone is not determined by other grammatical features; on the contrary it is, as we shall see below, an independent grammatical selection in its own right. It is therefore not surprising that the vast majority of utterances in English could be replaced by other utterances, distinct in formal and contextual meaning, which differ only in tone. In some cases only certain of the tones are possible, but it is not difficult to construct utterances which can vary through all seven primary tones, and many secondary ones as well, all other features remaining constant. For example:

†// <u>Peter</u>'s / helping them / now //

as one single tone group, with tonic beginning at 'Peter' (and second tonic, where appropriate, at 'now'), can be spoken on all seven primary tones. When in addition the secondary tones, the tone group boundaries, the starting point of the tonic, and even the rhythm are allowed to vary, the number of possible utterances becomes very large indeed.[16] But this number is simply the product of the interaction of different systems each of which, taken by itself, represents a choice among only a very small number of contrasting terms.

4

It can be seen, therefore, that in any utterance in English three distinct meaningful choices, or sets of choices, are made which can be, and usually are, subsumed under the single heading of 'intonation'. These are: first, the distribution into tone groups – the number and location of the tone group boundaries; second, the placing of the tonic syllable (in 'double tonic' tone groups, the two tonic syllables) – the location, in each tone group, of the pretonic and tonic sections; third, the choice of primary and secondary tone. I propose to call these three systems 'tonality', 'tonicity' and 'tone'. The three selections are independent of one another. They are not of course independent of the system of rhythm, the distribution of the utterance into feet: as long as the rhythm is kept constant, the number of possible choices in the second system, that of tonicity, is equal to the number of strong syllables – that is, the number of 'complete' feet as defined above.

It has sometimes been suggested that the division of an utterance into tone groups is congruent with its division into grammatical units. There is no agreement, however, as to which of the grammatical units is co-extensive with one tone group; and this is not surprising, since in fact the tone group bears no fixed relation to any of the grammatical units of spoken English. There is a tendency for the tone group to correspond in extent with the clause; we may take advantage of this tendency by regard-ing the selection of one complete tone group for one complete clause as the neutral term in the first of three systems. That is to say, a clause which consists of one and only one complete tone group will be regarded as 'neutral in tonality'.[17]

But in fact the tone group is regularly more than one clause, and also regularly less than one clause; in these cases it is most frequently two (occasionally more) complete clauses in one sentence or one complete group in a compound clause.[18] It does not even necessarily correspond to any grammatical unit at all: it may, for example, extend over the final element in one clause and the whole of the next. What matters is to recog-nize that two utterances, distinct in meaning, may be identical in every respect except that one consists (say) of one tone group and the other of two or even more – quite apart from the other possibility, that each con-sists of (say) two tone groups but with the boundary at a different place. Both these distinctions are contrasts in tonality.

For example:

// 1 this of course de/pends on the / country where they / <u>live</u> //

commutes with

†// 1 this of course de/<u>pends</u> on the // 1 country where they / <u>live</u> //

and this in turn with

†// 1 this of course de/pends on the / <u>country</u> where they // 1 <u>live</u> //

The three systems, tonality, tonicity and tone, play different roles in English grammar. But in any given utterance they are of course operating in interaction with one another, so that we cannot always give a clear account of the meaning of a particular selection in one system in isolation from the others. Moreover it is *not* the case that a given selection always carries the same grammatical meaning. The grammatical meaning of tone 2, for instance, is quite different if the clause which carries it is affirmative in mood from what it is if the clause is interrogative; and both differ from its meaning if the clause is moodless. Furthermore, tone 2 with one type of interrogative clause has a different meaning according to whether the tonic begins on the initial element in the clause or on the final element.

If therefore we attempt a summary of the place of intonation in the English language, what we are summarizing is in fact the grammatical systems that are expounded by the phonological systems of intonation.

What we can abstract as common to the grammatical meaning of a given choice in one of the (phonological) intonation systems may be extremely limited; it may in fact be nothing at all. In the brief account that follows, the attempt has been made to discuss the major contrasts carried by the three systems each in turn; but it must be remembered that the statements made are only conditionally valid. That is to say, it is only in the context of their occurrence in combination, both with each other and with grammatical systems *not* expounded by intonation, that we can fully account for the operation in English of tonality, tonicity and tone.

5

In tonality, the choice is that of the number of tone groups in the utterance. If, as suggested above, we regard the occurrence of one tone group for each clause as 'neutral' tonality, then we need state only the conditions under which the selection is other than neutral. 'Each clause' here means 'each clause operating in sentence structure'; for rankshifted clauses the 'neutral' is to share a tone group with the rest of the items in the same (non-rankshifted) clause. There are then two 'marked' possibilities: that the tone group is more than one clause, and that the tone group is less than one clause.

The former arises principally in two types of sentence (actually sequences of elements of sentence structure linked by presupposition): reporting clause followed by reported clause, and conditioned clause followed by conditioning clause.

For example:

//<u>4</u> ∧ but I / don't see / why they should lose / <u>marks</u> for / this //
//1 ∧ I / think . . . you'll / find that it's / just that it's / <u>new</u> //
//<u>4</u> ∧ it's / all right if you're / photo/<u>gen</u>ic //1 what / happens if you're / <u>not</u> //
//<u>4</u> ∧ this / wouldn't count a/gainst you when you / did your / <u>maths</u> paper //

If a conditioning clause precedes the conditioned clause which it presupposes, the two may still sometimes share a single tone group; usually, however, sentences of this structure have neutral tonality, with a tendency for all clauses except the last to select tone 4; for example

//4 ∧ and and / since the / credit mark is a / <u>hun</u>dred //1 + ∧ you / couldn't very well / <u>mark</u> out of a / hundred //

Similarly in the sequence conditioned–conditioning, there may be neutral tonality:

//1 ∧ per/haps it's / <u>eas</u>ier when you're //1 marking / <u>lang</u>uage //

The fact that in general relative clauses do not take a separate tone group whereas additioning (so-called 'non-defining relative') clauses do is merely consistent with neutral tonality: relative clauses are rankshifted and do not operate in sentence structure, whereas additioning clauses are not rankshifted and therefore do enter into sentence structure. Compare for example:

//1 ∧ in / fact you / end / up with a / pure / culture of / something you / didn't / <u>start</u> with //

//1 ∧ if you've got / something that / grows / rapidly it / kills off the / <u>oth</u>er thing //

//1 ∧ I'm / marking a / <u>thous</u>and . . . //4 ∧ of which / three are from / <u>home</u> centres and . . .//

The second possibility, where the tone group is less than one clause, occurs mainly with the break (into two tone groups) coming after the first elements of clause structure other than fully grammatical elements: that is, the first element that contains a lexical item. In other words, the break occurs after the 'theme'.[19] An affirmative clause with subject first is 'neutral' in theme; any element, other than a fully grammatical item, occurring before the subject in affirmative clause is 'thematic'. While a break into two tone groups can occur between any two elements of clause structure, and any one element may be assigned a tonic and therefore demand a new tone group, lexical adjuncts and complements in thematic position are particularly likely to carry a separate tone group: they are already marked by sequence, being away from their neutral position after the predicator, so that with marked tonality their thematic status is further reinforced. (Notice however that the two selections are independent: a marked theme does not necessarily carry a separate tone group, nor is it the case that the only place where a clause can break into two tone groups is immediately after the theme.) Examples:

(with break after unmarked theme)

//4 all the / <u>dia</u>lect forms are //1 + marked / <u>wrong</u> //

(with break after marked theme)

//4 ∧ but / in A/<u>meri</u>ca they they //1 <u>lay</u>er / things //

(with break other than after theme)

//4 ∧ they can / change / overnight / <u>then</u> //1 ∧ into / something completely / <u>diff</u>erent //

A break other than after the theme is most commonly found immediately before a clause-final adjunct, as in the above example.

Selection for tonality can be regarded as the distribution of 'information points',[20] though if this view is taken it is important to keep in mind the relation of tonality to clause structure, and to the various other systems operating at the rank of the clause. Each tone group is considered to contain one major information point, 'double tonic' tone groups having one major followed by one minor. The minor information point is frequently associated with final adjuncts (the clause thus having neutral tonality), for example:

|| 13 ∧ it / seems / <u>odd</u> though to / <u>me</u> ||
|| 1 + 3 ∧ they they / <u>change</u> peri/<u>od</u>ically ||
(note that 1 + 3 is <u>not</u> ' 1 plus 3 ' but ' 13 with tone 1 wide ')

or with conditioning clause following conditioned (this being marked tonality, since the two clauses share one tone group), for example:

|| 13 ∧ they don't / <u>have</u> to / move if they / only take in / <u>food</u> like / that ||

But these are not the only possibilities, and a minor information point may occur on any element of structure that is in suitable position in the tone group.

|| 13 ∧ it was a / <u>live</u> / <u>broad</u>cast ||
|| 13 ∧ no / <u>I</u> saw the / <u>first</u> one ||

6

The system of tonicity is clearly linked to the preceding system: the choice of how many tone groups, and where their boundaries are, goes a long way towards determining the choice of how many tonics, and where they are located. But it does not go the whole way; we can still vary tonicity while keeping tonality constant.

In tonicity also, we can recognize a neutral term. A tone group is neutral in tonicity if the tonic falls on the last element of grammatical structure that contains a lexical item. In fact this could be formulated even more simply by direct reference to lexis: the tonic, in neutral tonicity, falls on the last lexical item in the tone group. The statement via grammar is, however, theoretically more accurate, and makes the statement of marked tonicity easier.

If the tone group is a clause, 'last element of structure' means of course last element of clause structure; so also if the tone group is more than one clause. If it is less than one clause, 'last element of structure' can be taken to refer to 'last element of group structure'. No contrasts of tonicity within the word occurred in the texts, though it is easy to construct them. For purposes of discussion we need consider tonicity only in relation to neutral tonality: what is said applies, *mutatis mutandis*, to tone groups that are more or less than a clause.

In neutral tonicity, then, the tonic begins at the final element of clause structure unless this contains only 'fully grammatical items': that is, on final adjunct (if any) other than items such as 'there', 'to him'; otherwise on complement (if any) other than personal pronouns or items such as 'it', 'some', and the substitute 'one'; otherwise on predicator (if any) other than those consisting of auxiliaries only or with the substitute 'do' (unless the subject is a pronoun, in which case even a fully grammatical predicator – one consisting only of fully grammatical items – will, if final in the clause, carry the tonic). Any other placing of the tonic is 'marked' tonicity. Examples of neutral tonicity are:

//5 ∧ I / very often / meet him in the / <u>squa</u>re //
//2 did they ever / get a / hundred per/<u>cent</u> //
//1 ∧ how / long do these / changes / <u>take</u> //
//1 ∧ they / <u>grade</u> them //
//1 + ∧ that's / why it's so / awful to / have to get / <u>rid</u> of it //
//1 + ∧ I was / just going to sug/gest that . . . you / left home / after /
    <u>Mich</u>ael / did then //

Marked tonicity occurs, in general, under either (or both) of two conditions. Either some element other than the one just specified is 'contrastive'; or the element just specified (and possibly also other elements before it) is 'given' – has been mentioned before or is present in the situation. An element marked by tonicity as contrastive may, of course, be either a lexical element that is not final or a final element that is not lexical. Examples of marked tonicity are:

//1 what / happens if you're / <u>not</u> //
//4 ∧ it / <u>may</u> be that it's //1 just the / general / rule that //1 <u>all</u> the /
    G.C.E. / papers have to be / marked out of / two / hundred //

There is one clause class in which the tonic so regularly (at least with one of the tones) begins *before* the final lexis-bearing element that, although such a clause can still be regarded as marked in tonicity, it needs to be specially mentioned. This is the class 'interrogative clause' (in the system of 'mood': see below), secondary class 'non-polar' (the '*wh-*' or 'information questions'). The neutral tone for this class (see below) is tone 1; items in this class can however be marked for tone by the use of tone 2. If so, they carry a distinct (and unique) two-term sub-system of tonicity: either the tonic is in its usual place on the final lexical element, or it starts on the interrogative element (the '*wh-*' item). The interrogative element in this structure has thematic position, either (unmarked) as subject or (marked) before the subject. The second type, or 'echo question', is therefore a special instance of the tonic starting on the thematic element in clause structure; in the case of this class of interrogatives the contextual meaning is 'I have forgotten', 'I didn't hear' or 'I don't believe you'. For example:

(neutral tone)
 // 1 ∧ and / where's / <u>he</u> from //
(marked tone, neutral tonicity)
 //2 ∧ oh / what did they / <u>say</u> //
(marked tone and tonicity) (echo question)
 //2 <u>what's</u> it / called //

A final set of (constructed) examples may be used to illustrate the range of variety afforded by the two systems of tonality and tonicity.

Neutral tonality:
  Neutral tonicity:
  †//1 ∧ there's a/nother one in the / <u>kit</u>chen //
    (one information point, major)
  †//13 ∧ there's a/<u>noth</u>er one in the / <u>kit</u>chen //
    (two information points, major and minor).
  Marked tonicity:
  †//1 ∧ there's a/<u>noth</u>er one in the / kitchen //

Marked tonality:
  †//1 ∧ there's a/<u>noth</u>er one in the //1 <u>kit</u>chen //

In the first instance, the information point is on the final element, which is therefore 'new' but not contrastive: in the second, 'another' is contrastive, but 'kitchen' is retained as a minor information point. In the third instance, 'kitchen' is marked as given – the previous one was also in the kitchen; in the fourth, 'kitchen' is a major information point in addition to the contrastive 'another', suggesting that the previous one was not in the kitchen.

7

Any discussion of the place of the tone system in English starting from the phonological end – asking not 'how are these grammatical systems expounded?' but 'what grammatical systems do these tones expound?' – can only be partial, since in the last resort the comprehensive grammatical statement is presupposed as explicit throughout. Here the initial step is taken of ranging the tones in grammatically contrastive sets, with labels to assist identification. It seems simplest to start from the clause system of 'mood', since this determines which tone is neutral in a given instance. There are four terms in the mood system: affirmative (subject before predicator), interrogative (subject after first word of predicator), imperative (with predicator but no subject) and moodless (with no predicator). This is a primary system (first degree of delicacy); for tone, however, we have to distinguish within interrogative mood, at one further degree of delicacy, the secondary classes of 'polar' and 'non-polar' – 'polar' being the 'yes-no' or 'confirmation' interrogative, non-polar the '*wh-*' or 'information' interrogative.

TONES I AND 2 IN CONTRAST

Tone 1 can be regarded as neutral for all terms in the mood system except polar interrogatives. Leaving aside the latter for the moment, we will first consider the systemic contrast between neutral tone 1 and marked tone 2. If we take the total set of contextual sentence functions to be 'statement', 'question', 'command', 'answer', and 'exclamation', the mood system combines with these tones to operate normally as follows:

1. *Affirmative clauses*

    Tone 1: statement or answer (neutral)
    Tone 2: statement or answer (contradictory) ('challenging', 'aggressive', 'defensive', 'indignant', etc)
    // — 2 I don't / <u>know</u> // (in reply to 'how extraordinarily inefficient')

An affirmative clause on tone 2 is (at least in British English) very rarely a question, in spite of the frequent assertion that this is a regular way of forming questions in English. There are no examples in the texts of a tone 2 (or any other) affirmative clause as question. Moodless clauses on tone 2, on the other hand, are frequently questions.

2. *Imperative and moodless clauses (except '*wh-*' moodless)*

    Tone 1: command (imperative), answer (moodless) or exclamation: (neutral)
    Tone 2: question (less often, but especially in negative, contradictory answer or negative command)
    //2 right / <u>length</u> // (in reply to 'it's about the right length')
    //2 <u>seven</u> // (in reply to 'they start at seven in America don't they?')

3. *Interrogative clause (non-polar) and '*wh-*' moodless clause*

    Tone 1: question (neutral)
    Tone 2
        (*a*) tonicity neutral (final element tonic): request question ('I'd like to know')
        //2 ∧ oh / what did they / <u>say</u> //
        (*b*) tonicity marked (*wh-*element tonic), repeat or 'echo' question ('I've forgotten', etc)
        //2 <u>what's</u> it / called //

In '*wh-*' moodless clause this distinction is neutralized, since the *wh-* element is the only, and therefore also the final, element. An example of the (*b*) in the text is:

> //2 <u>how</u> many// (in reply to 'you've got probably about six foot of intestine I suppose – all coiled up')

By contrast for polar interrogatives tone 2 is neutral:

4. *Interrogative clause* (*polar*)

Tone 2: question (neutral)
Tone 1: demand question ('I insist on knowing'; 'I disapprove'; 'admit it!')
   //1 <u>did</u> you now //

A special secondary class of polar interrogative clause is the tag, which displays a sub-system of its own according to whether the polarity of the preceding clause is kept constant or reversed. The four common types are illustrated here by constructed as well as textual examples:

Polarity reversed
   Tone 2: question (neutral) ('I think I know the answer')
      //1 ∧ and in fact / most of the / <u>Zoo</u> department were / there //2 <u>weren't</u> they //
      †//1 <u>Jack's</u> been here //2 <u>hasn't</u> he //
   Tone 1: demand question ('I know the answer; admit it!')
      //1 − ∧ this / isn't quite / <u>true</u> //1 − <u>is</u> it //
      †//1 <u>Jack's</u> been here //1 <u>hasn't</u> he //

Polarity constant
   Tone 2: echo statement ('I've just gathered')
      //1 used to be . . . the / habit in / <u>China</u> //2 <u>did</u> it //
      †//1 <u>Jack's</u> been here //2 <u>has</u> he //

   Marked tonality; tag forming one tone group with preceding clause
   Tone 1: echo statement ('I've just learnt'; 'I see')
      †//1 <u>Jack's</u> been here / has he //

TONES 1, 3 AND 5 IN CONTRAST

Affirmative and moodless clauses, and rarely polar interrogative clauses, are marked in a different system by the use of tone 3 and tone 5. It is useful to distinguish two sub-systems, of which the first, where the clause is short and the tone group usually consists of tonic only, is the more common of the two.

5. *Moodless clause; short affirmative* (*or polar interrogative*) *clause*
(no pretonic)

 Tone 1 (tone 2 if interrogative): answer (etc) (neutral)
 Tone 3: non-committal answer ('disengagement'; 'unconcerned',
  'discouraging')
   //3 <u>six</u> / foot //3 <u>I</u> don't / know // (in reply to 'how many' in 3 above)
   // −3 ∧ it's / quite / long e/nough //
 Tone 5: committal answer ('involvement'; 'assertive', 'superior',
  'encouraging')
   //5 ∧ I / <u>certainly</u> / do //
   //5 ∧ it / <u>did</u> //
   //5 ∧ it's / <u>very</u> / interesting //
   //5 ∧ oh I'm / <u>sure</u> it / was //

6. *Affirmative clause* (with pretonic)

 Tone 1: statement (neutral)
 Tone 3: statement (confirmatory, dependent) ('this is not the whole
  of it', 'I confirm what you have just said')
   //3 that's / <u>right</u> //
   ... //3 ∧ and he mentioned his / <u>name</u> and // ...
 Tone 5: statement (unconditional, independent) 'I'm telling you!')
   //5 ∧ he was a / very / famous / <u>man</u> //
   //5 look what / <u>I've</u> made //

The special use of tone 3 following tone 1 or tone 5 in 'double tonic'
tone group has been mentioned above. The 'double tonic' tone groups
form a small system of their own:

7. *Affirmative clause with final adjunct* (or other instances of major
followed by minor information point)

 Tone 13: statement (neutral)
   //13 ∧ though I / don't think it / <u>can</u> be come to / <u>think</u> of it //
   //13 ∧ I / don't know / <u>why</u> they / <u>do</u> it //
   //13 ∧ no / <u>I</u> saw the / <u>first</u> one //
   //13 ∧ well they / <u>haven't</u> you / <u>see</u> but then //
 Tone 53: committal statement ('assertive', 'forceful')
   //53 <u>I</u> didn't / <u>think</u> so //
   //53 ∧ they / do in / <u>some</u> uni/<u>versities</u> //

TONES I AND 4 IN CONTRAST

In the samples studied, tone 4 was the next most frequent after tone 1.
The contrast between the two is best stated in terms of two distinct
systems, in one of which tone 1 is the neutral term and in the other tone 4.

8. *Affirmative or moodless clause*

Tone 1: statement or answer (neutral)
Tone 4: statement or answer with reservation ('there's a "but" about it')
   //4 ∧ I / don't know / whether it's / <u>true</u> //
   //4 ∧ no there / was a / Russian in the / <u>first</u> one //
   //4 ∧ yes . . . I I / don't think you can / do much a/<u>bout</u> it //
   //4 ∧ but the / Japa/<u>nese</u> did it //

9. *Conditioning clause preceding conditioned clause* (or thematic element in clause structure having separate tone group)

Tone 4: neutral (forward linking)
   //4 if its / father was a / mathema/<u>tician</u> then it //4 <u>obviously</u> was
      //1 + going to get a / hundred percent in / <u>maths</u> //
   //4 ∧ in the / case of the / <u>British</u> . . . e/xam //4 ∧ say in / <u>Russian</u>
      a/gain //1 ∧ I / don't know / whether it / <u>does</u> //
   //4 ∧ oh the ma/<u>terial</u> was //5 <u>excellent</u> //
Tone 1: (discrete)
   //1 ∧ after / <u>all</u> this is a //1 + great / <u>puzzle</u> //

Tone 1 here is limited in the texts to a small set of adjuncts including 'anyway', 'in any case', 'of course'. Contrast (*a*) sequences of linked free clauses and (*b*) clauses with more than one tone group but no marked theme, such as the following, in which tone 1 is neutral:

   (*a*) //1 last night's was re/<u>corded</u> . . . and em . . . //1 ∧ they / got they /
        ran over / <u>time</u> and //1 had to cut / various things / <u>out</u> and //1 cut
        down what / people were / <u>saying</u> and //
   (*b*) //1 well you see / he'd just / <u>organized</u> a / big em sym/<u>posium</u> in //1
        <u>Moscow</u> //1 couple of / <u>years</u> back on the //1 − origin of . . . / life on /
        <u>earth</u> //

SECONDARY SYSTEMS

10. *Tone 1, tonic*

Tone 1: new non-contrastive (neutral)
Tone 1 +: new contrastive
Tone 1 −: given
   //1 <u>no</u> in fact the //1 + smaller ones / eat the / <u>bigger</u> ones //
   //1 + ∧ I /don't know / whether it / <u>does</u> level / up //
   //1 − ∧ perhaps / <u>so</u> //
   //1 − ∧ I'm / not / sure that it's / <u>worth</u> it //

11. *Tone* 1, *pretonic* (*a*)

  Tone 1: neutral
  Tone −1: forceful
  // −1 ∧ it's / rather / <u>in</u>teresting //
  // −1 ∧ and / this is a / bit / <u>hard</u> //

12. *Tone* 1, *pretonic* (*b*)

  Tone 1: neutral
  Tone . . . 1: listing
  // . . . 1 ∧ it's grade / one / two / three to / <u>nine</u> //
  // . . . 1 ∧ of / vitamins and / this and / that and . . . / sugars and / salts
     and . . .

13. *Tone* 2, *tonic*

  Tone 2: neutral (question)
  Tone <u>2</u>: 'new' question ('point of query new or shown as information
     point'; 'element of surprise')
  //<u>2</u> ∧ and / do they give the / lectures over / tele/<u>vi</u>sion in //<u>2</u> stead of /
     <u>live</u> //
  //<u>2</u> is your / flat / <u>fur</u>nished / by the uni/versity //
  //<u>2</u> did you see the / <u>first</u> //

14. *Tone* 2, *pretonic*

  Tone 2: neutral (question)
  Tone −2: 'given' question ('point of query given'; 'element of
     casualness')
  // −2 was this de/<u>lib</u>erate //

15. *Tone* 3 (*pretonic*) (see 5 and 6 above)

  Tone 3: neutral (dependent or confirmatory statement or answer)
  Tone −3: casual (non-committal statement or answer)
  // −3 ∧ they / just find a / comfortable / place in your / <u>gut</u> and they
     // −3 stick their / <u>hooks</u> in and //1 <u>stay</u> there //

16. *Tone* 4

  Tone 4: neutral
  Tone <u>4</u>: contrastive
  //<u>4</u> no worse than / anyone / <u>else</u> //
  //<u>4</u> seemed to / <u>think</u> it was / very / good //
  //<u>4</u> ∧ but he / wasn't / <u>se</u>rious a/bout it //
  //<u>4</u> ∧ well . . . they / did when / <u>I</u> did it //

8

The set of phonological systems in English that are referred to collectively as 'intonation' can be summed up mnemonically as follows:

Tonality marks one kind of unit of language activity, and roughly where each such unit begins and ends: one tone group is as it were one move in a speech operation.

Tonicity marks the focal point of each such unit of activity: every move has one (major), or one major and one minor, concentration point, shown by the location of the tonic syllable, the start of the tonic.

Tone marks the kind of activity involved, by a complex pattern built out of a simple opposition between certain and uncertain polarity. If polarity is certain, the pitch of the tonic falls; if uncertain, it rises. Thus tone 1 is an assertion, or a query not involving polarity; and tone 4, which falls and then rises, is an assertion which involves or entails some query. Tone 2 is a query, 2 being a query about a specific assertion; and tone 5, which rises and then falls, is a dismissed query, one countered by an assertion. Tone 3 avoids a decision; as an assertion, it is at best confirmatory, contingent or immaterial.

Such a summary has, clearly, a very limited value. It may be useful if only as a reminder that no very precise statement can be made of the 'general meaning' of English intonation: the meaning of a choice of tone is bound up with other grammatical choices in the utterance. But the first step is to display the range of choices available; and in this paper I have tried to show how the study of texts in spoken English may help to throw light on the contrastive use of intonation resources, and how this in turn may contribute to the analysis of the resources themselves. The alignments suggested here are as it were pregrammatical; the next step is their organization into grammatical systems.

The phonological contrasts treated here have been presented as systems of discrete terms: this applies both to the phonological systems themselves and to the grammatical contrasts in which the phonologically identified terms act as exponents. It is possible to describe English intonation in this way, and justifiable on the grounds that in present-day linguistic theory we can handle discreteness more effectively than non-discreteness, at least at the level of grammar. So for example it is useful to recognize a three-term secondary system at tone 1, having the terms 1 + 1 and 1 −, because by selecting a criterion which yields clearly differentiated exponents we keep the terms discrete. But this discreteness is, at least in some cases, arrived at by a more or less arbitrary cutting of the continuum; and if the theory of grammar can be extended to include systems which are not made up of discrete terms but rather form a 'cline', systems expounded by intonation will be the first to be re-examined. We should not, however, wait until then before bringing such systems fully within the scope of the description of English grammar.

Notes

[1] 'English English' rather than 'British English' since, whether or not the systems described here are valid for all varieties of English in England (probably not), they are certainly not valid for many varieties of Scots. The textual material used in this study consisted of natural live conversation by speakers of 'RP': three speakers in the main sample, one of these and three others (in different combinations) in the remainder. All were aware they were being recorded – and quite accustomed to it.

My thanks are due especially to David Abercrombie, K. H. Albrow, J. C. Catford and J. McH. Sinclair for valuable help in discussion. Since this paper was first written as a series of lectures, previous works on the subject are not referred to in detail: the debt to them will be clear, but the following especially should be mentioned:

Lee S. Hultzén, 'Information Points in intonation', *Phonetica*, iv, 1959.
Roger Kingdon, *The Groundwork of English intonation*, Longman, 1958.
W. R. Lee, 'English intonation: a new approach', *Lingua*, iv, 1956.
Maria Schubiger, *English intonation: its form and function*, Niemeyer, 1958.
Alan E. Sharp, 'Falling-rising intonation patterns in English', *Phonetica*, ii, 1958.
Robert P. Stockwell, 'The role of intonation in a generative grammar of English', *Language*, xxxvi, 1960.
Elizabeth Uldall, 'Attitudinal meanings conveyed by intonation contours', *Language and Speech*, iii, 1960.

The important book *Intonation of Colloquial English*, by J. D. O'Connor and G. F. Arnold, Longman, 1961, appeared after this paper was first written for publication. I would not have adopted their analysis into ten 'tone groups' (=my 'tones') since it seems to me to conflate contrasts belonging for grammatical purposes at different degrees of delicacy. But the detailed analysis, the wealth of examples, and the phonetic description are quite invaluable. More recent still is the paper 'The correspondence of prosodic to grammatical features in spoken English', by Randolph Quirk and others, presented by Professor Quirk to the Ninth International Congress of Linguists (Boston 1962) and due to appear in the forthcoming *Proceedings*. This last paper describes the first results of a study in the correlation of intonation patterns with certain grammatical units and structures in a sample of English from unscripted broadcasts. The work of which this forms a part will be a major contribution to the study of spoken English.

[2] This of course depends on the purpose of the description. Machine analysis, for data retrieval or machine translation, requires a description that keeps as close to 'direct exponence' as is compatible with reasonable generality; but the description that is best for machine analysis is unlikely to be the best for other purposes.

[3] *Cf* my 'Categories of the theory of grammar', *Word*, xvii, 3, December, 1961.

[4] See David Abercrombie, 'Syllable quantity and enclitics in English', in the forthcoming volume of papers dedicated to Daniel Jones. [Abercrombie, D., *et al*, eds, *In Honour of Daniel Jones*, Longman, 1964. Eds.]

[5] Only the *first* tonic in a 'double tonic' tone group can thus be preceded by a pretonic. This is in fact the reason why such tone groups, having tones 13 and 53, are regarded as single tone groups with double tonic, rather than as sequences of two tone groups: the fact that it is not possible for a pretonic to tone 3 to occur here following tone 1 or tone 5. Other very common

sequences, as for example tone 4 followed by tone 1, are not considered as 'double tonic' tone groups, precisely because any of the possible varieties of pretonic to tone 1 may occur in between the two tonics.

6 'Tonic syllable', or 'tonic foot', could be referred to by the familiar term 'nucleus'. I have avoided this merely in order to stress the unity of the tonic element in the tone group.

7 The exact way in which the pitch movement is distributed over the tonic depends on the tone. In general, a tonic with a single pitch movement tends, if extended, to flatten, whereas one with a change of movement tends to continue the movement in the final direction.

8 What is often accounted for by 'juncture' can, alternatively, be stated partly as foot and syllable division and partly (an important part) as rules for the relative duration of syllables in the foot. See Abercrombie, op cit.

9 It is thus a little misleading to ask anyone if he can 'hear the four degrees of stress'. The answer may well be that he can hear, and tell apart, what are being *called* four degrees of stress, but would analyse them as something else; but the question is so framed as to preclude this answer.

10 There is of course, after the tonic syllable in certain tones, the possibility of 'selecting' a second tonic; since this must always take tone 3, no further selection of tone is involved.

11 There is however sandhi: a tone 1 tone group usually rises in pitch at the end of the tonic if the first strong syllable in the next tone group (tonic or pretonic) is high.

12 Underlining indicates the part of the movement which carries the greatest intensity.

13 To be read 'one three', 'five three' (not 'thirteen', 'fifty-three').

14 The criteria for the three terms in this system are in fact as follows: in 1 (neutral), the tonic starts on the same pitch as the final syllable of the pretonic (or proclitic weak syllable); in 1 +, it starts at a higher pitch, and in 1 − at a lower pitch.

15 In general, the neutral pretonic remains fairly level (mid-high) before the neutral tonic, works up towards the 1 + tonic and down towards the 1 −.

16 With tonality and rhythm constant, and taking into account only primary and not secondary contrasts, the number of tonal possibilities for any tone group, at the degree of delicacy specified here, is $n(2n + 7)$, where n is the number of feet.

17 The fact that, since a tone group boundary must be also a foot boundary, it does not necessarily coincide exactly with the boundary of the clause is immaterial; it is always clear whether or not there is an equivalence of clause and tone group. In any case it must be insisted that the location of the tone group boundary is a theoretical decision: the best description is obtained if a new tone group is considered to begin at the foot boundary immediately preceding the first strong syllable of its tonic or pretonic, as the case may be. But what matters is that the boundary between any two tone groups can be shown to lie within certain limits, so that it is clear how many tone groups there are in any stretch of utterance, and where – that is, in association with which elements of grammatical structure – their contrasts are made.

18 'Compound' means 'consisting of more than one of unit next below'; a compound clause is one whose structure is made up of two or more groups.

19 The category of 'theme' has been introduced by J. McH. Sinclair.

20 *Cf* Lee S. Hultzén, *op cit.*

Eugénie J. A. Henderson

Prosodies in Siamese:
A study in synthesis

The term 'prosodic feature' is applied in this paper to certain properties of modern spoken Siamese which may be regarded as abstractions apart from the consonant and vowel systems.[1] Such abstractions may be made at the syllable, word, or sentence level. Syllable prosodies include tone, quantity, and those properties which mark the beginning or end of a syllable. Word prosodies include tonal and quantitative features, stress, and the means whereby syllable is linked with syllable. Sentence prosodies include sentence tone, and the means used to mark the beginnings and ends of phrases and sentences, and to connect phrase with phrase or sentence with sentence. Italic type is used to show the consonant and vowel units, and to name the prosodies, while a rather larger roman is used for phonetic transcription in general terms.

The phonetic structure of Siamese is based primarily upon the monosyllable. A high proportion of words is monosyllabic, and all polysyllables may be pronounced as a succession of monosyllables, each conforming in structure to the pattern appropriate to monosyllables uttered in isolation. I have called this style of speech the 'isolative style'. It is that commonly used for monosyllabic words and for the slow, deliberate pronunciation of polysyllables, and is that shown in dictionaries.[2] The structure of the syllable, which is also that of the monosyllabic word, is determined by reference to the isolative style only. A study of words of more than one syllable shows that in connected speech, or what may be called the 'combinative style', the syllable structure proper to the isolative style is modified in some degree. This degree of modification is a prosodic feature, since it characterizes a connected group, whether compound word, polysyllable, or phrase. Such prosodies are appropriate to the combinative

First published in *Asia Major*, New Series, Vol I, Pt II: 189–215, 1949.

style, and clearly cannot be a feature of the isolative style. In addition to 'isolative style' and 'combinative style', it is sometimes necessary when examining certain word and sentence prosodies to take into account yet another style, which I have called 'rapid combinative style'.

Types of consonant sound

The types of consonant sound which may be heard at the beginning of a syllable may be represented in general phonetic terms, as follows:

	glottal and pre-glottal	*velar*	*alveolar and alveolo-palatal*	*labial*
voiceless plosive	ʔ	k	t	p
voiceless aspirated plosive		kh	th	ph
voiced plosive			d	b
voiceless affricate			tɕ	
voiceless aspirated affricate			tɕh (or ɕh)	
voiceless fricative	h		s	f
nasal		ŋ	n	m
semi-vowel		(w)	l, r, j (often dj)*	w

The following consonant clusters are also heard initially: kr, kl, kw, khr, khl, khw, tr, pr, pl, phr, phl.

The types of consonant sound which may be heard at the end of a syllable are as follows:

	glottal	*velar*	*alveolar*	*labial*
stop (without voice or plosion)	ʔ′	k′	t′	p′
nasal		ŋ	n	m

It will be seen that *plosion, aspiration, affrication, friction, voice* (except when accompanied by nasality), and the presence of the sounds r or l, are properties of the syllable initial only, and mark the beginning of a syllable whenever they occur. These features may, therefore, be regarded as belonging to the prosodic system, while what is common to both syllable parts, initial and final, may be postulated as the consonant system.

The consonant system

The units of this consonant system will be represented by the symbols k, t, p, $ŋ$, n, m, $ζ$,[3] the last being used to indicate *zero* consonant unit. The glottal plosive is regarded as being the realization of $ζ$ accompanied by *plosion.* Initial l and r are held to be realizations of ʓ accompanied by prosodic features which may, for lack of better terms, be called *lateralization* and *rhotacization.* Initial j is not regarded as the realization of ʓ with *yotization,* since it has been found convenient to postulate *yotization* as a feature of the syllable as a whole. Initial j, which is often pronounced with alveolo-palatal closure, is treated as the phonetic expression of t accompanied by *voice* and *affrication.* The w-element of kw and khw is a feature of the syllable rather than of the initial since these consonant clusters are never heard before the back vowels u, o, ɔ, ɯ, and ɣ. This syllabic feature, which is distinct from what is in this paper regarded as *labiovelarization* of the syllable,[4] may be termed *labialization,* and is restricted to syllables beginning with the consonant unit k. Initial w cannot be regarded as a feature of the syllable as a whole, since it is heard before all vowels except ɯ.[5] I have regarded it as a prosody of syllable beginning, restricted to syllables beginning with zero consonant unit.[6] The distribution among the consonant units of the prosodies of syllable-beginning and syllable-ending is set out in detail when the prosodies of the monosyllable are dealt with.

Types of vowel sound

The vowel sounds of Siamese may be represented in general phonetic terms, as follows:

FRONT		BACK			
		unrounded		*rounded*	
long	*short*	*long*	*short*	*long*	*short*
iː	i	ɯː	ɯ	uː	u
eː	e	ɣː	ɣ	oː	o
ɛː	ɛ	aː	a	ɔː	ɔ
	iə		ɯə		uə

The front vowels may be heard as the starting point of closing diphthongs moving towards a close back vowel position, which may be represented iu, eu, eːu, ɛu, ɛːu, iəu.

The vowels aː and a may be heard as the starting point of closing diphthongs moving towards either a close back or a close front vowel position, which may be represented aːi, ai, aːu, au.

The remaining back vowels may be heard as the starting point of closing diphthongs moving towards a close front vowel position, which may be represented ɣi, ui, oi, ɔi, ɯəi, and uəi.

This distribution clearly suggests the treatment of the i- and u-elements of these diphthongs as prosodic features of the syllable as a whole. Syllables characterized by the i-element are described in this paper as yotized, and those characterized by the u-element as labiovelarized.

Vowel quantity, which is closely bound up with word tone, is also abstracted as a prosodic feature at the syllable level.

The vowel system

The vowel units postulated for this study are, therefore: *i*, *e*, *ɛ*, *a*, *ɯ*, *ɤ*, *u*, *o*, *ɔ*, *iə*, *uə*, *ɯə*.

These vowel units are of three types, which we may call *front*, *back*, and *mid*, according to whether they may combine with yotization or labio-velarization of the syllable. Front vowel units, which may form part of a labiovelarized syllable, are *i*, *e*, *ɛ* and *iə*. Back vowel units, which may form part of a yotized syllable, are *u*, *uə*, *o*, *ɔ*, *ɯ*,[7] and *ɯə*. The mid vowel unit *a* may form part of both yotized and labiovelarized syllables.[8]

The structure of monosyllables

As has been stated above, the prosodic features of the syllable uttered in isolation are shared by single monosyllabic words. These features may be considered in three groups:

1. prosodies of syllable-beginning;
2. prosodies of syllable-ending;
3. prosodies of the syllable as a whole.

1. It has already been observed that the presence of one or more of the following properties is always the signal of the initiation of a syllable: *plosion*, *aspiration*, *voice* (except with nasality), *affrication*, *friction*, *lateralization*, *rhotacization*, and *labialization* (except with velarity). These properties may accompany *k*, *t*, *p* or *ʧ* and may be grouped in fifteen different ways. The possible applications of these fifteen groups are shown below:

Initial prosody or group of prosodies	Consonant units affected			
(1) *plosion*	*k*	*t*	*p*	*ʧ*
(2) *plosion* with *lateralization*	*k*		*p*	
(3) *plosion* with *rhotacization*	*k*	*t*	*p*	
(4) *plosion* with *aspiration*	*k*	*t*	*p*	
(5) *plosion* with *aspiration* and *lateralization*	*k*		*p*	
(6) *plosion* with *aspiration* and *rhotacization*	*k*		*p*	
(7) *plosion* with *voice*		*t*	*p*	
(8) *affrication*		*t*		
(9) *affrication* with *aspiration*		*t*		
(10) *affrication* with *voice*		*t*		
(11) *friction*		*t*	*p*	
(12) *aspiration*				*ʧ*
(13) *lateralization*				*ʧ*
(14) *rhotacization*				*ʧ*
(15) *labialization*				*ʧ*

It will be noted that ʒ is never accompanied by more than one prosodic feature, and that *affrication* is only combined with *t*.

2. *Closure without plosion* is a prosodic feature marking the end of a syllable. When the final consonant is ʒ, the presence or absence of such
closure is closely linked with syllable prosodies. If closure is present,
its realization is glottal.

3. The prosodies of the syllable as a whole are *tone, quantity, labialization,
labiovelarization,* and *yotization*.[9] There is a maximum of five differentiating tone units,[10] whose phonetic expression may be described as
(1) mid-level, as in -khaː 'to dangle'; (2) low level, as in _khaː 'Kha';
(3) falling, as in ˎkhaː 'price'; (4) high rise-fall,[11] as in ˄khaː 'to trade'
(hereafter called for brevity the 'acute' tone); and (5) rising, as in ˊkhaː
'leg'. These tone units may henceforth be referred to by number.

The characteristics of a long syllable are:
(1) length of vowel;
(2) the realization of final ʒ always as phonetic zero;
(3) the reduction of the possible tone alternance to tones 2 and 3 only,
    when the final consonant unit is accompanied by closure without
    plosion.[12]

The characteristics of a short syllable are:
(1) shortness of vowel;
(2) the realization of final ʒ as a glottal stop except in yotized and
    labiovelarized syllables;
(3) the reduction of the possible tone alternance to tones 2 and 4 only,
    when the final consonant is accompanied by closure without
    plosion.

The great majority of syllables containing the vowel units *iə, uə,* and *uɨə*
exhibit the last two characteristics ascribed to long syllables, and such
syllables are thus held to be long. There are, however, a few words such as
˄khiəʔ, _phluəʔ, _tɕhuəʔ, _phuəʔ which exhibit the last two characteristics
proper to short syllables. The last three examples cited above are, however, onomatopes. The first example is a botanical name, and may be of
foreign origin. A similar phonetic construction is found in another
botanical name, ˄kiəʔ (_pluək -baːŋ). I suggest that shortness in syllables
of this pattern may be a special feature proper to onomatopes and certain
foreign words, and not of general application. The special prosodies
appropriate to these two classes of word are discussed later in this
study.[13]

It is of some interest to note that quantity is extremely rarely of lexical
significance in syllables containing the vowel units *e, ɛ,* or *ɔ,* except where
these precede ʒ. The incidence of e, eː, ɛ, ɛː, ɔ, and ɔː appears to correlate

with tone to some degree, the acute and mid-level tones tending to be combined with vowel length, while with the falling tone there is some preference for the short series. Systematic examination of the recorded instances also showed that while syllables ending with the phonetic pattern *long close vowel + stop* are of fairly frequent occurrence, there is a remarkable paucity of words or syllables ending in iːm, iːn, uːm, uːn, uːŋ. No instances at all were found of iːŋ, only two of iːm, and four of uːŋ. Examples of iːn, uːn, and uːm were more plentiful, but all occurred in borrowed words. Historical study of all instances of final complexes of the *close vowel + nasal* type might show that length in such syllables must be interpreted as a term in a special prosodic system appropriate to certain borrowed and 'foreign' words.

No such clear relation exists between the syllable initial and the distribution of tone and quantity as between the final complex and these features.[14] There appears to be no correlation between the syllable initial and quantity, but there are indications that there may be some correlation between certain syllable initials and tone. It is rare for a syllable beginning with a consonant unit accompanied by *plosion* only, or by *plosion* with *voice*, or *plosion* with *affrication* to be characterized by either *tone* 4 or *tone* 5. Of those syllables that are so characterized, a high proportion are borrowed words, and others are onomatopes.[15] In others again, the incidence of either of these tone units is to be regarded as the result of sentence tone, and is dealt with in its proper place as a prosody of the sentence.[16]

The prosodic structure of onomatopes and certain foreign words

There are certain attributes common to some onomatopes, and to certain monosyllabic foreign words, usually of English origin, which do not conform to the pattern prescribed above for the structure of monosyllables. These properties may be described as 'irregular' groupings of *tone*,

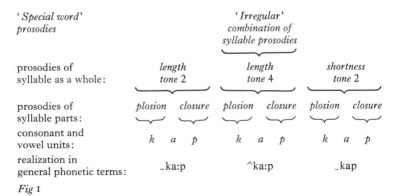

Fig 1

quantity, and *consonant units*. They serve to single out the onomatope or foreign word from the surrounding words of 'regular' pattern in much the same way as English printers may use italic type to show a foreign word, or an exclamation mark to single out an onomatope.

Examples of a possibly 'irregular' combination of shortness and certain vowel units have already been commented upon in the discussion of the regular distribution of tone and quantity,[17] and will not be enlarged upon here. Examples of other onomatopes and foreign words are set out below with an indication of the way in which they are 'irregular' when their structure is compared with that of the vast majority of monosyllables:

Foreign words			*'Irregularity' of structure*
เชิ๊ด	^tɕhɤːt	'shirt'	The phonetic pattern *long vowel + stop* is not normally pronounced on any but low level or falling tones.[18]
ก๊าส (19)	^kaːt	'gas' ⎱	As for tɕhɤːt, except that syllables of this pattern with initial ʔ or k would usually be pronounced on on low level tone only.
โอ๊ก	^ʔoːk	'oak' ⎰	

Onomatopes			
ปิ๊ป	^piːp	'cheep!'	As for ^kaːt and ^ʔoːk
กุ๊ก	^kuːk	'(call of a night-bird)'	As for ^kaːt and ^ʔoːk
แจ๊ด	^tɕɛːt	'chirrup!'	As for ^kaːt and ^ʔoːk
เจี๊ยวจ๊าว	^tɕiəu ^tɕaːu	'chatter, chatter!'	It is rare for syllables with an initial tɕ to be pronounced with the acute tone.[20]
ตุบตับ	˅tup ˅tap	'(noise of pounding)'	Syllable of the pattern *short vowel + stop* are normally restricted to either the low level or the shortened acute tone.[21]
โจ๋ง	ˊtɕoːŋ	'(noise of Malay drum)'	It is rare for syllables with this initial to be pronounced with the rising tone.[20]
เป๋ง	ˊpeŋ	'(noise of hammering sheet iron)'	As for ˊtɕoːŋ

Fig 1 opposite shows the relative structures of _kaːp 'outer fibre', _kap 'with', and ^kaːp[22] 'quack!'

Prosodies of compound words

By compound words are meant words of more than one syllable whose component syllables are themselves meaningful in isolation. The compound words whose structure it is proposed to examine in some detail here contain two such components.

There are certain attributes of compound words which serve in the combinative style to bind the two components together, creating a transitive relation between them. These attributes may be termed linking prosodies.[23] They operate by modifying the prosodic structure which would be proper to one or both of the components taken by themselves. Such modifications commonly affect (a) *tone*, or (b) *quantity*, as demonstrated below:

Word		Pronunciation in isolative style	Pronunciation in combinative style[24]
ที่ไหน	'where?'	ˋthiːˊnai	-thiˑˊnai
ที่นี้	'there'	ˋthiː^niː	-thiˑ^niː
สาวสาว	'young girls'	ˊsaːuˊsaːu	-sauˊsaːu
ว่างว่าง	'at your leisure'	ˋwaːŋˋwaːŋ	-waŋ ˋwaːŋ
ต้องการ	'want'	ˋtɔŋ-kaːn	ˋtɔŋ_kaːn
เท่าไร	'how much'	ˋthau -rai	ˋthau_rai[25]
น้ำชา	'tea'	^naːm -tɕhaː	^nam-tɕhaː
น้ำตาล	'sugar'	^naːm -taːn	^nam -taːn
สีขาว	'white'	ˊsiːˊkhaːu	-siˑˊkhaːu

Another linking prosody proper to compound words affects the realization of the junction of the two medial consonant units. The word อย่างไร 'how', which in the isolative or in 'careful' style is pronounced _jaːŋ-rai, is pronounced -jaŋ-ŋai in the combinative style. Texts attempting to show colloquial pronunciation may nowadays indicate this pronunciation orthographically, viz, ยังไง but the word is even in this context still felt to be a compound of _jaŋ and -rai.[26] In a more rapid and familiar style of speech -jaŋ-ŋai may be replaced by -jaŋai, a form which it is no longer possible to split up into two syllables of regular structure. The occurrence of a single consonant sound intervocalically after a short vowel, which is not permitted in the isolative style, must always be regarded as a prosody of junction.

The prosodic behaviour of the three utterances, _jaːŋ-rai, -jaŋ-ŋai, and -jaŋai is demonstrated in *Fig 2* on *p* 135.

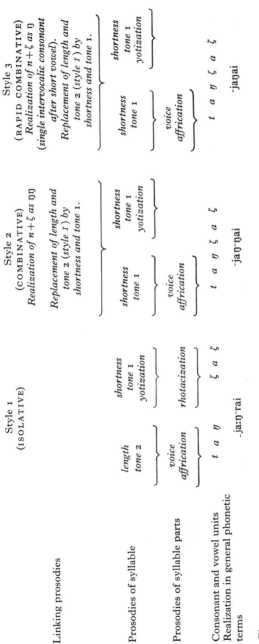

Fig 2

Other pronunciations which might be similarly analysed are _jaːŋ^niː, -jaŋ^niː, ja^ŋiː (where the syllable ja is pronounced with neutral tone[27]) for the word อย่างนี้ 'this way, like this', and _jaːŋ^nan, _jaŋ^ŋan, ja^ŋan for อย่างนั้น 'that way, like that'. The form ^ŋiː, however, which was quoted to me by a Siamese informant as a contraction of _jaːŋ^niː that might occur in the rapid combinative style, as in /khau \tɔŋ_kaːn ^ŋiː \maːk 'he wants as many as this', would probably require to be treated as an independent word.

Attention must be drawn to a special class of compound words of which the first component is of Pali or Sanskrit origin, in which junction is marked by the interpolation of a linking syllable pronounced with a neutral tone:[28]

Orthography	meaning	Pronunciation of components by themselves					Pronunciation in junction
ชลธาร	'stream, water course'	-tɕhon	'water',	-thaːn	'stream'		-tɕhonla-thaːn[29]
ผลไม้	'fruit'	/phon	'fruit'	^mai	'wood'		/phonla^mai[29]
นพเก้า	'set of nine precious stones (eg, on a ring)'	^nop	'stone',	\kaːu	'nine'		^noppha \kaːu
ราชยาน	'royal palanquin, barge, etc'	\raːt	'king'	-jaːn	'vehicle'		\raːttɕha-jaːn
พลรบ	'combatants'	-phon	'troops'	^rop	'fight'		-phonla^rop[29]

Prosodies of polysyllables

A Siamese polysyllable is separable in the isolative style into a sequence of syllables, each of which fulfils the requirements for the structure of monosyllables. The prosodic features peculiar to polysyllables serve to link the syllables of the word with one another, and cannot, therefore, operate in the isolative style. The operation of the prosodies of polysyllables in the combinative style can most simply be demonstrated by an examination of the prosodic behaviour of disyllables.

Disyllables are of two types.

The first type of disyllable may be split up in the combinative no less than the isolative style into two syllables conforming to the rules for the structure of monosyllables, but excluding the possibility of a short first syllable ending in zero consonant, unless accompanied by labiovelarization or yotization. There is no effective difference between the isolative pronunciation of these words and that of connected speech. Examples are อัมพิต -ʔam-phin, วิชชา ^wit-tɕhaː, อัปป _ʔap_paʔ, ชนพู -tɕhom -phuː, โกณ -koː^naʔ, นารี -naː-riː, ขัณฑา -khan-taː. It will be seen that where there is a junction of two similar consonant units, a long medial stop or nasal results in pronunciation. There is, however, no need to regard gemination as a special feature here. The structure of words in which it occurs is already adequately accounted for by the analysis of the word into consonant and vowel units, with accompanying prosodies of syllable-beginning or ending. The structure of อิทธิ _ʔit'ʌ thiʔ is illustrated below:

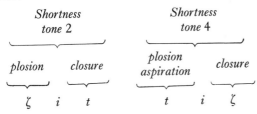

In the second type of disyllable the first syllable is realized in the isolative style as *consonant + short vowel + glottal stop*. In the combinative style, the first syllables of the words of this very numerous class may be joined to the second syllables by the following means:

1. A relatively weak stress; that is to say, a stress differentiation is introduced, in which there may be said to be two differential units: *stress* and *lack of stress*.
2. What may be called 'neutral' tone;[27] this is in effect a one-unit tone system, as contrasted with the usual five-unit tone system. Disyllables of this type operate a special tone differentiation of which the two differential units may be said to be *neutral tone* and *five-tone system*. This special tone differentiation is closely bound up with stress, and is always connective. The neutral tone is left unmarked in phonetic transcription.
3. The absence of final glottal closure. Whenever a short syllable unaccompanied by labiovelarization or yotization realizes final ζ as phonetic zero, linguistic suspense is created which binds that syllable closely to the following one. Moreover, this type of pronunciation results in the occurrence of a single intervocalic consonant after a short vowel, which has already been stated as a linking prosody.[30]
4. Vowel quality. When the vowel unit of the first syllable is *a*, a vowel sound that is appreciably closer and more centralized than that used in the isolative style is often heard.

Examples of disyllables of the second type are:

Orthography		Isolative style	Combinative style
ทะเล	'sea'	ʌthaʔ-leː	tha-leː
กตาย			

ระยะ	'interval'	^raʔ^jaʔ	ra^jaʔ
คะเน	'conjecture'	^khaʔ-neː	kha-neː
แขยง	'loathe'	_khaˊjeːŋ	khaˊjeːŋ
พระหาม	'dawn'	^phraʔˊhaːm	phraˊhaːm
ละอาด	'clean'	_saʔ_ʔaːt	sa_ʔaːt[31]
กระทรวง	'Ministry'	_kraʔ-suəŋ	kra-suəŋ
อินัง	'take an interest in'	^ʔiʔ-naŋ	ʔi-naŋ
พิธี	'rite'	^phiʔ-thiː	phi-thiː
ธุระ	'business'	^thuʔ^raʔ	thu^raʔ
สุภาพ	'gentle'	_suˋphaːp	suˋphaːp
อุชุ	'honourable'	_ʔuʔ^tɕhuʔ	ʔu^tɕhuʔ
อุทาร	'exalted'	_ʔuʔ-thaːn	ʔu-thaːn
กุดั่น	'filigree jewellery'	_kuˋdan	kuˋdan
กิเลน	'fabulous'	_kiʔ-leːn	ki-leːn

The examples ทะเด, ถถาย and คะเน, แขยง show that no difference is made in the combinative style in this context between certain syllables which in the isolative style are distinguished by tone. คะเน and สุภาพ have been selected at random to demonstrate the analysis of the prosodic features of words of this type. (See *Fig 3* on *p* 140.)

Words of more than two syllables may be treated as combinations of the disyllable types already presented. In general, the prosodic treatment of short syllables of the type *vowel unit + zero consonant* [32] is aimed at attaching them to the next following 'prominent' syllable, which may be a long syllable, or a short syllable ending in a consonant unit other than zero. Two or three short syllables may be linked to a following 'prominent' one. Where the last syllable of a word or before a pause is a short one of the type *vowel unit + zero consonant* [32] it retains its isolative structure, and functions as a 'prominent' syllable. Examples are:

Orthography		*Isolative style*	*Combinative style*
อริยะ	'venerable, sage'	_ʔaʔ^riʔ^jaʔ	ʔari^jaʔ
อรหะ	'deserving'	_ʔaʔ^raʔ_haʔ	ʔara_haʔ
อุทริยะ	'stomach'	_ʔut^taʔ^riʔ^jaʔ	ʔuttari^jaʔ
อุษณ	'heat'	_ʔuʔ_saʔ^naʔ	ʔusa^naʔ

ศาสนา	'scriptures, religion'	ˈsaː_saʔˈnaː	ˈsaːsaˈnaː
เมขลา	'goddess of lightning'	-meː_khaʔˈlaː	-meːkhaˈlaː
กรณ	'act of doing'	_kaʔˈraʔˈnaʔ	karaˈnaʔ
กิริยา	'verb'	_kiʔˈriʔ-jaː	kiri-jaː

Examples of longer compound words (of Pali and Sanskrit origin) are:

พระพุทธศาสนา, 'the Buddhist religion', isolative: ˈphraʔˈphutˈthaʔ ˈsaː_saʔˈnaː, combinative: phraˈphutˈthaʔsaːsaˈnaː

ปราชาปัตยวิวาหะ, '(a form of marriage)', isolative: -praː-tɕhaː_pat_taʔ ˈjaʔˈwiʔ-waː_haʔ, combinative: -praː-tɕhaː_pattaˈjaʔwi-waː_haʔ

ชนกาธิบดี,'the father of a King' isolative: -tɕhonˈnaʔ-kaːˈthip-bɔː-diː, combinative: -tɕhonna-kaːˈthipbɔ-diː

Sentence prosodies

Sentence prosodies are of three kinds, namely: 1. those affecting small groups or 'pieces' within the sentence;[33] 2. those relating to the sentence as a whole; and 3. those which link one sentence with another, or the part of a sentence with another part.

1. The prosodies affecting pieces within the sentence operate in much the same way as those affecting compound words and polysyllables, serving to bind together certain groups of words within the wider group, which is in turn held together by appropriate sentence prosodies. Among the pieces of a sentence which appear to be regularly linked by prosodic features are the following:

(a) The future particle จะ _tɕaʔ and the following verbal. A group like จะไป 'will go' is bound together by the same prosodic means as di-syllables of the second type;[34] that is to say, จะ is pronounced with relatively weak stress, neutral tone, centralized vowel quality, and without final glottal closure: tɕä-pai, as opposed to _tɕaʔ-pai in the isolative style.

(b) The negative particle ไม่ ˈmai and the following verbal ไม่ is usually linked to the following word by relatively weak stress and neutral tone. In rapid combinative style there is also a marked shortening of the utterance in relation to the following word, and the diphthong heard may start from a considerably closer vowel position than would be permissible in the isolative or slower combinative style. In certain contexts it is the verbal form which is pronounced with

COMBINATIVE STYLE
Realization of ζ + n as n.
Stress relationship.
Relationship of neutral tone and five-tone system.
Centralized quality of a.

Linking prosodies

	shortness neutral tone lack of stress		length tone 1 stress
Prosodies of syllable			
Prosodies of syllable parts	plosion aspiration		
Consonant and vowel units	k a ζ	n	e ζ
Realization in general phonetic terms		khä‑ne:	

Realization of ζ + p as p.
Stress relationship.
Relationship of neutral tone and five-tone system.

Linking prosodies

	shortness neutral tone lack of stress	length tone 1 stress
Prosodies of syllable		
Prosodies of syllable parts	friction	plosion aspiration · closure
Consonant and vowel units	t u ζ	p a p
Realization in general phonetic terms	suupha:p	

ISOLATIVE STYLE

Linking prosodies

	shortness tone 4	length tone 1
Prosodies of syllable		
Prosodies of syllable parts	plosion aspiration · closure	
Consonant and vowel units	k a ζ	n e ζ
Realization in general phonetic terms	^khä²‑ne:	

Linking prosodies

	shortness tone 2	length tone 3
Prosodies of syllable		
Prosodies of syllable parts	friction · closure	plosion aspiration · closure
Consonant and vowel units	t u ζ	p a p
Realization in general phonetic terms	– su²pha:p	

relatively weak stress and with neutral tone, while ไม่ is pronounced as in the isolative style. The intonation pattern of ไม่ได้หยุด 'without stopping', which in the isolative style would be pronounced ˇmaiˇdaːi_jut, might be represented (ˇ . .)

(c) Words in genitive relation. Where this relation is shown by the use of the word ของ khɔːŋ between two nominals, as in พ่อของเขา 'his father', ของ and the following word may be linked by the tonal and quantitative features that serve to link compound words of similar pattern: ˇphɔː-khɔŋˊkhau.[35] In rapid combinative style ˇphɔːŋˊkhau may be heard. Where the genitive relation is shown by the juxtaposition of the two nominals the close relation between the two is expressed rhythmically. Thus, the rhythm of the sentence -khraiˊkhaːi_khai_kai[36] 'who is selling hen's eggs?' may be represented ♩ ♩ ♪ ♪.

(d) A numeral and the following classifier. The link here is usually rhythmic.

2. The prosodies affecting the sentence as a whole include (a) *intonation* and (b) *sentence tone*.

(a) *Intonation.* In rapid combinative style it is possible to detect certain intonational tendencies which may be mentioned here. A sequence of mid level tones tends to be pronounced on a descending scale, with a fairly marked fall in pitch in the last syllable before a pause. A fall in pitch may be postponed until a word of sufficient semantic import is reached. The words preceding or following an important fall in pitch may, if their content allows it, be pronounced on a fairly low pitch, even if their lexical tone is not low level. Examples of some of these intonational tendencies in rapid combinative style are given side by side with the pronunciation of the same text in combinative style:

Orthography	*Pronunciation in combinative style*	*Intonation in rapid combinative style*
เป็นอย่างไร	-pen-jaŋ-ŋai · ·	‾ ‾ ⌐
ใจเดียวกันทีเดียว	-tɕai-diəu-kan-thiː-diəu ·	‾ ‾ ‾ ‾ ⌐
แพงเกินไป	-phɛːŋ-kɤːn-pai · ·	‾ ‾ ⌐
อยู่ในกรุงเทพฯ	_juː-nai-kruŋˇtheːp · ·	‾·‾ ＼
เราเดินมานานแล้ว	-rau-dɤːn-maː-naːn^lɛːu ·	‾ ‾ · _ ∧
ราคาแปดบาท	-raː-khaː_pɛːt_baːt ·	‾ ‾ _ ⌐

ราคาแปดบาทครับ   -raː-khaː_pɛːt_baːt_ʌkhrap ·

คุณกำลังจะไปไหน   -khun-kam-laŋ tɕa-paiˌnai

เรากำลังจะไปกินข้าว   -rau-kam-laŋ tɕa-pai-kin
                      ˋkhaːu   ·   ·   ·

ดิฉันไม่ค่อยว่างหมู่นี้   diˌtɕhanˏmaiˋkhɔiˏwaːŋ
                      _muːʌniː   ·   ·

(b) *Sentence tone.* When due account has been taken of such intonational tendencies as are described above, however, and of the
variations of tone and quantity in isolative and combinative contexts, it becomes clear that on the whole the lexical or isolative
patterns remain fairly constant in the phrase and sentence. Nevertheless, spoken Siamese, by the ingenious use of certain particles,
commands a flexibility of expression comparable to that achieved
in the English sentence by the modulations of stress and intonation.
The majority of such particles are used at the end of a phrase or
sentence, the most important exception being the anaphoric particle
ก็ , which is often found at the beginning of the second part of a
two-part sentence, or at the beginning of a sentence which refers
back to some earlier one. Such particles serve several purposes.
Firstly, by their presence they mark the end of a sentence, or, in the
case of ก็ , signal the beginning of a clause or sentence which is
linked with one that has gone before. They also add something to the
general meaning of the sentence. They may, for instance, soften a
command, indicate a question, or proclaim the sex and social
status of the speaker. They have, moreover, the special property of
carrying what we may call the *sentence tone.* The sentence tone is a
complex of the syllable prosodies of tone and quantity, and is
usually realized as one of the five tones proper to monosyllables,
combined with either shortness or length.[37] Particles bearing sentence tone are distinguished from other monosyllables in the sentence in one important respect: the disposition of tone and quantity is determined not by the phonetic structure of the particle itself,
but by the requirements of the sentence as a whole.† We thus find as
particles such forms as ˏkhaʔ, ˏkɔʔ, -si, which are inadmissible from
the point of view of word-tone.[38] It is not the aim of this study to
attempt a detailed statement of the semantic function of the particles themselves, or of the sentence tones they may carry, but some
general observations on their use may usefully be made. The following table sets out seven sentence tones, showing the syllable prosodies of which they are a synthesis, and attempting to give some

approximate indication of the way in which they may colour the
sentences to which they are applied:

Sentence tone	Synthesis of syllable prosodies	Notes on general effect
A	Tone 1 and *shortness*[(39)]	The most 'neutral' sentence tone. May give impression of casualness.
B	Tone 2 and *shortness*	Suggestion of impatience, abruptness, exasperation; or mild command.
C	Tone 3 and *length*	Assertion, or assent. More formal than *D*.
D	Tone 3 and *shortness*	Assertion, or assent, or command.
E	Tone 4 and *length*	Intensity, emphasis, or urgency.
F	Tone 4 and *shortness*	Interrogation, invitation; less formal than *G*.
G	Tone 5 and *length*	Interrogation in slow, careful, or very formal style.

In the following examples the particles that may bear sentence
tone are underlined. It will be seen that two such particles can occur
together at the end of a sentence. When this happens, it is usually
the last of the pair that bears the sentence tone, the first one being
bound to the second by appropriate linking prosodies, which
may include the neutral tone. Where the first particle of the sentence is felt to have more importance than the second for the
sentence as a whole, however, both particles may bear an appropriate sentence tone. Thus, the sentence 'How are you?' may be
expressed politely by women speakers either by sa‿baːi-diː꞉ˊ‿ˆkhaʔ or
sa‿baːi-diːꞋˊruː꞉ˆkhaʔ. The syllable ˆkhaʔ in both indicates politeness and the fact that the speaker is a woman. It bears sentence tone
F, to indicate enquiry. The syllable ˊruː in the second sentence is an
interrogatory particle bearing sentence tone *G*, and could be final
in the sentence if the speaker did not choose to add the special sign

of formal politeness. It should be noted that a sentence may consist solely of a final particle or particles, as: ˏkhaʔ (indicating polite assent by women); ˊtɕaː 'Yes?' (as to a child, or servant); and ˌthɤʔ-na 'Do (this) for me, please!'; where ˌthɤʔ is a particle expressing a request or mild command, and -na a particle expressing polite entreaty or persuasion, here bearing sentence tone *A*.

Examples of sentence tone *A*

ˏkhaːu -maː -<u>si</u>	'Come in!'
ˋdaːi -<u>si</u>	'All right!'
ˋtɕiŋ -<u>si</u>	'Indeed!'
ˊkhɔː -pai -<u>thi</u>	'Please let me pass!'
ˊkhɔː -<u>thi</u>	'Give it to me, please' or 'Do it for me, please'
ˌpɤːt pra-thuː-<u>thi</u>	'Please open the door!'

Examples of sentence tone *B*

ˋthau ˆnan ˌlɛʔ	'That's all'
ˊphuːt ˆsam ˌjuːˆnan ˌlɛʔ	'You've said all that before!'
ˊphom -ɕa-paiˆdiəu ˆniː ˌlɛʔ	'I'm going now'
ˋnan ˌlɛʔ	'That's it!'
ˋphuːt -pai -jaŋˆŋan ˌlɛʔ	'How you do go on (talking)!'
-duː ˋnan ˌnɛʔ	'Just look there!'
ˆlɛːu -khun ˌlaʔ	'And what about you?'
ˋtɕhaːŋ ˌthɤʔ	'It doesn't matter (= No, thank you)'
ˋnaŋ-loŋ ˌthɤʔ	'Sit down!'
-pai ˌthɤʔ	'Let's go!'

Examples of sentence tone *C*

ˋniːˋnɛː	'Here it is!'
-tham-pen ˋlen-pai ˋnaː	'Don't play the fool, now'
ˋtɕau ˋkhaː	'Yes, sir' (respectful, used by women)

Examples of sentence tone *D*

-duː ˋnan ˋnɛʔ	'Just look at that!'
ˋniː ˋkhaʔ	'Here you are' (polite, used by women)
-tɕhɤːn-khun ˌsaŋ-ʔaːˊhaːn siˋkhaʔ	'May I invite you to have something to eat?'
ˆlɛʔ ʔa-rai ˌʔiːk ˋlaʔ	'Is there anything more you require?'

Examples of sentence tone *E*

ˋkhau -maː ˆsiː	'Do please come in!'
ʔaˆrai[(40)]	'What!'

Examples of sentence tone *F*

-tɕhɤːn ˋnaŋ ^siʔ	'Please won't you sit down?'
sa_baːi -diːˊrɯːˆkhaʔ	'How are you?' (used by women)
ˊkhau _juː ˊmaiˆtɕaʔ	'Is he in, please?'
sa_baːi -diː ^rɯʔ	'How are you?'
^phop -kan _mai ^naʔ	'We'll be seeing each other again (won't we?)'
-pai si ^naʔ	'*Do* go!'
-loŋ-kan -thiˋniː ^lɛʔ	'Here's where we get down!'
ˋnan ^lɛʔ	'That's quite right!'
ˋnoːn ^nɛʔ	'That one over there!'
-au si ^waʔ	'Take it, then!' (vulgar)
-pai ˊnai ^waʔ	'Where are you going?' (vulgar)
ʔa -rai ^waʔ	'What is it, then?' (vulgar)

Examples of sentence tone *G*

-pai si ˊnaː	'Won't you please go?'
ˋtɕau ˊkhaː	'Yes, sir?' (very respectful)
ˊtɕaː	'Yes?' (used among intimates)

That the same particle may carry different sentence tones is shown by the following:

ˋkhaːu-maː -si	'Come in, (please)!'
ˋkha(ː)u -maː ^siʔ	'Come in, won't you?'
ˋkha(ː)u -maː ^siː	'*Do* come in!'
ˋkhaːu -maː _siʔ	'Come in, (please)!'
ˋkhaːu -maː si ^khaʔ	'Won't you come in, please?' (used by women)

In the passage ฉันมาหาคุณดำจ้ะ เขาอยู่ไหมจ๊ะ 'I've come to see Mr Dam. Is he in, please?' as it might be spoken to a servant answering the door, the particle tɕa is used twice, the first time with a sentence tone appropriate to statements and assertions (*D*), and the second time with one appropriate to enquiries (*F*): ˊtɕhan -maː ˊhaː-khun -dam ˋtɕaʔ ˊkhau _juː ˊmaiˆtɕaʔ. Similarly, in a conversation between two women, the answer to sa_baːi-diː ˊrɯːˆkhaʔ 'How are you?' is sa_baːi-diː ˋkhaʔ 'Quite well, thank you'.

The sentence tones which may combine with any one particle are restricted in some degree by the semantic function of the particle itself. The interrogative particle rɯ, for instance, may normally be expected to carry one of these sentence tones associated with enquiry, namely, *F* and *G*. The final particle ^khrap appears to be subject to a restriction which is not imposed by semantic function. This particle is used by male speakers in the same way as kha by women, but in contrast with the variable tone and quantity of the latter, is always pronounced with *tone* 4. Two factors may here inhibit the working of sentence tone, namely, phonetic form and historical origin. The great majority of final particles have zero final consonant, and it is possible that the presence in this word of final *p* is less conducive to prosodic change. From the historical point of view, ⌃khrap has been described as a fairly recent contraction of a two-word expression ⁄khɔː⌃rap,[41] and it may be that awareness of the tone pattern of the original phrase is still acute enough to prevent the acceptance of the contracted form as a particle carrying sentence- rather than word-tone.

It has been observed that where phonetic form and position in the sentence are favourable other words may be characterized by the prosodic features proper to final particles. The pronunciation of รู้ 'know', which is ordinarily ⌃ruː, may be ⌃ruʔ in such expressions as จนอะไรก็ไม่รู้ 'Whatever sort of man *is* he?' In certain emphatic contexts อะไร, usually pronounced ʔa-rai in combinative style, may be heard as ʔa⌃rai. It may be speculated whether the so-called interrogative particle ⁄mai may not be regarded as the negative particle ˎmai with a superimposed sentence tone *G*.[42] I am inclined to believe, moreover, that the incidence of *tone* 4 in certain words expressing notions of distance, size, colour, speed, etc, may properly be accounted for by sentence rather than word tone, and may be referred to the emphatic and intensifying connotation of sentence tone *E*.[43] Among such examples I would include นี่ ⌃niː 'this', นั่น ⌃nan 'that', and โน่น ⌃noːn 'that over there' (as compared with นี่ ˎniː, นั่น ˎnan and โน่น ˎnoːn), and the following less familiar words: ปรี๊ด ⌃priːt 'extremely (tall or fast)', จ๊วก ⌃tɕuak '(expressing superlative degree of whiteness)', จิ๊ด ⌃tɕiːt 'smallest', and ล้า ⌃la 'late', (as compared with ล่า ˎlaː, also meaning 'late'). Such forms as ปรี๊ด, จ๊วก, จิ๊ด could not ordinarily be accompanied by *tone* 4 as a word-tone.[44] Their prosodic structure may be accounted for either by sentence-tone or by the prosodies for 'special words' already examined.[45] My inclination is to treat their 'irregular' features as the expression of a sentence prosody comparable with emphatic stress and intonation in English.

The anaphoric function of the particle ก็ has already been mentioned.[46] The lexical pronunciation of ก็ is ˎkɔː, but this is rarely heard, ˎkɔʔ being the commoner pronunciation even in the isolative style. The combination in this latter pronunciation of *tone* 3

and syllabic shortness, which is 'irregular' as monosyllabic structure, may be interpreted as sentence tone. When linking the two
parts of a sentence, ก็ is pronounced at the beginning of the second
part, being attached to the first word of the second part by prosodies
such as obtain for disyllables of the second type.[47] It thus comes
about that the function of this particle as a bearer of sentence tone
is frequently subordinated to its function as an anaphore. Examples
of the use of ก็ as a link between sentence parts are given below:

˅phuːt-diː kɔ-diː-pai	'Talking about it will do me no good.'
˄nɯəˌrɯəŋ kɔ-phɔː-duː	'The *story* (eg, of a film) is all right.'
˅phuːt˄lɛːu kɔ_cep-cai	'Even talking about it is painful to me.'
sa_botˌhai kɔˌdaːi	'I can swear to it.'
-khraiˌtɕhɯə kɔˌtɕhaːŋ	'Let him believe it who can.'
-tham ʔa-rai kɔ mai˄ruː	'I don't know what to do!'

ก็ may occur at the beginning of a sentence when its function is to
refer that sentence back to something that has been said or implied
earlier, often by another speaker. Thus, the answer to an enquiry
about someone's health may be ก็เรื่อยเรื่อย kɔˌrɯəiˌrɯəi 'So so'.
This function of referring back to some earlier utterance leads to the
English translation of ก็ as 'too' or 'also' in many instances. The
sentence   เขาว่ากับข้าวไทยก็ดี   ˌkhau ˌwaːː_kap ˅khaːu-thai
kɔ-diː may perhaps best be translated 'They say Siamese food is
good too' (previous conversation having perhaps been about the
excellence of Chinese food).

In conclusion, *Figs* 4 and 5 on *pp* 151–153 attempt to demonstrate some of the prosodic features discussed in this paper as they
apply to a Siamese speaker's pronunciation of the following two
short exracts of conversational passages from a Siamese novel:[48]

(i) '˅ʔaːu ! wi-mon na-ʔeːŋ.   -maː ˄rot-khrai ˄naʔ?'
    'Ah! There you are, Wimon!   Whose car did you come in?'
    'kɔˌtɕhan na-si.'
    'Yes, here I am!'

(ii) '-rɔŋˌhai kɔ˄rɔːŋ-pai-khon-diəu-si, -thamai ˅tɔŋ
    'Go on and cry if you want to, but why must you bang
    kraˌthɛːkˌnan kraˌthɛːkˌniː _nuək ˌhuː maiˌtɕhai ˄rɯʔ?'
    things about? The noise is pretty awful, you know!'
    'kɔ-khrai ˌkhau ˄tɕhai ˌhai ma-faŋˌlaʔ, ˌkhau _juː
    'Who asked you to come and listen to me then? I'm in my
    n(a)i ˌhɔŋ -khɔŋˌkhau.'
    own room!'

'ʔuˇbaʔ! kɔˇkhau -nɔːn_juː n(a)iˇhɔŋ.'
'But *I* sleep in this room too!'

Reasons of space have made it necessary in *Figs* 4 and 5 to indicate many prosodic features by abbreviations. A key to the abbreviations used is given below:

Aff	= *affrication*	*NT*	= *neutral tone*
Asp	= *aspiration*	*P*	= *plosion*
C	= *closure without*	*R*	= *rhotacization*
	plosion	*S*	= *stress*
F	= *friction*	*Sht*	= *shortness*
L	= *lateralization*	*SC*	= *single medial consonant*
Lb	= *labialization*		*after a short vowel*
Lv	= *labiovelarization*	*T*1, *etc*	= *tone* 1, *etc*
Lth	= *length*	*V*	= *voice*
L of S	= *lack of stress*	*Y*	= *yotization*
NT : 5 *T*	= *relationship between neutral tone and five-tone system*		
L of S : *S*	= *stress relationship*		

The abbreviations *T*5 > *T*1 *in Syll.* 1 means that the prosodic feature in this case is the fact that in junction the first syllable has *tone* 1, whereas in isolation it would have *tone* 5. Other abbreviations of this type are to be similarly interpreted.

Notes

[1] See 'Sounds and Prosodies', by J. R. Firth, in 1948 volume of the *Transactions of the Philological Society of Great Britain*. [Reprinted in this volume *pp* 47–65, Eds.]

[2] *eg* McFarland's *Thai-English Dictionary*, to which I am indebted for much linguistic material, and the ปทานุกรม .

[3] The symbol ζ has been chosen as being less likely to cause confusion than *Z* or *O*.

[4] See below.

[5] McFarland's Dictionary records one instance only, หวือ ˇwɯː, an onomatope, 'from the sound of chips or splinters flying past the ear'.

[6] There would be some gain in clarity of exposition if two additional consonant units, *y* and *w*, could be postulated to account for initial j and w and for the final elements of the closing diphthongs described below. The limited vowel alternation that would obtain before final *y* and *w*, however, does not tally with what is observed before other final consonant units, and points to some other interpretation of the syllables concerned.

[7] ɯi does not occur in Siamese. *ɯ* is, however, assumed to be of the same type as *ɯə* by analogy with *u*, *uə*; *i*, *iə*.

[8] It is possible to reduce the number of vowel units by abstracting such properties as *closeness*, of which there might be said to be three degrees, *roundedness, unroundedness, etc.* These properties would not, however, be features of the syllable but of the vowel alternation only, and it has not, therefore, been thought useful to make such abstractions in this study.

[9] Only prosodies of the syllable in isolation are under discussion here. A

syllable in a combinative context may be characterized by other features (see *pp* 134, 138–139).

[10] For tone of syllables in combinative contexts, see below, *pp* 134, 137–140.

[11] On short syllables closed by a stop the acute tone comprises a short high rise or a short high-level pitch.

[12] Long syllables with final ζ and *tone* 4 or 5 are often pronounced with some final glottal closure. This is, however, a syllabic feature, and is distinct from the glottal stop, which is frequently the realization in short syllables of final ζ accompanied by the syllable-ending prosody *closure without plosion*.

[13] See *pp* 132–133.

[14] The so-called 'high consonants' of Siamese orthography and the use of ห นำ suggest that at some time there may have been a correlation between *aspiration* and *tone* 5.

[15] See next paragraph for a discussion of the special properties of certain onomatopes and foreign words.

[16] See *pp* 143–145.

[17] See *p* 131.   [18] See *p* 131.

[19] This word, which is given in the ปทานุกรม and in McFarland, was unknown to a Siamese informant whom I recently had occasion to ask about it.

[20] See *p* 132.

[21] See note 11.

[22] Usually repeated in utterance, as in English.

[23] See 'Sounds and Prosodies', by J. R. Firth, in the 1948 *Transactions of the Philological Society of Great Britain*.

[24] In the rapid combinative style, words of this type may be further modified from the isolative pattern so as to incorporate such features as stress and the neutral tone (see *pp* 136–137). A word like ที่ไหน may in the rapid combinative style exhibit the same phonetic features in utterance as a disyllable of the second type (see *p* 137) in the combinative style.

[25] It is of interest here to note that in a colloquial text I wrote out recently for recording purposes the word เท่าไร, which occurred several times, was corrected by a Siamese informant to เท่าไหร่, a spelling which implies a low level tone in the second syllable. No such spelling as เท่าไหร่ is, however, recognized by dictionaries I have consulted.

[26] I have not yet found the form ยังไง in a dictionary, although I have seen it written fairly often. It may be speculated whether the word ทำไม ⁻tham⁻mai 'why', which is always so spelt in dictionaries I have seen, does not represent the combinative pronunciation of a word whose isolative pronunciation was once ⁻tham⁻rai.

[27] The actual pitch of the neutral tone may vary according to context, but is most commonly mid level.

[28] The initial consonant of the linking syllable can, of course, be predicted by recourse to the spelling, which reflects the foreign original in some degree. A full study of the phonetic treatment of Sanskrit and Pali words in Siamese is needed in order to show how far and how many of such words have been 'naturalized' into Siamese. Many still retain two possibilities of utterance, one in accordance with the usual principles of Siamese syllable structure, and one pedantic or 'alien' pronunciation.

[29] I have heard these words pronounced ⁻tɕholla⁻thaːn, ˌpholla^mai, ⁻pholla ^rop. The gemination here is, of course, a prosody of junction.

[30] See *p* 134.

[31] It will be noted that the glottal stop, which is in the isolative style the realization of the final ζ of the first syllable, is not present in the combinative style, whereas the glottal plosive, which is the realization of the initial ζ of the second syllable, is common to both styles.

[32] Excluding yotized or labiovelarized syllables.

[33] See article by J. R. Firth, quoted above.

[34] See *p* 136.

[35] See *p* 134.

[36] A well-known Siamese 'tongue-twister'.

[37] Special effects may, as in other languages, sometimes be obtained by means which are less readily analysed, since they are highly individual. To give an instance: the normal polite way of asking a friend what he said is ˈphuːtˌwaːʔaˌrai^naʔ, but if the polite particle ^naʔ is uttered on an unusually high pitch and with appropriate voice quality, sarcasm or irony may be implied.

[38] See *p* 131.

[39] This sentence tone is heard as a short open syllable without final glottal closure. Siamese orthography has no way of indicating this pronunciation. Short syllables with zero final consonant, unless realized as diphthongs, are always pronounced with a final glottal stop before a pause, and can never be accompanied by a mid level tone in this position. Written texts I have seen appear to represent this sentence tone by a spelling which indicates a mid level tone, but implies a long final vowel. I have, however, so far not heard a Siamese speaker pronounce a long vowel in this context.

[40] For the use of sentence tone *E* without a final particle, see *p* 146.

[41] McFarland and the ปทานุกรม only recognize ขอรับ /khɔː^rap.

[42] One of my Siamese informants was put to some difficulty to explain how the word for 'silk' (the lexical meaning of /mai) could come to be used as a sign of interrogation! The relevant entry in McFarland's *Dictionary* suggests that the interrogative /mai is equivalent to /rɯː ˌmai 'or not'.

[43] See in this connection 'Techniques of Intensifying in Thai', by Mary R. Haas, in *Word*, Vol II, No 2.

[44] See *p* 131.

[45] See *p* 132.

[46] See *p* 142.

[47] See *p* 136.

[48] *Phu Di*, by Dok Mai Sod.

* [I now believe that the sound I heard preceding the j was not d but a weak glottal stop (see 'Marginalia to Siamese Phonetic Studies' in *In Honour of Daniel Jones*, D. Abercrombie *et al* (eds), London, 1964, *p* 419). If I had recognized this at the time, I should almost certainly have modified the presentation offered in this paper. – Author 1968.]

† [I should now add syllable-ending prosodies to the features so determined. Since this paper was written, greater familiarity with the usages of conversational Thai (Siamese) has convinced me that final glottal closure is far less common in particles than I had earlier supposed, and that it is in many situations socially unacceptable. (See 'Marginalia to Siamese Phonetic Studies', *pp* 421–422.) If I were rewriting the paper today, many of the final glottal stops shown for particles in the examples that follow would be deleted, with consequent changes in the syllable-final prosodies on *pp* 151–153. – Author 1968.]

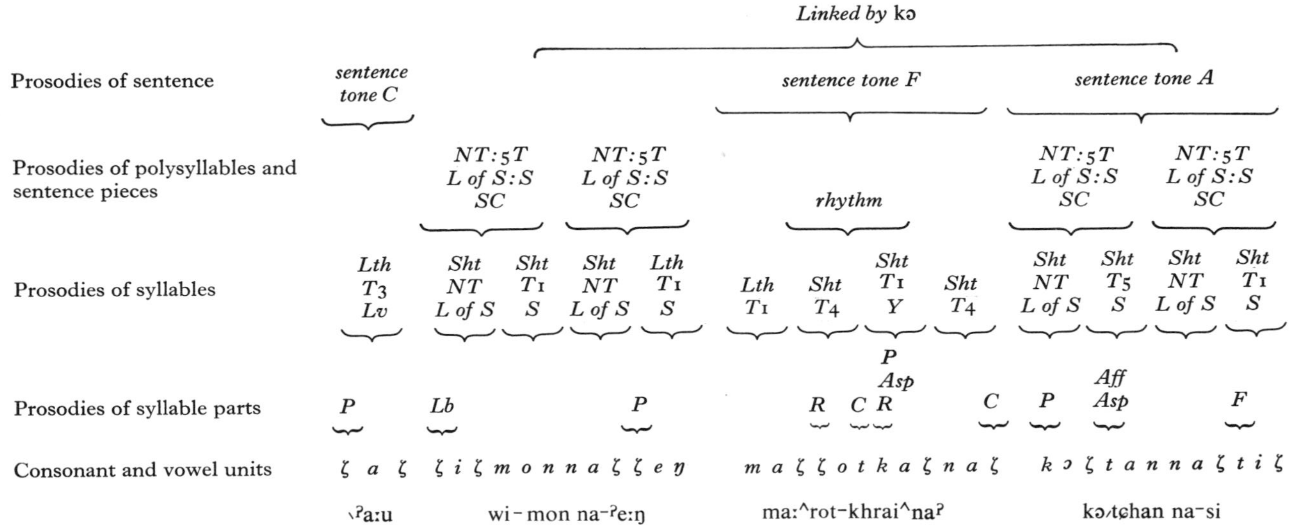

Linked by kɔ

Prosodies of sentence	sentence tone C	sentence tone F	sentence tone A

Prosodies of polysyllables and sentence pieces

| | NT:5T L of S:S SC | NT:5T L of S:S SC | | rhythm | | NT:5T L of S:S SC | NT:5T L of S:S SC |

Prosodies of syllables

| Lth T3 Lv | Sht NT L of S | Sht T1 S | Sht NT L of S | Lth T1 S | Lth T1 | Sht T4 | Sht T1 Y | Sht T4 | Sht NT L of S | Sht T5 S | Sht NT L of S | Sht T1 S |

Prosodies of syllable parts

| P | Lb | P | R | C R | P Asp | C | C | P | P Asp | Aff | F |

Consonant and vowel units

| ✓ʔaːu | ɹaɬ ɬiɬmonnaɬɬeŋ | maɬɬotkaɬnaɬ | kɔɬtannaɬtiɬ |

wi‑mon na‑ʔeːŋ

ma:‑ʔrot‑khrai‑ʔnaʔ

kɔ‑tchan na‑si

Fig 4

sentence tone A

Prosodies of sentence

Prosodies of sentence parts   *linked by* kɔ

Prosodies of
polysyllables and   *Lth > Sht in syll.* 1   *NT:5T*
sentence pieces   *T4 > T1 in syll.* 1   *L of S:S*   *SC*   *NT:5T*   *NT:5T*
   SC   *L of S:S*   *L of S:S*
   SC   *SC*

Prosodies of syllables
   Sht T1 Y   Sht NT L of S   Lth T4 S   Sht T1 Y   Sht T1   Sht T4
   Sht T1 Y   Sht T1 L of S   Sht T3 S   Sht T1 Y   Sht NT L of S   Lth T4 S   Sht T1 Y   Lth T1 Lʋ   Sht T1
   Sht NT L of S   Lth T3 S   Sht T3 L of S   Lth T4

Prosodies of syllable parts
   R Asp P R P Asp   P V F   P Asp   P R Asp C   P R Asp C   P P R Asp C

Consonant and vowel units
   ʔ ɔ ŋ a ʔ k ɔ ʔ ʔ ɔ ŋ p a ʔ k o n t i a ʔ t i ʔ   t a m m a ʔ i ɔ ŋ k a ʔ t e k n a n k a ʔ t e k n i ʔ
   ‾rɔŋ ˌhai kɔ^rɔːŋ‾pai‾khon‾diɔu‾si   ‾thamai ˌtɔŋ kra ˌthe:k ˌnan kra ˌthe:k ^mi:

linked by kɔ

---

sentence tone F   *sentence tone D*

Prosodies of sentence   *T3 > T1 in syll.* 1

Prosodies of
polysyllables and   *T3 > T1 in syll.* 1   *NT:5T*   *NT:5T*
sentence pieces   *L of S:S*   *L of S:S*
   SC   *SC*

Prosodies of syllables
   Lth Lth   Sht Sht   Sht T1 Y   Sht NT L of S   Sht T1 S   Sht T4 Y   Sht T5 Lʋ   Sht Aff   Sht NT L of S   Sht T1 S   Sht T1 Y   Sht T3
   T2 T5   T1 T3 Y   T4   F

Prosodies of syllable parts
   C Asp   Aff Asp   P R Asp P Asp Asp   P R Asp P Asp   F   L C

Consonant and vowel units
n wǝ k l u k m a l t a l l w l   b ɔ ʔ b ɔ ʔ t a ʔ ʔ a r m a ʔ ʔ a r

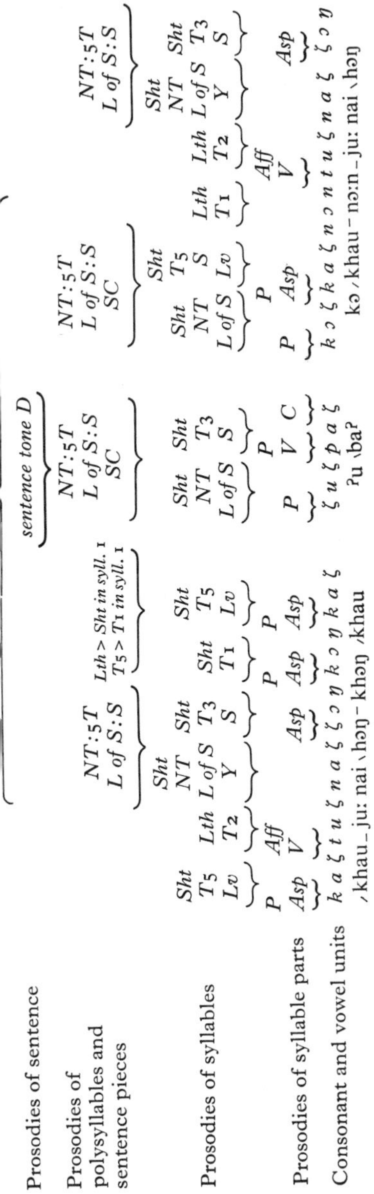

		sentence tone D		

Prosodies of sentence

Prosodies of polysyllables and sentence pieces

$$NT:5T$$
$$L\ of\ S:S$$

$\begin{Bmatrix}Lth > Sht\ in\ syll.\ 1\\ T5 > T1\ in\ syll.\ 1\end{Bmatrix}$

$$NT:5T$$
$$L\ of\ S:S$$
$$SC$$

$$NT:5T$$
$$L\ of\ S:S$$
$$SC$$

$$NT:5T$$
$$L\ of\ S:S$$

Prosodies of syllables

Sht / $T5$ / Lv — Lth / $T2$ / Y — NT / $L\ of\ S$ — Sht / $T3$ / S — Sht / $T5$ / Lv — Sht / $T1$ / Lv — Sht / $T5$ / Lv

Sht / NT / $L\ of\ S$ — Sht / $T3$ / S — Sht / NT / $L\ of\ S$ — Sht / $T5$ / S — Lth / $T1$ / Lv — Lth / $T2$ / Y — Sht / NT / Y — Sht / $T3$ / S

Prosodies of syllable parts

P — Asp / Aff / V — Asp / P — Asp / P — P / V / C — P / Asp — P / Asp — P / Aff / V — Asp

Consonant and vowel units

kaʒtuʒnaʒɔŋkɔŋkaʒ

ˌkhau‿ju: nai ˎhɔŋ‿ˎkhɔŋ‿ˎkhau

ʒuʒpaʒ

ʔu ˎbaʔ

kɔˎkaʒncntuʒnaʒ ʒɔŋ

kɔ ˎkhau‿nɔ:n‿ju: nai ˎhɔŋ

Fig 5

Daniel Jones

The 'word' as a phonetic entity

In *Le Maître Phonétique* April 1930, *p* 24, Passy remarked 'il est bien entendu, n'est-ce pas, que l'espace blanc laissé entre les mots n'a pas de valeur phonétique'. Bloomfield in the same number (*p* 28) seemed to take it for granted that 'words' are not phonetic entities. The object of Bloomfield's article was, however, to show that 'words' and even some suffixes[1] should be treated as entities for the purpose of the definition of a phoneme.

Bloomfield's view on this latter subject is, I believe, sound. But I would go further, and say that a 'word' *is* a phonetic entity – that the blank spaces between written words do have phonetic significance. Passy himself has given instances of this: 'dans un parler tant soit peu lent, on distinguera *trois petites roues* (trwa ptit'ru) et *trois petits trous* (trwa pti'tru)' (*Sons du Français, p* 61), 'l'anglais peut faire la différence entre *an aim* (ən'eim) et *a name* (ə'neim)' (*Petite Phonétique Comparée, p* 46).

In the case of trwa ptit ru and trwa pti tru the difference is mainly one of sound formation, consequent no doubt upon the point of incidence of the stress. In pətit ru the final t of pətit is weak and the r is fully voiced; in pəti tru the t is strong and r is partially or completely voiceless. A similar difference between the t sounds may be observed in comparing partu with n ɛ̃pɔrt u; it seems that the t in partu is strong and with some French speakers slightly aspirated, while the t of n ɛ̃pɔrt u is weak and never aspirated.

When we compare the English ən eim with ə neim, we find no appreciable difference of sound-quality; the distinction is made almost entirely by means of stress. Word-divisions involving differences of sound are, however, also found in English quite frequently. An excellent

First published in *Le Maître Phonétique*, 3rd series, No 36: 60–65, 1931.

example suggested by Miss E. Quick is seen in the expressions *blacked eye* (blækt ai), *black tie* (blæk tai); in the second of these the t is strong and aspirated, but in the first it is weak and unaspirated – with the result that blækt ai is often almost indistinguishable from *black die* (blæk dai).

It will be found that the phonetic value of word-division varies considerably. Sometimes, as we have seen, it has relation merely to the incidence of the stress; sometimes differences of sound are involved; very often word-division determines the length of sounds, and probably in some cases it is a determining factor in intonation.

The following are some examples from English illustrating the above points.

1. Incidence of stress. The differences in these cases are often barely audible.

ən 'eim (an aim)	ə 'neim (a name)
'siː ðəm 'iːt (see them eat)	'siː ðə 'miːt (see the meat)
'geim 'eit (game 8)	'gei 'meit (gay mate)
ai l 'eid (I'll aid)	ai 'leid (I laid)

2. Differences of sound without appreciable differences of length.

(a) Weaker s in first column, stronger s in second column.

'ðæt s 'tʌf (that's tough)	'ðæt 'stʌf (that stuff)
its 'nouz (its nose)	it 'snouz (it snows)
'wits 'end (wits' end)	'wit 'sʌndi (Whit Sunday)
'ðæt s 'ink (that's ink)	'ðæt 'sink (that sink)

(b) Flapped r in first column, fricative r in second column.[2]

'ouvər-'ɔː (overawe)	'ouvə-'rɔːt (over-wrought)
ouvər 'iːtʃ (over each)	'ouvə'riːtʃ (overreach)
'fɔːr 'eisiz (four aces)	fɔː 'reisiz (four races)

(c) Unaspirated consonant in first column, aspirated consonant in second column.

'mist 'eit (missed eight)	'mis 'teit (Miss Tate)
'wəːst 'ækt (worst act)	'wəːs 'tækt (worse tact)
'dʒʌst 'eibl (just able)	'tʃes teibl (chess table)
'drest 'ai (dressed eye)	'dres 'tai (dress tie)

See also 3 (c), where length is also involved.

(d) Fully voiced consonant in first column, partially or completely voiceless consonant in second column.

'ʌp 'leit (up late)	ə'pleit (a plate)
ðei 'tɔːkt 'ræʃli (they talked rashly)	ðei 'tɔːk 'træʃ
	(they talk trash)

ðei 'laikt 'ruːθ (they liked Ruth)

ðei 'laik 'truːθ
(they like truth)

'signit-riŋ (signet-ring)

'simitri (symmetry)

ə bit 'reizd (a bit raised)

bi'treiz (betrays)

ʌp-'reiz (upraise)

ə'preiz (appraise)

hiː 'sed ðət 'rein wəz kʌmiŋ
(he said that rain was coming)

hiː 'sed ðə 'trein wəz kʌmiŋ
(he said the train was
coming)

ət 'wil (at will)

ə 'twil (a twill)

ət 'juːtə (at Utah)

ə 'tjuːtə (a tutor)

ðei 'laikt 'juːnis (they liked Eunice)

ðei 'laik 'tjuːnis
(they like Tunis)

See also 3(d), where length is also involved.

3. Differences in length.

(a) Without appreciable difference of sound. Vowel or liquid consonant in first column shorter than the corresponding sound in
second column.

'siːsiŋ (ceasing)

'siː-sik (sea-sick)

'tiːpət (tea-pot)[3]

'siː-pɔːt (sea-port)

'biːstiŋz (beestings)

'biːstiŋz (bee-stings)

'heisti (hasty)

'hei-stæk (haystack)

('kiːp jɔː) 'feis kuːl (face cool)

'dei skuːl (day school)

ðə 'kauslips (the cowslips)

ðə 'kau slips (the cow slips)

'ɔːstriə (Austria)

'ɔː-strʌk (awe-struck)

'hɔːs-trʌk (horse-truck)

'hɔːs-treinə (horse-trainer)

'tiː-streinə (tea-strainer)

'nais 'triːt (nice treat)

'bai-striːt (by-street)

ə 'nais 'trein (a nice train)

ən 'ai-strein
(an eye-strain)

'meltiŋ (melting)

'bel-tauə (bell-tower)

'ɔːltə'geðə (altogether)

'ɔːl tə'geðə (all together)

'selfiʃ (selfish)

'ʃel-fiʃ (shell-fish)

'instənt (instant)

'in-step (instep)

'wulfiʃ (wolfish)

'bul-fintʃ (bull-finch)

'mænsfiːld (Mansfield)

'mæn-slɔːtə
(man-slaughter)

(b) Without appreciable difference of sound. n or l rendered syllabic by
length in first column.

'iːtn 'ɔːt (eaten ought)

'iːt 'nɔːt (eat nought)

'kʌpl it (couple it)

'kʌplit (couplet)

'aidl 'eid (idle aid)

ai d 'leid (I'd laid)

(c) Combined with difference in aspiration. Unaspirated consonant in first column, aspirated consonant in second column. Vowel or liquid consonant in first column shorter than the corresponding sound in second column.

'meik 'il (make ill)	'mei 'kil (may kill)
'meik 'ɔːl (make all)	'mei 'kɔːl (may call)
'fɔːk 'ʌp (fork up)	'fɔː 'kʌps (four cups)
'ʃɔːt 'auə (short hour)	'ʃɔː 'tauə (shore tower)
'greit 'ai (great eye)	'grei 'tai (grey tie)
'brait-aid (bright-eyed)	'hai 'taid (high tide)
'liŋk 'ʌp (link up)	'kiŋ-kʌp (king-cup)
'boult 'ʌp (bolt up)	'roul 'tɔp (roll top)

(d) Combined with difference in voicing. Fully voiced l, r, or w in first column, partially or completely voiceless l, r, or w in second column.

'diːp 'leid (deep laid)	'riː-'pleid (replayed)
'mait 'rein (might rain)	'mai 'trein (my train)
'rait 'riːzn (right reason)	'hai 'triːzn (high treason)
'greit 'raut (great rout)	'grei 'traut (grey trout)
'fɔːst-'reit	('put jɔː) 'fɔː streit
(first-rate)	(fur straight)
'ouk-wud (Oakwood)	'krou-kwil (crow-quill)
'laik 'waiət (like Wyatt)	'lai 'kwaiət (lie quiet)

(e) Affricate in first column, sequence of corresponding sounds in second column. Each sound of the sequence is longer than the corresponding element of the affricate. (In the first two examples there is also a difference in the length of the preceding vowel.)

'wai 'tʃuːz (why choose?)	'wait 'ʃuːz (white shoes)
'tuː 'tʃɔps (two chops)	'buːt ʃɔps (boot shops)
'mitʃəl (Mitchell)	'nʌt-ʃel (nut-shell)
ai 'dred (I dread)	aid 'red (I'd read)
wiː 'drest (we dressed)	wiːd 'rest (we'd rest)

In German, two notable features of pronunciation are indicated by word-division, namely the use of c as an initial and the use of the glottal stop. As Bloomfield pointed out, the suffix -çən should be treated as a separate 'word', and as a result the sound ç is to be regarded as a member of the x- phoneme. (In broad transcription when x and ç are represented by the single letter x, the suffix -çən (written -xən) must sometimes be hyphened off to show that the consonant is 'initial'; *Frauchen, Kuhchen* will thus be written frau-xən, kuː-xən – while *rauchen, Kuchen* will be written rauxən, kuːxən. In most cases it would not be necessary to insert the hyphen.)

It seems that in cases like these there is a difference of vowel-length in addition to the difference of consonant-sound, the au of frauçən being apparently somewhat longer than that of rauxən.

As to the glottal stop, it need not be considered as belonging to any phoneme at all in German. It is merely an indication of word-beginning, and its presence can be taken for granted without writing it, if the word-division is shown. In the case of compounds, this can be done by hyphens or by stress-marks. Thus *Verein*, *Spiegel-ei* can be written in broad transcription fɛr-ain, ʃpiːgəl-ai or fɛr'ain, ʃpiːgəl'ai, while *herein*, *Ziegelei*, would be written hɛrain, tsiːgəlai or hɛ'rain, 'tsiːgə'lai. Here again, it would rarely be essential to insert the hyphen.

In German, cases are found similar to the English examples 2(*d*) (compare unt rəyə, untrəyə, fraŋk-raiç, riŋ-krɑːgən), but it is doubtful if German has anything comparable to the other English examples.

The extent to which word-division has phonetic significance appears then to vary considerably with different languages. Distinctions such as those mentioned in this article are fairly common in English; they are presumably less common in German, and still less common in French; possibly they are non-existent in Italian and Spanish. Could any members familiar with these and other languages give us their views on the subject? It would be particularly interesting to know whether phenomena of the kind here referred to are any guide to the problem of word-division in languages hitherto unwritten.

Notes

[1] To which may be added prefixes.

[2] This is my pronunciation. With those who do not use a flapped r the difference is one of incidence of stress.

[3] 'tiːpət and 'tiːspuːn are apparently not thought of as compounds; I don't think they are ever pronounced 'tiː-pət, 'tiː-spuːn.

Daniel Jones

Chronemes and tonemes
[a contribution to the study of the theory of phonemes]

When[1] one surveys the work that has been done since the idea of the phoneme first began to take shape – that is to say during a period of more than 70 years – a striking fact emerges, namely that we find no commonly accepted definition of what a phoneme is. Possibly it is indefinable like the fundamental concepts of other sciences (*eg* numbers in mathematics, consciousness in psychology, matter in chemistry). But whether it is definable or not, it is worth noting that three quite different methods of definition have been attempted. Some (including Baudouin de Courtenay, the originator of the term) have regarded it as a *mentalistic* conception: they suggest that phonemes are abstract sounds which one aims at producing, but which emerge in actual speech as a number of differing concrete sounds depending upon the phonetic environment. Others have regarded it as a *physical* conception: they express the view that a phoneme is a family of sounds, each of which is appropriate to one or more phonetic contexts, and is unpronounceable in other contexts (in a particular language). Others again maintain that phonemes are *phonological* conceptions ('phonological' in the sense attributed to the term by the Prague School): those features of speech which serve to distinguish one word from another, or 'utilizable semantic counters' as some have called them.

Those who have favoured definitions of the first and second types appear to have confined their investigations chiefly to sound-*qualities* (timbres) and their determination by neighbouring sounds in words. They have to a certain extent taken into consideration the other 'sound-attributes', *duration* (length), *stress* (force of utterance of a syllable), and *intonation* (voice-pitch), but, if I am not mistaken, they have not applied the term 'phoneme' to these attributes: they have, I believe, restricted

First published in *Acta Linguistica*, Vol IV, Fasc 1: 1–10, 1944.

the term 'phoneme' to sound-qualities (timbres). Some of them refer to other attributes as 'prosodic' features of speech.

But those, or some of those, who favour the third type of definition of the phoneme naturally put duration, stress and intonation on the same footing as quality, since there are many languages in which words are distinguished by these features. Professor Bloomfield of Yale, in particular, does this; he applies the term 'phoneme' to duration, stress and intonation as well as to quality.[2]

Personally I am one of those who feel drawn towards the original mentalistic conception of the phoneme, but as I have found certain difficulties in working with it in practice, I am at present adopting the second type of definition (if it can be so called) of the phoneme. I find it convenient to restrict the use of the term to sound-*qualities*, and to consider each phoneme as a family of sounds, each member of which is used in particular phonetic environments. Members of phonemes are mutually exclusive in regard to their environments: one never occurs in the same phonetic setting as another. For instance in French the k of ki does not occur before o, nor does the k of ko occur before i; the voiceless l occurs in French finally but not initially; in Southern English the l phoneme comprises a 'dark' variety used finally and before consonants and 'clearer' varieties used before vowels; the a phoneme of Russian comprises 'front', 'back', 'middle' and 'obscure' varieties, the use of each variety being determined by the nature of the adjoining sounds (whether they are 'hard' or 'soft' consonants, strongly or weakly stressed, etc). Each of these families of sounds counts for linguistic purposes as if it were a single sound, or at least a single entity of some sort – the thing we call a phoneme.

Further, I find it convenient to treat duration, stress and intonation separately from timbre and not to call them phonemes. There is a special reason for this, and it is this reason which forms the subject of this article.

The reason may be explained by an examination of the way in which *duration* (to take this attribute first) is employed in languages which use it for differentiating words. In each language of this type many degrees of length are to be found. If words are distinguished, say, by long and short vowels, we find that the long vowels are not always of exactly the same degree of length, but that the lengths vary according to circumstances. Similarly the lengths of the short vowels are not always exactly the same. In such languages it is the *relative* lengths of vowels which are always preserved, the *absolute* lengths being conditioned by the nature of adjoining sounds, by the position the syllable occupies in the word, by the degree of stress of the syllable, or by other features of the phonetic context.

We find in fact that various different lengths count for linguistic purposes as if they were the same length, in the same sort of way as we find that various timbres have to count as if they were one (the phoneme). Put otherwise, different degrees of length have to be grouped together into families (generally only two families 'long' and 'short') in the same sort of way that different sound-qualities have to be grouped together into the families that are called phonemes (regarding the phoneme in the second of the ways mentioned above).

Chronemes

We need a terminology to express this. I have suggested therefore adopting the term *chrone* to denote any particular degree of length, and the term *chroneme* to denote a set of lengths which count as if they were one and the same. In this way we should have chrones and chronemes parallel to phones (sound-qualities) and phonemes.

A few examples are given below in illustration. It must be observed in the first place that the most striking examples are to be found in languages such as British English, in which distinctive lengths are linked with certain quality differences. In normal Southern English there are a very large number of chrones (absolute lengths) applicable to vowels, but it is easily seen that these are reducible to two chronemes: long and short. These two are associated with differences of vowel-quality. For instance when the long chroneme is applied to the i-phoneme, a closer variety of i is used; when the short chroneme is applied to it, an opener i is used. But, as has often been pointed out, each of these chronemes comprises several chrones depending upon the nature of the sound following. Thus in the case of the long chroneme, the actual lengths of the vowel in *bead, bean* and *beat* are easily heard to be different – that in *bead* being the longest, that in *bean* being less long, and that in *beat* being still less long. The lengths of the vowels in all these words are, however, recognized as 'long', *ie* belonging to the long chroneme. The same kind of thing applies to vowels having the short chroneme, for instance *bid, bin, bit, rod, Ron, rot.* The vowel in *bid* is short, but that in *bin* is shorter, and that in *bit* still shorter. The vowels of such words have often been measured experimentally. They were measured by E. A. Meyer nearly 50 years ago: see his *Englische Lautdauer*, 1903. I measured these words containing [iː] and [i] in 1917 (see Proceedings of the Royal Institution, 1919, *pp* 8–18), and my colleague D. B. Fry measured them again in 1939: these later measurements will be given in my forthcoming book on *The Phoneme, its Nature and Use.* The experimental measurements corroborate the rough estimates of vowel length that we make by aural perception.

In Southern English the lengths of 'long' vowels in strongly stressed syllables depend not only on the type of sound following but also to a large extent on the number of weakly stressed syllables following them. The long [iː], for instance, is very long in words like *me* or *mead* when they are said by themselves. But the same vowel is not nearly so long in *immediate* [i'miːdjət], and it is still less long in *immediately* [i'miːdjətli]. The same applies to *muse* [mjuːz], *music* ['mjuːzik], *musical* ['mjuːzikl], *morn, morning*, and so on. The principle also applies to the short chroneme, though it is of course less noticeable: compare *wed, wedding, leg, legacy, rob, robber, robbery*.

The same thing may be noticed in sentences. *Days* said by itself has a very long [ei].[3] In the expression *for days on end* the [ei] is less long, and in *the days of the week* it is still less long.

It is easy to see why this is. There is a tendency in English to make the strong stresses follow each other as nearly as possible at equal intervals of time. Consequently when there is a sequence consisting of a strongly stressed syllable followed by one or more weakly stressed syllables, English speakers instinctively try to cram this sequence into the same space of time as a single strongly stressed syllable. For instance when we count, *one, two, three* . . . and *thirteen, fourteen, fifteen* . . ., our rhythm remains approximately the same. The [oː] of *fourteen* is therefore necessarily much shorter than that of *four*, and so on. But it is still a 'long' [oː]; the short chroneme in such a position would be shorter still.

Yet another factor determining the absolute length of a vowel is the degree of its stress. In English when a vowel with the long chroneme is in a weakly stressed position immediately preceding a strongly stressed syllable, its length is noticeably less than what it would be if the syllable were said by itself. The word *tube* [tjuːb], for instance, has a very long [uː], but the [uː] in *tuberculous* [tjuːˈbɔːkjuləs] is less long. Similarly with the [iː] in *economy* [iːˈkonəmi] or *aesthetic* [iːsˈθetik],[4] the [ou] in *rotation* [rouˈteiʃn] and the [ai] in *identity* [aiˈdentiti].

The idea of the chroneme may apply to consonants as well as to vowels. Its application to consonants may be illustrated from Italian. As is well known, the Italian language contains long and short consonants: *fatto* has a [t] with the long chroneme, *fato* has a [t] with the short chroneme. That is clear enough. But there are situations where [t] has intermediate length – after [n] for instance, as in *conto* ['konto], *tanto*. These words are written in ordinary spelling with a single *t*, but the pronunciation is not ['kon-to], ['tan-to], but something approaching ['kontto], ['tantto]. These lengths must obviously be considered as belonging to one of the two chronemes. If these *t*'s have the short chroneme, as is suggested by the spelling, they are rather long members of it. (Personally I am disposed to think they should be regarded as having the long chroneme, since they are nearly if not quite as long as the [tt] of *fatto*.)

In Estonian there are three chronemes applicable to both vowels and consonants. [jama] (*jama*, nonsense), [jaːma] (*jaama*, of the station), [jaːːma] (written also *jaama*, to the station); [lina] (*lina*, flax, sheet), [linna] (*linna*, of the town), [linnna] (written also *linna*, to the town). In such a language as this there is not likely to be much in the way of variations of chrone within the chroneme. But Miss L. Krass in her thesis on *The Phonetics of Estonian* (for the London MA, 1944)[5] has called attention to some cases in which the extra long chroneme is not quite so long as usual.

The subject of variations of chrone within the chroneme is one that merits further investigation, particularly in languages like Italian and Japanese or Czech (in the case of the vowel a) where word distinctions are made by length without any accompanying differences of quality. Enough has, however, been said to show what I mean by the idea of the chroneme – a set of different lengths which for linguistic purposes have to be counted as if they were the same – and why it seems to me in consequence that significant length had better not be called a phoneme but is better treated as a separate and independent feature of speech with a special terminology to denote it.

Tonemes

Analogous considerations frequently apply to 'tones' (voice-pitches) in languages which employ tones for distinguishing one word from another. In such languages the exact values of the tones are very often dependent upon the nature of tones on syllables preceding and following. Sometimes too their values are affected by the position which the syllable occupies in the sentence. For instance, a particular mid-level pitch might count as being a high tone if the preceding and following tones were low, or it might count as a low tone if the tones on each side of it were high.

The following is an example of the grouping of tones. In the Cantonese dialect of Chinese (as spoken by a native Chinese with whom I worked for some time) the word [ˋto] (much) has what is commonly called the first tone. Its normal value is what we should call 'high-falling':[6] if this word is said by itself, it has a pitch which may be represented graphically thus [\]. If, however, the word is immediately followed by another word having the same tone, the value of the tone is high but there is no perceptible fall, at any rate in quick speech. [ˋtoˋto] (very much) has an intonation which would be represented graphically thus [‾\]. Similarly [ˋsin] [\] (previously) but [ˋsinˋsaŋ] (previously born = Mr) [‾\]. These two different tones count as if they were the same. We must accordingly presuppose that there is such a thing as a *toneme*, in the same sort of way as two phones (sounds) can be members of one phoneme.

The Pekingese expression corresponding to this last is [‾ʃien ‾ʃeŋ],[7] both words having the first Pekingese tone. In actual speech the second word is said with a much lower pitch than the first, thus [-]: for example ₌li ‾ʃien ‾ʃeŋ (Mr Li). In this language a strong stress is apparently put on the first syllable, and the lower tone of the second is conditioned by the fact that it has weaker stress.

Good examples illustrating the toneme principle are found in the Tswana language of South Africa. The following words illustrate the chief tonal characteristics of the language. The tones indicated here are those which the words have when said in isolation. They are shown by a 'narrow' system of tone-marking: ‾ high-level, ˋ high-falling, ˎ mid-falling, _ low-level, + lowered high-level; unmarked syllables have mid-level tone.

tʃhǫlǫ (dishing up food), tʃhòlǫ (act of offering hospitality), tʃhòlɔ́ (hard fat, suet)
ņtsi̱ (a fly), ǹtsi̱ (many)
ɲènà (ear-ring), ɲ ̣ènà (you people)
sehùdi (wild duck), sehùdi̱ (man who shoots very straight), sehųdi̱ (animal that eats grass)
tshēkìʃɔ́ (purification), tsheki̱ʃǫ (legal prosecution)
modirèdi̱ (servant, pastor), modirẹdi̱ (person who cuts up meat)
moxōlòdi (deliverer, Saviour), moxolǫdi̱ (blue crane)

In connected speech two tones, the high-level and the mid-level, are much more frequent than any others; most of the other tones are confined to final and penultimate syllables of sentences. For instance in the saying xō lēsiwa bō tholoxīleņ (people should leave that[8] which is spilt) there are four high-level tones and four mid-level tones; only the two last syllables have other tones, mid-falling and low-level.

With few exceptions the tones of final and penultimate syllables are never the same as the ordinary high and mid tones of preceding parts of the sentence. If a Bechuana says 'I am searching' he pronounces ke a bątlạ, but if he says 'I am searching for some meat' he pronounces ke batla nạmạ. In the first of these cases batla (searching) has a mid-falling tone on the first syllable and a low-level tone on the last, but in the second case the same word has two mid-level tones; in this latter example it is the final word nama which is pronounced in the way batla was in the previous sentence. Mid-level tones in fact occur in final or penultimate syllables in Tswana statements; these other tones replace them in such situations. And, what is more, these other tones never occur in any other situations except these. So these three different tones – the mid-level, the mid-falling, and the low-level – count (from the linguistic and phonological point of view) as if they were one and the same. I submit that this treatment of tones is parallel to the treatment of phones (sound-qualities) in different phonetic contexts: three tones have to be grouped together into a single toneme.

The case I have just mentioned concerns 'variants' of the mid or low tone (whichever we like to call it). In Tswana the high tone also has 'variants' in the same sort of way. For instance when words like mosī (smoke) or taū (lion) begin a sentence they have a mid-level tone on the first syllable and high-level on the second, as here marked. But when they end a statement, the tones are much lower and the first one has a fall: mǫsi tạ̀ù [ˇ]. Similarly the words which would appear at the beginning or in the middle of a sentence as tsālā (friend), kxōpē (obstacle) would be pronounced tsàlâ, kxòpê, with [ˋ-], at the end of a statement. Thus the 'lowered high-level' tone, the 'high falling to low' and the 'high falling to lowered high' are variants of the 'high-level' conditioned by the position of the word in the sentence and by the nature of the adjoining tone: they all belong to a single toneme, and a single tone-mark (with conventions) suffices to indicate them in writing.

The above examples will, I think, suffice to show that we cannot do otherwise than make groupings of tones into tonemes (in 'tone' languages) in the same sort of way as sound-qualities have to be grouped into phonemes. And for this reason it does not seem practical to call tones 'phonemes'. They are, to my way of thinking, special linguistic phenomena requiring separate treatment and separate terminology.

There is one further point to which some reference may be made here, namely that there appears to be nothing, or hardly anything, in *stress* (force accent) of a comparable nature to what is applicable to timbre, duration and voice-pitch. There are, as we all know, degrees of stress, and such degrees are used for differentiating words in some languages (such as English, German, Spanish, Greek). And we can, or think we can, distinguish fairly easily three degrees of stress or even four.[9] There does not, however, appear to be any way of grouping different degrees of stress into single entities comparable to phonemes, chronemes or tonemes. Nor indeed is there any need for groupings of this kind. For stress, in all ordinary cases, works in a manner quite different from timbre, duration or voice-pitch. In ordinary stress-languages every word of two or more syllables has to have a strong stress on one of the syllables. Words are differentiated by the *location* of the strong stress: examples are English 'insʌlt, in'sʌlt, 'impɔːt, im'pɔːt; Spanish [termino] (end), [ter'mino] (I finish), [termi'no] (he finished); Greek ['poli] (city), [po'li] (much), etc. In this there is nothing to be grouped. It does not even seem possible to group secondary stress either with the strong stresses or with the weak stresses, since in most stress languages secondary stresses may have various locations – they are not as a rule determined in any way by the strong stresses.[10]

It would seem that the only kinds of stresses which might possibly be susceptible to groupings comparable to those of phones (timbres), chrones and tones, are those which are not merely strong or weak but which have a special characteristic such as crescendo or diminuendo. Such types of stress are believed to occur in Serbo-Croatian and in Somali, but even here it would be difficult to make precise observations, since in both these languages the special stresses are linked with tones. It is *possible* that in such a language as one of these when a syllable has crescendo stress and the following syllable a weak stress, the crescendo stress might be adequately suggested in speech by a stress of constant force (*ie* what might be represented graphically by – · in place of < ·), and that as long as the stress were not diminuendo (> ·) it would be understood by the hearer as being crescendo. If a constant stress would do duty for the crescendo stress in this particular sequence, the two might be grouped together as if they were one. As far as I know, however, no attempt has been made to group the stresses of these languages in this manner, and it would seem to be very difficult, if not impossible, to arrive at any conclusions on these lines, on account of the elusive character of stress when separated from other attributes.

For these reasons I submit that the only attributes of speech sounds capable of being grouped in the manner I have described are phones (which, as we all know, can and must be grouped into phonemes), chrones (which are similarly groupable into chronemes) and tones in tone languages (which have to be grouped into tonemes).

These groupings are, I believe, necessary to an understanding of the linguistic structure of languages, and they also provide the basis for establishing the simplest methods of representing languages in writing – one letter for each phoneme, an accent or other mark to show one of the chronemes, accents or other devices for showing each toneme.

Notes

[1] This article is an English adaptation of a lecture delivered in French before the *Société Genevoise de Linguistique* at Geneva on 28 September 1946.

[2] 'Chinese uses features of pitch as primary phonemes,' *Language, p* 91. 'Secondary phonemes of pitch in English,' *Language, pp* 114, 115. 'There are two phonemes of stress – strong stress and weak stress [in the Serbo-Croatian dialect of Svirće]' (G. L. Trager, a follower of Bloomfield, in *Le Maître Phonétique*, January 1940, *p* 14).

[3] The English diphthongs have the long chroneme.

[4] Most of the words containing [iː] or [uː] in this position have an alternative pronunciation with the short chroneme (combined with a different vowel quality). For instance many English people pronounce [tjuˈbəːkjuləs, iˈkonəmi, isˈθetik] – the latter with the same vowel as *estate* [isˈteit].

[5] This thesis can be consulted in the Library of the University of London.

[6] The Cantonese themselves call it [ˌphiŋ] which means literally 'level' (the corresponding tone in Pekingese *is* level, and that is presumably where the terminology comes from).

[7] More narrowly [ˉɕien ˉʃʌŋ].

[8] The use of bō showing that porridge (boxˋɔbɛ) is meant. This saying is the equivalent of our saying 'It's no good crying over spilt milk'.

[9] *Movie-auditorium* was quoted by Trager and Bloch in their article 'The Syllabic Phonemes of English' (in *Language*, Vol 17, No 3, July 1941) as a word containing four essential degrees of stress.

10 Russian may perhaps be an exception to this, since it is generally considered that every syllable immediately preceding a strong stress has a secondary stress. But even here we are up against the fact that stress is a very elusive feature of speech and is bound up (in the case of Russian) with vowel-quality. In other languages stress is almost always linked to something else, generally intonation, so that it is extremely difficult – perhaps impossible – to disentangle it from general prominence in which other attributes (timbre, length, intonation) also take part. It has in fact been shown that, when other attributes are eliminated, stress alone is not very effective as a means of distinguishing words (see N. C. Scott, 'An Experiment in Stress Perception' in *Le Maître Phonétique*, July 1939, *p* 44).

Daniel Jones

Some thoughts on the phoneme

It seems to me that the most important thought suggested by a consideration of the theory of phonemes is one of a very general nature, namely that
the fundamental concepts upon which all sciences are based are incapable of definition. Either a so-called 'definition' implies a reference
to the thing to be defined, or it has loopholes for exceptions and is therefore not a complete definition. Take for instance a case from zoology, say
a dog. We can attempt a definition of it as a four-footed mammal having
certain characteristics, but the definition is not complete. It would, I
imagine, always be possible that an animal might exist having all the
characteristics that one could put into a definition, and yet which was not
a dog, or that an animal might be found differing considerably in appearance from the dogs hitherto known but which nevertheless was undoubtedly a dog. I was once talking to Professor Otto Jespersen on this
subject, and he told me of a 'definition' of a dog which he had heard: a
four-footed mammal, etc, *which is recognized by another dog as such*. This
is conclusive proof that a particular animal is a dog, but it is no definition.
The 'definition' in the *Oxford English Dictionary* is no better: a quadru-
ped of the genus *Canis*.

One can produce different kinds of dogs to exemplify what they are,
and one can describe their appearances and habits up to a certain point.
But this is not the same thing as giving a definition.

To give another example, most, if not all, sciences are concerned in
some way or other with numbers. Yet numbers are not definable except
in terms of themselves; in other words they are not definable at all. We
think we know what the number 2 means, but there appears to be no way
of defining it without using some such word as *and* or *with* or *next* which

First published in *Transactions of the Philological Society*, 119–135, 1944.

already involves the conception of *two*. The whole of mathematics is therefore based on the unproved assumption that the number 2 exists and that people know what it means.

Here again we can give plenty of illustrations of numbers and explain what can be done with them, but that is not the same thing[1] as defining them. Similarly in physics one can give examples of colours, but they cannot be defined except in terms of themselves or in terms of numbers.

The fact that all sciences are based upon concepts or units which are undefinable, and which therefore cannot be said to form a firm foundation, does not mean that scientific studies should be abandoned. On the contrary, they should be pursued and developed in every possible way, and that for an excellent reason: such studies are part of the search for truth, part of the task which man is presumably in existence to perform. Moreover scientific studies can and do give results of value to us, results that work, results which, if we do not abuse them, are conducive to the well-being of humanity. Owing, however, to the undefinable nature of our units and the vagueness of our words (see note 1 below), it seems to me that we cannot escape from the conclusion that 'scientific proof' of a thing is not so valuable as many people consider it to be.

General considerations such as these are suggested by observations in the science of phonetics as in other sciences. We make use of terms denoting fundamental concepts such as 'words', 'speech sounds', and 'phonemes', but it is found upon examination that no unassailable definitions can be given of any of these things.[2] But, as with other sciences, we can get valuable results from phonetic science in spite of our inability to give precise definitions of these terms. Particularly valuable results of applied phonetics are the improvement of means of communication between people of different nations by speech and by writing.

Now phonemes, the subject of this paper, are certain essential units which form, or appear to us with our present limited knowledge to form, the basis of the structure of spoken languages. They are also the units that need representation when a language is written alphabetically. I believe the majority of those interested in the science of speech are in agreement so far. But beyond this we find differences of opinion concerning the exact nature of these units we call phonemes. So much so that a suggestion has been made that we might leave the question of definition at this point, and say that a phoneme is any element or family of elements of a given language which it is found advisable to represent by a single letter in writing. Such a rough and ready manner of defining the phoneme will serve practical needs up to a point, but there are certain objections to it, as I shall show later.

Although I believe phonemes to be undefinable, like the fundamental units in other sciences, it is nevertheless needful for the purposes of linguistic study to examine in some detail the nature of these elements, and if possible to produce a so-called 'definition' of the phoneme of a more precise kind than the one I have just mentioned.

Before proceeding further it is necessary to point out that the phoneme may be viewed in at least two different ways. Some authorities have looked at phonemes in what may be called a 'psychological' manner. They regard them as 'ideas' or 'mental concepts', or whatever may be the appropriate psychological term. Personally I feel drawn towards this view,[3] but I find it difficult to work with in practice. Others have taken a what may be called 'physical' view of phonemes, regarding them as families of sounds actually uttered. This way of regarding phonemes I find to give good results in practice, in spite of certain difficulties which are to be found in connection with it. A third view has been expressed by the American writer on linguistic subjects, W. Freeman Twaddell, who considers that phonemes have no real existence either 'physically' or 'mentally', but are merely 'abstractional fictitious units' – whatever that may mean.

As the 'physical' view of the phoneme leads to satisfactory practical results in my experience, I will now give you a few examples of phonemes considered in this light – for, as we have already noted, it is possible to give illustrations of fundamental units even though we cannot define them. These examples will give you a fair idea of what we are talking about. After that I will call attention to some of the difficulties encountered when we attempt to formulate a precise definition of what a phoneme is.

If one isolates the sounds of *g* in the words *goose* and *geese*, one hears them to be different, and one can feel that they have different tongue articulations: the second has a fronter articulation than the first. But from the point of view of the structure of the language the two sounds count as if they were one and the same. In the terminology I find it convenient to use they are 'members of a single phoneme'. One of the sounds is the variety appropriate in English to a following [uː], while the other is conditioned to the following [iː]. The two sounds count as if they were one, and in every ordinary phonetic transcription they would be written by the same letter. It is obviously unnecessary to complicate a transcription by using two different signs: we use one sign, and state or imply once for all that the variety of [g] used is always adapted to the vowel which follows.

The following are some further examples. In French (ordinary conversational Northern French), when words like *boucle, simple* occur with a pause after them, the sound of the *l* is voiceless [l̥]; it is a sound acoustically very different from the ordinary French [l] of *loup* or *aller*. But in spite of the wide difference of sound no French person thinks of this [l̥] otherwise than as an *l*; he probably will not notice any difference between these very different sounds unless his attention is specially called to it. If he hears the difference, he will regard the [l̥] as a slightly modified [l], a particular variety used in this special position. The two sounds [l̥] and [l] thus count in French as if they were one. In our terminology we say that they 'belong to the same phoneme'.

In Italian and some other languages our English *ng*-sound occurs, but only in specific phonetic contexts, namely before [k] and [g]; it is used in these contexts to the exclusion of [n]. Thus the *n*'s in the Italian words *banca* and *lungo* are pronounced [ŋ], and an Italian never uses an ordinary [n] in such a situation. He is not like a Russian who uses [n] before [k] and [g] as well as in other positions. The result is that an Italian whose attention has not been called to the fact is unaware that the sound of *n* before [k] and [g] is in any way different from that of any other *n*. To him these nasal consonants are one and the same, and for all linguistic purposes they count as if they were one and the same - the sounds [n] and [ŋ] are 'members of the same phoneme' in Italian. (They are not so in English or in German.)

The examples given above are of consonantal phonemes. There are likewise cases where easily distinguishable vowel sounds have to be grouped together and count linguistically as if they were one and the same. Very notable cases of this are found in Russian, where the qualities of vowels vary considerably according to whether they are next to 'hard' or 'soft' consonants. For instance the [a] of ['jabləkə] (яблоко, apple) differs noticeably from that in ['jaʃtʃek] (ящик, box). Russian shows differences of this kind better than any other European language, but examples are also to be found in French, Spanish, Danish, and to some extent English. There is, for instance, the well-known case of '[e] moyen' in French, which is undoubtedly not a separate phoneme; it, so to speak, takes the place of '[e] fermé' in non-final syllables: the two vowels of *été* are not the same, the first being the '[e] moyen', a sound intermediate between close [e] and the opener sound [ɛ]. In Danish the [a] in *Sand* [san'] (sand) is noticeably different from that in *Sang* [saŋ'] (song), a more retracted variety being used before [ŋ]. In Spanish [e] preceding [r] is opener than in other positions; for instance the first [e] in *fuerte* is opener than the [e] in *mes*. In my kind of English the [ei] of *stay* is not the same as that in *station*, though for linguistic purposes the two sounds must obviously count as if they were one – two members of one phoneme.

Examples like those quoted above give a rough idea of what a phoneme is. And you will see incidentally that different members of the same phoneme can never be used for the purpose of distinguishing words. You cannot for instance change one Italian word into another by substituting [n] for [ŋ], or distinguish French words by substituting [l̥] for [l]. Words are distinguished by phonemes and not by sounds.

Now I want to put before you a few propositions for your consideration, to which, as it seems to me, serious attention must be given before we can understand more definitely what the term 'phoneme' can mean.

Proposition 1

It is necessary to give a special restricted meaning to the expression 'a language' when speaking of the phoneme. We cannot take the term 'a language' with the signification generally given to it, which is, I suppose, some typical form of speech together with various other forms diverging from this. In my view a theory of phonemes can only be based upon the speech of one particular person. Other speakers of the same 'language' may use different sounds, they may distribute their phonemes differently, and they may even have a different number of phonemes. I will give a couple of examples to illustrate the kind of thing I mean.

1*st example:* In South-Eastern English as I speak it there is no difference in sound between *horse* and *hoarse;* I pronounce them both [hɔːs]. But in Scotland and many parts of England the words are differentiated by different vowel sounds: in Scotland [hɔrs] and [hors], in the West of England [hɔɹs] and [hoəɹs]. Whether you make this distinction or not, you are speaking the English language in the general use of the term 'language'. But in considering the nature of the phoneme these two ways of pronouncing must, in my view, be considered as belonging to two different languages. Whatever view you may take of the phoneme, you cannot get away from the fact that in these words some speakers use two different phonemes while others use only one.

2*nd example:* Here is an example from French. There are, as is well known, several shades of *a*-sound used in French. Some French speakers use two well-defined shades, a 'front' [a] and a 'back' [ɑ] for distinguishing certain words, *eg: moi* [mwa] and *mois* [mwɑ], *fois* [fwa] and *foie* [fwɑ], *la* [la] and *las* [lɑ]. Others, however, do not distinguish these or any other pairs of words by means of different varieties of a-sound. We are therefore forced to the conclusion that some Frenchmen have two *a*-phonemes and others only one.

For reasons such as these I submit that when we speak of 'a language' in discussing the nature of phonemes we must confine ourselves to the pronunciation of a particular speaker. In fact I think we should go even further, and restrict ourselves to the pronunciation of a particular person speaking in one particular style, since the pronunciation of someone talking rapidly is often different from what he would use when saying the same words slowly.

Proposition 2

This brings me to my second proposition, which is that the only kind of speech that can be reduced to phonemes at all is a *consistent* style of utterance. Many people's way of speaking is to some extent *erratic*, words being sometimes pronounced in one way and sometimes in another, apparently at random – without any assignable reason.

Erratic pronunciation may often be observed in the speech of people who have lived in different parts of a country, in different regions where the same 'language' (in its broad sense) is spoken, *eg* people of Scottish parentage who have lived for a long time in Southern England and have what is called a slight Scottish accent. They may for instance be erratic in their way of saying such a word as *coat*, giving it sometimes the pure vowel sound characteristic of Scottish speech or sometimes a more or less diphthongal sound approximating to that used in the south. Their vowel in this and similar words is unstable. Similarly they may sometimes use the Southern English short [u] in such a word as *book*, and sometimes the Scottish sound. They may sometimes roll their *r*'s before consonants and sometimes not, and so on. It would appear that erratic speech due to mixture of dialect is particularly prevalent in the USA.[4]

Erratic pronunciation also arises from a mixture of the different styles of speaking that one uses – the formal precise style, the rapid colloquial with its multitude of contractions and assimilations ('telegraphic' style in which one suppresses or slurs over everything that is not essential to intelligibility in conversation), and intermediate styles.

I submit that it is quite impossible to devise any system of phonemes that will apply to erratic pronunciation – that phonemes can only be established in a consistent form of a language such as Paul Passy's 'prononciation familière ralentie' (slow conversational style) or possibly in some kinds of formal style. Rapid conversational speech is generally erratic, and cannot be reduced to phonemes; and mixed dialect cannot be reduced to phonemes for the same reason.

The examples of phonemes already given show that the whole idea of the phoneme is to consider as a single entity two or more distinct sounds the use of which is conditioned by *phonetic environment*. We cannot, in my view, make a phoneme also include sounds which are not so conditioned, such as the sounds of a speaker who pronounces the word *coat* sometimes with a Scottish vowel and sometimes with an English one. Moreover, if one takes a 'psychological' view of the phoneme, it is evident that one cannot assume that one speaker aims at exactly the same sound as another; the phoneme can therefore only appertain to the pronunciation of a single speaker and one whose pronunciation is consistent.

If it is true that everyone's speech is erratic in some degree, we must still further limit the signification of the term 'a language', and take it to mean the speech of an imaginary 'average' person speaking consistently in a particular style.

Proposition 3

My third proposition is that a system of phonemes should as a general rule be based upon the pronunciation of single isolated words and not upon connected speech. I have to assume that you know what the word 'word' means, though as in the case of other fundamental units I believe it to be impossible to give a definition of it which is not subject to exceptions. It has often been pointed out that there are no interruptions in 'speech-chains' – that we do not pause between words except for a special purpose, *eg* to take breath, or at the ends of sense-groups. Apart from these pauses the stream of speech-sounds is continuous. Phonetic texts have been published by Sweet and others, in which the words were run together, in order to demonstrate this. But the fact that there are no pauses between words does not mean that there are never any indications of word division in continuous speech. There often are such indications.[5] My attention was first called to this fact by noticing a transcription somewhere in Sweet of the expression *well-to-do*, which he wrote ['weltə'duu], and I realized at once that the first two syllables were pronounced quite differently from the word *welter* which he would have equally transcribed ['weltə]. On examining the question further it became clear to me that not only were lengths involved, as in this case, but that connected speech may contain sounds which are not found in isolated words, and that consequently if we try to evolve a system of phonemes from connected speech we may have to admit a larger number of phonemes than in a system based on single words.

The type of difficulty we should be confronted with is illustrated by the expression *plum pie*. There is no pause after *plum*, but if for this reason the words were written together as one [plʌmpai], the writing would be ambiguous. In the absence of some written indication of word division, this sequence might be read as *plump eye*. There are two main differences in pronunciation between these two expressions. One is that the [m]'s are of different length; the other is that the second has an unaspirated [p], while in the first the [p] is aspirated, at any rate in Southern English speech. There may also be a subtle difference in the point of incidence of the stress. Accordingly, if we were to base a system of phonemes on connected speech, and if the idea of the phoneme is restricted to sound-qualities only (and not extended to include length and stress), we should find ourselves in the position of having to consider aspirated and unaspirated [p] as two separate phonemes in English.

To give another example from English, in colloquial speech we sometimes find nasalized vowels at word junctions without any adjacent nasal consonant, as in the expression [aidoũwontit] (reduced form of *I don't want it*). If this style of speech were to be taken into consideration, the nasal diphthong [oũ] would have to be regarded as a phoneme of the language. But it is clearly not advisable to regard it thus, both on the ground that the sound occurs without an adjacent nasal consonant solely in connected speech, and on the ground that the style of talking in which such a form would occur would almost certainly be erratic.

Examples can be found in foreign languages illustrating the same kind of thing. For instance the vowel and consonantal values of the French written *u*, (*ie* the sounds generally transcribed [y] and [ɥ]), belong to a single phoneme if we classify on the basis of words; for the two sounds never occur in identical situations in French words, and consequently the substitution of one sound for the other is never used as a means of distinguishing one word from another. Whether a written *u* is pronounced [y] or [ɥ] in a word is merely a matter of rule, of phonetic context.[6] If, however, phonemic grouping were to be determined by connected speech, these two sounds would have to be considered as separate phonemes, since sequences like [yi], and single consonant + [yɛ], occur at word junctions: compare [tyɛ] (*tu es*), [tɥɛ] (*tuait*), [i(l)layisi] (*il l'a eu ici*), [ilaɥisi] (*il a huit scies*), [ilapyiale] (*il a pu y aller*), [ilaɽɥi] (*il aɟɟuie*) [tyiɛ] (*tu y es*), [tɥio] (*tuyau*).

It would seem too that voiced and voiceless [r] would have to be considered as two separate phonemes in French, if connected speech were to be taken into account. For, as Paul Passy once pointed out,[7] many French people distinguish between [trwɑptitɽu] (*trois petits trous*) and [trwɑptitru] (*trois petites roues*), the latter expression being pronounced with a completely voiced [r].

Another example illustrating the kind of thing I mean is, I believe, to be found in Portuguese. Those who know that language will remember that when [l] terminates a word it has a 'dark' or velarized value [ɫ], but that an ordinary [l] of medium resonance is used when a vowel follows in the same word: for instance *mil* (a thousand) has a 'dark' [ɫ], quite different from the French [l] in *mille*, but *militar* has an ordinary [l] like the French one. These two sounds therefore belong to a single phoneme if we classify on the basis of single words. It appears, however, that in connected speech dark [ɫ] may occur when a word ending with an *l* is followed by a word beginning with a vowel. I find, for instance, the transcription [tɑɫ ĩtɹes] (for *tal interesse*) and other similar examples in Viana's *Portugais*.[8] This indicates that ordinary [l] and velarized [ɫ] would have to be regarded as separate phonemes if we made our phonemic classification of these Portuguese sounds on the basis of connected speech.

In some languages, of which German is the most noteworthy, it appears necessary to base the phonemic classification on something less than the word, and to regard certain prefixes and suffixes as separate word-like entities. The average North German speaker appears to have an unusually distinct feeling for word division, and he evidently feels too that these prefixes and suffixes are very much like separate words. It is for this reason that the glottal stop [ʔ], although of very frequent occurrence, need not be held to constitute a phoneme at all. It is simply, as Trubetzkoy pointed out,[9] a signal that there is a division between words or to show that there is a prefix. The point is illustrated by such a word as *Wohnort*, which is pronounced in North German with [ʔ] between the [n] and the [o], thus ['voːnʔort], because the second part of this compound is *Ort*; there is no such word as ['voː-nort]. Similarly *Verein* is pronounced in North German as [fɛr'ʔain] because *ver-* is one of the prefixes which North Germans apparently feel as separate from whatever follows. The prefix *her-*, however, (if it is a prefix) is one which presumably they do not feel in this way, *herein* and other similar words being pronounced without [ʔ]: [hɛ'rain], [hɛ'runter], etc.

The question whether the German *ich*-sound is to be held to be a separate phoneme from the 'back' sounds of *ch* heard in such words as *Bach* and *Buch* depends upon the word-like nature of the diminutive suffix *-chen*. If this is regarded as a 'word' or as a word-like entity, we find that [ç] and the various shades of [x] should in all probability be assigned to a single phoneme. For [ç] is then found to occur in definite phonetic contexts from which the back [x]-sounds are excluded.[10] The words ending in *-chen* include some in which this suffix is immediately preceded by a back vowel, such as *Frauchen*. This shows that if *-chen* were not considered as a sort of 'word' [x] and [ç] would have to be classed as separate phonemes: *Kuchen* ['kuːxən] and *Kuhchen* ['kuːçən] are distinguished by these consonants. It is therefore only by regarding *-chen* as a separate word that we can assign them to the same phoneme. (In writing one could show the word division by inserting a hyphen: if [x] were used to denote the phoneme, these words could be distinguished phonetically as ['kuːxən] and ['kuː-xən].)[11]

We may put the matter in another way. If we did not know where German words began and ended, we should be obliged to class [x] and [ç] as separate phonemes, since it is possible for such sequences as [-oːxryː-] and [-oːçryː-] to occur in connected speech.

So much for the proposition that the basis for any theory of phonemes is to be found in the pronunciation of single words (or word-like entities) and not in connected speech.

Proposition 4

The term 'phonetic context' should be held to comprise not only the nature of neighbouring sounds but also lengths of sounds (both of the sounds under consideration and those near by in the sequence), the stress of syllables and, in the case of tone languages, voice pitch. I mention this because Bloomfield and others in America have used a different terminology, employing the term 'phoneme' to mean anything that may serve to differentiate one word from another – a defensible terminology, but not that intended as far as I know by the originators of the phoneme theory. I find it preferable to treat length and voice pitch separately, since they too are subject to variations conditioned by phonetic context, so that parallel to the theory of 'phonemes' there are separate theories of what may be termed 'chronemes' and 'tonemes'. (There does not appear to be any analogous theory applying to stress.)

Proposition 5

Except possibly in certain very uncommon special cases it is absolutely inadmissible that a sound should belong to more than one phoneme. For instance, it will not do to say, as has been suggested to me by one colleague, that [ŋ] is generally a separate phoneme from [n] in English, but should be considered as belonging to the [n] phoneme in *ink* [iŋk]. I maintain that if these sounds belong to different phonemes in *sing* [siŋ] and *sin*, they must be held to belong to separate phonemes wherever they may occur in the language. Any other supposition appears to me to involve insuperable difficulties: one of them is that [m] might with equal right be considered to belong to the [n] phoneme in *lamp*, since such a sequence as [lanp] is impossible in English.

The possible exceptions are (1) when one phoneme overlaps another (as French [ɔ] and [œ]),[12] (2) where there is no more reason to assign a sound to one phoneme rather than to another (as Japanese [dz] in the syllable [dzu] which from the phonetic point of view may be assigned either to the [d] or to the [z] phoneme).[13]

Proposition 6

The sounds belonging to a phoneme must have some sort of fairly near relationship to each other. Thus it would be clearly undesirable, as has often been pointed out, to assign [h] and [ŋ] to the same phoneme in English on the ground that the two sounds never occur in the same phonetic context: they are too different from each other, the only feature they have in common being that they are both continuants. It is, however, apparently impossible to lay down any general rule as to what the degree of relationship must be: one has to be guided by the conditions in each particular language. It is worth while pointing out, however, that the relationship may be either acoustic or organic. Thus the different values of [h] in English are organically very distinct; they differ from each other in the same sort of way that one vowel differs from another, though acoustically the differences are hardly perceived. On the other hand the acoustic difference between the French sounds [l̥] and [l] is very considerable though the organic difference is merely a matter of making the vocal cords vibrate or leaving them apart.

The question as to what constitutes sufficient 'relationship' has, I think, to be left unanswered. We have to use common sense about it. And I submit that this admitted vagueness does not in any way invalidate the theory of phonemes or diminish its usefulness.

Bearing all these propositions in mind, we can formulate a sort of definition of a phoneme in these terms: *a family of sounds in a given language which are related in character and are used in such a way that no one member ever occurs in a word in the same phonetic context as any other member.*

This is a 'physical' definition. It is, however, important not to forget that it may be found possible, as already mentioned, to regard phonemes in quite a different light, namely on what may be called a 'psychological' basis. We might take them to be abstract sounds that one so to speak aims at producing but which in actual utterance come out as one sound in one context and another in another context. This was I believe the original idea of Baudouin de Courtenay, the first exponent of the phoneme theory. However, for the ordinary purposes for which the theory of phonemes is employed, *ie* in analysing languages, teaching their pronunciation and devising phonetic transcriptions and orthographies, I find the 'physical' conception suggested by the above definition to be of greater practical use.

Notes

1 From this expression we see very clearly the truth of L. R. Palmer's apt remark (*Introduction to Modern Linguistics*, *p* 82) that 'speech is nothing more than a series of rough hints which the hearer must interpret in order to arrive at the meaning which the speaker wishes to convey'. The words *same* and *thing* are both undefinable words. We can give synonyms for them, but we cannot define them. Yet I assume that you know what I mean when I use the expression 'the same thing'.

2 The best definition of a 'word' is, I believe, that given by L. R. Palmer (*Introduction to Modern Linguistics*, *p* 79): 'the smallest speech unit (=constantly recurring sound pattern) capable of functioning as a complete utterance.'

3 See my paper on 'Concrete and Abstract Sounds' in the *Proceedings of the Third International Congress of Phonetic Sciences*, Ghent, 1938, *p* 4.

4 For instance in *American Speech*, December 1941, *p* 291, we find that a certain speaker is recorded as pronouncing the second syllable of *America* in one place with a vowel written [æ] and in another with a vowel written [ɛт],

while the first vowel of *guarantee* is written [ɛ]; this speaker evidently uses varieties of [ɛ] and [æ] before [r] indifferently, *ie* the variants are not conditioned in any way by phonetic context. Again, according to a transcription on *p* 42 of *Phonetic Transcriptions from 'American Speech'*, edited by Jane Dorsey Zimmerman, 1939, the pronunciation of a well-known radio speaker is shown to be erratic in the sound given to stressed *er;* it is recorded in that transcript sometimes with the symbol [ɜ], sometimes with [œ] and sometimes by a special sign [ɝ] meaning a retroflexed variety of the sound denoted by [ɜ].

⁵ See my article 'The Word as a Phonetic Entity' in *Le Maître Phonétique*, October 1931, *p* 60. (Reprinted in this volume, *pp* 154–158. Eds.)

⁶ Always [y] finally and before consonants. Before vowels the rules are as follows:

   1. Always [ɥ] before [i], *eg: lui, pluie, instruit.*

   2. Always [ɥ] before other vowels if a single consonant precedes, *eg: tuer, nuage.*

   3. Always [y] before other vowels if two consonants precede, *eg: cruel, influence.*

⁷ *Sons du Français* ⁷, *p* 61.

⁸ Teubner, Leipzig.

⁹ *Grundzüge der Phonologie, p* 244.

¹⁰ The rules for the use of the two sounds are: 1. [x] only occurs at the ends of syllables, and then only when an [a], [o] or [u] sound precedes; 2. [ç] occurs in all positions other than these, namely (*a*) at the beginnings of syllables and (*b*) at the ends of syllables when a front vowel or a consonant precedes. Examples are: 1. *Bach, hoch, Buch*; 2 (*a*) *Chemie* [çeːˈmiː], *Chrysalis* [ˈçryːzaːlis], *archaisch* [arˈçaːiʃ] and all the words ending with the termination *-chen*; (*b*) *ich, tüchtig, recht, durch.*

¹¹ An exceptional word is *Wacholder* [vaxˈolder] (juniper). Our theory concerning [x] and [ç] can only be maintained on the supposition that in this word the [x] is held to terminate the first syllable in spite of the absence of glottal stop before the [o]. It is, however, said (*eg* in *The Advancement of Science*, Vol III, No 9, 1944, *p* 17) that only such hypotheses as are compatible with all the known facts are valid, and as soon as a single fact is found to be incompatible with it, the hypothesis, and maybe with it a whole theory, must be dropped. Ought we therefore to take it that the unusual form of the single German word *Wacholder* causes the collapse of the theory that [x] and [ç] may be assigned to a single phoneme, and with it the possible corollary that the whole of the theory of phonemes must fall to the ground? I think not.

¹² The retracted variety of [œ] used before [r], in such a word as *heurter* [œrte], has much the same quality as the advanced variety of [ɔ] used in such words as *note* [nɔt], *possible* [pɔsibl].

¹³ The Japanese now treat the sound as belonging to the [z] phoneme, and write it in all words with the letter *z* in their new romanic orthography. Formerly, for reasons connected with dialectal speech and the history of the language, they used to write it with *z* in some words and *d* in others.

Daniel Jones

The London school of phonetics

1 Historical note

The School of Phonetics in the University of London may be said to have
started in 1903, when Dr E. R. Edwards[1] was invited to give evening
lectures at University College on phonetics as applied to French. He
gave these courses for two sessions, but was obliged to discontinue the
work on being appointed an Inspector of Schools. At about the same time
Dr R. A. Williams, then Reader in German at University College, was
asked to lecture on general phonetics with special reference to English
and German. He did this for a few years, but his courses came to an end
in 1907 when he left London to take up the Chair of German at Dublin.[2]

It so happened that, mainly as the result of a letter of recommendation
from my teacher, Professor Paul Passy, it fell to me to revive the courses
previously conducted by Dr Edwards, and I gave my first lecture at
University College (on phonetics as applied to French) in January 1907.
In the autumn of the same year the College authorities asked me to take
over in addition the work previously done by Dr Williams. The time was
propitious. The principles of phonetics had been preached in England
by Henry Sweet, of Oxford,[3] during the preceding thirty years, and
were being popularized among school teachers by Walter Ripman.[4]
Many English school teachers were also being trained in phonetics by
Professor Wilhelm Viëtor, of the University of Marburg, by Paul Passy
at the Ecole des Hautes Etudes, Paris, and above all by that great linguist
and teacher William Tilly in his Language Institute at Marburg and
(subsequently) Berlin.[5] The result was that from the first the phonetics

First published in *Zeitschrift für Phonetik und allgemeine Sprachwissenschaft*,
Vol II, 3/4: 127–135, 1948.

courses at University College were well attended – mostly by language teachers. Phonetics began to 'catch on', and a demand soon arose for courses on the phonetics of English for foreign students and for instruction in the phonetics of languages other than English, French and German, including some non-European languages. The result was that round about 1910 I found myself involved in researches into the phonetics of Italian, Spanish, Hindustani and Cantonese; a few years later Russian, Tswana (Chwana) and Sinhalese had to be added, since favourable opportunities presented themselves for studying these. From about 1910 too it became necessary to give some attention to historical aspects of phonetics, and a start had to be made with experimental phonetics. The work in fact became far too heavy for one man to cope with. Fortunately the value of phonetics was recognized by that great and far-seeing administrator Dr (afterwards Sir) Gregory Foster, who was Provost of the College at that time, and through his encouragement and help assistance was gradually provided. At first owing to financial difficulties only part-time assistants for evening work could be appointed. There was no full-time assistant for phonetics until 1918, when Miss L. E. Armstrong became a member of the staff. Then conditions improved rapidly, with the result that by 1921 (the year in which I received the title of Professor) the Department of Phonetics reached the dimensions which it maintained until 1939, namely nine full-time assistants in addition to myself. After 1939 there was a period during which the Department was of necessity greatly reduced in staff and in output of work. However, in the autumn of 1943 it was found possible to recommence courses on a limited scale. From then onwards there has been a period of steady expansion. Applications from intending students have been very numerous during the last few years, and fortunately it has been possible to secure competent assistants to cope with the new conditions. The assistant staff now numbers eleven full time academic members, and there is in addition a technical assistant for laboratory work.

In 1926 phonetic work in the University of London was strengthened by the establishment of a Department of Phonetics in another University institution, namely the School of Oriental and African Studies. (Previously the necessary phonetic work there had been carried out by visiting teachers from the Department at University College.) The separate Department there was started by the appointment of my late colleague A. Lloyd James as lecturer. The work prospered under his direction; assistants soon became necessary, and he was promoted to a professorship in 1933. Since his death the phonetics in that institution has come under the direction of J. R. Firth, Professor of General Linguistics. The staff there now numbers six full-time academic assistants in addition to the Professor.

2 The work of the school

The work of the Department of Phonetics at University College consists of 1. Teaching and 2. Research.

1. *Teaching*

The aim is to teach students to acquire the greatest possible skill in pronouncing languages. English students are taught how to pronounce accurately French, German, Spanish, Russian and other European languages, also certain non-European languages (*eg* Hindustani, Cantonese, Tswana). Foreign learners are taught the phonetics of English with a view to enabling them to pronounce the language as nearly as possible as English people do. General Phonetic theory is also taught with special application to many languages of Europe, Asia and Africa. Much of this takes the form of discussions on such topics as the theory of phonemes, the principles to be followed in constructing phonetic transcriptions, the theory of the alphabetic representation of languages for current purposes, the nature of the syllable.

'Ear-training' (or more accurately 'cultivation of the auditory memory') constitutes a very important part of the teaching given in the Department. It is found that skill in pronunciation cannot be acquired without skill in *hearing*, *ie* skill in the correct recognition of sounds and a good memory for sound qualities, intonation and the other elements of spoken language. The student must be trained to bring to his mind correct acoustic images of the sounds he has to learn; he must not confuse one sound of the foreign language with another, nor must he identify foreign sounds with those of his mother tongue. To this end a great deal of time (one hour per week in a full course) is devoted to '*Ear training exercises*'. These exercises consist of the dictation by the teacher of invented words, which have to be written down phonetically by the students. At first and for a long period the invented words are composed entirely of sounds of the language the student is learning. For instance, if an English student is learning German, invented words like the following are dictated to him (the phonetic symbols having the values attached to them in German): bøːfoːrgəʃtriçts, laŋkʃeːçtjopf, çaimuːxənɛzilk. When the student can write words of this sort without mistake, more difficult ones are given in which German sounds are placed in situations where they would not occur in German. Words of this kind would be sɛptʃyvŋyxolb, ŋiugŋɛxtʃaːyoh.[6] Later, words are invented containing not only German sounds but also English ones and other sounds not occurring either in German or in English. Such would be miːstlə̰ːgyɔ̰ːθøːfx, ɛrŋdzvoṵpmɛi-ʒa̰l, ɣaŋguːlkɛː ɹβoçɲḭə.[7] The student has to write down all such words by means of a phonetic system such as that exemplified in the foregoing examples, in order that the teacher may know whether he has heard the dictated sounds correctly or whether he has misheard some of them. When the teacher finds a mistake, he repeats the invented word (or parts of it) a number of times, alternating the original pronunciation with the pronunciation shown by the student's transcription. By that means the student gradually familiarizes himself with the acoustic differences between the sounds he is liable to confuse with each other.

When learning a tone language students also require 'tone dictations'. 'Intonation dictations' may also be given to train students to recognize the intonation patterns of languages not possessing significant tones.

In addition to ear-training students are required to do a great deal of *mouth-training* (mouth gymnastics), to enable them to get into the way of using their vocal organs in unaccustomed foreign ways. Exercises are devised to help them to make the sounds of the foreign languages, and these exercises have in some cases to be practised for long periods (weeks or even months) when a sound proves particularly difficult to acquire. The difficult foreign vowels and consonants are practised first separately and then in various combinations. The methods of teaching foreign sounds are described in books on phonetics, and need not be explained here in any detail. It should be noted, however, that many of the methods described in books are approximate only, and require development or modification to suit particular students. The teachers have to be continually on the look-out for unexpected difficulties for which no suggestions are to be found in books; they have to be prepared to invent new exercises. For instance I find it impossible to state any infallible method for teaching the Zulu ɓ (implosive b), a sound which is exceedingly difficult for some students to learn; I have to use different methods with different students.

At appropriate places during the teaching of the sounds of a foreign language it is necessary to explain to students the usage of that language in the matter of lengths of sounds, especially vowel lengths, and the stressing of syllables. And if the course is a long one, considerable attention is given to intonation (the rise and fall of the pitch of the voice), since it is found that wrong intonations not only give a general foreign effect to the student's speech, but may affect meaning or suggest sentiments which are not intended by the speaker.

In teaching phonetics it is of course necessary to make extensive use of *phonetic transcription*. Students are required to read aloud frequently from phonetically transcribed texts, and they do written exercises every week which are corrected and commented upon by their teachers. The object of the transcriptions is to show the learner in an unmistakable way which sounds of the language are used in particular words and sentences, and the written exercises are to test their knowledge of this. The type of transcription employed depends upon the purpose of the course. When the course deals with the phonetics of a single language (as in teaching the pronunciation of English to foreign learners) I recommend the use of a 'broad' or 'phonemic' transcription such as that adopted in MacCarthy's *English Pronunciation* and other recent books. In comparative work it is sometimes advisable to narrow the transcription to some extent, *eg* by writing the English short *e*, long and short *o* and long *a* by the special symbols ɛ, ɔː, ɔ, aː; it is convenient to do this, for instance, in the courses on historical English phonetics, where comparisons have to be made between present-day pronunciation and the pronunciation of English at earlier periods of the language.

2. *Research*

Research into problems of speech may be carried out 1. by auditory analysis, 2. by laboratory experiments. Both these methods are in use in the University College Department of Phonetics.

The analysis of the phonetic structure of particular languages has been one of the main activities of the London School ever since it was inaugurated. The analysis is carried out in the main by auditory methods, the findings being from time to time checked by experimental investigations. Researches of this type are generally undertaken with pedagogical requirements in view, *ie* with the object of discovering how best to learn to pronounce the language correctly. Sometimes also such research has for its aim the provision of a good form of current spelling for the language analysed. In the course of the last 25 years, I and my colleagues have analysed over 30 languages in this manner, besides examining in greater detail particular features of languages which had already been analysed by others (*eg* the intonation).

The method as applied to languages hitherto untouched is as follows. The investigator (who must of course have a very well trained ear) asks a native helper to say words and sentences many times over. He takes these down in phonetic transcription – a very 'narrow' form to begin with, marking with minute accuracy the precise shades of sound. If it is found, or thought likely, that the language has significant 'tones', a graphic representation of voice-pitches is added. The results have to be checked and re-checked many times. To do this checking, the observer has to endeavour to reproduce himself the words and phrases which are being analysed, and to see whether his attempts satisfy his native helper or not. If they do not satisfy him, then clearly his analysis is wrong in some respect, and he must investigate the relevant sounds more closely. If the observer's reproduction does satisfy the native helper, it means that his analysis *may* be correct. (He has to explain to the native speaker that nothing is to be accepted as correct unless it sounds *exactly* like the speech of a native. Unless and until this explanation is given, they often express satisfaction with attempts which are really only approximations to the actual pronunciations.)

The phonetic analysis of a language does not end with an accurate description of the sounds and a notation of them by a 'narrow' system of transcription. It is necessary further to discover how the sounds are grouped into phonemes, and in consequence how to convert the 'narrow' transcription into a 'broad' one showing the true linguistic structure of the language – a system which not only indicates the pronunciation accurately with the minimum number of letters, but one which can also serve, if needed, as a basis for the construction of a simple orthography for the language. It is recognized that an orthography may have to differ considerably from a phonetic transcript. Accurate (though 'broad') representations of languages are indispensable to those who wish to learn to pronounce them correctly and to understand their phonetic make-up. Orthographies, being intended for current reading and writing, must satisfy the requirements of easy visual apprehension. Thus in an orthography different pronunciations of the same word are as far as possible ignored in order that each written word shall always have the same written form. For instance it would not be practicable in a reformed orthography for English to take account of the 'strong' and 'weak' forms of such words as *at, from, for*, though indications of the weak forms are essential in transcriptions designed to teach the pronunciation of the language to foreign learners. To give other examples, it would not be feasible in a phonetic orthography for Dutch, or in a romanic orthography for Hindustani, to indicate the numerous assimilations which occur at word junctions in these languages. Nor can an adequate orthography for such a language as Ganda in Central Africa take into account the numerous elisions of final vowels of words. Moreover orthographies often have to serve for many varieties of a language and must therefore often embody compromise spellings; while a phonetic transcription for language learners gives an accurate representation of one particular variety of the language and the question of compromising with other varieties does not arise. All such work is of necessity based on the theory of phonemes, a subject which has occupied my attention for over 30 years and upon which I hope to publish a book before long.[8]

Experimental Phonetics has been carried out on a modest scale since 1911 when a small laboratory fitted with apparatus similar to that used by Rousselot was installed. For many years the laboratory was used mainly giving experimental demonstrations of the mechanisms of utterance to students of other branches of phonetics, and for corroborating observations made by auditory methods. Some pieces of research work of value were also produced in the Laboratory during that period. Among them may be mentioned J. W. Jeaffreson's investigations into the mensuration of French verse,[9] researches in palatography by A. P. Rudolf,[10] an examination of the phenomenon of 'double voice' by Stephen Jones,[11] x-ray photographs of tongue positions of sounds,[12] and work with sensitive flames and their application in the teaching of speech to the deaf.

During the last few years the scope of the work of the laboratory has been greatly extended by the present Superintendent, Dr D. B. Fry, and much new apparatus has been acquired. The laboratory is at present being equipped with the electronic and photographic apparatus necessary for the examination of speech wave-forms and the analysis of the frequency complexes occurring in speech, and plans have been made for the provision of an insulated and non-reverberant room. A programme of experimental work on 'tone-deafness' is just being completed, and future plans include the investigation of the contribution of various physical factors to the intelligibility of speech sounds, of the effect of aural harmonics on the perception of sound and, particularly, of the response of the ear to low intensity signals and the pitch-intensity relationship in hearing.

Notes

[1] At that time a French master at University College School. He had been a pupil of Viëtor and Passy, and had made a name for himself in the phonetic world by his book *Etude Phonétique de la Langue Japonaise*, which gained him his doctorate of the University of Paris. He died in December 1947.

[2] Professor Williams remained in Dublin for over 25 years, and was eventually appointed to the Chair of German at Cambridge. He retired about three years ago.

[3] Died 1912.

[4] Died 1947.

[5] It was Tilly who first taught me phonetics. Readers who may be interested to know something of this great man are referred to my note on him in *Le Maître Phonétique*, October 1935.

[6] Short y denotes the sound of *ü* in *hübsch*.

[7] The underlined letters denote English sounds differing from German ones written with the same letters. They should be underlined in the students' transcriptions to show that they recognize the differences. Thus underlined a would mean the English short a (æ), and underlined l would mean the English 'dark' l. l is voiceless l.

[8] *The Phoneme, its Nature and Use*, to be published by Heffer and Sons, Cambridge, 1950.

[9] Thesis in the library in the University of London. Also a summary in the *Transactions of the Philological Society*, 1938.

[10] Mr Rudolf's palatograms have not been published. They are preserved in the Department of Phonetics, University College.

[11] See the *Proceedings of the Second International Congress of Phonetic Sciences*, London, 1935.

[12] See *Proceedings of the Royal Institution of Great Britain* 1918. Also *Le Maître Phonétique*, July–September 1929. Also 'Radiography and Pronunciation' in *The British Journal of Radiology*, Vol II, New series, No 15, March 1929.

Daniel Jones

The history and meaning of
the term 'phoneme'

1. At the request of our editor I am writing this article primarily to give some account of the origin and use of the term 'phoneme' as it has been employed in the Department of Phonetics at University College, London, during the last 40 years or so – the principle of which was passed on to me by pupils of Baudouin de Courtenay and collated with the work of Henry Sweet and Paul Passy, and made more specific in the Department itself as the result of applying the basic idea to a number of languages which had not previously been examined from this point of view. A few remarks on cognate matters are also included, and a suggestion is made for introducing a new term, which, if adopted, will go a long way towards bringing about uniformity of phonemic terminology in various countries.

2. First it must be said that the idea of the phoneme, as distinct from the formulation of the theory, is very ancient. In fact by its nature it must date back to the times when people first bethought themselves of writing down languages by an alphabet instead of using a pictorial system. For people possess what the eminent American linguistician Edward Sapir (1884–1939) called 'phonemic intuitions', which come into action as soon as they begin attempting to write their own languages alphabetically. They work with phonemic intuition as long as they are phonetically unsophisticated and as long as they remain uninfluenced by alphabetic traditions (which always grow up sooner or later). They know by a sort of instinct which differences between speech-sounds are capable of distinguishing words[1] in their own languages, and as a rule they do not notice other phonetic differences which may exist but which are not capable of dis-

First published as a supplement to *Le Maître Phonétique* in 1957, and issued as a pamphlet by the International Phonetic Association. It is also printed as an appendix to D. Jones, *The Phoneme*, 3rd edn, Heffer, Cambridge, 1967.

tinguishing words. In other terms, it is natural that in their early attempts at representing their languages by means of an alphabet men should write them phonemically.

3. The fact is well demonstrated by the system by which the Korean language is written. It is alphabetic, and was devised by the Korean king Se-Jong about the year 1450 AD. This monarch quite evidently possessed a feeling for the phonemes of the Korean language. To give but one instance, he represented the sounds p' (slightly aspirated p) and b by a single letter. He is believed to have been quite a good phonetician, and doubtless realized that the two sounds were different; but as the sounds only occur in Korean in complementary distribution (b occurring to the exclusion of p' between voiced sounds, and p' being used to the exclusion of b in other situations), they have a kind of 'sameness' to Koreans. That 'sameness' is phonemic: the two sounds belong to a single phoneme, and that is why it is proper to represent them in writing by a single letter.[2]

4. The existence of 'phonemic intuitions' was insisted upon repeatedly by Sapir. It came to his notice in the course of teaching American Indians to write their languages. He observed how they continually and naturally noted differences of sound which 'mattered' (to them) and took no account of differences that did not 'matter' (to them): to put the case in modern terminology, they recorded differences of sound which were phonemic but ignored those which were not. Hence Sapir's frequent use of such expressions as 'psychological values' of sounds, the 'inner' or 'ideal' system of a language (as contrasted with its objective system of sounds),[3] 'phonemic intuitions' and 'the psychological difference between a sound and a phoneme'.[4]

5. People's natural sense for phonemes is also observable when teaching children to spell. For instance, it does not occur to a child who speaks my kind of English that the l-sound in *leaf* ought to be written with a different letter from the l-sound in *field*. It can be shown to him (if the teacher thinks there is any point in doing so) that the sounds are not the same – one being a 'clear l' and the other a 'dark l', but we speakers of Southern English feel them to be in some way 'the same'. This feeling of 'sameness' arises from the fact that the two sounds are in complementary distribution: 'clear l' is used (to the exclusion of 'dark l') before iː and other vowels, whereas 'dark l' is used (to the exclusion of 'clear l') before consonants and finally. The two sounds belong to a single phoneme, which means that the distinction just 'doesn't matter' as far as the child learning to read is concerned.

6. Turning now to the question of formulating the theory of phonemes, it must be stated to begin with that the first linguistician to enter this field of enquiry and to point out the distinction between the 'phone' (speech-sound, Russian *zvuk*) and the 'phoneme' (Russian *fonema*) was

almost certainly Jan Baudouin de Courtenay (1845–1929).[5] He was a philologist of Polish origin who established himself in Russia, first as a privat docent at St Petersburg, then as Professor for eight years (1875–83) at Kazan, where he created his famous school of linguistics. Later he held professorships at Dorpat (1883–93), Cracow (1893–1900) and eventually St Petersburg (1901–1918) where he continued to develop his school. He spent the last years of his life in Poland. He appears to have worked out the fundamental principle of the phoneme during the 1870s. He did not, however, write much on this theme, and in fact no clear exposition of it appeared in print until 1894 when he published his *Próba Teorji alternacyj fonetycznych* (Cracow). A German version of this, *Versuch einer Theorie phonetischer Alternationen*, was published at Strassburg in 1895. His teachings, however, eventually permeated into Western Europe, and especially to England, mainly orally through his pupils.[6]

7. The idea of the phoneme was recognized independently, also in the 1870s, by the English pioneer Henry Sweet (1845–1912), though he did not employ the term 'phoneme'. His realization of the principle was shown by the distinction he drew between 'broad' and 'narrow' types of phonetic transcription – a distinction that corresponded in one fundamental aspect to what we now call 'phonemic' and 'allophonic' transcriptions.[7] As C. L. Wrenn has said: 'Sweet may virtually be regarded as a co-equal with Baudouin de Courtenay in discovering the phoneme. One cannot be sure whether Sweet or de Courtenay was the first to realize this new and most important conception, since they worked – the one in London and the other in Kazan in South Russia – in entire ignorance of each other's studies'.[8]

8. Paul Passy (1859–1940) too, though he did not employ the term 'phoneme',[9] was aware at an early period of his career of the basic principle underlying the phoneme theory. I think he came to it independently, but he probably clarified his ideas on the subject in the 1880s by studying the works of Sweet, for whom he had great respect. He is known to have had considerable correspondence with Baudouin de Courtenay from 1900 onwards, but no records of this have been preserved, as far as I know. An early reference to the phonemic principle is to be found in the first formal statement of the aims of the *International Phonetic Association* (IPA)[10] which was drafted by Passy and was agreed to by the Council in 1888. The relevant paragraph ran as follows: 'There should be a separate letter for each distinctive sound; that is, for each sound which, being used instead of another, can change the meaning of a word'.[11] He repeated the principle subsequently on many occasions. The following is a characteristic quotation: 'On a déjà inventé trop de signes pour des variétés de sons n'ayant pas de valeur distinctive; c'est une manie funeste, qui risque de nous entraîner de plus en plus loin – il n'y a pas de raison pour

s'arrêter – et qui finirait par rendre les textes phonétiques illisibles. *Ne noter dans les textes que les différences significatives:* c'est une règle d'or, dont on ne devrait jamais se départir'.[12]

9. The phoneme idea was thus known in England, and to a very limited extent in France,[13] at the time when I was first appointed to lecture on phonetics at University College, London (January 1907). But it was some time before we in England realized the full import of the concept, and in spite of Passy's exhortations still more time elapsed before the theory came to be regarded as a basic feature in the teaching of phonetics here.

10. The word 'phoneme' in the sense attributed to it by Baudouin de Courtenay was first brought to my notice by L. Ščerba (one of his pupils) in 1911, who referred to the concept in his pamphlet *Court Exposé de la Prononciation Russe* published by the IPA in that year.[14] About two years later the theory was explained to me more fully by another of Baudouin de Courtenay's followers, Tytus Benni of Warsaw. The immense importance of the theory then became very clear to me, especially in its relation to the construction of phonetic transcriptions, to the devising of alphabets for languages hitherto unwritten or unsuitably written, and in general to the practical teaching of foreign spoken languages. Consequently by about 1915 the theory began to find a regular place in the teaching given in the Department of Phonetics at University College.

11. The term 'phoneme', though known to phoneticians in England round about 1916, did not become current in books for some little while. The theory was still in the process of being clarified, and the terminology was incomplete. I used to manage at that time without employing the term. For instance, I wrote on *p* xiv of the *Sechuana Reader* by myself and S. T. Plaatje (University of London Press, 1916): 'The consonant sounds c, ɬ, ɥ, and the vowel sound ʉ are probably[15] "non-distinctive" in respect to the sounds t, l, w and u. By this we mean that the substitution of the sounds t, l, w, u, respectively, for the sounds c, ɬ, ɥ, ʉ would probably[16] never change the meaning of any word'. A year or two later I would have said that the sounds c, ɬ, ɥ, ʉ 'belong to' or 'are members of' the t, l, w, u phonemes.

12. At this point I must make mention of a decision that had to be taken about that time. The term 'phoneme' as used by Baudouin de Courtenay was a phonetic one,[17] and I have never seen any reason to consider it otherwise.[18] A comparison between his work and that of Sweet and Passy showed that this phonetic concept can be viewed in two ways, the 'psychological' and the 'physical'. Viewed 'psychologically' a phoneme is a speech-sound[19] pictured in one's mind and 'aimed at' in the process of talking. The actual concrete sound (phone) employed in any particular speech-utterance may be the pictured sound or it may be another sound having some affinity to it, its use being conditioned by some feature or features of the phonetic context. This was the view taken by Baudouin de

Courtenay and his immediate followers. Benni told me (about 1913) that they consequently recognized two kinds of phonetics: one was called by them 'psychophonetics' and related to the pictured sounds; the other was called 'physiophonetics' and related to the concrete sounds actually uttered. Corresponding to these were two types of phonetic transcription: the 'psychophonic' (representing only phonemes)[20] and the 'physiophonic' (representing sounds actually uttered).[21]

13. Viewed from the 'physical' angle a phoneme is a family of uttered sounds (segmental elements of speech) in a particular language[22] which count for practical purposes as if they were one and the same; the use of each member of the family (allophone) is conditioned by the phonetic environment, ie no one member ever occurs in the situation appropriate to another.[23] To use a modern technical term (invented, I believe, by M. Swadesh), the members of the family are in 'complementary distribution'.[24] We can see from the writings of Sweet and Passy that they would have subscribed to this view. Z. Arend, one of the followers of Baudouin de Courtenay, was also not averse to it.

14. Both these ways of regarding the phoneme were thus in existence at the time to which I am referring (round about 1916). They are not incompatible; in fact they lead to the same practical results. Together they formed the foundation upon which a complete theory of the phoneme had to be built. Since little had been done at that time towards applying the theory to any language except Russian, it fell mainly to the members of the staff of the Department of Phonetics at University College, London (because no one else in Western Europe or America seemed to be interested at that time) to start the further development of the theory with the aid of materials obtained by examining the phonetic features of a number of other languages.

15. Here I must interpolate a short explanation concerning the use of technical terms. I am of opinion, especially in view of what was said in §§ 2–5 above, that it is perfectly justifiable to take into account 'mind', 'feeling', 'impressions', 'notions', 'picturing' and other undefinable psychological terms in investigating the nature of the phoneme. I consider it justifiable too to postulate axioms (unproved assumptions).[25] Besides which, I hold that though observations capable of 'exact' measurement[26] may have their uses, it would be erroneous to place reliance on them as sole admissible criteria in the determination of phonemes.

16. When speaking or writing, all of us (including those who strive after 'exactness') make constant use of inexact, ambiguous and undefinable terms and axioms. This does not prevent our words from being very useful, and indeed indispensable, since people are endowed not only with reason but also with common sense (direct perception, intuition), and they rely to a large extent on these powers when listening or reading. We are accordingly generally able to make ourselves understood in spite of in-

exact wording and the use of undefinable terms. As L. R. Palmer puts it in his *Introduction to Modern Linguistics*,[27] *p* 82: 'speech is nothing more than a series of rough hints, which the hearer must interpret in order to arrive at the meaning which the speaker wishes to convey'.

17. For the above reasons I regard the psychological view of the phoneme as a tenable one. This is not, however, to say that the physical view is to be rejected. That view is equally tenable. In fact, when it became necessary for me to come to a decision between the two, I found it in the end impossible to escape the conclusion that the physical view of the phoneme is on the whole better suited to the needs of ordinary teaching of spoken languages and (in spite of Sapir's experiences) for those who are called upon to reduce to writing languages hitherto unwritten or to improve upon existing unsatisfactory orthographies. I find the physical view more easily comprehensible to the ordinary student of languages than any other. At the same time I do not hesitate at times to resort to psychological criteria.

18. Reverting now to the use of the word 'phoneme', I should like to put on record the fact that the first occasion on which I employed the term outside the class-room or in private conversation with my colleagues was in a lecture on *The Sechuana Language* given to the Philological Society on 4 May 1917. Unfortunately the part of that lecture dealing with the general conception of the phoneme was omitted from the *Proceedings*. It may therefore be of some historical interest, as exemplifying the state of our knowledge of the phoneme at that date, if I reproduce here the words I used on that occasion. They are copied from the lecture notes which I happen to have kept. They include words and forms of expression which were shortly afterwards found to be inadequate; these are printed here in italics, and the wordings which would have been used later are put in the notes:

It is rather difficult to say precisely what the number of speech-sounds is in Sechuana. It depends how you define a speech-sound. We know that in every language *certain so-called speech sounds vary in value to some extent according to their surroundings.*[28] (Examples: English k in *key, call*, n in *bun, month*, e in *get, well*.) But in counting up the English sounds, we do not generally count these varieties as separate sounds; we ignore such *incidental variations because they are not*[29] what is called 'significant'; the meaning of words does not in any way depend upon them.

In order to make matters clear, it will be found convenient in dealing with any language to make a distinction between 'speech-sounds' proper and what may be termed 'phonemes' or the significant *phonetic*[30] elements of speech. Speech-sounds should be considered as definite sounds incapable of variation; a phoneme might be defined as a normal sound of the language together with all its incidental variants. These two k's in English [in *key* and *call*] are different sounds *but the same phoneme*.[31]

In such languages as English and French, phonemes *do not as a rule differ greatly from speech-sounds*.[32] Incidental variations are on the whole slight. But in other languages cases may be found where very different speech-sounds *count as being*[33] the same phoneme. Russian is of course the most notable instance of this kind of language; there each vowel phoneme, for instance, has a whole set of easily distinguishable *values*[34] depending on its situation in the word or sentence. [Here followed two examples from Tswana (Sechuana): the l-phoneme, which has a member ɟ (a phone sounding between l and d) used to the exclusion of ordinary l before i and u, and the u-phoneme which has as a member a very advanced variety 'approaching French y' used exclusively when a following syllable contains i.]

19. By 1918 the terminology was straightened out, as will be seen from the short but very nearly adequate explanation of the phoneme given in §§ 4–9 of the Introduction to the *Colloquial Sinhalese Reader* written in that year by the Sinhalese phonetician, psychologist and educationist H. S. Perera and myself and published early in 1919.[35] As that book is now difficult to come by, I reproduce here the section relating to the phoneme; it is headed 'Sounds and Phonemes':[36]

4. A *speech-sound* is a sound of definite acoustic quality produced by the organs of speech. A given speech-sound is incapable of variation.

5. Most languages contain a very large number of distinguishable speech-sounds. But fortunately it is not necessary in phonetic writing to have separate symbols for each sound, owing to the fact that many of the sounds fall into groups called phonemes.

6. A *phoneme* is defined as a group of related sounds of a given language which are so used in connected speech that no one of them ever occurs in positions which any other can occupy.

7. Thus the k's in the English words *keep, call* are distinct speech-sounds but belong to the same phoneme (the English k-phoneme). This is because the first variety of k only occurs before the sound iː, and the second does not occur in that position in English. The two kinds of k can without ambiguity be written with the same letter (k) in phonetic writing. Likewise the n's in the Sinhalese words kanːdə ('hill'), kanːɖiə ('mound'), are different sounds but they belong to the same phoneme, *viz* the Sinhalese n-phoneme. The first kind of n only occurs in Sinhalese before t and d; the second only occurs before ʈ and ɖ.

8. Speech-sounds which belong to the same phoneme cannot distinguish one word from another; failure to distinguish them on the part of a foreign learner may cause him to speak with a foreign accent, but

it will not as a rule make his words unintelligible. On the other hand, if the foreign learner confuses one phoneme with another, he will confuse different words of the language.

9. It is generally only necessary in phonetic writing to have symbols for the phonemes. The use of the different sounds belonging to any given phoneme is, in most languages, determined by simple rules which can be stated once for all, and which can be taken for granted when reading phonetic texts.

20. The above explanations with a few verbal amendments to the definition (see below) hold good today, and the theory as it then stood has formed the basis of the phonetic work at University College ever since.

21. Further developments in phonetic theory followed very shortly. One of the most noteworthy was initiated by the American phonetician D. M. Beach, who came to work in the Department in 1919. He continued to study and do research work there for nearly four years, gaining a PH D for a remarkable thesis on *The Phonetics of Pekingese*.[37]

22. Beach was, I believe, the first to show that groupings analogous to those of phones into phonemes are to be found in connection with one of the 'sound attributes'.[38] One day – it was, as far as I remember, about February 1921 – he gave a lecture in the Department of Phonetics at University College, London, on the Phonetics of Pekingese, in the course of which he demonstrated that each of the four so-called 'tones' of that language had 'variants' conditioned by the tones of syllables adjoining them in connected speech, and sometimes by other factors. The word 'toneme' was coined on that occasion at my suggestion: it was readily accepted by Beach and the members of the staff of the Department at the time.[39] The purpose of the introduction of the term was to be able to express the fact that the actual 'tones' employed in the tone languages are groupable into families called 'tonemes' in the same sort of way that 'phones' are groupable into 'phonemes'.[40]

23. While Beach was still in London, he invented the terms 'tonetic' (pertaining to the tones of tone languages), 'tonetics' (the study of tones) and 'tonetician' (a person specializing in this study). He employed these terms, as well as 'toneme', in his thesis on *The Phonetics of Pekingese* (1923), and in the article mentioned in note 39. In this article he also introduced the term 'tonology' to denote 'the comparative and historical study of tones'.

24. It is noteworthy that K. L. Pike re-invented the term 'toneme' independently in the early 1940s, giving to it the same meaning as Beach had done.[41]

25. It may be added here that Beach appears to have been one of the first (if not the first) to employ the term 'prosodies' to denote what had previously been called 'sound attributes', the chief of which are length, stress

and voice-pitch. See the section headed 'Classification of Prosodical Elements' in his thesis on *The Phonetics of Pekingese*, pp 76–91.[42] Others who subsequently employed the same term in the same sense were Trubetzkoy, R. Jakobson and K. L. Pike;[43] later also J. R. Firth, who, however, used the word with extensions of meaning.[44]

26. The theory of the phoneme and the toneme had thus become established on a firm foundation in England in the early 1920s. A fairly adequate positive definition of the phoneme had been worked out on physical lines and appeared in print first in 1919, as stated above. It was repeated (with different examples) in 1923.[45] Minor improvements in the wording of the same definition, to make it more precise, were made in my paper 'On Phonemes' in *Travaux du Cercle Linguistique de Prague*, IV (1931), p 74, and in my paper 'The Theory of Phonemes and its importance in Practical Linguistics' published in the *Proceedings of the First International Congress of Phonetic Sciences*, Amsterdam, 1932, p 23,[46] and again in my book *The Phoneme, its Nature and Use*.[47] In the latter publication the definition of the phoneme, which is I think as precise as words can make it, runs as follows: '*a family of sounds in a given language which are related in character and are used in such a way that no member ever occurs in a word in the same phonetic context as any other member*'. (For the words 'in such a way . . . other member' we may substitute 'in complementary distribution', a convenient expression believed to have been invented by Morris Swadesh and first used by him in print in 1934,[48] and now widely employed by those interested in the phoneme.) The precise meanings attached to 'a language', 'phonetic context' and 'related in character' need not be repeated here; they are to be found in *The Phoneme*, §§ 28–33.

27. In more popular expositions of the phoneme idea I prefer to use the simpler description enunciated in § 13 (which means the same thing as the precise definition just given).[49] In any case, whether the phoneme is defined psychologically or physically, I adhere to Baudouin de Courtenay's statement that the term 'phoneme' is a phonetic one. In fact, since I came to the phoneme entirely through phonetics, I cannot do otherwise than regard phonemics as an essential part of phonetics. We must not overlook the facts that phonetics can neither be studied nor applied without the use of phonetic transcriptions, and adequate systems of transcription cannot be constructed without the theory of phonemes.[50]

28. Some of those who interest themselves in linguistics may feel some surprise that the above definitions contain no reference to the function of phonemes in connection with meanings. It is my considered opinion that any reference to meaning is out of place in a physical definition of the phoneme. It is incumbent on us to distinguish between what phonemes *are* and what they *do*. Phonemes are *what is stated in the definition*. *What they* do *is to distinguish words from one another*. Different sounds belonging to the same phoneme cannot do this. (See *The Phoneme*, Chap IV, §§ 48–

53.) It follows also from the physical definition that *phonemes are of necessity units of linguistic structure.*

29. Somewhere about 1940 our American colleagues improved the terminology relating to the phoneme by adopting the term 'allophone' to denote a member of a phoneme.[51] Not that there is anything the matter with the term 'member', but 'allophone' has the advantage of providing us with a corresponding adjective 'allophonic'. So we can now speak of 'allophonic transcription' (phonetic transcription in which special symbols are employed to denote allophones),[52] 'the allophonic use of ḷ in French', etc.

30. The above terminology being established in connection with the phoneme, we can now in a similar manner improve upon Beach's original terminology relating to tones by adding 'tonemic' (pertaining to tonemes, as in 'tonemic marking of tones'), 'tonemics' (the study of the grouping of tones into tonemes), 'allotones' (tones belonging to a particular toneme) and 'allotonic' (as in 'allotonic' or 'narrow' representation of tones).[53]

31. It eventually became evident that similar terminology is applicable to another of the sound attributes, namely length, and is of value in connection with languages possessing significant degrees of length. If a particular degree of length is called a 'chrone', then we find that several chrones may be groupable into a single 'chroneme' (a family consisting of two or more chrones in complementary distribution, and therefore counting as if they were the same, the differences of length being conditioned by the phonetic environment). For instance in my sort of English, where the close i (as in *bead*) may be considered to be the 'long' of the open i (as in *bid*), there are two chronemes, long and short, applicable to certain vowels. Each chroneme comprises several easily distinguishable chrones; thus the three degrees of vowel length heard in biːd (*bead*), biːn (*been*), biːt (*beat*) all belong to the long chroneme, while those in bid (*bid*), bin (*bin*), bit (*bit*) belong to the short chroneme.

32. The degrees of length belonging to a particular chroneme may be called 'allochrones'.[54] And in transcriptions we can have 'chronemic' (broad) marking of length, which has to be distinguished from 'allochronic' (narrow) marking of length. Allochronic representations of length show differences of length which are not significant.

33. Similar terminology is rarely applicable to stress, though there are often 'significant' degrees of stress. The reasons for this are set out in detail in my article 'Chronemes and Tonemes' in *Acta Linguistica* (Copenhagen), IV, No 1, dated 1944,[55] and in Chap 24 of *The Phoneme*, especially §§ 468, 469.

34. During the later 1920s impetus was given to the study of the phoneme by the group of Eastern European scholars who, on the initiative of V. Mathesius in 1926, formed themselves into the Cercle Linguistique de Prague. Foremost among them, in addition to Mathesius, were N.

Trubetzkoy (1890–1938), R. Jakobson and S. Karcewski. They were not pupils of Baudouin de Courtenay nor even pupils of his pupils, but they were of course familiar with his work. The remarkable achievements of these scholars and of others who joined them are well known, and their conclusions are to be found in the series of *Travaux du Cercle Linguistique de Prague* which commenced in 1929 and culminated in Trubetzkoy's masterly *Grundzüge der Phonologie* published in 1939 shortly after his premature death.[56]

35. The activities of the Prague School covered the whole field of linguistic theory, but the contributors were naturally obliged to devote much attention to phonemes, which when defined as explained above, cannot help constituting the chief means of distinguishing one word from another in every language, and are therefore fundamental linguistic units. Actually they did not follow Baudouin de Courtenay's description of the phoneme as a phonetic conception. They took the opposite course of treating phonemes as units of structure which were 'realizable' as speech-sounds.[57] Fortunately this change of front did not affect materially the all-important practical applications of the phoneme theory.

36. In one important respect the findings of the Prague School were in accord with the intentions of Baudouin de Courtenay and with the work that was being done in London. The term 'phoneme' as understood in the Prague School had to do solely with vowels and consonants.[58] The sound or syllable 'attributes' (length, stress, voice-pitch, etc)[59] and the 'boundary signs' (indications of syllable separation, beginnings and ends of words, etc) were treated separately in distinct categories. As Karcewski put it in *TCLP*, IV (1931), *p* 194: 'La notion de *phonème* repose sur la division de la chaîne phonique en unités *qualitativement* différentes, qui sont les oppositions de *timbre*'.[60] For the separate treatment of sound and syllable attributes and boundary signs readers are referred to the long sections on these subjects in Trubetzkoy's *Grundzüge* (*pp* 166*ff* and 241*ff*).[61]

37. In America little interest was shown in the phoneme theory during the 1920s. I have a feeling, however, that Sapir (see § 2 of this article) was on the track of it when his book *Language* appeared in 1921. He did not make use of the term 'phoneme' in that work, nor was any sort of formulation of the idea expressed there. But hints of it are to be found in his chapter on sounds (Chap 3). In 1925 the principle appeared more clearly in his article 'Sound Patterns in Language'.[62] There he spoke of 'individual variations' of sound and 'conditional variants', the latter being 'dependent on the phonetic conditions in which the fundamental sound ("point of the pattern") occurs'. By 'individual variations' he evidently meant what I should call 'members of a diaphone', and by 'conditional variants' what are now called 'members of a phoneme' or 'allophones'. By 'point of the pattern' he presumably meant what we now call the 'principal member' or 'norm' of a phoneme. He regarded these features of

speech from a psychological angle, and did not hesitate to use such expressions as 'intuitively felt phonetic systems' and 'the psychological equivalent of a single sound'.[63]

38. By 1933 it became clear from his article 'La Réalité Psychologique des Phonèmes'[64] that Sapir had then (and doubtless had had for a long time previously) a full understanding of the phoneme idea, viewed psychologically. It is probable that he worked out the theory independently, without reference to, and possibly without knowledge of, the work previously carried out in this field by Baudouin de Courtenay and his followers.[65]

39. After 1930 interest in the phoneme theory became widespread in America. It may be said to have originated with the appearance in 1933 of Leonard Bloomfield's now classical book *Language*,[66] *ie* comparatively recently when considered in relation to the whole history of the phoneme. We owe a great debt of gratitude to him and to the many American linguisticians who have followed him for their prolific work dealing in one way or another with the phoneme, and particularly for their continuous efforts to make known far and wide the difference between phonemes and speech-sounds – a distinction which is even now found difficult to grasp by many non-specialist students of languages.

40. Confusion between the two is naturally fostered by the fact that written symbols have to be used sometimes for denoting speech-sounds and sometimes for the representation of phonemes. And what has helped perhaps more than all verbal descriptions to emphasize the distinction has been the use in American publications of slant lines / / to enclose symbols denoting phonemes and sequences of phonemes – a usage which is, I am glad to say, now beginning to find its way to Europe and elsewhere. This simple and exceedingly effective device was the invention of Bernard Bloch, the editor of the journal *Language*.

41. Our American colleagues will, I am sure, pardon me if I put forward as a recommendation that in future work they should define the phoneme in a manner in keeping with the intentions of the European pioneers. By some mischance some of them have extended the meaning in a way not previously contemplated, namely by applying the term to length and other prosodic features (when significant) and even to significant features of juncture.[67] This innovation was, in my opinion, an unnecessary and unfortunate one. It appears to have originated from a terminology employed by Bloomfield, who, however, had taken the precaution of distinguishing significant prosodic features from the segmental elements previously known as phonemes by calling the former 'secondary phonemes'. Owing to the excellence of his book *Language* in other respects and to the immense influence it deservedly exerted, this terminology was soon adopted by others. These followers, however, omitted Bloomfield's im-

portant qualifying word 'secondary', and as a result the word 'phoneme' came to have different senses in Europe and America.

42. The situation is, however, remediable. What seems to me really to lie at the back of the present difference of usage has been the absence of an appropriate comprehensive term to denote 'any speech feature whatever (segmental or otherwise) which can be used for distinguishing meanings'. It is, I believe, the lack of a suitable term for this that has led many American writers to employ the unsuitable word 'phoneme' to denote it. We need an unequivocal term, and I submit that such a term should be related to 'significance' and not to 'phone'. An appropriate term is 'signeme'.[68] The use of this word will enable us to distinguish conveniently the different types of significant difference by employing the terms 'signemes of phone', 'signemes of length', 'signemes of stress', 'signemes of pitch' and 'signemes of juncture'. Then the term 'phoneme' (which would be equivalent to 'signeme of phone') can be retained for the purpose for which it was originally invented in the school of Baudouin de Courtenay and adopted by those who have based their work on his.

Notes

1 Sapir pointed out, after long experience of reducing American Indian languages to writing, that untrained native speakers generally have no difficulty in deciding what portions of connected speech constitute 'words'. See particularly his book *Language*, p 35, footnote 6.

2 The Korean language also possesses a completely unaspirated (sometimes glottalized) p and a strongly aspirated ph. These sounds belong to separate phonemes and are therefore properly written in the Korean alphabet with separate letters.

3 See Sapir, *Language* 1921, *pp* 56–58.

4 See Sapir, 'La Réalité Psychologique des Phonèmes' (in the *Journal de Psychologie*, xxx, Nos 1–4, Jan–April, 1933, *pp* 247–265). An English translation of this article is contained in the *Selected Writings of Edward Sapir*, edited by D. G. Mandelbaum, University of California Press, 1949.

5 Baudouin de Courtenay stated more than once that the word *fonema* was the invention of a student of his named Kruszewski. The formulation of the theory was, however, the work of Baudouin de Courtenay.

6 I am indebted to Dennis Ward, Head of the Department of Russian in the University of Edinburgh, for many of the above particulars. They are for the most part taken from the article on Baudouin de Courtenay in the *Bol'shaya Sovetskaya Entsiklopediya* (Large Soviet Encyclopedia), 2nd edn, 1951, Vol v, *p* 366. Ward has translated this article into English and has kindly given me a copy with permission to quote from it.

The following is his translation of the paragraph in the article which deals with Baudouin de Courtenay's work on the phoneme:

'His chief merit in world science is the construction of the theory of phonemes and phonetic alternations. He had been working out this theory from 1868, thus forestalling Western European linguistics by nearly

40 years. He starts from the position that the role of sounds "in the mechanism of a language, for the feeling of the people" does not coincide with their physical nature, and that this non-coincidence obliges one to distinguish "phonemes" from "speech-sounds"; in his theory he subordinates the phonetic side of speech to the social function of language as a means of communication and a form of thinking. He states not only the mutual relationships of phonemes, but also the ways in which they are formed historically. A radical failing of this theory, as laid down by Baudouin de Courtenay in his basic works, is the psychological concept of the phoneme; nevertheless in one of his works (*O nekotorych Otdelakh sravnitel'noi Grammatiki slovyanskikh Yazykov* [Some Branches of the Comparative Grammar of the Slavonic Languages], 1881) he showed the possibility of working out a theory of phonemes and phonetic alternations without recourse to any subjective idealistic premise.'

Some further particulars concerning the early work of Baudouin de Courtenay are to be found in Z. Arend, 'Baudouin de Courtenay and the Phoneme Idea' in *Le Maître Phonétique*, January 1934, *p* 2; J. R. Firth, 'The Word Phoneme' in *Le Maître Phonétique*, April 1934, *p* 44, and C. L. Wrenn's article on 'Henry Sweet' in the *Transactions of the Philological Society*, 1946, *p* 189 (footnote). To tell the full story (if it can be discovered at all) would require close reading of the works in Russian, Polish and German mentioned above, together with the Polish memoir of Baudouin de Courtenay by Ulaszyn (Poznań, 1934), and searching for other relevant material.

7 See Sweet's *Handbook of Phonetics*, Oxford, 1877, especially *pp* 103, 104. See also the article on 'Types of Phonetic Transcription' which forms Appendix A to the 8th edn of my *Outline of English Phonetics*, Heffer, Cambridge, 1956, especially *pp* 331, 332.

8 *Trans. Phil. Soc.*, 1946, *p* 189.

9 Except on one occasion, in *Le Maître Phonétique*, January 1931, *p* 3, when he repeated 'the golden rule of the practical phonetician' in these terms: '*n'indiquer dans les textes que les différences distinctives*, ou si l'on aime mieux *ne représenter par des lettres différentes que les phonèmes différents*.'

10 Then called *The Phonetic Teachers' Association*.

11 *The Phonetic Teacher*, August 1888.

12 *Le Maître Phonétique*, October 1925, *p* 29.

13 French philologists had for a long time previously been using the term 'phonème', but always in the sense of 'speech-sound' (synonymous with 'son' or 'son du langage'). The technical sense assigned to it by Baudouin de Courtenay was almost unknown in France (except to Passy), and remained so until André Martinet came on the scene. The word 'phonème' is believed to have been invented (independently) with the meaning of 'speech-sound' by Louis Havet, who used it in 1876, if not before. 'Speech-sound' was the only meaning given to the term in Marouzeau's *Lexique de la Terminologie Linguistique*, 1933. The 2nd and 3rd editions of this work (1943 and 1951) were improved by the addition of a paragraph referring to what was described as an English use of 'phonem' [*sic*].

F. de Saussure, the Swiss pioneer in linguistics, likewise used the term 'phonème' regularly to mean 'speech-sound'. It would seem, however, from a passage on *p* 164 of his *Cours de Linguistique Générale* (first published in 1916) that he was beginning to get an inkling of the concept of the phoneme as we know it and also of the diaphone. But his explanation was obscure and of a negative character, and he never reached the point of recognizing the existence of allophones.

14 His reference to the phoneme in that pamphlet was not made sufficiently explicit, and some confusion arose owing to two very unfortunate misprints in his sound chart. The symbols ɯ and ɑ were printed in black type (the type used to designate the phonemes) when they should have been in ordinary roman (to show that the sounds belonged to the same phonemes as i and a – facts which must have been known to Ščerba as they were to Baudouin de Courtenay; see R. Jakobson's note on *p* 102 of *Trav. Cercle Ling. de Prague*, II, 1929).

15 Further research showed that the word 'probably' should have been deleted.

16 The words 'would probably' should have been deleted.

17 It was stated by him to be so in his *Próba Teorji alternacyj fonetycznych* and in his *Versuch einer Theorie phonetischer Alternationen*.

18 The phonetic character of the phoneme was also recognized much later by the American linguistician Morris Swadesh, who wrote in 1934 'The description of the phoneme in terms of norm and deviation belongs to the science of phonetics' (*Language*, x, No. 2, *p* 117).

19 A 'linear' or 'segmental' element of speech.

20 Now called 'phonemic' or 'linguistically broad' transcription.

21 Now called 'allophonic' or 'linguistically narrow' transcription.

22 'Language' here meaning one particular and *consistent* variety of a spoken language – presumably what is meant by an 'idiolect' in modern American terminology.

23 *Eg* in English the k-sound of *call* never occurs before an i; nor does the k-sound of *king* ever occur before ɔ:.

24 Not 'free variation'. I find it necessary to postulate that a sound not belonging to a specified form of a language (idiolect) must be held to belong to another 'language' (idiolect). Free variants must, in my opinion, be treated in separate categories; they belong to what I have called 'diaphones'. See *Proceedings of the First International Congress of Phonetic Sciences*, Amsterdam, 1932, *p* 23; also the Explanations in the 1956 and subsequent editions of my *English Pronouncing Dictionary*, p. xxxv, and the 'Glossary of Phonetic Terms' in the same work, *p* 536; also Chap 27 of *The Phoneme* (published by Heffer, Cambridge; 2nd edn, 1962).

It should be noted that the *diaphone* is a much less definite concept than the *phoneme*, owing to the fact that a particular speech-sound often belongs to two or more diaphones. For instance the sound ʌu belongs to the ou diaphone in types of London English, but to the au diaphone in Scottish English.

25 H. J. Uldall's 'primitive ideas'. See his *Outline of Glossematics*, Copenhagen, 1957, *p* 36.

26 In reality there appears to be no such thing as an exact measurement. All measurements are approximate.

27 Published by Macmillan [1936 Eds].

28 *certain different though related sounds of a given language count as if they were one and the same, the use of one or another being prescribed by the phonetic context.* In more modern terminology they are said to be in 'complementary distribution' and are called 'members of the phoneme' or 'allophones'.

29 *incidental use of variant sounds, because the differences between them are not . . .*

30 *segmental* or *linear*.

31 *but they belong to the same phoneme.*

32 *do not as a rule comprise many members (allophones) and in only a few cases do they comprise members differing widely from the 'norm' (principal member).*

33 *belong to.*

34 *members (allophones).*

35 Manchester University Press.

[36] The symbols ʈ and ɖ (first proposed by the Rev J. Knowles) were employed to denote retroflex t and d, the IPA having at that time not come to a definite decision as to the mode of representing these sounds. The traditional though unsatisfactory ţ and ḑ had been used previously. The present IPA symbols (ʈand ɖ) were decided upon in 1927.

[37] This thesis has never been published. It may be consulted in the Library of the University of London.

Beach took his first degree at Harvard in 1915, majoring in chemistry. He then went to China, where he obtained an appointment as a teacher of chemistry, English and other subjects, near Peking. He soon discovered through teaching English and learning Chinese that he had talent for linguistic studies, and that in fact these studies had greater interest for him than chemistry. It was after four years in China, during which time he had attained an excellent knowledge of Pekingese, that he came to London to specialize in phonetics. In 1923 he was appointed Senior Lecturer in Phonetics in the University of Cape Town, and a few years later a professorship was conferred on him there.

[38] Now often called 'suprasegmental' or 'prosodic' features of pronunciation.

[39] The term 'toneme' was subsequently employed again by Beach in his important article 'The Science of Tonetics and its application to Bantu Languages' in *Bantu Studies*, December 1924, *pp* 75–106, and later in his book *The Phonetics of the Hottentot Language*, Heffer, Cambridge, 1938. Lilias E. Armstrong used it in the *Burmese Phonetic Reader* which she wrote in collaboration with Pe Maung Tin, University of London Press, 1925, and C. M. Doke used it in his book *The Phonetics of Zulu*, University of the Witwatersrand Press, 1926.

[40] As Beach put it in his above-mentioned article: 'The key to all tonetic transcription is the principle of the *toneme*, just as the key to all phonetic transcription is the principle of the *phoneme*'; and again on a later occasion (*The Phonetics of the Hottentot Language*, published by Heffer, Cambridge in 1938, *p* 127): 'Just as phonetic transcription depends on the phoneme-principle, so tonetic transcription must depend on the toneme-principle.'

[41] See his *Tone Languages*, University of Michigan Publications, Linguistics, 4, 1948. At the time when Pike re-invented the term 'toneme' he had apparently not seen that M. Swadesh had already used the word in his important article 'The Phonemic Principle' in *Language*, x, No 2 (1934), *p* 117.

[42] It is possible that Beach got the term 'prosodic' from Sapir who used it (in the sense of 'rhythmic') in his *Language*, *p* 187.

[43] The latter in his *Phonemic Work Sheet*, Summer Institute of Linguistics, Glendale, California, 1938.

[44] See Firth, 'Sounds and Prosodies' in *Trans. Phil. Soc.*, 1948, *pp* 127–152.

[45] In the *Pronunciation of Russian* by M. V. Trofimov and myself (Cambridge University Press, 1923). This book was prepared during 1916–17, and the manuscript was sent to the printer on 31st December, 1917. Circumstances prevailing at the time delayed its appearance until 1923.

[46] I was pleased to see that the gradual improvement in the wording of the physical definition of the phoneme between 1923 and 1932 was noticed by W. Freeman Twaddell in his monograph *On defining the Phoneme* (Linguistic Society of America, 1935). (He did not accept the definition, but propounded another, taking the view that the phoneme should be regarded as an 'abstractional fictitious unit'.)

[47] Published by Heffer, Cambridge, 1950; 2nd edn, 1962. I started writing this book in 1937. The greater part of the manuscript was ready about 1941, but the conditions prevailing at the time prevented me from completing it until

the end of 1945. It was in the printer's hands in January 1946. The necessary type-cutting, printing and proof correcting took four years.

[48] In his article 'The Phonemic Principle' in *Language*, x, No 2 (1934), *p* 123.

[49] See for instance the 'Glossary of Phonetic Terms' in my *English Pronouncing Dictionary*, 11th edn, 1956, *p* 537.

[50] I am unable to subscribe to Trubetzkoy's proposal to treat phonemics as a science on its own, quite separate from phonetics (*Grundzüge der Phonologie*, *pp* 12–17, and Cantineau's translation, *pp* 6–15), so that the phonetician is prohibited from concerning himself with meanings of words, while apparently the phonemicist need not trouble himself overmuch with the ways in which words are pronounced. Such a separation is, for me, impossible. The two subjects are, to my mind, part and parcel of a single science, which, ever since serious studies of them began, has been called 'phonetics'. There is, however, no reason why specialized books should not be written on phonemics, as there are on intonation or other branches of phonetics. K. L. Pike has written an excellent one (*Phonemics*, University of Michigan Press, 1947). Incidentally I am not sure that Pike did not go a little too far when he made the pronouncement that 'phonetics gives us our raw material; phonemics cooks it' (*Phonemics*, *p* 57).

[51] This term was invented by B. L. Whorf, probably about 1934, and was passed on by him to Morris Swadesh and others. The first use of it in print was, as far as I know, in the article by Trager and Bloch entitled 'The Syllabic Phonemes of English' in *Language*, XVII, No 3 (1941), *pp* 243–246.

[52] First suggested, I believe, by D. Abercrombie. See his article 'Phonetic Transcriptions' in *Le Maître Phonétique*, July 1953.

[53] The tone-marking in the *Sechuana Reader* by myself and Plaatje is allotonic. That in the Tswana (Sechuana) text on *p* 49 of the *Principles of the IPA*, 1949, is tonemic.

[54] I have had occasion to employ this term in my article, 'The Hyphen as a Phonetic Sign' in the *Zeitschrift für Phonetik*, IX, No 2, 1956.

[55] This article was actually written in 1946. (Reprinted in this volume, *pp* 159–167. Eds.)

[56] It was seen through the press by Jakobson. The book is now available in a French translation by J. Cantineau, *Principes de Phonologie*, Klincksieck, Paris, 1949.

[57] Easily intelligible definitions of the phoneme on this basis are difficult to formulate. See, for instance, those by Mathesius in *Trav. Cercle Ling. Prague*, I (1929), *p* 68; Jakobson in *TCLP*, II (1929), *p* 5; Trubetzkoy in his *Grundzüge*, *p* 34, and again on *p* 35 (in Cantineau's translation, bottom of *p* 37 and top of *p* 40).

[58] *ie* with what are now often called 'linear' or 'segmental' elements of speech.

[59] *ie* the 'suprasegmental' or 'prosodic' features.

[60] Karcewski's italics.

[61] In Cantineau's translation, *pp* 196 and 307.

[62] In *Language*, I, No 1, *pp* 37–51.

[63] Incidentally he made use of the term 'phoneme' on three occasions in 'Sound Patterns in Language' with the meaning 'speech-sound' in each case. He also employed a term 'phonem' (a misprint?) on *p* 45, line 11, apparently meaning a 'sound sequence'. See also § 4 of the present article.

[64] See note 4 above.

[65] Sapir is undoubtedly to be numbered among the pioneers in the field of phonemics. Since, however, in his published works he made so few and such scattered references to the phoneme idea, we are liable to underrate his services to the subject.

[66] Published by Henry Holt and Co, New York, and (in an edition specially adapted to the needs of British readers) by Allen and Unwin, London.

[67] Not all American linguisticians have done this. For instance Einar Haugen has called significant suprasegmental elements of speech 'prosodemes' (quite a good term). In the course of an article entitled 'Phoneme or Prosodeme' in *Language* XXV (1949), *pp* 278–282 he expressed the opinion that 'there would seem to be an advantage in distinguishing the prosodemes from the phonemes as thoroughly as possible'. The term 'prosodeme' is also used by S. Potter in his *Modern Linguistics*, Deutsch, London, 1957. (It had been employed before by Trubetzkoy, who, however, restricted its use to 'prominence' of syllables. *Grundzüge, p* 180.)

[68] A suggestion of Dennis Ward of the University of Edinburgh.

Peter Ladefoged
with the assistance of
M. H. Draper & D. Whitteridge
[*Department of Physiology, University of Edinburgh*]

Syllables and stress

Stressed syllables are often discussed in phonetic literature. But in these discussions there is often little attempt to explain what is meant by stress, either in acoustic terms, or in terms of the activity of the speaker. It is simply assumed that the stress of an utterance is something which can be perceived. Similarly the syllable is often regarded as a unit which can be apprehended, but is not easy to define. In this article we wish to report the results of a preliminary instrumental investigation into the connection between these perceived features of speech and the action of the speaker's breathing mechanism.

A recent account of the mechanics of respiration has been given by Campbell (1958). But in physiological laboratories the involvement of respiratory muscles in speech activity has been almost entirely neglected. From the phonetician's point of view, some research is reported in Gray and Wise (1946); and there has been some recent work at Purdue University (Hoshiko, 1957). But the American psychologist, R. H. Stetson (1951), is the only well-known investigator in this field.

It will be obvious that in the research to be described, we are much indebted to Stetson, who had an intuitive appreciation of many points which, with the means at his disposal, he was unable to substantiate. Furthermore, his shrewd insight often suggested possibilities which we might have overlooked. Stetson's main conclusions were:

1. *Every* syllable is accompanied by a 'ballistic chest pulse' produced by the action of the internal intercostal muscles.

2. In 'open syllables' (*eg: tea, spa*) the collapse of the lung is checked by an active inspiratory effort by the external intercostal muscles.

First published in *Miscellanea Phonetica*, III, 1–14, 1958, and subsequently in a revised form, in P. Ladefoged, *Three Areas of Experimental Phonetics*, Oxford University Press, London, 1967.

3. In a stressed syllable the action of the intercostal muscles is reinforced by the abdominal muscles, led by rectus abdominis.

Since we disagree with some of these conclusions, it is necessary to give a brief review of Stetson's experimental technique. Stetson obtained most of his data from three sources:

1. Kymograph recordings of movements of the body wall. In our view recordings of such movements can hardly be regarded as valid indications of the use of specific muscles. Movements of the chest wall can be brought about in different ways; and the muscles nearest to the moving point are not necessarily in active contraction at all.

2. Recordings of the air pressure in the trachea of tracheotomized subjects. These likewise do not provide direct evidence concerning the muscles which are used to regulate the variations in air pressure.

3. Recordings of the pressure of the air in the lungs as shown by variations in the pressure of an air-filled balloon in the stomach. Recordings of this kind may be used to show that speech is not articulatory activity superimposed on a steady stream of air at an even pressure; but they cannot be used as a complete proof that certain kinds of muscular activity are involved in speech.

The most satisfactory method of obtaining direct evidence concerning the muscles involved in an action is by means of the technique known as electromyography. Some of the factors involved in this technique will be explained in the next section. We need note here that Stetson also made some recordings of this kind. In the publications we have examined (which include nearly all the articles by Stetson and his co-workers listed in the bibliography in the second edition of *Motor Phonetics*) there are only two illustrations of these, one showing the syllables *pup, pup, pup* spoken at a slow rate, and the other showing the same syllable *pup* spoken at an increasing rate. Even these recordings are technically inadequate, and it seems very doubtful whether they do in fact show the activity of the muscles indicated in the legends.

As Twaddell (1953) has pointed out, Stetson's writings are full of unsignalled transitions and other hazards. In addition, for those who are unaccustomed to assessing instrumental techniques, there is the difficulty of deciding whether Stetson is making a statement based on reliable evidence, or whether he is propounding a hypothesis. Furthermore, Stetson sometimes confuses the situation by his use of terms. Thus he often states that the movements of the chest associated with the syllable are 'ballistic' (which for him implies that they are the product of a sharp contraction of the intercostal muscles which is always of the same kind), as opposed to 'controlled' (which is the term he uses when there are variations in muscular tension throughout the movement). Few phoneticians seem to be aware that this dichotomy of types of skilled movement is not used by physiologists with these implications (Begbie, 1958).

The major part of Stetson's work should be considered as a theory attempting to explain how the respiratory muscles are involved in speech, rather than an account of the observed action of these muscles. In our experiments we have been able to substantiate a number of points in this theory; and (despite the criticisms noted above) it is a pleasure to be able to record here that if it had not been for Stetson's work, it is unlikely that we would have attempted any of this research.

In our experiments the activity of the respiratory muscles during speech was studied by means of electromyography. Since this technique has not been used to any great extent in linguistic research it seems advisable to give a short account of some of the factors involved. A more extensive account is given in Buchtal (1957).

All the muscles that are under voluntary control consist of a large number of elongated cells or fibres, each of which can contract. These fibres are organized into groups, each group being connected to a specific nerve cell in the spinal cord. This combination of a nerve cell and its associated muscle fibres is known as a motor unit. Each of the muscles with which we are concerned contains many thousands of motor units.

Every time a nerve cell discharges, all the muscle fibres in that particular motor unit contract for a few hundredths of a second and then relax again. (If there are further discharges of the nerve cell before the muscle fibres have relaxed, the twitches are more or less fused; complete fusion, when impulse frequency no longer alters muscle tension, occurs only when the nerve is discharging at a frequency higher than we observed in these experiments.) Normally, when a muscle is in a state of slight tension each active group of muscle fibres is being stimulated by its appropriate nerve cell at a fairly low rate (5–10 per sec), so that it is contracted for only small parts of the time during which the tension continues. Under these conditions, the muscle as a whole will contain at any given moment a comparatively small number of contracted fibres. When the tension of the muscle has to be increased, there are generally two processes involved; firstly, each active nerve cell discharges more frequently so that its associated group of muscle fibres is more often in a state of contraction, and thus contributes more to the state of tension of the muscle as a whole; and secondly, there is an increase in the total number of groups of muscle fibres which are being stimulated. By these means the degree of activity can be controlled over a very wide range.

When the muscle fibres making up a motor unit are being stimulated an electric discharge known as an action potential is produced by the muscle cells. It is possible to record this electrical activity in the muscle in two ways. In the one method electrodes consisting of silver plates about 5 mm in diameter are placed on the skin, immediately above the muscle; in the second method a hollow needle containing an insulated central wire is inserted into the muscle. In either case the electrical potentials which occur between the surface electrodes, or between the insulated wire and the outer shaft of the needle, can be amplified and displayed on a cathode ray oscilloscope which may be photographed. *Figs* 1–4 include recordings of muscular activity in which the action potentials appear as a series of sharp spikes indicating when the muscle fibres are contracting. (In one of these figures there are also some larger waves marked E, recurring at regular intervals of approximately one second, which are due to the electrical activity of the heart; and which of course are irrelevant to the present observations.)

The size of the impulse recorded on the oscilloscope is *no* indication of the tension produced by a motor unit. In the conditions with which we are concerned each group of muscle fibres either contracts or does not contract. The size of the action potential which is recorded depends on the distance between the electrodes and the active muscle fibres. Each recorded impulse (whatever its amplitude) simply indicates the contraction of a single motor unit.

Because the fibres of a muscle are very small, the electrodes are seldom placed so that the recording shows the activity of only a single motor unit; however, even when the activity of a large number of units is shown on the recording, the individual impulses produced by a particular motor unit can often be recognized by their amplitude or by some characteristic of their shape.

The precise changes in tension in a muscle may be expressed quantitatively by considering the frequency of the contractions of a particular motor unit. In recordings such as *Fig* 3 where there are a number of impulses of the same size which all seem to be characteristic of a single motor unit, it is possible to calculate the rate at which this particular group of muscle fibres is being stimulated. This information may be represented graphically as shown in the lower part of the diagram, where the points are related to the time intervals between consecutive impulses.

The general results of observation of recordings of this type are given in the next section. But we may note here that this particular group of muscle fibres becomes active just before the first word of the phrase, and has a number of peaks of activity during the phrase, one just before the word *old*, another during the first part of the word *man*, a large peak just before *doddered*, which was the word with the major sentence stress, a fourth peak during the second part of the word *along*, and two peaks for the last word *road*, which was pronounced with a very long vowel.

Many recordings (*eg Figs* 1, 2, and 4) show the activity of a large number of motor units. In these circumstances it is difficult to assess the precise variations in the state of tension of the muscle; but it is quite possible to get an overall picture of the degree of muscular activity.

We investigated the activity of various muscles by means of electro-myography. As a result we found that the respiratory muscles which are most active during speech are the *internal intercostals*. The fibres of these muscles run between the ribs, pulling downwards when they contract so that they increase the pressure of the air in the lungs.

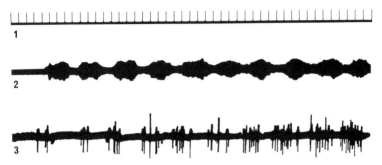

Fig 1 : Internal intercostal activity during the repetition of a single stressed
syllable recorded on a cathode ray oscilloscope. 1 Time marker,
1/10 seconds. 2 Microphone record showing the waveforms of ten
syllables. 3 Internal intercostal action potentials.

A typical pattern of activity of the internal intercostals during the pro-nunciation of a simple utterance such as the repetition of a single stressed syllable is shown in *Fig* 1. Two points are immediately obvious: firstly there is a general increase in the amount of muscular activity as the utter-ance proceeds; and secondly the muscular activity occurs mainly in bursts which immediately precede each syllable. The first of these features – the general increase in muscular activity – can be correlated with the decrease in the volume of air in the lungs which occurs during the utterance. As the thoracic cavity becomes smaller there is a corresponding increase in the degree of muscular activity which is required to produce a given air pres-sure in the lungs. (This point has been noted before by Roos (1936) and Hoshiko (1957); but these investigators did not obtain any quantitative data.) The measurements which we made are to be reported elsewhere (Draper *et al*, forthcoming).

The bursts of activity of the internal intercostals were first noted by Stetson. They are very obvious in a simple utterance such as *Fig* 1; but in normal speech they are far less evident. We made many recordings of the muscular activity which occurred when lists of words were read. These re-cords show that each segment of speech which is perceived as a syllable is not necessarily accompanied by a separate burst of muscular activity. Stetson oversimplifies the situation by considering the activity of the in-tercostal muscles in terms of a series of 'ballistic movements', each of which either happens or does not happen. But in fact there are many other possibilities. Not only can the tension of the intercostal muscles be varied over a large range, but also there can be variations in the rate of change of tension. Sometimes a single increase in tension spans a group of articulations including two vowels separated by a consonant closure (our records show that words such as *pity* and *around* may be spoken in this way); and sometimes there are two separate bursts of activity in what is normally regarded as a single syllable (*eg* in *sport*, *stay*, and other words beginning with a fricative followed by a plosive).

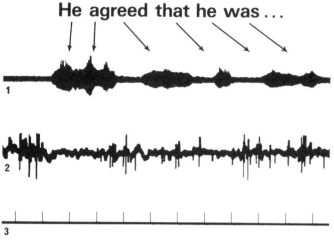

Fig 2: Internal intercostal activity during continuous speech. 1 Microphone record. 2 Internal intercostal action potentials. 3 Time marker, 1/10 second.

These results indicate that a consideration of the muscular activity which occurs when reading lists of words in a normal conversational style is unlikely to lead us to the segments which are usually called syllables. Very often there is not even a correlation between the number of bursts of muscular activity and the number of segments perceived as syllables in an utterance.

The activity of the internal intercostals during connected speech is shown in *Figs* 2 and 3. *Fig* 2 shows the first part of the sentence 'He agreed that he was very sorry for everything', said in a normal conversational style. It is obvious that the muscular activity is not constant throughout this phrase. There are striking increases in the muscular activity immediately before the first word and before the second syllable in *agreed*. But the latter syllable is also accompanied by a further burst of activity in the middle of the vowel (a pattern of activity which we often observed during long vowels). The last two words are also preceded by bursts of activity.

The activity of the internal intercostals during the phrase 'The old man doddered along the road' is shown in *Fig* 3. Here the variations in muscular activity may be expressed quantitatively, since on this occasion the activity of a single motor unit was recorded. The variations in muscular activity during this utterance are in accord with the variations in the perceived stress. Listeners who heard a tape recording of the utterance agreed

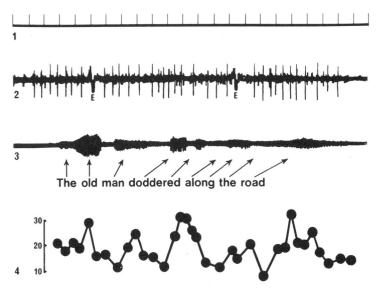

Fig 3: Internal intercostal activity during speech. 1 Time marker, 1/10 second.
2 Internal intercostal action potentials (electrical activity associated with the action of the heart indicated by E). 3 Microphone record.
4 Instantaneous frequencies of the single motor unit recorded in 2 in impulses per second.

that the greatest stress was on the first part of the word *doddered*, and the words *old man* and *road* were also stressed. It can be seen from the graph in the lower part of *Fig* 3 that the frequency of stimulation of the particular group of muscle fibres being recorded on that occasion is greatest just before *doddered*, and that it is also fairly high immediately before the words *old*, *man*, and *road*. Many of our other records also show an increase in the degree of muscular activity immediately before the syllables which were heard as being strongly stressed.

It is generally agreed that the stress of an utterance cannot be correlated with any single acoustic property. Thus a syllable which is perceived as having a strong stress does not necessarily have a greater intensity, nor a higher nor lower frequency, nor a longer duration, nor a specific quality.

But on the basis of our evidence it appears that the degree of stress is often related to the extra increase in muscular activity (*ie* the increase over and above the increase in activity which is associated with the decrease in the volume of air in the lungs). Thus differences in stress, like many consonantal differences (Liberman, 1957), can be ordered more simply in terms of the human behaviour producing them than in terms of the accompanying acoustic phenomena.

When a listening phonetician states that a syllable is stressed he may believe that he is assessing acoustic attributes of the sound; and, of course, his judgment may be based on an auditory interpretation of the acoustic cues. Nevertheless, statements about stress are usually best regarded as statements about the speaker's muscular behaviour (or about the action of the listener's muscles which would have to be made in order to produce similar sounds). This point of view was put by S. Jones (1932), who said that 'Accent is sui generis, depending for its perception on the kinaesthetic sense . . . the listener refers what he hears to how he would say it. Thus he translates exteroceptor into proprioceptor sensations, the kinaesthetic memory serving as stimulus'. However, even if this viewpoint is not accepted, there is no need to consider statements about stress as being different in kind from those about, say, the place of articulation. They are both difficult to interpret in acoustic terms; but the fact remains that they can both be easily correlated with the behaviour of the speaker's vocal apparatus.

The internal intercostal muscles are not the only respiratory muscles which are active during speech. But before discussing the activity of the other muscles, we must consider the general nature of the forces affecting the pressure of the air in the lungs. Not only are there expiratory muscular forces which can increase the pressure, and inspiratory muscular forces which can decrease it, but also the pressure will be considerably affected by the tendency of the elastic structures in and about the lungs to recoil. The lungs are in some ways like rubber balloons; they may be inflated as a result of one kind of effort; and another mechanism may be used to push the air out; but this latter effort can be supplemented by the recoil of the stretched elastic walls. The pressure which is exerted by this tendency of the lungs to return to the relaxed position is known as the relaxation pressure; it is largely dependent on the amount of air in the lungs. After a maximal inspiration, when the lungs are fully expanded, the relaxation pressure is far more than is needed for a normal conversational utterance. Accordingly, in these circumstances, the pressure cannot be regulated by the internal intercostals (which function so as to increase the pressure); instead inspiratory muscles come into action. Among the most important of the inspiratory muscles in this connection are the *external intercostals* which also lie in between the ribs. But their fibres run in a different direction from those of the internal intercostals; they may be thought of as a

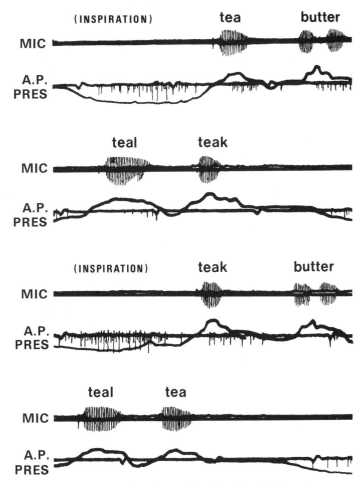

Fig 4: External intercostal activity when reading lists of words after a deep
    inspiration. The record, which is continuous, shows the waveforms of
    the words (MIC); the external intercostal action potentials (A.P.); and
    the pressure below the vocal cords (PRES).

sheet of muscles linking the ribs to the fixed first rib and the neck. Their
function is to lift the rib cage, thus enlarging the thoracic cavity.

When we talk quietly after a deep breath, the external intercostals regulate the pressure of the air in the lungs by checking the descent of the rib
cage. Some of our records of subjects reading lists of words show bursts of
activity of the external intercostals at the ends of words spoken after a deep
inspiration. Typical of these records is *Fig* 4, which is a simultaneous re-

cording of the sound waves, the oesophageal pressure (which will be discussed in a future paper), and the activity registered by a concentric needle electrode in the external intercostals. This muscle is clearly active during the inspiratory phase of respiration when the pressure of the air in the lungs is less than that of the outside air; and there are further bursts of activity towards the end of each of the first two or three words after each inspiration. These bursts occur irrespective of whether the word ends in a consonant closure or not. After the first inspiration the word *tea* is checked by inspiratory activity; but after the second inspiration, when the same word occurs later in the utterance, it is not followed by a burst of external intercostal activity. In the second breath group it is the words *teak* and *teal* which are checked.

Other records show that after a deep inspiration using the external intercostals some subjects continue to support the rib cage by maintaining these muscles in a state of varying tension throughout the first part of each utterance; in such cases the air pressure in the lungs is often increased immediately before each word by a slight slackening of the muscles supporting the rib cage.

It should be emphasized that in the majority of conversational utterances which we have recorded there is no action at all of the external intercostals. Activity is commonly observed only when talking quietly after a deep inspiration. There is no evidence for Stetson's statement that English syllables with a certain kind of phonetic structure are always checked by the action of the external intercostals.

The *diaphragm* is another inspiratory muscle which might theoretically be used in the same way as the external intercostals. It is a large dome-shaped muscle which is attached to the ribs and spinal column, and forms the base of the thoracic cavity; when it contracts it is drawn down and flattened so that the thoracic cavity is enlarged. Consequently it is one of the most important muscles of inspiration. But it should be noted that it can never actively push air out of the lungs, since its action can only decrease the pressure in the thoracic cavity.

The diaphragm was not active during the speech of the majority of our subjects. Even when talking softly after a deep inspiration during which there was a great deal of diaphragmatic activity, in nine out of eleven speakers the diaphragmatic activity ceased completely within the first 2–3 seconds.

The other two out of our eleven subjects used a very complex pattern of activity of the respiratory muscles. The diaphragm was active not only in inspiration, but also during speech. We were able to study only one of these subjects in detail. With this subject we often recorded activity of expiratory muscles such as the internal intercostals, at the same time as the diaphragm was exerting an inspiratory effort. Thus this subject was using some muscles to decrease the size of the thoracic cavity while he was simultaneously using other muscles to expand the cavity. He regulated the pressure of the air below the vocal cords by balancing the expiratory effort of one set of muscles against the inspiratory action of another. The other subject who maintained the diaphragm in action throughout most of his speech also used a similar complex pattern of muscular activity.

All the subjects whom we studied used additional muscles to supplement the intercostals in certain circumstances. The *external obliques, rectus abdominis,* and *latissimus dorsi* are among the muscles which assist expiration towards the end of a long utterance. These muscles are mainly concerned with altering or maintaining the position of the body. Thus the external obliques are used to support the trunk when leaning over to one side; rectus abdominis is used when sitting up from a supine position; and latissimus dorsi is used for pulling up on the arms. But each of these muscles can help to reduce the size of the thoracic cavity. Accordingly they often come into action when the volume of air in the lungs is small and the internal intercostals can no longer produce the required pressure.

In the case of those who do not use the diaphragm while talking, the sequence of muscular activity during a long conversational utterance after a deep inspiration is therefore: first decreasing activity of the external intercostals; then increasing activity of the internal intercostals; and finally increasing activity of the accessory respiratory muscles, probably beginning with the external obliques, and then bringing in rectus abdominis, and then, right at the end, latissimus dorsi. In louder utterances, such as when talking in a large lecture room, the sequence is the same; but because an increased mean pressure is required, the expiratory actions of the internal intercostals begin when there is more air in the lungs; and the actions of the supplementary muscles also begin earlier. When talking very loudly indeed, or when shouting, the external intercostals do not check the descent of the rib cage at all, since even after deep inspiration the relaxation pressure is less than is needed in such an utterance.

Stetson believed that rectus abdominis reinforced the action of the internal intercostals in stressed syllables. This does not in fact happen except perhaps in cases of very emphatic stressing, when the pressure in the lungs may be unusually high. Our observations are that in normal conversational English the abdominal muscles are in action only at the end of a very long utterance. In most utterances the air pressure is regulated solely by the intercostals. Of course on the parade ground, or in other languages (Pike, 1957), the abdominal muscles do play a more important part.

There are probably two reasons why Stetson imagined that the abdominal muscles function in ordinary speech. Firstly it is very easy to be deceived by subjective impressions. During speech, there are movements of the body wall in the abdominal region, particularly in the neighbourhood of rectus abdominis. Stetson recorded these movements and considered that they provided evidence for his theory that stressed syllables involved a pulsing action of the abdominal muscles. But our electromyographic records show that these muscles are not active during most normal speech; consequently, when the internal intercostal muscles contract, the increase in the pressure of the air in the lungs may cause a passive movement of adjacent parts of the body wall. An analogy of this situation is provided by an inflated balloon with a squeaker in the neck. Squeezing the sides of the balloon will squeeze more air out (and make a louder or higher pitched noise); but it will also push the bottom of the balloon down. There are, therefore, movements of the abdominal muscles which may be coordinated with the occurrence of stressed syllables; but they are passive movements, not involving the activity of these muscles.

The second reason why Stetson found it necessary to consider the abdominal muscles was because of a simplified view of the action of the internal intercostals. It was assumed that the intercostals could either contract or not contract, each contraction constituting a 'ballistic pulse'. Therefore some other mechanism had to be found to account for observable linguistic phenomena such as stress. But, as we have seen, the internal intercostals can contract in a variety of ways. They can regulate not only the degree of stress, but also the manner of onset of stress. Possibly their activity can also be correlated with vowel length and many other prosodies of the syllable and the breath group. However, speculation on this subject is somewhat pointless, since objective evidence can be recorded by any team of physiologists and phoneticians who care to insert an electrode into the relevant muscle.

Bibliography

BEGBIE, H. 'Accuracy of assessing in linear hand movements.' *Q.J. Exp. Psych.*, in press. [Vol XI, 1959. Eds.]

BUCHTAL, F. 'The functional organization of the motor unit.' *Premier Congrès International des Sciences Neurologiques*, 1957, 17–41.

CAMPBELL, E. J. M. *The respiratory muscles and the mechanics of breathing*, 1958.

DRAPER, M. H., LADEFOGED, P. and WHITTERIDGE, D. 'Respiratory muscles in speech.' *J. Speech and Hearing Research* (forthcoming). [Vol II, No 1, March 1959. Eds.]

GRAY, G. W. and WISE, C. M. *The Bases of Speech*, 1946.

HOSHIKO, M. S. 'An electromyographic study of respiratory muscles in relation to syllabification.' PHD *Thesis*, Purdue University, 1957.

JONES, S. 'The accent in French – what is accent.' *Le Maître Phonétique*, 40, 1932, 74–75.

LIBERMAN, A. M. 'Some results of research on speech perception.' *J. Acoust. Soc. Am.*, 29.1, 1957, 117–123.

PIKE, K. L. 'Abdominal pulse types in some Peruvian languages.' *Language*, 33.1, 1957, 30–35.

ROOS, J. 'The physiology of playing the flute.' *Arch. Néer. Phon. Exp.*, 12, 1936, 1–26.

STETSON, R. H. *Motor Phonetics*, 2nd edn, 1951.

TWADDELL, W. F. 'Stetson's model and the "supra-segmental phonemes".' *Language*, 29.4, 1953, 415–453.

Peter Ladefoged

The value of phonetic statements

It is odd that linguists, who pride themselves on the rigour and scientific nature of many of their concepts, should nevertheless be so tolerant of vague, unverified statements in some parts of their field. To take an example, Bloch has made many contributions to linguistic theory in a long series of excellent publications,[1] but he does not appear to have adopted any scientific procedure to check the validity of the phonetic statements (*eg* those about tongue positions during vowel sounds) which often occur in these works. It seems as if he regards the justification of phonetic statements as outside his field as a linguist. Thus he says,[2] 'Qualities are identified by ear; but in linguistic works they are traditionally defined in terms of their assumed production by the vocal organs.' This uncritical acceptance of the traditional descriptive techniques is, as we shall show, inadvisable. Disclaimers such as 'articulatory terminology is used only because a usable auditory terminology has not yet been developed' (*loc cit*) are not sufficient excuses for making seemingly dogmatic assertions about physiological facts. When Bloch states (*loc cit*) that [a] in the Japanese word [ha-ko-bu] 'carries' is to be interpreted as 'low back (slightly advanced towards central position)', there is no description of any rigorous experimental procedure used in establishing this 'fact'; nor is there a reference to previous work on which the statement might be based. In any case, even if the terminology is regarded as specifying simply auditory qualities, there is no published evidence indicating that a description of this kind is actually meaningful – *ie* capable of interpretation by other linguists who are also trained phoneticians.

First published in *Language*, Vol XXXVI, No 3: 387–396, 1960, and also incorporated in P. Ladefoged, 'The Nature of Vowel Quality', *Revista do Laboratorio de Fonetica Experimental*, Coimbra, 5: 73–162, 1960. It was subsequently published in a revised form, in P. Ladefoged, *Three Areas of Experimental Phonetics*, Oxford University Press, London, 1967.

Bloch is, of course, not alone in making statements of this form. The great majority of linguists (including the present author) constantly use loose unverified descriptions in all their work; and most linguists would agree with Joos, who, on their behalf, says:[3] 'We have no quarrel with [Bloch's procedure in this respect]. We all do that, and shall continue to do it no matter how convinced we may yet be that it is unjustified.' But we should note that this traditional cavalier treatment of physiological facts largely accounts for the difficulties which our colleagues in the experimental sciences have in recognizing us as fellow scientists. Furthermore, it seems probable that our lack of knowledge of what we are doing when we make phonetic descriptions is actually hampering our own work as descriptive linguists.

We need valid phonetic descriptions for two principal reasons. First, a linguist cannot give a comprehensive account of the phonology of a language unless he knows all the phonetic facts; if the original observations made in the field are inadequate, the subsequent analysis is liable to be faulty. Secondly, a linguist usually wants his analysis to be capable of interpretation in phonetic terms. This is obviously the case if the analysis was made for a practical purpose such as teaching the pronunciation of a language. But even if no such purpose is intended, it is still desirable; any account of a language which states simply the phonemic system is obviously not as complete as one which both states that and also gives a phonetic description of the actual sounds in different contexts.

A phonetic description can be considered to be adequate only if it has the same meaning for all who use it. It is, of course, impossible to find out whether a given description will actually be interpreted in the same way by all the linguists who are likely to read it. But it is quite possible to see whether the members of a particular group of linguists are capable of making descriptions which are meaningful within that group. One of the purposes of this article is to assess the extent to which this can be done for vowel sounds.

Vowels can be described in terms of three different kinds of properties: a fieldworker listening to an informant can try to specify the position of the speaker's vocal organs, or the acoustic structure of the sound, or the auditory nature of the sound in comparison with other sounds. Despite Bloch's present claim that he is using articulatory terminology simply because no satisfactory auditory terminology has yet been developed, most fieldworkers probably still believe (as is implied by Bloch's earlier work) that the first of these methods is the most accurate.

Our present method of classifying the positions of the vocal organs during the pronunciation of vowel sounds was largely originated by the nineteenth-century phonetician A. M. Bell. In his early work[4] Bell had used a form of description (based on that of Wallis,[5] a seventeenth-century grammarian) in which vowels were classified in terms of two series, 'labials' and 'linguals', plus an intermediate series 'labio-linguals'. But when he was working out his system of Visible Speech,[6] Bell realized that this form of description was inadequate, in that certain vowels (*eg* that in *sir*) could not be conveniently placed in these categories. Accordingly he devised a scheme which specified the position of the tongue by means of two parameters. The height of the tongue was described as being high, mid, or low; and the highest point of the tongue was described as being at the front of the mouth, at the back, or 'mixed' (*ie* with both the front and the back of the tongue raised). This resulted in a scheme in which there were nine 'cardinal' tongue positions (this is the first use of the word 'cardinal' in the description of vowels), which Bell usually discussed in terms of a three-by-three arrangement.

This two-dimensional scheme was taken over (with certain modifications) by other leading phoneticians and linguists, such as Sweet, Sievers, Passy, and Jespersen; but it should be noted that none of them had any exact knowledge of the tongue positions during vowels. Similarly when Jones,[7] and much later Bloch and Trager,[8] set up their descriptive schemes, they did not begin by making a complete series of experimental observations of articulatory positions, but apparently assumed that it was useful to describe vowels in terms of the highest point of the tongue in a two-dimensional system simply because they had been specified in these terms for so many years (just as, for 200 years before Bell's new system, phoneticians had considered it possible to specify vowels in terms of the categories which Wallis had set up). Later on Jones did have a number of x-ray photographs taken; but he published only four of these,[9] because (as he told the present author in a recent conversation) 'people would have found the others too confusing'. Subsequently Stephen Jones, a senior member of Daniel Jones's staff, published a complete set of x-ray photographs showing the tongue positions in all the cardinal vowels.[10] There is no scale attached to these photographs, but it is apparent that out of the seven intervals between the eight cardinal vowels only two involve equal movements of the tongue, and some are so different from the others that it is hard to see how any linguists and phoneticians could persist in maintaining that in making these sounds the tongue moves in a series of even approximately equidistant steps.

An alternative to giving articulatory descriptions of vowels is to make physical measurements of the actual sounds. After the publication of Joos's excellent monograph on acoustic phonetics (see note 3), many linguists believed that it was possible to specify vowels in acoustic terms. Joos himself was careful to point out at the time that his work was largely speculative, rather than a normal piece of scientific research in which hypotheses are set up and then tested by means of reliable and valid experiments, and he has elsewhere described himself as 'a notorious dilettante'.[11] But many linguists who had not been trained in the methods of the experimental sciences did not appreciate this point; they overvalued Joos's deservedly renowned work, because they could not tell when he was making a statement which had been the subject of rigorous experimental verification, and when he was just making an intelligent guess. It has now become clear that it is not at all easy to specify vowels in acoustic terms. Despite much intensive research no one has been able to publish a formula showing how the quality of every vowel could be measured.

We are then left with the third method of specifying vowel sounds, *viz* by means of statements about their relative auditory quality. Bloch and many other linguists now claim that they are making auditory statements when they describe vowels. But it is doubtful whether some of these statements are actually meaningful. As I have noted elsewhere,[12] a written auditory description cannot be interpreted precisely unless both the writer and the reader know the exact reference points in terms of which the other sounds are described. Just as a musician cannot tell another musician about the pitch of a sound unless they both know what is meant by the pitch of some reference sound (such as Concert Pitch A), so a linguist cannot meaningfully describe the vowel in a word as 'the cardinal higher low front unrounded lax vowel'[13] unless both he and his readers know the *sound* referred to by this label.

In the systems commonly in use in America, the reference sounds are described solely in terms of their articulatory formation, and this is not a valid method of describing sounds accurately. Consequently most of the auditory-articulatory descriptions of American linguists are simply personal impressionistic remarks.

Many British linguists, on the other hand, use a somewhat different scheme of auditory description, namely that devised by Daniel Jones. As we have seen, Jones, like Bloch, based his classification on presumed articulatory positions. But he always emphasizes the fact that 'a knowledge of the organic formation of vowels . . . is not in itself sufficient'.[14] In his definitions of the eight primary cardinal sounds which form his reference points, he makes as little use as possible of articulatory prescriptions. Only two of the eight (numbers 1 and 5) are defined in terms of positions of the vocal organs; the other six are specified in terms of a property which Jones (following the nineteenth-century usage) calls acoustic (and we nowadays would call auditory) equidistance. Moreover, he himself is well aware of the inadequacy of his formal definitions. As he says, 'the values of the cardinal vowels cannot be learnt from written descriptions; they should be learnt by oral instruction from a teacher who knows them.' In other words, despite the constant use by both Jones and his followers (including the present author, who is a pupil of a pupil of Jones)[15] of articulatory terminology, Jones's system is a true auditory one, employing eight precisely determined auditory reference points. It is, of course, a very arbitrary system, utilizing vowels standardized by one man; but it is nevertheless a meaningful one, allowing linguists to communicate with one another, and to make useful statements about part of their subject matter. Thus when Ida Ward publishes a chart showing the qualities of the vowels in a number of words in Efik,[16] it may be presumed to be meaningful to a large group of other linguists who have also been trained in the British school of linguistic phonetics, and who consequently know the reference points on the chart.

It might be objected that there are no grounds for presuming that descriptions of this kind are actually meaningful; British linguists might be deceiving themselves in imagining that they would all specify a given vowel sound in the same way. Because of this possibility, a controlled experiment was conducted. A recording was made of the following ten Gaelic words as pronounced by a native speaker: A *bèid*, B *sgò*, C *cùl*, D *reub*, E *lon*, F *bìg*, G *fàl*, H *laochan*, I *stagh*, J *gaoth*. These words contained vowels which were as monophthongal as possible, but which differed greatly in their phonetic quality. Eighteen linguists were asked to plot the vowels in these words on cardinal-vowel diagrams, and to state the degree of lip rounding associated with each of the plotted vowels. Fifteen of these subjects had been trained in the British tradition of linguistic phonetics, and consequently had had extensive practice in performing cardinal vowels and assessing the quality of other vowels in terms of them. The other three subjects were experienced phoneticians well acquainted with the theory of cardinal vowels; but they had not undergone the rigorous formal training in the use of the system which had served to provide the first group of subjects with fixed reference points. Each subject listened to the recording by himself, playing it back as often as he wished and in any way that he found convenient. None of the subjects was acquainted with this variety of Gaelic.

It was hoped that this procedure was sufficiently standardized to ensure that each subject was assessing the same phonic data and presenting his results in the same way; but that it nevertheless corresponded as much as possible to the typical situation in which a fieldworker needs to be able to describe vowels for purposes of linguistic research.

The consolidated results of this test are shown in *Fig* 1. The points representing the vowels in the first seven words are shown in the three diagrams on the left of the figure. The filled points are those of the fifteen subjects trained in the British tradition of linguistic phonetics; and the open circles correspond to the points plotted by the other three subjects. In the first words there were only minor disagreements about the degree of lip-rounding; *eg* some subjects described the vowel in word B (*sgò*) as having 'rather open rounding' whereas others thought this vowel had 'open to close rounding'. In these words no subject ever thought that any vowel had a spread or neutral lip position when other subjects thought that the same vowel had open or close lip-rounding. This was not true of

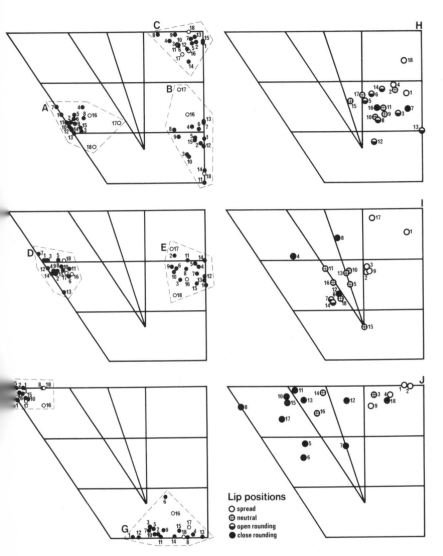

Fig 1: The judgments of eighteen linguists of the qualities of the vowels in ten
Gaelic words. In the diagrams on the left of the figure, the filled points
indicate the judgments of the subjects (1–15) trained in the British
tradition of linguistic phonetics, and the open circles those of other
professional linguists. In the diagrams on the right of the figure, the
degree of lip-rounding has been indicated by the kind of point, no
difference being made between the two groups of subjects.

the vowels in the last three words, the points for which are shown in the last three diagrams on the right of the figure. In these words the degree of lip-rounding has been indicated by the kind of point, no distinction being made between the points of the different groups of subjects.

The first thing to note about these results is that the judgments of the subjects trained in the British tradition seem to be usually more in agreement than those of the three other subjects and any twelve of the first fifteen subjects. This is especially true for the vowels in words A, B, E, and F. The points representing the qualities of these vowels according to subjects 16, 17, and 18 are comparatively widely scattered. These subjects do not agree with each other in their descriptions of these vowels, nor do they agree very closely with most of the other subjects. All the last three subjects were well known linguists, accepted scholars in their fields, with a knowledge of many different languages and considerable experience of dialectology. Each of them had spent many years doing fieldwork and research, and had published articles involving descriptions of the sounds of speech. They thus had a higher professional standing and a great deal more experience than subjects 6–9, who were post-graduate students of the University of Edinburgh. But they are relatively unable to communicate in writing with one another in an unambiguous way about the quality of a vowel sound.

The superiority of the agreement among subjects trained in the British tradition of linguistic phonetics cannot be explained as being due to aspects of their linguistic background which had nothing to do with their phonetic training. Admittedly eleven of them were speakers of that variety of English known as RP; but of the others subject 2 was an American, subject 7 a Dutchman, subject 8 a Scot, and subject 9 a Yorkshire girl. Yet despite these diverse backgrounds, these subjects were not in disagreement with the other eleven, as were subject 16 a Swede, subject 17 an American, and subject 18 an Englishman, who had had no formal training in the cardinal vowel system. We may conclude, therefore, that in so far as there is agreement among the subjects who have graduated in the British tradition, it is to some extent due to the rigorous training which they have all undergone.

There are, however, disagreements even among these subjects. Some of these are between the group of subjects who were or had recently been members of the Phonetics Department of University College London (subjects 10–15) and the group who were associated with the Phonetics Department of the University of Edinburgh (subjects 1–9). Thus most of the Edinburgh subjects considered the vowel in word A (*bèid*) to be more central and more close than was indicated by most of the London linguists. The same is true of the vowel in word B (*sgò*). The variations between the two groups can be summed up by saying that the London subjects had a greater tendency to regard vowels as peripheral. In the first seven words there were thirty-four judgments indicating that a subject thought that a vowel had a peripheral quality. Twenty-two of these judgments were made by the six London linguists, and only twelve by the nine from Edinburgh. This difference is statistically very significant ($\chi^2 = 10 \cdot 5$, $p < 0 \cdot 1$). So it would appear that there is a danger that even groups of British linguists who meet only occasionally may diverge in their descriptions. But it should be emphasized that these differences are very small in comparison with the differences among the subjects not trained in the British tradition of linguistic phonetics.

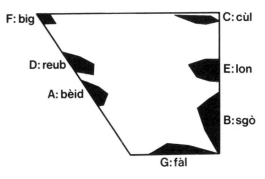

Fig 2: The minimum areas containing the points indicating the judgments of at least fourteen out of the fifteen linguists trained in the British tradition of linguistic phonetics for the vowels in the first seven Gaelic words.

It is also apparent that in some words the agreement is much greater than in others. *Fig* 2 shows for each of the first seven words the minimum area which will contain the points representing the judgments of at least fourteen of the fifteen subjects trained in the use of the cardinal vowel system. Comparison with *Fig* 1 will show how these areas have been drawn. *Table* 1 shows the size of the area for each of the ten vowels, expressed both in square mm and as a percentage of the total area of the diagram. When the judgments of the vowels in the first seven words are compared in this way, it may be seen that the degree of agreement is often very great (far greater than might appear from *Fig* 1, where the size of the points and the attached numbers tend to exaggerate the spread of the points).

Some interesting facts emerge from a study of the rank ordering of these areas. Thus the vowels in words C (*cùl*) and F (*bìg*) are both of the kind in which it is difficult to locate the exact centre of the first formant because of its proximity to the fundamental. But nevertheless these are the vowels concerning which subjects are in the greatest agreement; and the major part of what disagreement there is in the case of word C (*cùl*) is in judgments of the front-back dimension, which, according to the usual formant theories for vowels of this type, can be correlated with the frequency of formant 2. This agreement of judgments of the close-open dimension in the case of vowels in which it is difficult to locate the centre of the first formant suggests the hypothesis that these vowels are assessed in terms of some auditory quality other than the pitch of formant 1.

After the judgments of the vowels in words F (*bìg*) and C (*cùl*), the next best agreement is in the judgments of the vowels in words A (*bèid*) and D (*reub*). These vowels are of the type which it is comparatively easy to analyse and specify in terms of their formant frequencies. The vowels in words G (*fàl*), E (*lon*), and B (*sgò*), however, are more difficult to specify in this way; and there is also more disagreement in the judgments of their qualities.

It is also readily apparent that subjects have a great deal of difficulty in assessing the qualities of the relatively unfamiliar vowels in the last three words. As in the case of the vowels in the first seven words, they would no doubt have found the task easier if they had been listening to the informant himself instead of a recording. There might then have been less disagree-

Table 1

word	minimum area sq mm	% total area	rank order
A *bèid*	84	1·5	3
B *sgò*	206	3·8	7
C *cùl*	60	1·1	2
D *reub*	90	1·6	4
E *lon*	135	2·5	6
F *bìg*	30	0·6	1
G *fàl*	114	2·1	5
H *laochan*	396	7·3	8
I *stagh*	604	11·1	9
J *gaoth*	1449	26·7	10

ment about the degree of lip-rounding; and this in its turn would probably have resulted in greater agreement in the judgments of the other aspects of vowel quality. Nevertheless it should be noted that in each of these three vowels there is a wide scatter of judgments, even among those who agree in their estimates of the lip positions.

Since subjects often disagree about the degree of lip-rounding, it appears that this quality is not easy to assess in auditory terms alone. This conclusion is supported by the fact that although eleven out of the eighteen subjects considered that the vowel in word J (*gaoth*) had close lip-rounding, all the subjects who met the informant after the experiment then considered that this vowel has a spread or neutral lip position. Furthermore the judgments of this vowel and of the vowel in word I (*stagh*) indicate that the degree of lip-rounding is not always considered an independent variable. There is a very significant correlation ($\chi^2 = 17.3$, p <

o·o1) between the judgments indicating open or close rounding which are
associated with points in the left-hand section of the chart, as opposed to
judgments indicating a spread lip position which are associated with
points in the right-hand section of the chart. The reasons for this are not
quite clear. It has already been pointed out that the terms indicating positions of the tongue which are used to specify two of the auditory parameters are definitely imitation labels,[17] despite the ardent belief to the
contrary of some subjects. The third parameter (the degree of lip-rounding) might be supposed to be a genuine articulatory description; but in
fact this is probably not so. No formal experiment on this point has been
carried out, but observation of linguists assessing vowel quality in the presence of an informant suggests that the normal procedure does not involve
first looking at the informant and deciding on the description of the lip-
position, and then assessing the 'tongue position'; instead the quality of
the vowel is assessed as a whole in terms of three auditory parameters. As
a result, a precise statement about the degree of lip-rounding of a vowel is
usually a statement about what the vowel sounds like, and not necessarily
about what it looks like.

We are now in a position to summarize the value of phonetic statements
involving the use of Jones's cardinal vowel system. Considering the judgments of the vowels in the ten Gaelic words, we may conclude that the
traditional training in the use of the system enables linguists to make very
adequate judgments of at least those vowels which are judged as having lip
positions like those of similar primary cardinal vowels. It is difficult to
produce a valid statistic based on the experimental data reported here; but
we can attempt to summarize part of it by saying that the mean minimum
area for the judgments of the vowels shown in *Fig 2* is under 2 per cent of
the total vowel area. In other words, the degree of agreement between adequately trained linguists in judging vowels of this type is of the order of
one part in fifty.

There is at the moment no other way in which vowels can be specified
with equal accuracy. Even the forty-two symbols and additional modifiers
suggested by Bloch and Trager (*op cit*) will be of no avail unless they constitute auditory reference points which are prescribed in such a way that
they are accurately known to all users of the system. But at present no
linguist relying solely on the written descriptions could produce the required vowel qualities with certainty; the articulatory statements (*eg*
about tenseness and laxness, as well as about tongue positions) are too insufficient and vague – or even meaningless – from a physiological point of
view. No doubt the authors and their immediate associates know exactly
what vowel sounds are intended by the symbols and the descriptions; but
they could convey this information to other linguists only by oral instruction in their reference points. Students being trained in the British tradition of linguistic phonetics spend many hours receiving instruction in the

precise values of the cardinal vowels which serve as reference points. Consequently their statements about vowel quality are often, as we have seen, meaningful to other linguists who have been similarly trained. It would obviously be helpful if the form of description used by this group did not involve articulatory terms, which are apt to be misleading to those who do not realize that they should not be taken literally. Instead there should be a system of auditory terms indicating vector quantities from the agreed reference points. But this is irrelevant to the point that these linguists are using a system which seems to be the only practical method of specifying vowels at all accurately. This will remain the state of affairs until it is possible to use acoustic measurements for specifying vowels; and it seems that we are a long way from a simple acoustic specification which is applicable to vowels of all types, and which allows for the personal features of a speaker's vowels, which a linguist automatically recognizes and discounts.[18] Consequently the traditional rigorous training in the performance and use of known reference points will remain for some time an essential for all who wish to make useful phonetic statements about vowel sounds.

Notes

[1] See those in *Readings in linguistics*, ed M. Joos, Washington, 1957.

[2] 'Studies in Colloquial Japanese IV, Phonemics', *Lg* 26.86–125, 1950.

[3] Martin Joos, *Acoustic Phonetics*, Language Monograph 23, 1948.

[4] A. M. Bell, *Principles of Speech*, London, 1849.

[5] J. Wallis, *Grammatica linguae anglicanae*, London, 1653.

[6] A. M. Bell, *Visible speech*, London, 1867.

[7] D. Jones, *An English Pronouncing Dictionary*, 1st edn, London, 1917.

[8] B. Bloch and G. L. Trager, *Outline of Linguistic Analysis*, Baltimore, 1942.

[9] *Proceedings of the Royal Institution*, 22.1, 1919.

[10] S. Jones, 'Radiography and pronunciation', *British Journal of Radiology*, 2.149–50, 1929.

[11] *Readings in linguistics*, 356.

[12] 'The classification of vowels', *Lingua*, 5.2, 1956.

[13] G. L. Trager and H. L. Smith Jr., *An Outline of English Structure*, Norman, Okla., 1951.

[14] D. Jones, *An outline of English phonetics*, Cambridge, 1956.

[15] David Abercrombie, who has offered many helpful comments on parts of this paper.

[16] Ida Ward, *The phonetic and tonal structure of Efik*, Cambridge, 1933.

[17] K. L. Pike, *Phonetics*, Ann Arbor, 1943.

[18] P. Ladefoged and D. E. Broadbent, 'Information conveyed by vowels', *Journal of the Acoustical Society of America*, 29.98–104, 1957.

John Lyons

Phonemic and non-phonemic phonology: some typological reflections

American linguistics has proudly and more or less consciously adopted the pragmatic position; the philosophy of justification by results, of first getting things done and only then, if at all, asking what in fact has been done.[1] In the preface to his collection of articles by American linguists, Martin Joos brings out this point well. He goes on to remark: 'Altogether there is ample reason why both Americans and (for example) Europeans are likely on each side to consider the other side both irresponsible and arrogant. We may request the Europeans to try to regard the American style as a tradition comme une autre; but the Americans can't be expected to reciprocate: they are having too much fun to be bothered, and few of them are aware that either side has a tradition.'[2] As a representative of one European tradition in the enviable position of having secured a captive American audience for an hour or so, I propose to put before you views that absorption in the fun might otherwise prevent you from considering. To those of you who, having heard these views, might feel inclined to say that they are 'of only theoretical interest' and that the linguist's job is to describe what actually occurs in particular languages without troubling himself about what might occur (for I have heard this said), I would suggest that the history of science is full of examples to support the opinion that the actual cannot be properly described, perhaps not even recognized, except in the framework of what has previously been envisaged as possible. At the same time, of course, the sphere of what is thought of as possible is being constantly revised under the impact of discoveries made in the description of actual languages. Such is the relation between the theoretical and the applied. And, as a consequence of this, linguistic typologies should be built of a judicious mixture of

First published in *International Journal of American Linguistics*, Vol XXVIII, No 2: 127–133, 1962.

induction and deduction. This view is at least defensible; and it underlies what I have to say here on phonological typologies.

The concept of the phoneme is so widely accepted nowadays, especially in America, that it may seem perverse to question it. The use of the same terminology, it is true, tends to conceal a number of differences both of theory and of practice among the several schools of phonemicists. These differences, however, important though they are, do not concern us in the present connection. There is a common core of doctrine upon which all phonemicists are agreed and which sets them apart from non-phonemicists: this is expressed in their aim to describe language-utterances, on the phonological level, as a unidimensional sequence of discrete units, every one of which is in opposition with every other of the inventory in at least one pair of distinct utterances of the language.[3]

A radically different kind of phonological analysis has been developed and practised in recent years by what might be called 'the London school' of linguistics headed by J. R. Firth.[4] To this they give the name 'the Prosodic Approach'.[5] Since this type of phonological analysis is less familiar to American linguists than the phonemic, I shall first give a brief exposition of what seem to me to be its main distinguishing characteristics. Though this cannot claim to be either an authoritative or an adequate statement of prosodic theory, it will have served its main purpose if it arouses the interest of readers sufficiently for them to turn up and study the several articles listed in the bibliography. After discussing and illustrating the prosodic approach by comparison with the phonemic I shall suggest that neither the one nor the other is completely satisfactory as a general theory of phonological structure, but rather that the applicability of the one rather than the other model to the description of a particular language can be used as a means of typological classification along a continuous scale ranging from one extreme point, the cardinally phonemic, to the other, the cardinally prosodic, and that, in fact, there is probably no language that is either cardinally phonemic, or cardinally prosodic.[6] Other independent variables may then be sought for the typological classification of the phonology of different languages. If this approach is pursued we are led to the view that the phonological system of a given language (or its phonological subsystems) may be thought of as a point (or set of points) in a multidimensional space – the number of selected variables giving the number of dimensions in the hyperspace. Classical phonemic theory would fit perfectly only languages whose phonological systems were placed by this kind of classification at one 'corner' of the hyperspace. That there is probably no such language does not mean that phonemic description is never appropriate: it will be more or less appropriate according as the language being described is more or less close to the phonemic 'corner'; and in no language will each of the phonemes have equal claim to legitimacy.[7]

The two main differences between the prosodic approach and the phonemic seem to be these:

1. whereas the phonemicist maps the phonic data onto a unilinear sequence of phonological segments (phonemes), the prosodist describes the data in terms of two fundamentally different kinds of elements, PHONEMATIC UNITS and PROSODIES, the former being ordered with respect to one another in terms of successivity, the latter having as their 'domain' a variable, but determinate, number of phonematic units;

2. the prosodist, unlike the phonemicist, does not set up one overall inventory of phonological units for the language he is describing, but a number of different subsystems, each relevant for different phonological structures or for different places in these structures.[8]

These differences may be summarized by saying that the phonemic model is UNIDIMENSIONAL and MONOSYSTEMIC, and the prosodic TWO-DIMENSIONAL and POLYSYSTEMIC. Though both of these characteristic features of prosodic analysis have been associated with it from the beginning and are insisted upon equally by prosodists, they are clearly independent of one another and may be discussed separately.

The idea of describing the phonology of a language in terms of a two-dimensional model is not new to American linguists. In an early article, Zellig Harris pointed out that 'Two independent breakdowns of the flow of speech into elements are physically and logically possible. One is the division of the flow of speech into successive segments. . . . The other is the division of each segment into simultaneous components.'[9] He went on to show that in many languages the 'simultaneous components' recognized in the analysis extended over more than one segmental phoneme and could frequently be associated with the whole of a higher-level structure: eg, tongue-retraction in Moroccan Arabic, nasality in Swahili, etc. This point of view, which is essentially that of the prosodist, does not seem to have commended itself to the majority of American linguists; and Harris himself appears unwilling to draw from it its full implications, at least in the practical description of languages.[10]

To illustrate the difference between the phonemic and the prosodic approach to analysis we may briefly consider what is generally called 'vowel harmony' in Turkish. It seems that any phonemically-based analysis of Turkish must recognize eight vowels: viz, /i ï u ü e a o ö/. Any one of these vowels may occur in monosyllabic words: in words of more than one syllable, however, there are systematic restrictions on the co-occurrence of the several vowel phonemes. Thus, in words of native Turkish origin, front vowels, /i ü e ö/, and back vowels, /ï u a o/, do not occur together; nor do rounded vowels, /ü ö u o/, and unrounded vowels, /i e ï a/. Moreover, the phoneme /o/ occurs generally only in the first syllable of a word (with the exception of certain verbal forms). A phonemic representation of polysyllabic words is therefore very highly redundant, since it represents each vowel in the structure as a selection from eight contrasting units, whereas all but two of the eight vowel phonemes are excluded from occurrence by the occurrence of any other given vowel phoneme of the word. The phonemicist may of course take account of the limitations upon the co-occurrence of vowel phonemes in his statement. It is to be noticed, however, that the redundancy is of his own making, and the corrective distributional statement a consequence of the phonemic preconceptions of the analysis in the first place. Redundancy at a particular point in a language can be measured only by reference to the set of 'choices' permitted by the language at that point.[11] By introducing the two binary PROSODIC contrasts of front/back and rounding/non-rounding, and admitting only two contrasting segmental PHONEMATIC UNITS, high/low, not only do we secure economy in the inventory of phonological elements, but we produce a much more satisfying description of the language – one based on the patterns actually operative in the language.[12]

The advantages of the prosodic approach in a description of Turkish are especially apparent as soon as one moves from phonology to morphology. The phonemicist must either make use of morphophonemes in his representation of the Turkish suffixes or list the allomorphs of each suffix and append a statement of the rules governing the automatic conditioning in different PHONOLOGICAL environments. C. F. Voegelin and M. E. Ellinghausen, in their account of the structure of Turkish, set up two morphophonemic variables to handle 'vowel harmony' in the suffixes, x^2 and x^4, the former taking the two phonemic 'values' /e/ and /a/, and the latter the 'values' /i ü ï u/. The 'value' taken by the variables is then said to depend on the phonemic shape of the preceding vowel. 'The phonemic shape of the determined vowel may be any of the four high vowels or either of the two unrounded low vowels . . . ; the rounded low vowels o and ö are never determined in vowel harmony, but may serve as influencing vowels.' Determination by the preceding vowel is expressed graphically as follows:

(*a*) in vowel harmony of the x^2 type:

i   ü   ï   u
↓ ↙   ↓ ↙
e ←ö   a←o

eg, with the plural suffix -lx^2r: /kibritler/ : /kollar/, etc.

(*b*) in vowel harmony of the x^4 type:

i   ü   ï   u
↑   ↑   ↑   ↑
e   ö   a   o

eg, with the possessive suffix -x^4m: /kibritim/ : /evim/ : /üzümüm/, etc.[13]
For comparison, we may consider a prosodic representation of words

containing the same suffixes, using lower case letters for phonematic units and upper case for prosodies. Prosodies will be put before phonematic units: but this, it may be noted, is simply a matter of arbitrary decision – they might just as well be written above or below, at the end of the word, or even in the middle.[14] For the phonematic contrast between the high vowel and the low vowel, I use $i:a$; for the prosodies of front/back and rounding/non-rounding, I use $F:B$ and $R:N$ respectively. (One might equally well, of course, treat one of each pair of prosodies as the absence of the other and so dispense with two symbols.) With the exception of R when it 'combines' with a, the domain of these prosodies is the whole word (independently definable in Turkish in terms of stress): in combination with a the domain of R is the first syllable, in succeeding syllables N necessarily occurs (and, therefore, need not be written).[15]

The following table brings together for comparison the morphophonemic, phonemic and prosodic representation of selected words:

$gözlx^2r$	/gözler/	FRgazlar
$evlx^2r$	/evler/	FNavlar
$kollx^2r$	/kollar/	BRkallar
$adamlx^2r$	/adamlar/	BNadamlar
$güllx^2r$	/güller/	FRgillar
$kibritlx^2r$	/kibritler/	FNkibritlar
$bulutlx^2r$	/bulutlar/	BRbilitlar
$kïzlx^2r$	/kïzlar/	BNkizlar
$gözx^4m$	/gözüm/	FRgazim
evx^4m	/evim/	FNavim
$kolx^4m$	/kolum/	BRkalim
$adamx^4m$	/adamïm/	BNadamim
$gülx^4m$	/gülüm/	FRgilim
$kibritx^4m$	/kibritim/	FNkibritim
$bulutx^4m$	/bulutum/	BRbilitim
$kïzx^4m$	/kïzïm/	BNkizim

It will be observed that the prosodic representation here, and elsewhere, does away with the need for morphophonemics. And this still holds true (with a few exceptions, which must be treated as exceptional in any description) however many suffixes occur: thus what is morphophonemically $gözlx^2rx^4mx^4zdx^4n$ and phonemically /gözlerimizden/, is prosodically FRgazlarimizdan. That is to say, both stems and suffixes have everywhere the same phonological form. That this gives a 'truer' picture of the language seems impossible to deny. If it is objected that prosodic formulae are difficult to read, it may be replied that it is worth making the effort, if thereby we come to see things as they are.[16] If it is objected that the prosodic formulae are longer than the phonemic, it may be pointed out that even shorter formulae than the phonemic may be secured by using a syllabic notation. The only relevant criterion is that of phonological opposition; and if this is consistently applied in the analysis of Turkish, it will lead us to something like the statement given here, according to which the prosodies are 'long components' (not of sequences of phonemes, but of words as structural units on the phonological level of analysis) and phonematic units are minimal segmental elements following one another in serial order within morphemes and words.[17]

What is customarily called 'dissimilation' is no less suggestive of prosodic treatment than is 'assimilation', of which 'vowel harmony' is one instance. Suppose, for instance, there was a language in which (phonetically speaking) the occurrence of a front vowel in any given syllable excluded the occurrence of a front vowel in contiguous syllables within the same word, and likewise in the case of back vowels. It would seem to be quite justifiable to set up a pair of contrasting word-length prosodies whose phonetic realization would be contrasting frontness and backness in alternate syllables: that is $P_1 : P_2 = bfbfb \ldots : fbfbf \ldots$, where P_1 and P_2 are the prosodies in question, $=$ denotes phonetic realization and f/b represents a syllable marked by frontness/backness. And of course we can envisage prosodies with a far more complex phonetic 'realization'. There is no reason to fight shy of recognizing phonological units of a quite 'abstract' nature or of great phonetic complexity.[18]

Enough has been said to make clear the distinction between phonemic and prosodic analysis. It should be clear also that some languages are more satisfactorily described by the one than the other. This being so, it may be suggested that the goodness of fit of one model of analysis rather than the other should be made a criterion in the typological classification of the phonology of languages. It will be evident that there will be a continuous 'line' separating the cardinally phonemic from the cardinally prosodic languages.

We may now ask whether there is not good reason to divide what the London school handles under the head of prosodies into two different kinds of phonological units. The one would comprise those features that are called 'prosodic' in the more general usage of linguists (namely: tone, quantity and stress); the other would cover suprasegmental consonantal and vocalic features operating as 'long components'. If this division is made, we may decide to restrict the term 'prosody' to the former, and the term 'suprasegmental' to the latter, kind of phonological unit. The division itself is justified by the fact that prosodies (the term now and henceforth being used in the restricted sense) rest upon syntagmatic contrast, while suprasegmentals, like phonematic units, depend upon paradigmatic opposition, being what Jakobson calls 'inherent' features.[19] Indeed, if the matter is pressed, there seems to be no reason to group together prosodies and suprasegmentals as against phonematic units. We may therefore use three, rather than two, cardinal points for the phonological typology, each point representing the employment of one of the phonological variables to the exclusion of the others. It is easy to construct at least rudimentary languages that make exclusive use of only one of the phonological variables (and this establishes their theoretical independence). It is improbable in fact that there exists any natural language that is cardinally of any one of the three types: but this does not invalidate the proposed typology, any more than the fact that few languages, if any, are purely agglutinating, isolating or fusional invalidates the particular morphological typology implied by these terms.[20] The phonological systems or subsystems of given languages can be represented as points within the triangle formed by lines joining the cardinal extremities. To the present writer at least, this appears to be a much more satisfactory system of typological classification than that of forcing all languages into the same phonemic mould, often at the price of arbitrariness, and then comparing them as to the number of phonemes, the ratio of consonants to vowels, etc. That it is always *possible* to phonemicize a language does not prove that one always *should* phonemicize.[21]

There are at least two other theoretical questions touching on phonological analysis upon which linguists are divided. The first is the question of 'coexistent phonemic systems',[22] or, better, coexistent *phonological* systems: the second is that of 'grammatical prerequisites'.[23] As has been said above, the view that the phonology of a language cannot be described satisfactorily in terms of one, overall system, but should be considered as a set of subsystems, is an integral part of the London school approach; and it is accepted by linguists of the London school that the sphere of relevance of a given subsystem may be, though is not necessarily, grammatically, as well as phonologically determined. The 'orthodox' American view seems to be : (*a*) that the phonology of any given language is a uniform system; and (*b*) that phonological analysis can, and should, be carried out independently of grammatical analysis. Neither of these propositions is acceptable.[24] A more reasonable point of view would be that the phonology of a given language may or may not form a uniform system and that, in a given case, it may or may not be desirable to do the phonological analysis independently of the grammatical. In Turkish, for example, it would be desirable to set up a different phonological system or different systems to handle those words to which 'vowel harmony' does not apply (in the manner described above), since such words form a minority and, being loan-words, may have other 'non-Turkish' features. Methodological differences among linguists may here again reflect an inherent difference in languages. And, if this is so, the possibility or non-possibility of (*a*) describing the phonology of a language satisfactorily in terms of a uniform system and (*b*) carrying out the phonological analysis independently of the grammatical could be used to provide a further pair of (two-valued) variables in the phonological typology. And of course these variables could be given more values by quantizing the complexity of the phonological subsystems and of the grammatical correlations.

Further variables may suggest themselves: but the five mentioned above, especially the first three, would seem to have a good claim to inclusion in any reasonably comprehensive phonological typology of languages.

Bibliography

When citing journals, abbreviations will be used as follows: *TPS = Transactions of the Philological Society; BSOAS = Bulletin of the School of Oriental and African Studies*, University of London; *SILA = Studies in Linguistic Analysis*, Special Volume of the Philological Society, Oxford, 1957.

ALLEN, W. S.

    'Notes on the Phonetics of an Eastern Armenian Speaker', *TPS*, 1950, 180–206.

    'Phonetics and Comparative Linguistics', *Archivum Linguisticum*, 3, 1951, 126–136.

    'Some Prosodic Aspects of Retroflexion and Aspiration in Sanskrit', *BSOAS*, 13, 1951, 939–946.

    Phonetics in Ancient India, London, 1953.

    'Retroflexion in Sanskrit: Prosodic Technique and its Relevance to Comparative Statement', *BSOAS*, 16, 1954, 556–565.

    'Aspiration in the Harauti Nominal', *SILA*, 68–86.

    'Structure and System in the Abaza Verbal Complex', *TPS*, 1956, 127–176.

CARNOCHAN, J.

    'A Study of Quantity in Hausa', *BSOAS*, 13, 1951, 1032–1044.

    'Glottalization in Hausa', *TPS*, 1952, 78–109.

    'Gemination in Hausa', *SILA*, 149–181.

FIRTH, J. R.

    'The Semantics of Linguistic Science', *Lingua*, 1, 1948, 393–404.

    'Sounds and Prosodies', *TPS*, 1948, 127–152. [Reprinted in this volume, *pp* 47–65. Eds.]

    'General Linguistics and Descriptive Grammar', *TPS*, 1951, 69–87.

    'A Synopsis of Linguistic Theory', *SILA*, 1–32.

HENDERSON, E. J. A.

    'Prosodies in Siamese', *Asia Major* (new series) 1, 1949, 189–215. [Reprinted in this volume, *pp* 127–153. Eds.]

    'The Phonology of Loanwords in some South-East Asian Languages', *TPS*, 1951, 131–158.

    'The Main Features of Cambodian Pronunciation', *BSOAS*, 14, 1952, 149–174.

MITCHELL, T. F.

    'Particle-Noun Complexes in a Berber Dialect (Zuara)', *BSOAS*, 15, 1953, 375–390.

    'Long Consonants in Phonology and Phonetics', *SILA*, 182–205.

PALMER, F. R.
'The "Broken Plurals" of Tigrinya', *BSOAS*, 17, 1955, 548–566.
'"Openness" in Tigre: A Problem in Prosodic Statement', *BSOAS*, 18, 1956, 561–577.
'The Verb in Bilin', *BSOAS*, 19, 1957, 131–159.
'Gemination in Tigrinya', *SILA*, 139–148.
ROBINS, R. H.
'Notes on the Phonetics of the Georgian Word' (with Natalie Waterson), *BSOAS*, 14, 1952, 55–72.
'The Phonology of the Nasalized Verbal Forms in Sundanese', *BSOAS*, 15, 1953, 138–145.
'Formal Divisions in Sundanese', *TPS*, 1953, 109–142.
'Vowel Nasality in Sundanese. A Phonological and Grammatical Study', *SILA*, 87–103.
SCOTT, N. C.
'A Phonological Analysis of the Szechuanese Monosyllable', *BSOAS*, 18, 1956, 556–560. [Reprinted in this volume, *pp* 299–304. Eds.]
SHARP, A. E.
'A Tonal Analysis of the Disyllabic Noun in the Machame Dialect of Chaga', *BSOAS*, 16, 1954, 157–169. [Reprinted in this volume, *pp* 305–319. Eds.]
SPRIGG, R. K.
'Verbal Phrases in Lhasa Tibetan', *BSOAS*, 16, 1954, 134–156, 320–350, 566–591.
'The Tonal System of Tibetan (Lhasa Dialect) and the Nominal Phrase', *BSOAS*, 17, 1955, 134–153.
'Junction in Spoken Burmese', *SILA*, 104–138.
WATERSON, NATALIE
'Some Aspects of the Phonology of the Nominal Forms of the Turkish Word', *BSOAS*, 18, 1956, 578–591.

Notes

[1] This paper was given at one of the regular Ethnolinguistic Seminars at Indiana University in March 1961. In preparing it for publication, at the kind invitation of C. F. Voegelin, I have left the exordium more or less unchanged, although I realize that its style is more appropriate to a seminar talk than to a formal article. My intention is quite selfish: I wish to be reminded more vividly, whenever I see this paper later, of the enjoyable and instructive year I spent at Indiana University and of the seminars that form such a vital part of linguistic activity there.

[2] *Readings in Linguistics*, Washington, 1957, *p* vii.

[3] As used throughout, the term 'phoneme' is to be understood as referring to what are generally called 'segmental' phonemes in America, as distinct from the so-called 'suprasegmental' phonemes. It is in any case doubtful whether the extension of the term 'phoneme' to include phonologically distinct degrees of stress, tone and quantity is justifiable: for it tends to obscure the important distinction between paradigmatic opposition and syntagmatic contrast. (*Cf*, *eg*, R. Jakobson and M. Halle, *Fundamentals of Language*, *pp* 25–26, on the comparison of 'inherent' and 'prosodic' features.)

⁴ Most of the linguists practising this kind of analysis are, or have been, at the School of Oriental and African Studies in the University of London and have published their work generally in either *Transactions of the Philological Society (TPS)* or *Bulletin of the School of Oriental and African Studies (BSOAS)*. A list of such works is given at the end of this article.

⁵ It should be emphasized that the term 'prosodic' as used in this connection covers much more than, and something different in kind from (though it may include), what is generally held to fall within the scope of the term by other linguists. For the London school usage *cf* primarily J. R. Firth, 'Sounds and Prosodies', *TPS*, 1948, 127–152: for the more general usage *cf*, *eg*, Jakobson and Halle, *p* 22.

⁶ This approach to typological classification may be compared with that exemplified for morphology in C. E. Bazell, *Linguistic Typology*, London, 1958.

⁷ The practical advantages of phonemic description for typing and printing should not of course be allowed to influence the theory of phonological structure. It has been argued that phonemic theory has been built on the 'hypostatization' of letters of the roman alphabet: *cf* Firth, *op cit*, *p* 134.

⁸ A terminological distinction is made by prosodists between 'structure' and 'system'. Briefly, the distinction is this: a SYSTEM is a set of TERMS in paradigmatic opposition (a substitution set); a STRUCTURE is a sequence of ITEMS occurring in the stream of speech and considered as a unit at some level of analysis (a syllable, morpheme, word, phrase, etc). *Cf* R. H. Robins, 'Formal Divisions in Sundanese', *TPS*, 1953, 109; W. S. Allen, 'Retroflexion in Sanskrit: Prosodic Technique and its Relevance to Comparative Statement', *BSOAS*, 16.556, 1954.

⁹ 'Simultaneous Components in Phonology', *Lg*, 20.181–205, 1944 = Joos, *Readings*, *pp* 124–138. The quotation is from Joos, *p* 124.

¹⁰ His reason is interesting: 'The components are merely generalizations of the phonemes extending the very development which gives us phonemes out of sounds . . . Analysis into components completes what phonemics can only do in part: the transfer of the limitations of sounds from distributional restriction to positional variation in phonetic value. This is not an argument for the use of components: phonemics is undoubtedly the more convenient stopping point in this development, *because it fits alphabetic writing;* but we must recognize the fact that it is possible to go beyond it.' (Joos, *p* 137: my italics.) The prosodist would deny that the recognition of 'long components' (prosodies) is an extension of phonemic analysis and subsequent to it.

¹¹ It may be observed in passing that many of the generalizations made about the degree of redundancy in languages are vitiated by the failure to allow for redundancy artificially introduced into the description by the choice of model for the analysis. As an instance of this, *cf:* 'a maximally efficient code, in the information-theory sense, would employ just the number of features necessary to distinguish its phonemes, *eg* the 32 phonemes of English would require only five distinctive binary features. . . . However in English, nine binary features are actually employed. The efficiency of English in respect to phonology is therefore about five-ninths, or 56 per cent. Investigation of several languages suggests the generalization that the phonetic efficiency of languages is distributed around the 50 per cent point.' J. H. Greenberg, Ch. Osgood, James Jenkins, 'Memorandum Concerning Universals', Preprint for the SSRC Conference on Language Universals held at Dobbs Ferry (April, 1961).

¹² For a more complete account of Turkish phonology in terms of prosodic analysis, *cf* N. Waterson, 'Some Aspects of the Phonology of the Turkish Word', *BSOAS*, 18.578–591, 1956.

[13] C. F. Voegelin and M. E. Ellinghausen, 'Turkish Structure', *JAOS*, 63.34 *ff* 1943. The quotation is from *p* 37.

[14] Prosodists usually write the prosodies above or below the phonematic units and make their domain explicit in the symbolization.

[15] *Cf* Waterson, *p* 580, where the domains of these prosodies are described, together with the additional fact that R may occur with *i* in a syllable following one in which N occurs with *a*, provided that there is labiality before the *i* in question. (Thus: BNkarRpiz, /karpuz/, etc. This fact, of course, requires a slight, though general and systematic, modification of the statement given above, where it was omitted for the sake of simplicity.)

[16] Prosodists seem generally to prefer the 'hocus pocus' philosophy of language (*cf, eg*, R. H. Robins, 'Aspects of Prosodic Analysis', *Proceedings of the University of Durham Philosophical Society*, Series B (Arts), 1.2–3, 1957). It seems, however, that on this question (as on so many theoretical questions of linguistics) it is possible to adopt an intermediate position. Where the structure of the language being described is clearly determinate and all linguists can reach agreement on the 'facts', one might claim to be dealing with 'God's truth'; but where the language is indeterminate and does not compel one analysis rather than another, the linguist may choose arbitrarily one of the alternative solutions, providing that he makes clear what he is doing. This, if I understand him correctly, is the position of C. E. Bazell in *Linguistic Form* (Istanbul, 1953) and in many articles. At the same time it should be emphasized that a good deal of 'hocus pocus' is rendered unnecessary by the proper choice of linguistic model.

[17] In a full prosodic analysis of Turkish phonology further consonantal and junctural prosodies are required: *cf* Waterson, *op cit.*

[18] There is abundant exemplification from the analysis of real languages in the articles listed in the bibliography. Of particular interest is R. H. Robins, 'Vowel Nasality in Sundanese: a Phonological and Grammatical Study', *Studies in Linguistic Analysis*, Philological Society, Oxford, 1957, *pp* 87–103.

[19] *Cf* note 3.

[20] *Cf* Bazell, *Linguistic Typology.*

[21] C. F. Hockett observes: 'The danger which we encounter in letting ourselves become too firmly attached to any one arbitrary unit (feet, Trubetzkoy's principle, Bloch's postulates) is that we fail to realize the extent to which our generalizations are dependent on the frame of reference.' (*Manual of Phonology*, 1955, *pp* 2–3.) The attachment of most linguists, including Hockett himself, to the concept of the phoneme would seem to fall within the scope of this warning.

[22] *Cf* C. C. Fries and K. L. Pike, 'Coexistent Phonemic Systems', *Lg*, 25.29–50, 1949.

[23] *Cf* K. L. Pike, 'Grammatical Prerequisites to Phonemic Analysis', *Word*, 3.155–172, 1949 and 'More on Grammatical Prerequisites,' *Word*, 8.106–121, 1952.

[24] Hockett's argument that the use of grammatical criteria in phonological analysis necessarily involves circularity is not convincing (*cf SIL*, 7.40, 1949).

J. D. O'Connor and J. L. M. Trim

Vowel, consonant, and syllable – a phonological definition

1 Introduction

There is a general tendency, in the early development of a discipline, to extend its gains as rapidly as possible with the help of any concepts which may prove useful, whether their bases are clearly understood and formulated or not. There must come a time, however, if the discipline is to progress, when the theoretical validity of such concepts must be more critically examined, and their bases firmly and rigorously established.

Two concepts which we feel to be still in this situation are those of the syllable and the vowel/ consonant dichotomy. Their past, and continuing, usefulness to phonology is not in question, for they have, from the earliest times, been employed in the anatomy of words, whilst the syllable has also been used as the basic unit in the description of the prosodic systems of languages and in verse forms based on prosodic patterns.

And yet it would seem to us that the bases of these ideas are not yet fully understood, and until they are understood progress must be hampered. Such is their importance to linguistic analysis that many definitions have been attempted, but as criticism has shown, none hitherto propounded will stand up to close inspection in the light of the ways in which the terms are subsequently used. Such definitions may be divided into two types:

1. *Purely phonetic definitions*, consisting of straightforward acoustic-organic statements such as can be found in most phonetic textbooks, *eg* 'a vowel is a voiced, central-oral frictionless sound', 'a syllable is a sequence of sounds containing one peak of prominence (syllabic)'.

2. *Phonological definitions* based on formal linguistic criteria. For example, the syllable may be defined as some sort of unit of accent placement;[1]

First published in *Word*, Vol IX, No 2: 103–122, 1953.

vowel and consonant can then be either derived from the syllable as its central and marginal constituents,[2] or treated independently as units of widely different distribution.[3]

Purely phonetic definitions are of undoubted value in describing the sound features of the utterances of a language. They generally provide units corresponding fairly well to the phonological units otherwise elicited; but obviously such a relationship can only be a rough and never an exact correspondence. The many cases in which a phonetic syllable can be correlated with no phonological syllable and vice versa, the case of the 'fricative vowel', and the like, are too well known to require quotation here.

Turning to the phonological treatment of these concepts, the syllable as a unit of accent placement is found to be an attractive proposition. There is obviously a connection between syllable and accent – where phonological accent occurs. But two grave disadvantages seem to us in-herent in this approach. The first, and more important, may be illustrated from Hjelmslev's paper (see note 1). There he says of the word /dɒktə/ that it bears two different accents. True; but when he goes on, with no overt justification, to relate one accent to the sequence /dɒk/ and the other to the sequence /tə/ the whole solution becomes suspect, since there is no reason, accentually, to make the division after rather than before the /k/. The delimitation of the syllable is assumed before the syllable is even established, and it is hard to see how this basic error can be avoided in such an approach. Accentuation may tell us about syllabics – but not, we believe, about syllables.

The second disadvantage of this method is that, as Hjelmslev says, in languages where no phonological accent is found, such as French, there can be no syllable, and, if vowel and consonant are derived terms, no vowel or consonant. This disproves nothing, of course, but it is incon-venient, because the ideas of syllable and vowel and consonant have been found useful in dealing with non-accentual languages, too, and indeed Hjelmslev mentioned the concepts of 'pseudo'-syllable, -vowel, and -consonant, in order, presumably, to account for the distributional relations of French phonemes.

We believe that the solution of the problem of vowel and consonant lies in the possibility sketched by Pike (see note 3) that they are classes of sound-units having very different distributions in speech forms. Such a notion, though never explicitly formulated, has often been used in the solution of analytical problems, but it has generally led in the past to the setting up of 'obvious' vowels and consonants on a phonetic basis, leaving a residue of 'dubious' items, which are then parcelled out be-tween the obvious classes on the grounds of their similarity of distribu-tion. Thus, fricative [i], a dubious item, may be classed with obvious vowels such as [ɑ] because they appear in similar contexts. Although this may give roughly satisfactory results in practice, it is quite clearly not a proper procedure theoretically, because it utilizes two different criteria for the establishment of one class.

It is almost twenty years since Bloomfield said that phonology 'defines each phoneme by its role in the structure of speech forms',[4] but his pioneer work in this direction has not been developed as it might have been. Bloomfield showed that no two phonemes in English have all their contexts in common, and therefore that each can be defined in terms of the contexts in which it does occur. If it is possible to do this, then it should be possible to do a great deal more by a systematic comparison of the distribution of all the phonemes. From such a project might emerge classes much more nearly comparable with our unexplained, yet nonetheless clear, ideas of what vowel and consonant are. Having done this, it might be possible to reverse the more usual procedure and define the syllable in terms of vowel and consonant.

We shall try in the following pages to show, with reference to the 'Received' Southern British dialect of English:

(a) that a study of phoneme distribution is the proper theoretical basis for the establishment of the vowel and consonant classes; and

(b) that the syllable is best regarded in phonology as a structural unit most economically expressing the combinatory latitudes of vowels and consonants within a given language.[5]

2 Vowel and consonant

Two main assumptions underlay our investigation, namely:

1. that the comparison of a large number of utterances enables us to abstract those free forms which we call words. Words, and not utterances, are the stuff of the investigation.

2. that the method of commutation furnishes an inventory of linguistic units which we shall call, without prejudice, phonemes. Words may then be characterized in terms of phonemes having a position in the word. We have taken no account in our work of prosodic features (eg length, stress, pitch).

The initial phoneme list used was as follows: /p t k b d g č j f θ s š h v ð z ž r l m n ŋ j i ɪ e æ a ɒ ɔ u ʊ ʌ ɜ ə/. Note that /y/ and /w/ are not differentiated from /i/ and /u/ (the symbols are used to identify and in no case to classify units). There might be reasons for making these distinctions, but there are arguments against so doing, and we have thought fit to make our task less rather than more simple at the outset.

The method followed was to list all those phoneme combinations actually occurring, with no preconception as to vowel and consonant, syllabic and non-syllabic, in the first two and the last two places in words, places which we shall call *initial, post-initial, pre-final,* and *final.* It was convenient so to restrict our investigation for two reasons: first, because it is then possible to take complete account of all the possibilities in these places; otherwise, if all positions in the word were considered, it would be necessary to work with a sampling of the available words only, with the consequent risks to accuracy. And secondly, if a syllable is a unit expressing most economically the combinatory latitudes of phonemes, then combinations will occur at syllabic junctions which are not permitted within the syllable. Only the mutual relations between initial and post-initial and between final and pre-final were considered, and not the relations between post-initial, pre-final, and any following or preceding place respectively; so, for example, in the word 'spawn' /spɔn/, the context of /p/ is /s-/ and not /s-ɔ/, whilst that of /ɔ/ is /-n/ and not /p-n/. It is to be observed also that we were interested, not in the *frequency* of occurrence of any two phonemes in a given order, but simply in the fact of such occurrence.

In compiling the word list exemplifying the various phoneme combinations, we rejected – somewhat arbitrarily, it must be allowed – certain words which would have provided additional examples. Is one, to put the problem in its extreme form, to accept words such as *phthisis, voodoo, oof, Dnieper,* which, so far as we are aware, provide the only examples of the initial groups /fθ/, /vu/, /uf/, /dn/? We thought not, and the words which we excluded fall into the following categories:

(a) PROPER NAMES. This involves the exclusion, for consistency's sake, of even such commonplace items as *Osborne, Orpington, Ezra,* and *Czar.*

(b) LEARNED AND SCIENTIFIC TERMS, *eg: eschscholtzia, osmium, bdellium, argentiferous.*

(c) ANGLICIZED FOREIGN WORDS, *eg: tsetse, zariba, ragout, putsch.*

(d) RARE AND ARCHAIC WORDS, *eg: argent, doth, zoril, orpiment.*

(e) SLANG AND INTERJECTIONS, *eg: oof, schnozzle, yah!, pst!.*

(f) UNUSUAL PRONUNCIATION VARIANTS, *eg: psychology* /ps/, *hoof* /uf/, *either* /ið/.

In all these categories, (a) perhaps excepted, the line is difficult to draw and must to a certain extent be a matter of purely subjective judgment. However, we shall shortly have cause to observe that the 34 combinations rejected under one or another of the above categories would have had no significant effect upon our results. It is also probable that in our search for examples we have missed acceptable words which would show combinations not in fact dealt with. We are confident that such words would simply reinforce our conclusions. The total of possible combinations in both initial and final positions, using our list of 34 phonemes, is $34 \times 34 = 1156$. Of these 424 were actually found as initial combinations, and 387 as finals.

Table 1

Common contexts in initial place

Listed horizontally and diagonally are the phonemes of 'Received' English. Above or to the left of each phoneme, in *italics*, is the number of different two-phoneme combinations in which the given phoneme occurs in word-initial combination; thus, *6* next to z means that /z/ occurs initially before six different phonemes. The figures inside the table show the number of identical contexts in which two initial phonemes occur. Thus, 3 at the crossing of d and ə means that there are 3 phonemes before which both /d/ and /ɔ/ occur initially (*eg* before /r/: *draw, aural,* etc). **Bold-face numbers** stress the fact that the number of common contexts for two phonemes equals or exceeds half the number of different combinations in which at least one of the two phonemes

Table 2 is printed sideways (rotated 90°) as an upper-triangular matrix of co‑occurrence counts. Each phoneme is listed with its italic diagonal value, followed by its common‑context counts with the subsequent phonemes in the row order p t k b d g č j f θ s š h v ð z r l m n ŋ i e æ a ɒ o u ʌ ə.

phoneme	diag	p	t	k	b	d	g	č	j	f	θ	s	š	h	v	ð	z	r	l	m	n	ŋ	i	e	æ	a	ɒ	o	u	ʌ	ə
p	46		42	45	39	39	33	32	32	42	34	41	32	17	30	13	28	6	23	40	40	10	13	32	10	7	9	7	14	23	12
t	52			44	40	40	34	31	32	31	40	26	16	30	14	13	6	24	41	40	11	18	37	9	5	5	6	20	21	17	10
k	49				31	35	34	29	34	34	37	29	12	31	16	13	6	25	43	42	11	24	33	7	3	7	6	11	24	12	8
b	43					34	34	27	32	26	28	40	29	24	29	14	13	6	23	39	40	10	13	26	9	5	3	12	20	14	8
d	52						34	32	24	24	34	26	31	26	16	28	19	6	22	34	39	10	13	24	7	2	5	5	10	14	9
g	37							28	29	29	24	33	24	12	17	16	13	7	20	31	33	8	12	14	6	0	4	2	9	16	8
č	35								30	31	28	35	27	28	26	10	26	0	16	32	28	7	9	15	5	2	0	6	6	4	0
j	36									31	29	34	26	15	24	13	11	7	18	29	29	9	20	20	5	1	3	7	9	5	5
f	44										33	40	26	32	27	11	25	5	15	15	28	6	12	16	6	7	6	2	6	4	4
θ	40											36	26	17	30	13	21	7	9	15	28	4	25	20	5	5	0	7	12	4	2
s	59												32	16	24	13	29	6	32	31	30	12	42	23	21	13	23	11	23	6	5
š	33													17	12	13	21	6	31	33	31	8	8	18	6	3	1	3	16	5	2
h	17														12	9	9	7	16	16	12	9	9	6	2	0	5	2	7	1	0
v	32															14	22	15	17	32	30	4	2	7	0	6	2	7	8	4	5
ð	15																9	11	28	30	12	5	15	5	3	2	4	1	6	5	4
z	38																	7	15	29	31	14	28	24	11	3	11	14	12	4	17
r	34																		30	24	25	5	13	13	13	14	2	3	4	6	4
l	61																			44	45	14	29	26	27	26	23	12	13	11	11
m	46																				41	12	30	33	24	23	33	13	27	23	27
n	47																					13	30	22	13	8	22	8	24	8	15
ŋ	14																						15	10	9	6	13	8	11	8	6
i	78																							73	55	51	62	46	56	47	58	63
e	102																								56	55	63	62	51	64	54	52	59	71
æ	59																									53	46	51	40	52	36	50	48	47
a	58																										46	43	57	44	35	50	48	47
ɒ	66																											52	44	24	47	42	52	57
o	52																												44	24	34	23	43	42
u	69																													24	47	25	54	59
ʌ	43																														35	45	44
ə	59																															79

bloc 1

bloc 2

Table 2

Common contexts in all four places summated

In each of the four places considered, every phoneme was compared with every other phoneme in respect of the contexts occupied in common. Thus, in the words *spar* and *saw*, /p/ and /ɔ/ have a common context in post-initial place, since they are both preceded by /s/. In the words *pray* and *oral*, /p/ and /ɔ/ again have a common context, this time in initial place, both being followed by /r/. The number of contexts occupied in common by every pair of phonemes in each of the four places was determined and the results examined. The results for initial place are shown in *Table* 1.[6] As a random illustration, /p/ in initial place has a total of 14 occurrences; 13 are held in common with /t/, 12 with /h/, 14 with /ɪ/, 11 with /ʊ/, and 0 with /ɑ/ and /u/. It is possible to reach the tentative conclusion that in this place /p, t, h, ɪ, ʊ/ may be regarded as a group having similar combinatory latitudes, from which /u/ and /ɑ/ are excluded. In other places such groupings naturally vary. In post-initial place, for example, /p/, occurring 9 times, has 8 contexts in common with /t/, 1 with /h/, 4 with /ɪ/, 3 with /ʊ/, 2 with /ɑ/ and /u/ – a less clear picture.

It is necessary, in order to gain an idea of the overall combining power of the phonemes in all the places studied, to total the results obtained for the single places. This was done and the totals are set out in *Table* 2. In assessing the similarities and differences in the distributions of two phonemes, three figures must be taken into consideration, namely, the number of contexts held in common and the total number of occurrences of each of the two phonemes. So it is not possible to make an accurate assessment of the distributional relations of /p/ and /h/ on the basis simply of common contexts, since, if it is known that of a total of 46 occurrences, /p/ has 17 in common with /h/, 41 with /t/, and 16 with /ɔ/, one might be tempted to class /p/ with /t/, and /h/ with /ɔ/. In fact, as can be seen from the figure above /h/ in *Table* 2, /h/ occurs in a total of only 17 contexts, so that /h/ has all its contexts in common with /p/, and none at all with /ɔ/.

Bold type has been used in all the tables to show that the figure in question is not less than half the total number of occurrences of at least one of the phonemes compared. Thus, in *Table* 2 the number of contexts which /p/ and /ŋ/ hold in common is 10, and this figure is set in bold type because it is more than half the total number of occurrences of /ŋ/, *ie* 14 (although it is much less than half the total occurrences of /p/). As a statistical treatment this is no doubt crude, but it is nonetheless effective, since, as the contrast in types shows, it clearly divides the phonemes into two main groups. It is particularly interesting to note how the picture of the two groups is clarified by the summation effected in *Table* 2. Two groups can indeed already be discerned in outline in *Table* 1 and the corresponding tables for each of the other positions, but it is not until these results are brought together that the simplicity of the grouping is made evident. With regard to *Table* 2 two points should be noticed:

1. There are odd pairs of phonemes which, when examined separately, must clearly be classed in the same bloc, but which have fewer than half the total occurrences of either in common, *eg* /h/ and /ŋ/. There is no doubt, on the remaining evidence, that they must be classed together.

2. There are two phonemes which adhere to both blocs, *ie* /ɪ/ and /ʊ/, /ɪ/ more obviously than /ʊ/, but both quite clearly.

We must now examine the functioning of these two phonemes, in order to see whether it is possible to analyse the reason for its anomaly.

It is at once apparent that the percentage of common occurrences with bloc 2 (/i, e, æ/ etc) is much higher than with bloc 1 (/p, t, k/ etc), and it is therefore convenient to say that /ɪ/ and /ʊ/ are primarily members of bloc 2, but have some distributional characteristics similar to members of bloc 1.

This happens in cases where /ɪ/ or /ʊ/ follow or precede a member of bloc 2. Initially we find /ɪ/ preceding all members of this bloc, but following only /ɪ, e, ɔ, ʊ, ʌ/; /ʊ/ precedes all but /ə/, and follows only /ɪ, ʊ, ʌ, ɜ/. Finally, /ɪ/ precedes /i, ɑ, ɔ, u, ə/ (*ie* all members occurring finally except /ɪ/ and /ɜ/) and follows /e, ɔ, u, ʌ/, whilst /ʊ/ precedes /i, ɔ, u, ɜ, ə/ (*ie* all possible except /ɪ, ɑ/) and follows /ʌ/ and /ɜ/.

If we say that in the sequences /ɪɪ, ʊɪ, ɪʊ, ʊʊ/ the first term is in bloc-1 function and the second in bloc-2 function, we have the situation that in both initial and final groups /ɪ/ and /ʊ/ may occur before almost any member of bloc 2, and thus have in these cases a distribution indistinguishable from any typical member of bloc 1. But /ɪ/ may follow only /e, ɔ, ʌ/, and /ʊ/ only /ʌ/ and /ɜ/, both in final and initial groups. In this case it is not possible to say that /ɪ/ and /ʊ/ have a distribution substantially identical with members of bloc 1. That we are here dealing with a different phenomenon is made more likely by the parallel behaviour of /ə/, which may never precede a member of bloc 2, but may follow /i, ɪ, e, ə/ in initial groups, and /i, ɪ, e, ɔ, ʊ, u/ in final groups. Of these /iə, uə/ are found to occur only in some few isolated cases (*aeon, freer, fewer*). This is also the case with the remaining sequences of two members of bloc 2, /iɒ/ in *aeon*, /ui/ in *evacuee*, /uɒ/ in *jaguar*, /uɪ/ in *dewy*. On the other hand the sequences /eɪ, ɔɪ, ʌɪ, ʌʊ, ɜʊ, ɪə, eə, ɔə, ʊə/, if taken as close-knit units, are found to have a widespread distribution substantially identical with that of the members of bloc 2. For reasons which will be clearer if stated later, it is also more convenient to treat the sequences /ɪu/ (or /yu/) and /ɪʊə/ (or /yʊə/) similarly.

In this way we arrive at a more complete inventory of distributional units.[7] Whether these units are regarded as phonemes or not is a matter of definition which does not fall within the scope of this paper, and the term 'simple' distribution units will be used for those appearing on the first list (*p* 245), and 'compound' distributional units for those added here. The complete list of distributional units now appears as follows:

Table 3
Summation of common contexts in all four places (with extended inventory)

bloc 1

bloc 2

/p t k b d g č ǰ f θ s š h v ð z ž r l m n ŋ y w i ɪ e æ ɑ ɒ ɔ u ʊ ʌ ɜ ə eɪ ɜʊ ʌɪ
ʌʊ ɔɪ ɪə eə ɔə ʊə yu yuə/. *Table* 3 shows the common occurrences of all
these units, bold type once again being used to show where these amount
to half or more of the possible total.

It may here be remarked that though we have treated /č/ and /ǰ/ as
simple distributional units, we could by identical methods have established them as compound distributional units, had we assumed from the
start that they were composed of a sequence of /t + š/ or /d + ž/.

It may be worth while to inspect a little more closely at this point the
anomalous cases visible in *Table* 3 as bold type in a block of plain or vice
versa. We will take first those within bloc 1 in *Table* 3. They may be
abstracted from the whole table as follows:

Table 4

	30	34	53	19	33	14	
	ð	h	r	y	w	ŋ	
55 θ		×					
60 z		×	×	×	×		× = less than half
7 ž		×	×	×	×	×	the total of
14 ŋ	×	×	×	×	×		either participant

An examination of these 8 units and their relations shows that 3 of them
have a very limited distribution, namely, /ž, ŋ, y/. The paucity of occurrence of these phonemes increases the risk of purely random gaps in the
overall pattern due to chance failure of the contexts in which they occur
to coincide in more than a few cases, and the gaps in which the 3 units
mentioned above are concerned are no doubt explicable in this way. On
the other hand the number of contexts they hold in common with other
members of this bloc is clear evidence of where the affinities of these
phonemes lie.

This explanation can hardly hold good, however, for the pairs /θ:r,
z:h, z:r, z:w/, whose occurrences are sufficiently numerous to exclude,
prima facie, doubts on their reliability as a sample. In each of these pairs
it may be observed that one participant does not occur at all in final
place, *ie* /r, w, h/. If allowance is made for this and the total number of
occurrences calculated only in the places in which both participants actually occur, excluding, that is to say, 31 occurrences of /z/ and 20 of /θ/
finally, we then find this position:

	55	34	33
	r	h	w
35 θ	24		
29 z	23	14	14

In other words, /θ:r/ and /z:r/ would then have more than the critical
number of common contexts, but /z:h/ and /z:w/ still would not. An

examination of the results in individual places suggests the reason for this, the figures being as follows:

	/h/	common contexts	/z/	common contexts	/w/
initial	21	8	8	8	17
post-initial	1	1	12	1	6
pre-final	11	5	9	5	10
final	—	—	31	—	—

/z/ and /h/ are seen to have more than 50 per cent common contexts within the limits set by the paucity of occurrences of one or other of them in each individual place. This is also true of /z/ and /w/ except in post-initial place. This indicates, not so much a random result, as a difference of combining power on the part of the various units (but within the framework of the main bloc, as a glance at the /z, w, h/ lines in *Table* 3 will show). In any event the 50 per cent dividing line used here as an arbitrary standard must in no way be considered sacrosanct. It may well be found that in different languages the line should be drawn higher or lower in the percentage scale. In Burmese, for example, according to Troubetzkoy's reckoning,[8] the line could be drawn at 100 per cent, since the structure of words is always of the type CV or V, and all combinations are realized.

In bloc 2, the anomaly /u:yuə/ can be accounted for (*a*) by the small number of occurrences of the participants, and also (*b*) by the non-occurrence of /u/ in final place.

In the bloc showing predominantly the lack of contextual correspondence, the anomalies – here those cases in which the number of common contexts *is* 50 per cent or more of the total occurrences of one participant – can all be accounted for by the paucity of occurrence of one of the units as compared with the great frequency of the other. It is not surprising that those which are scarce of occurrence, /ž/ – 7, /ŋ/ – 14, /u/ – 20, should happen by chance to share a few contexts with some of the large numbers found for /l/ (95), /i/ (77), /ɪ/ (87), /ə/ (84), /ɜu/ (81).

What we have succeeded in doing so far is to establish a repertory of free combining units in English, and to divide them into two classes, members of the same class having distributional characteristics showing an overall similarity. We have reached the stage foreshadowed by Hjelmslev when he wrote: 'It would sometimes be possible to distinguish two types of constituents by studying their mutual government.'[9] These two classes correspond exactly to the traditional vowel/consonant division and for this reason, with no thought of ascribing any ulterior function to our classes, we propose to retain these terms rather than add yet more to the present overburdened vocabulary.[10] 'But,' says Hjelmslev, 'it would never be possible to determine which are to be called consonants and which are to be called vowels, and in many cases even the distinction would turn out to be impossible.' Whether this last assertion is true is a matter on which judgment must be suspended until the net of research has been cast more widely; we are content to say here that the distinction is possible for English.

Our contention is that these two blocs into which the units fall can be very useful in the statement of the phoneme combinations of English. The members of one of the blocs can be used as the central point of a unit of classification larger than the phoneme which will forward the statement of word structure. If we generalize our statement of initial and final pairs, using C and V, respectively, to represent any phoneme belonging to these classes, we arrive at the following result:

| | number of occurrences | |
type	initial	final
CV	421	276
VC	209	277
CC	26	59
VV	10	22

These figures show that:
1. an alternation of C and V (1183 occurrences) is many times more frequent than CC or VV (117 occurrences).
2. CC (85 occurrences) is more common than VV (32 occurrences).
3. C predominates finally and initially, V in post-initial and pre-final place.

	initial and final	post-initial and pre-final	total
C	783	570	1353
V	517	730	1247

The conclusions to be drawn from these figures are:
(a) V has more claim to be considered as a central unit and C as a marginal unit even from the sequential aspect (see 3 above).
(b) The fact that V units stand side by side far less frequently than C units makes a statement of distribution in terms of discrete units with V as a central element and C as marginal element more economical than one in which C were taken as central and V as marginal.

At this point it is immaterial which bloc is called central so far as the *exhaustiveness* of the final statement is concerned. In the event of the consonantal bloc being chosen, the word /spɑks/ would have to be stated as consisting of 4 units: /s+p+ɑk+s/ (or /s+pɑ+k+s/), whereas the word /iɒn/ would be analysed as one unit. If the vowel bloc is chosen, then /spɑks/ is one unit, but /iɒn/ is two: /i+ɒn/. By choosing the second alternative the statement of combinability is made much more conveniently and economically.

However, the existence of monophonemic words whose structure is exclusively V (12 occurrences) clinches the issue, and makes the choice of this bloc imperative if the statement is to be exhaustive.

To sum up, if the vowel is regarded as that one of the two classes of phonemes elicited by the above method which, because of its more restricted occurrence side by side with other members of the bloc and because of its ability to stand alone, is most usefully employed as the nucleus of a unit of phoneme combination, then we shall find that the notion has a high correlation with traditional and intuitional views of the vowel, and we shall have come back, via a strictly phonological route, to the view of consonants as those phonemes which 'sound together' with vowels.

3 Syllable

If it is possible to analyse words in terms of discrete units containing one vowel unit only, preceded and followed by a number of consonant units, then the structure of such units is best investigated by an examination of the one-vowel word. All combinations of o to 3 consonant units preceding the vowel unit with o to 4 following are found, except VCCCC. However, the types of consonant combination are very restricted, and reveal a definite structure.

1 Possibilities of consonant initial

1. Zero consonant is possible before all vowels except /u, uə/.
2. All consonants except /ž/ and /ŋ/ may occur as normal initial simple consonant units.
3. Two-term initial consonant combinations:
   (a) /č, ǰ, h, v, ð, z, y/ are not found as members.
   (b) Each combination contains a normal 'initial', either preceded by a 'pre-initial' /s/ or followed by a 'post-initial' /l, w, r/. This may be illustrated diagrammatically as follows:

pre-initial	normal initial	post-initial
/s/	any consonant	/l r w/
before	except	following
p t k⁽¹¹⁾ f	ž ŋ	p t k f
m n		b d g θ š
(l w)		(s)

(Exceptions: /l/ not after /t, d, θ, š/; /w/ not after /p, b, f, g, š/.)
/sl, sw/ may be regarded either as pre-initial + initial or initial +
post-initial.

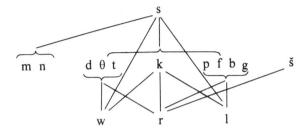

4. Three-term initial consonant combinations are possible only with the
normal initials /p, t, k, f/ which may be both preceded by pre-initial
/s/ and followed by post-initial /w, r, l/. Three-term types found are
/spl, spr, str, skw, skr, sfr/.[12] These may be shown as follows:

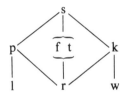

We decided when preparing *Table* 3 to deal with apparent VV sequences in the following way:

(i) Where one element combined freely with any vowel unit, and
thus had a 'consonantal' distribution, we gave it a consonantal
symbol and ranged it amongst the consonants ('semi-vowel' – *ie*
/y/ and /w/). Only under those circumstances is an analysis into
semi-vowel or vowel + semi-vowel permissible.

(ii) Where neither element is freely replaceable by another, but the
sequence as a whole has a distribution approximating to that of
simple vowel units, we rate it as a compound vowel unit (diphthong or triphthong). Thus /yu/ is treated as a diphthong because
in secondary position neither /y-/ nor /-u/ can be replaced by
other vowel units, and the group /yu/ shows the same distributional characteristics as do simple vowel units.

(iii) Where each element is freely replaceable by another, or where the
sequence has a restricted and apparently random distribution, it
is taken as a chance juxtaposition of two independent simple
vowel units.

It is possible that the same procedure may be applied to consonants. To test this we studied the distribution of vowels following initial consonant combinations and found the following:

Consonant combination: sp st sk sf pr tr kr br dr gr fr θr šr
No of vowels following: 21 19 16 5 14 14 17 15 16 15 14 10 9
pl kl bl gl fl sl sm sn tw kw dw θw sw (py ty ky by
13 15 15 14 15 13 11 15 9 14 3 3 14 2 1 2 1
dy fy θy sy hy vy ly my ny)
1 2 2 2 1 1 2 1 1
spl spr str skr skw (sfr spy sty sky)
8   11 11 10 8   1   2   1   1

The majority of consonant combinations have a combinability factor approaching that of simple consonant units, though a trifle reduced. It will be seen, however, that combinations of the types /Cy/ and /CCy/ have a particularly restricted distribution and cannot therefore be regarded as compound consonant units in the same way. They are moreover followed only by /u/ and /uə/. The groups /yu/ and /yuə/ are thus freely combinable with a wide range of simple and compound consonant units. This analysis gives overall economy in the inventory of vowel and consonant units.[13]

Other combinations of limited scatter are:

(*a*) /sf/ and /sfr/. All words with these initials are 'learned' words of Greek phonology. *Sphere* and *spherical* alone have wide currency. Their exclusion would, to some extent, simplify the pattern of initial consonant combinations.

(*b*) /θw/ and /dw/.

Against the treatment of initial combinations as compound consonant units speaks the fact that they are tied to the initial position and are not freely combinable in all positions.[14]

2 Possibilities of consonant final

1. Zero consonant is possible with all vowel units, simple and compound, except /e, æ, ɒ, ʊ, ʌ/.
2. All consonants except /h, r, w, y/ may occur as normal final simple consonant units.
3. The structure of final consonant combinations presents more difficulties than that of initials. The use of consonant suffixes as a morphological device makes for a greater variety of combination. The same phoneme may recur within a combination, and combinations of greater length are found. It might seem that a simpler answer would be attained by taking the morpheme into account, and analysing final combinations such as /θæŋks/ into /θæŋk + s/, /tenθs/ into /ten + θ + s/

and treating as compound units only those combinations which cannot be resolved in this way.

It seems to us, however, that it is methodologically preferable to make a phonological analysis independent of other levels of linguistic analysis. Analysis at each level should, in our view, be made self-consistent, and only then should correlations at different levels be established, and the degree of congruence determined. In addition, the difficulty of establishing morphemic division (*eg* in *spent, health, drift*) is well known, and in any case the structure of final consonant combinations involving added suffixes does not require separate treatment from that of other finals.

The suggested treatment is very similar to Bloomfield's,[15] but differs from it in one respect. The core of the final consonant group is the *normal final*. Any consonant may be found in this position except /h, r, w, y/ which do not occur as simple finals. The normal final may be preceded by a *pre-final* and followed by one or two *post-finals*. These latter are often suffixed morphemes, but need not be. The consonants occupying these positions are as follows:

pre-final	normal final	post-final	2nd post-final
l	any consonant	θ	t (d)[16]
m n ŋ	except	t d	s
s	h r w y	s z	

/l/ is found in final combinations only as a pre-final, and may precede any normal final except /g, ð, ŋ/, which never take a pre-final.

/m, n/ take only /l/ as pre-final. As pre-finals, /m/ occurs before /p, b, f/, /n/ before /t, (d),[17] č, ǰ, s, (z)/,[17] and /ŋ/ before /k/.

/s/ occurs as pre-final before /p, (t),[17] k/.

/k/ occurs as pre-final before /s/.

/θ/ occurs as post-final after /p, t, (k),[18] f, s, l, m, n, ŋ/.

/t/ occurs as post-final after /p, k, č, f, θ, s, š/.

/d/ occurs as post-final after /b, g, ǰ, v, ð, z, ž, l, m, n, ŋ/.

/s/ occurs as post-final after /p, t, k, f, θ/.

/z/ occurs as post-final after /b, d, g, v, ð, l, m, n, ŋ/.

/t/ occurs as second post-final after /s/.

/s/ occurs as second post-final after /t, θ/.

Two-term final combinations may be analysed as pre-final + normal final or as normal final + post-final. In most cases this will give an unambiguous analysis, but in the case of a possible pre-final + possible post-final the choice is clearly arbitrary.

The 48 three-term consonant combinations may be analysed as pre-final + normal final + post-final, or normal final + post-final + 2nd post-final. (Here too the choice may be ambiguous, as with /l, m, n, ŋ + θs; l, n, s, k + ts; l, n, k + st/.)

Only one three-term combination is found containing a sequence not permitted in two-term combinations. The combinations found show 10 consonants in the first position, 14 in the second, and 5 in the third, as shown in the following table:

	post-final + 2nd post-final																						
	θs	ts	st	ps	pt	ks	kt	čt	jd	dz	zd	bz	bd	vz	vd	mz	md	nz	fθ	fs	ft	sθ	tθ
pre-final																							
l	×	×	×	×	×	×	×	×	×	×	×	×	×	×	×	×	×	×		×	×	×	×
n	×	×	×			×	×	×	×														×
s			×	×	×	×	×																
ŋ	×					×	×																
m	×			×	×																		
k		×	×																			×	
normal final																							
p	×	×	×																				
f	×	×																					
t	×																						
d												×											

Seven four-term combinations are found: /lkts/ (*mulcts*), /mpst/ (*glimpsed*), /mpts/ (*exempts*), /ksts/ (*texts*), /lfθs/ (*twelfths*), /ksθs/ (*sixths*), /ntθs/ (*thousandths*). 'Alternative pronunciations', such as /glɑntst/ (*glanced*), /leŋkθs/ (*lengths*), /klendzd/ (*cleansed*) are not included, but on the other hand most of the words containing four-term combinations have an alternative pronunciation containing a three-term combination (/twelθs/), or contain a sequence analogous to the excluded 'alternative pronunciation' – /glɪmpst/ or /glɪmst/, /ɪgzempts/ or /ɪgzemts/, /θʌuzəntθs/ or /θʌuzənθs/. Apart from the very rare word *mulcts*, the only words containing a certain four-term combination are /sɪksθs/ and /teksts/. A case may fairly be made out, in view of the fact that /k/ occurs as pre-final only before /s/, for regarding /ks/ as a close-knit compound consonant unit functioning as a simple consonant unit.[19] Moreover, the combinations /ksθ, ksθs/ are the only three- or four-term combinations to contain a sequence (/sθ/) which is not found as a two-term combination. In this way it would be possible to eliminate the few four-term combinations altogether. Classification of final clusters could then be based on the structure of three-term finals, and the concept of 2nd post-final need not be introduced. It was perhaps this that led Bloomfield (*loc cit*) to prefer the idea of 2nd pre-final to that of 2nd post-final. However, the two post-finals system is clearly more economical, given the need to classify four-term final consonant combinations, since in them the possibilities of occurrence in the last two terms are more limited than in the first two.

1st term	2nd term	3rd term	4th term
k l m n	p t k s f	t θ s	t s

Further, those occurring as 4th term occur also as 3rd, whereas those occurring as 2nd term are of a different order from those found as 1st term, and involve phonemes it is not otherwise necessary to treat as pre-finals.

Having described the structure of one-vowel words, we can now apply the ideas of permitted sequence derived from them to the structure of plurivocalic words. That is, we may proceed to analyse longer sequences containing a number of vowels into a succession of discrete units, each composed of one simple or compound vowel unit, preceded and followed by zero, or a simple consonant unit or permitted consonant combination. Such a procedure accounts for the vast majority of cases, leaving only a very small residue requiring further elucidation.

For instance, in words such as /erə/ possible divisions into V|CV and VC|V each yield a syllable unit (/e/ or /er/) of a type not found in one-vowel words, since neither /e/ nor /r/ are found in final place. To account for these it is necessary to set up a syllable type which cannot occur finally in a sequence of syllables, or in isolation, just as there are phonemes which cannot occur finally in a sequence of phonemes. We prefer to regard sequences of /e, æ, ɒ, ʊ, ʌ + r + V/ as divided V|CV, so as to bring them into line with other VCV sequences, which, as shown below, are best divided in this way.

So far as we are aware, the only medial consonant cluster which is not reducible to permitted final + permitted initial consonant combination is /ŋgw/ as in *language*. This we prefer to divide /-ŋ|gw-/, thus setting up a syllable-initial conbination /gw/ not found in absolute initial except for proper names, as /gwen/, /gwɪn/, and exotic /gwɑvə/.

The point of syllable division is often unambiguous; thus, in /æŋgə/ it must be placed between /ŋ/ and /g/, the sequence /ŋg/ being permitted neither initially nor finally. In /æŋkšəs/, the division comes between /k/ and /š/, since the sequence /ŋk/ is permitted finally, but not /ŋkš/, nor are /ŋkš/ or /kš/ permitted initially. Similarly with /ɪn|reɪǰ/, /ɪks|čeɪnǰ/, /æθ|lit/.

Generally, however, there is a choice of syllable division. In the word /ekstrə/, for instance, only the possibilities /e|kstrə/ and /ekstr|ə/ are excluded. The divisions /ek|strə/, /eks|trə/, /ekst|rə/ all yield a permitted final + a permitted initial combination. Indeterminacy of syllable division as opposed to syllable nucleus has often been remarked in English.

Our thesis seems to us substantiated by the fact that the examples cited as indeterminate are always those where there are these alternative analyses into permitted final + permitted initial.

However, there is in these cases a certain preference for one division as against another. It is of course most disputable to what extent the intuition of native speakers may be taken into account in linguistic analysis. It is probable that many intuitive native linguistic judgments are based on a lifelong unconscious statistical discussion of speech material. On the other hand those of an educated speaker are likely to be coloured by taught linguistic ideas, such as school grammars or a particular method of learning to read. In a literate society these factors are very strong, and naïve speakers rare. 'Native intuition' is in these circumstances suspect. Nonetheless, a proffered linguistic analysis which correlates closely with intuitive judgment is likely to give a better account of the facts of a language than one which contradicts it.

The preference for one syllable division as opposed to another may be explained in terms of the frequency of occurrence of different types of syllable finals and initials. These were:

	number of occurrences	
type	*initial*	*final*
CV	421	276
VC	209	277
CC	26	59
VV	10	22
V	12	

Thus, if a sequence VCV may be analysed into VC|V or V|CV, the relative probabilities of division would be of the order of $277 + 12 = 289$ to $12 + 421 = 433$. This accounts for the often heard dictum: 'If possible a syllable should begin with a consonant.' If VCCV (*eg* /æstə/) may be 'permitted' as V|CCV, VC|CV, or VCC|V, the relative probabilities of these solutions would be of the order of $(12 + 26)\ 38 : (277 + 421)\ 698 : (59 + 12)$ 71. The 'preference' for the division VC|CV is clearly overwhelming.

A fuller statistical treatment of final clusters similar to that of initials on *p* 244 would be needed before the divisions could be determined in every case. However, there seems to be no reason why the principle should not be of general application.

4 Conclusion

The findings of this paper may be summarized as follows.

Given the possibility of providing an initial phoneme inventory for English by a method of commutation not involving considerations of vowel, consonant, or syllable, it is possible, by a study of the combinatory latitudes of each phoneme, to separate out two classes corresponding to the conventional vowel/consonant dichotomy. An examination of the various cases of phoneme ambivalence led to a procedure for establishing a repertory of free combining units, simple and compound, vowel and consonant.

Following on this, the syllable may be defined as a minimal pattern of phoneme combination with a vowel unit as nucleus, preceded and followed by a consonant unit or permitted consonant combination. All longer sequences are to be analysed as a succession of syllables, the relative frequency of occurrence of various syllable-initial and syllable-final consonant combinations furnishing a basis for determining the point of syllable division in cases where this is not immediately apparent from the above analysis. The syllable is thus established irrespective of accentual features, though it may subsequently be useful to relate the two together.

Whether this approach, or some modification of it, will be of value in the study of other languages,[20] remains to be seen. For English, however, we feel able to claim with some confidence that it gives a clearer result than any other method so far advanced.

Notes

[1] *Eg* Louis Hjelmslev: 'The Syllable as a Structural Unit,' *Proceedings of the Third International Congress of Phonetic Sciences*, Ghent, 1938, *p* 266.

[2] Hjelmslev, *op cit*, *p* 270.

[3] K. L. Pike: *Phonemics*, Univ. of Michigan Publications, Linguistics III, Ann Arbor, 1947, *pp* 60, 235, 254.

[4] *Language*, 8.8.

[5] Previous attempts at formulating the structure of the English syllable, such as the one by Benjamin Lee Whorf ('Linguistics as an Exact Science', *The Technology Review*, 43, 1940, 61–3, 80–3; reprinted in his *Four Articles on Metalinguistics*, Foreign Service Institute, Washington, 1950, *p* 12), had a more limited theoretical purpose. Whorf's contribution presented only the final model of the syllable without the process by which it was constructed; it did not extend to polysyllabic words, and was based on a different dialect of English ('standard midwestern American').

[6] Considerations of space have forced us to dispense with the tables for common contexts in the three places other than initial. The results of the missing tables and the differences between them and *Table* 1 may be summed up as follows:

1. *Post-initial place.* Number of different contexts in which each phoneme occurs: p 9, t 10, k 11, b 9, d 10, g 9, č 7, ǰ 6, f 8, θ 8, s 10, š 4, h 1, v 7, ð 1, z 6, ž 1, r 16, l 15, m 11, n 10, ŋ 4, i 22, ɪ 25, e 22, æ 21, ɑ 19 ɒ 21, ɔ 20, ʊ 18, u 19, ʌ 22, з 21, ə 21. Common contexts (50 per cent or more) shared by post-initial phonemes but not by initial phonemes (*Table* 1): ž + all but č, h, ð, i, ɪ, e, æ, ɑ, ɒ, ɔ, ʊ, u, ʌ, з, ə; r + i, e, æ, ɑ, ɒ, ɔ, ʊ, ʌ, з, ə; l + ɒ; ŋ + all but ǰ, h, i, e, æ, ɑ, ɒ, ɔ, u, ʌ, з, ə; ʊ + i, e, æ, ɑ, ɒ, ɔ, u, ʌ, з, ə; u + e, ɑ, ɒ, ɔ, ʊ, ʌ; ə + t, č, ǰ, f, θ, l. Common contexts (50 per cent or more) shared by initial phonemes (*Table* 1) but not by post-initial

phonemes: s + ᴅ, ʌ; ð + b, č, ǰ, f, θ, h, z, ž, r; ɪ + p, k, b, d, g, č, ǰ, θ, s, š, h, v, z, ž, m; ʊ + p, t, k, b, d, g, č, ǰ, f, θ, s, š, h, v, z, ž, m, n.

2. *Pre-final place.* Number of different contexts in which each phoneme occurs: p 9, t 8, k 9, b 8, d 7, g 6, č 7, ǰ 7, f 9, θ 5, s 11, š 6, h 4, v 6, ð 5, z 6, ž 2, r 6, l 22, m 11, n 13, ŋ 6, i 20, ɪ 24, e 18, æ 18, ɑ 17, ᴅ 18, ɔ 16, ʊ 12, u 22, ʌ 19, ɜ 17, ə 12. Common contexts (50 per cent or more) shared by pre-final phonemes but not by initial phonemes (*Table* 1): ž + all but h; ŋ + all but p, k, č, θ, š, h, r; l and n + i, e, æ, ɑ, ᴅ, ɔ, ʌ, ɜ; l + ə; i + g, θ, v, ð; e + t, b, g, f, θ, s, š, v, ð, z, m: ɔ + t, b, g, f, θ, s, š, v, ð, z, m; ʊ + i, e, æ, ɑ, ᴅ, ɔ, u, ʌ, ɜ, ə; u + e, ɑ, ᴅ, ɔ, ʌ; ʌ + g, θ, v, ð. Common contexts (50 per cent or more) shared by initial phonemes (*Table* 1) but not by pre-final phonemes: θ + b, h, v, ð, z, ŋ; s + ᴅ, ʌ; š + v; h + g, v, ð, ž, ŋ.

3. *Final place.* Number of different contexts in which each phoneme occurs: p 14, t 21, k 15, b 12, d 23, g 8, č 11, ǰ 12, f 13, θ 16, s 19, š 10, v 9, ð 3, z 20, ž 4, l 12, m 13, n 12, ŋ 4, i 20, ɪ 24, ɑ 18, ɔ 17, ʊ 2, u 17, ɜ 11, ə 27. The phonemes h, r, e, æ, ᴅ, ʌ do not occur; given this, the common contexts (50 per cent or more) shared by final phonemes but not by initial phonemes (*Table* 1) are: ž + all but ŋ, ɪ, ɔ, ʊ, u, ɜ, ŋ + all but ð, i, ɪ, ɑ, ɔ, u, ɜ, ə; i + t, d, ð; ɑ + t, d, ð, z, ž; ɔ + t; u + t, ɑ, ɔ; ɜ + t, s; ə + all but v, ŋ, i, ɪ, ɑ, ᴅ, u, ɜ. Common contexts (50 per cent or more) shared by initial phonemes (*Table* 1) but not by final phonemes: ɪ + k, b, g, č, f, š, v, ð, ž, l, m, n, ŋ; ʊ + ð.

⁷ Words such as *little, button, lissom,* have been analysed in the body of the paper as ending in /-əl/, /-ən/, /-əm/, and it is therefore necessary to show what would be the effect of the alternative analysis /l̩, n̩, m̩/. The changes involved in the pre-final and final lists would be:

Deleted: əl.

Added: pl tl kl bl dl gl čl ǰl fl θl sl šl vl ðl zl rl ml nl; pn tn kn bn dn gn čn ǰn fn θn sn šn vn ðn zn žn rn mn; sm ðm zm.

The effect of these changes is to add to the contexts of /l, m, n/ in final position a number (18 for /l/ and /n/, 3 for /m/) in common with bloc 2. In the case of /l/ and /n/ the number of such occurrences is sufficient to cause these phonemes to have a distribution more than 50 per cent common with both blocs. We therefore proceed as with /y/ and /w/, separating /l/ and /n/ into two units each, one adhering to bloc 1 and one to bloc 2. This is what is in fact done when 'syllabic *l, m, n*' are spoken of. The position of /m/ in these examples is clearly parallel to that of /l/ and /n/, but its extremely small occurrence in this place tends to obscure the picture.

It may be objected that the distribution of /l, m, n/ in these examples is similar to that of the post-finals /p, t, b, d, θ/. The essential difference is that these latter are limited in occurrence to a restricted range of preceding consonants, with which they form a close unity, whereas /l̩, m̩, n̩/ are independent of the preceding consonant.

⁸ *Grundzüge der Phonologie,* Travaux du Cercle Linguistique de Prague VII, 1939, *p* 220; French edn, *p* 264.

⁹ *Loc cit.*

¹⁰ However, care must be taken not to attribute automatically acoustic or articulatory characteristics to vowel and consonant units in the phonological system. An acoustic or articulatory analysis of a large number of utterances may well yield a classification into two classes according to the possession of common articulatory or acoustic features. But they are classes in an entirely different order of analysis. We may establish correlations between phonological, articulatory, and acoustic classes, and these may in fact be fairly

close, so that we find the same terms, vowel and consonant, applied to them. But there is no question of identity, and the correlation should not be expected to be exact. This problem is discussed in great detail by Eli Fischer-Jørgensen, 'The Phonetic Basis for Identification of Phonemic Elements,' *Journal of the Acoustical Society of America*, 24, 1952, 611–617. In this case we shall be dealing with some phonological consonants (or vowels) which do not correspond to such recurrent features of the utterance as would fall naturally into the consonant (or vowel) class yielded by an articulatory or acoustic classification. We must at all times be aware of the order of analysis within which our terms operate. The terms *vowel* and *consonant* as used here denote classes obtained by the analysis of the constraints which operate at the phonological level in English.

[11] We have accepted the traditional analysis into /sp, st, sk/ though aware of the problems involved (*cf* W. F. Twaddell: *On Defining the Phoneme*, Language Monographs 16, Baltimore, 1935, *p* 31). Our findings will apply, *mutatis mutandis*, to the alternative analysis.

[12] Only in the word *sphragistics*.

[13] It reduces initial CC to 26 types and CCC to 6, enabling us to dispense with 13 two-term and 3 three-term consonant combinations occurring only before /u/ and /ʊə/, and some involving consonants not otherwise found in initial combinations.

[14] We feel that it is probably best to confine the use of the term 'compound consonant unit' to cases such as /sp, st, sk/ which are found in all positions, and to use the term 'consonant combination' for other groups of consonants occurring either initially or finally. /spr/ etc could then be regarded as a two-term consonant combination consisting of a compound + a simple consonant unit (/sp + r/).

[15] *Language*, 8.4.

[16] Only in the linguistic curiosity *adzed*.

[17] The choice between analysing a possible pre-final + a possible post-final as pre-final + final or final + post-final is clearly arbitrary.

[18] Possibly in *length*. We prefer to regard the optional /k/ as a phonetic feature of utterances in which it occurs having no phonological relevance.

[19] But see note 14.

[20] A tentative approach to this method is to be seen in Otto v. Essen: 'Die Silbe – ein phonologischer Begriff,' *Zs. f. Phonetik*, 5, 1951, 199–203. Concerning syllable division see also Jens Holt: 'La frontière syllabique en danois,' *Travaux du Cercle Linguistique de Copenhague*, 5, 1949, 256–265.

R. H. Robins

Aspects of prosodic analysis

The object of this paper is to give some account and illustration of what would seem to be certain of the general principles of Prosodic Analysis, as being developed among the group of linguists working in London in association with Professor J. R. Firth. Prosodic analysis falls under the general rubric of phonology, and this in turn comes within the compass of descriptive linguistics.

The modern era of general and descriptive linguistics may perhaps be said to begin with the great Swiss scholar Ferdinand de Saussure, whose lectures, published posthumously in 1916 (*Cours de Linguistique Générale*, Paris, 1949, 4th edition), more than any one other factor served to broaden the academic study of language from its nineteenth-century preoccupation with the comparative and historical aspect, and to establish as well as christen the discipline of synchronic linguistics. In establishing synchronic linguistics de Saussure did much to inaugurate the application of structural analysis to language, which is emphasized by almost all schools of linguistics today.

Many of the main features of structural linguistics, on which the literature is now very extensive, can be traced back to de Saussure, whose ideas were developed on different lines by the Prague school and by Hjelmslev; *cf* especially Karl Bühler, 'Das Strukturmodell der Sprache', *TCLP* 6, 1936, *pp* 3–12, Ernst A. Cassirer, 'Structuralism in Modern Linguistics', *Word* 1, 1945, *pp* 99–120, Louis Hjelmslev, 'The Structural Analysis of Language', *Studia Linguistica* 1, 1947, *pp* 69–78, *Prolegomena to a Theory of Language* (trans Whitfield, as Supplement to *IJAL* 19, 1, 1953), *pp* 13–17.

First published in *Proceedings of the University of Durham Philosophical Society*, Vol 1, Series B (Arts), No 1: 1–12, 1957.

.

In developing the structural approach to language, de Saussure drew attention to the two dimensions that must be taken into account in linguistic analysis, the syntagmatic and the associative, in his own terms (*Cours*, *pp* 170–175) Rapports Syntagmatiques and Rapports Associatifs, the former referring to the relations obtaining between elements in parallel to the stream of speech ('in praesentia'), the letter to the relations ('in absentia') between different elements in the language that are associated in some way with the items at various points in stretches of speech. This latter set of relations was more appropriately designated Paradigmatic by Hjelmslev (*Actes du Quatrième Congrès International de Linguistes*, 1936, *p* 140), thereby avoiding the latent psychologism of de Saussure's term.

In connection with these two sets of relations, syntagmatic and paradigmatic, it is desirable to keep apart on the same lines the terms *Structure* and *System*, so often used almost interchangeably, and to employ *structure* and its derivatives (*structural*, etc) to refer to the syntagmatic relations and pieces in parallel with stretches of utterance in a language, and to reserve *system* and its derivatives (*systemic*, etc) for the paradigms of comparable and contrastive elements relevant to the various places in structures (see further Robins (3), *p* 109, Allen (5), *p* 556. Publications listed at the end of this paper will be referred to by name (and number) only). Thus syllables, words, and sentences constitute structures, and the relations between and within them are structural relations; the familiar vowel triangles and quadrilaterals of languages, and sets of consonants or consonant clusters applicable to particular places in syllables or words are examples of phonological systems, and the word classes (parts of speech) of a language and its sets of inflectional categories are grammatical systems.

During the period in which de Saussure's thought was making its impact on linguistics, the synchronic study of phonology was expressing itself in the development of the phoneme theory, or, as we might better put it from the standpoint of today, the various phoneme theories. The dominance of the phoneme concept on phonology at the present time may be seen in the array of phoneme-derived terms currently in use, particularly in the writings of American linguists (phonemic, allophone, phonemicize, rephonemicize, etc).

The origin of the phoneme as a linguistic concept must be seen in the search for economical 'phonetic transcriptions' of the type of Sweet's Broad Romic and Daniel Jones's Broad Transcription (*cf* Henry Sweet, *Handbook of Phonetics*, Oxford, 1877, *pp* 100–108, 182–183, Daniel Jones, *Outline of English Phonetics*, 6th edition, Cambridge, 1947, *pp* 48–51). Since these early days different interpretations and theoretical developments have made such growth that the need has been felt to formulate explicit statements of principle in regard to phonemic analysis; one may instance in particular Trubetzkoy's *Grundzüge der Phonologie* (*TCLP* 7, 1939, trans Cantineau, Paris, 1949), Bloch's 'Set of Postulates

for Phonemic Analysis' (*Language* 24, 1948, *pp* 3–46), Daniel Jones's
The Phoneme; its Nature and Use (Cambridge, 1950), and the all-too-
neglected monograph by W. Freeman Twaddell, *On Defining the
Phoneme* (*Language Monograph* 16, 1935).

During the development of the phoneme theories, considerable discussion took place on the status of the phoneme as an analytical term, on the
classical lines of the philosophical disputes between realists, conceptua-
lists, and nominalists. According to the realist view, espoused by Jones
and others (*cf* Jones, 'Concrete and Abstract Sounds', *Proc. 3rd Int.
Cong. Phon. Sci.*, 1936, *pp* 1–7), the phoneme has actual existence as an
'abstract sound' or structural entity in the language to which it belongs;
on the conceptualist view, favoured by Trubetzkoy for a time (*cf* 'La
Phonologie Actuelle', in *Psychologie du Langage*, Paris, 1933, *pp* 227–246,
'Zur Allgemeinen Theorie der Phonologischen Vokalsysteme', *TCLP*, 1,
1929, *pp* 39–67. But note his later views, *Principes de Phonologie* (trans
Cantineau), *pp* 41–46), the phoneme is a mental entity or conception as
against the sound, which is a physiological and acoustic entity. The
nominalist attitude, in contrast to both the above viewpoints, is that the
phoneme, like any other element of scientific analysis, is no more than an
appropriate term or operational fiction, with which to handle the mass of
observations and to make orderly statements about the gross data, in the
case of phonetics, the sounds of a language (*cf* Twaddell, *op cit, pp* 33–36).

It might be said that this controversy is of no concern to linguists as
such; but it has a relevance to linguistic work, not as an aspect of philosophical thinking, but as one of method and attitude to linguistic science.
In a fairly recent statement of the realist position, Pike writes (*Phonemics*,
Ann Arbor, 1947, *pp* 57–58): 'It is assumed in this volume that *phonemes
exist as structural entities or relationships*, and that *our analytical purpose is
to find and symbolize them*. This implies that there is only one accurate
phonemic analysis of any one set of data' (author's italics). This says in
effect that phonemes exist in some way in languages apart from the work
of the analyst, who is finding an existing structure or system lying behind
the phenomena of utterance, and that this structure or system is organized
in phonemes, which the linguist must discover and in his description and
symbolism represent as accurately as he can.

Methodologically there is much to be said for the nominalist point of
view. Such an attitude, which has been somewhat flippantly labelled
'hocus-pocus' in contrast to the 'God's truth' or realist position (*cf* Fred
W. Householder in *IJAL*, 18, 1952, *pp* 260–268), does not imply any
levity towards language as an object of study, nor any scientific irrespon-
sibility or disregard of the need for the most meticulous observation and
painstaking analysis that is possible. All that adherents of this view of the
subject would claim is that existence or reality are not properly predicable
of anything other than the actual phenomena or data under observation.

Terms and concepts used in analysis are in the nature of a set of words, and no more, employed by the analyst to talk about his data, and in so talking to make summary statements and analyses which account for and explain not only the data from which they are made, but also further data from the same field, in the case of the linguist, from the same language. Phonemes, like all other technical terms in linguistics, take their place as part of the linguist's 'language about language', and no more than that. In linguistics we are, in fact, putting language to an unfamiliar and relatively uncomfortable task, that of talking about itself. To summarize, one may quote Firth ('Personality and Language in Society', *Sociological Review*, 42, 1950, *p* 42): 'In the most general terms we study language as part of the social process, and what we may call the systematics of phonetics and phonology, of grammatical categories or of semantics, are ordered schematic constructs, frames of reference, a sort of scaffolding for the handling of events . . . Such constructs have no ontological status and we do not project them as having being or existence. They are neither immanent nor transcendent, but just language turned back on itself'.

The attitude summed up here is relevant to the purpose of this paper. If the terms and categories employed by the linguist are, as it were, imposed on the language in the process of analysis, it follows that linguistic structures and systems must likewise be thought of not as pre-existing or discoverable in any literal sense, but rather as the product of the linguist in working over his material. No one analysis, or mode of analysis, is the only one accurate or sacroscant, but any account of the language, in any terms, is an adequate statement and analysis, provided that, and to the extent to which, it comprehensively and economically explains what is heard (and read) in the language, and 'renews connection' with further experience of it. Questions of truth and falsity of 'what is there' and 'what is not there', only arise on the view here set out at the level of the barest phonetic observation and recording, before any analysis has taken place.

The last few paragraphs may seem like an unnecessary methodological digression, but it is necessary to make it clear that in developing phonological analysis on prosodic lines there is no suggestion that phonemic analysis is wrong, invalid, or untrue. In terms of the general theory of linguistic analysis just outlined, such statements have no meaning. Nor is it suggested that phonemic analysis is inapplicable or unhelpful.

It is however, legitimate to claim that from its origin the phoneme concept has been primarily tied to transcription, the representation of a language in terms of its phonic material by means of discrete and consecutive letters or symbols on paper (*cf* the sub-title of Pike's book *Phonemics, A Technique for Reducing Languages to Writing*), and that in consequence of this, phoneme theories have necessarily concentrated on minimal contrast in identical environment, emphasizing the paradigmatic aspect of phonological relationships at the expense of the syntagmatic or structural aspect (in the narrower sense of *structural* referred to at the beginning of this paper). Where a language is unwritten, or where the orthography is far from adequate as a key to pronunciation, a phonemic analysis may well be indispensable as the basis of a workable transcription unburdened with the excess of different symbols required in a narrow impressionistically 'accurate' phonetic transcription. But phonological analysis need not stop at or be based on phonemic transcription.

The aim of prosodic analysis in phonology is not that of transcription or unilinear representation of languages, but rather a phonological analysis in terms which take account not only of paradigmatic relations and contrasts, but also of the equally important syntagmatic relations and functions which are operative in speech. These syntagmatic factors should be systematized and made explicit in phonology, no less than paradigmatic contrasts.

The theory of prosodic analysis was put forward in a paper read to the Philological Society by Firth in 1948, and since then applications of the method there presented and theoretical developments have been undertaken with reference to a variety of individual languages. An attempt will be made here to state the principles of this sort of analysis very briefly and then elaborate them in the light of recent work and with the aid of examples.

Prosodic analysis is, in fact, an abbreviated designation of an analysis that makes use of two types of element, Prosodies and Phonematic Units (*cf* Firth (2), *pp* 150–152, Allen (5), *p* 556); the latter are not phonemes or phonemic units, and the analysis is carried out in terms other than phonemic. In this analysis, abstractions adequate to a full analysis of the phonological working of the language are made from the phonic data, or the raw material of the actual utterances, and these abstractions fall into the two categories of prosodies and phonematic units. Phonematic units refer to those features or aspects of the phonic material which are best regarded as referable to minimal segments, having serial order in relation to each other in structures. In the most general terms such units constitute the consonant and vowel elements or C and V units of a phonological structure. Structures are not, however, completely stated in these terms; a great part, sometimes the greater part, of the phonic material is referable to prosodies, which are, by definition, of more than one segment in scope or domain of relevance, and may in fact belong to structures of any length, though in practice no prosodies have yet been stated as referring to structures longer than sentences. We may thus speak of syllable prosodies, prosodies of syllable groups, phrase or sentence-part prosodies, and sentence prosodies; and since grammatically defined elements may also be characterized by prosodic features (*cf* Sharp, *pp* 168–169) we may have in addition word and morpheme prosodies. A structure will thus be stated as a syntagmatic entity comprising phonematic or segmental units and one or more prosodies belonging to the structure as a whole.

This abstract statement of principle may be illustrated from the application of prosodic analysis to Siamese (Henderson (1)), a basically monosyllabic and tonal language with fairly rigid patterns of syllable structure. Phonological analysis of a Siamese sentence involves among others, the following prosodic and phonematic elements:

Sentence prosody: intonation;

prosodies of sentence pieces: length, stress and tone relations between component syllables;

syllable prosodies: length, tone, stress, palatalization, labiovelarization;

prosodies of syllable parts: aspiration, retroflexion, plosion, unexploded closure.

Phonematic consonant and vowel units, in such classes as velar, dental, bilabial, nasal, front, back, rounded, unrounded.

After this very summary and incomplete illustration, more may be said in explanation and justification of the methods of prosodic analysis. Phonemic analysis essentially involves the allotment of all the phonic material that is regarded as relevant to individual segments or segmental phonemes, except for the special case of suprasegmental phonemes which are of limited application (*cf* below, *p* 273). But a great deal of the phonic material of languages seems clearly to belong to structures longer than single segments, and is very probably so perceived by the native speakers. Broadly speaking this may come about in two ways.

In the first case a feature may be spread or realized phonetically over a structure, such as a syllable, as a whole; examples of this type of syllable prosody are stress, pitch, and length, nasalization, in languages in which a nasal consonant is always followed by a nasalized vowel and a nasalized vowel is only found after a nasal consonant, and palatalization and velarization, when front or palatally articulated consonants are associated in the syllable with front type vowels and back type consonants with back articulated vowels, as in some Slavonic languages. In languages with 'vowel harmony' as a feature of word structure, for example Turkish and Hungarian, this is well treated as a prosodic feature of the word as a whole or word prosody; these word prosodies may be put in such categories as Front, Back, and Lip-rounded, and apply to the words concerned as structures, the articulation of the consonants being determined by the relevant prosodies no less than that of the vowels (*cf* Waterson, *pp* 578–580). Intonation sequences or 'tunes' that are associated with sentences or with divisions within sentences (clauses and the like) are stated as prosodies of sentences or of sentence parts. The typical English intonation tunes 1 and 2, as described by Daniel Jones (*Outline*, *pp* 258–276), are obvious examples.

Features of the type that have just been instanced can, of course, be analysed phonemically, but in such an analysis there is the risk of misrepresenting or distorting important aspects of the phonic material. Where a feature belongs in the manner described above to a syllable (for example) as a whole, this of necessity involves the phonemicist in saying that at one point in the syllable, say the consonant, the distinction between (say) palatalization and non-palatalization is phonemic or relevant (in Prague terms pertinent (*cf* Trubetzkoy, *Principes* (trans Cantineau), *p* 34)), while the same feature in the vowel, being a consonant concomitant of the consonantal feature, must be relegated to non-significance, non-pertinence, or 'redundancy'. Yet at what point are we to tell, if at any point, that the feature involved is perceived and so functions for the native listener? It is not of course, implied that linguistic analysis can or should be based on the Sprachgefühl or sentiment linguistique of native speakers; but it is desirable that the analysis should not be in violent disagreement with it. This may be illustrated from Jones's treatment of the palatalized (soft) and non-palatalized (hard) consonants in Russian (Daniel Jones, *The Phoneme, pp* 50–53, *cf pp* 25–26). Any phonemic analysis of Russian, it would appear, must recognize as phonemic the difference between the two sets of consonants in that language; this being so, the concomitant differences in the quality of adjacent vowels will necessarily be non-distinctive phonemically. But we are told that the difference between a palatalized and a non-palatalized consonant is in many words easier to recognize by the difference in the adjacent vowel than in the consonant itself. Thus we are involved in listening to the non-distinctive or irrelevant feature in order to catch what is distinctive or relevant. An analysis of palatalization and non-palatalization as syllable prosodies with phonetic realization in the syllable as a whole helps to avoid this rather paradoxical form of statement, though it is obviously necessary to differentiate, by the concept of Focus (*cf* Allen (3), *p* 943), or otherwise, palatalized syllables with initial palatalized consonants, those with final palatalized consonants, and those with both.

We must not be slaves to our machines in preference to the observations of the human ear, for which in the first instance speech is given utterance, but it may be relevant to notice that the tracings of the kymograph show scant regard for the phonemic segmentation of each and every phonetic feature that requires phonological notice. In kymograph tracings made of the utterances of a Georgian speaker (Robins (1), *pp* 66, 70; see also the kymograph tracings on *p* 269, below) it is clearly shown that the glottalized consonants, p', t', tʃ', k' and q', are followed in the syllable by vowels of a constricted or glottalized tamber, a feature also noticeable in listening. Glottalization in such syllables may be treated as a feature of the syllable and abstracted as a syllable prosody.

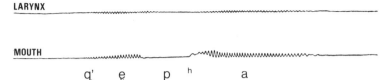

Fig 1: Tracings of vowels immediately following glottalized consonants exhibit a distinctive shape, the maximum amplitude of the vowel being reached late in the vowel segment. Such vowels were heard with some constriction.

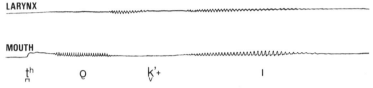

Fig 2: The vowel tracing following the glottalized consonant exhibits a shape similar to that in *Fig* 1.

The above examples are intended to illustrate the first case of prosodic treatment mentioned earlier, in which prosodies are abstracted as elements of structures in view of the extended realization of a feature therein.

In the second case may be mentioned features which are not realized phonetically over the whole or large part of a structure, but which nevertheless serve to delimit it, wholly or partly, from preceding and following structures, thus entering into syntagmatic relations with what goes before or after in the stream of speech. By virtue of their syntagmatic relations in structures, such features may be treated as prosodies of the structures they help to mark or delimit (*cf* Firth (2), *p* 129; for examples of prosodies of both types, with respect to monosyllables, see Scott).

Examples of these demarcative prosodies are found in the analysis of Siamese mentioned above. In Siamese, as in some other languages of South-east Asia, the audible release of stop consonants, or plosion, is confined to syllable initial position, final stop consonants being unexploded. In this language, therefore, plosion serves as a syntagmatic signal of syllable initiality and helps to delimit the syllable. So also do aspiration, affrication, and some other articulatory features (Henderson (1), *pp* 192–193). These are abstracted as prosodies of syllable initiality; though they may be realized phonetically at one place in the syllable, their relevance extends over the whole structure which they serve to mark off and bind together as a functional unit. In a similar manner features invariably associated with the final place in syllable structures may be abstracted as prosodies of syllable finality.

Obviously phonetic features which in one language are treated as prosodic may not be so treated, or may be so with reference to different structures, in other languages. It is the task of the analyst to decide what and how many prosodic elements and phonematic units he requires, to state the syntagmatic and paradigmatic relations relevant to the phonology of the language as completely, economically, and elegantly as he can.

The grammatical unit referred to as the word, fundamental to the traditional distinction between syntax and morphology, is in many languages marked off in speech, to a greater or less extent, by prosodic features of this second type. In English no word in normal speech has more than one full stress. Orthographically hyphenated words like *home-made*, which in certain contexts bear two full stresses, may for that reason be regarded structurally as two words, behaving phonologically like other comparable sequences of two words (*cf* 'This parsnip wine is 'home-'made/'well 'brewed' and 'This is a 'home-made/'well brewed parsnip wine',) and the difference between *greenhouse* and *green house*, *blackbird* and *black bird*, *Maryport* and *Mary Port*, can be at least partially explained in these terms. On the other hand the converse is not true; in connected discourse many words are not fully stressed, and certain words, such as the definite and indefinite articles, never bear stress in the forms in which they are most frequently found in speech (ðə and ə(n)). In at least two languages, which are quite unrelated, Swahili and Sundanese, full stress is confined in words of more than one syllable to the penultimate syllable (a few exceptions to this rule occur in Sundanese and may be covered by a separate statement (*cf* Robins (3), *pp* 125–126). In these languages, stress, which is a prosody by extension of the syllable which it characterizes, is a prosody by demarcation of the word whose boundaries it helps to delimit. Similar prosodic significance may be assigned to the word-initial stress of Hungarian and Czech.

In some languages particular aspects of consonantal articulation, which would be regarded as allophonic or phonemically irrelevant in a phonemic analysis, exhibit this demarcative function. In English word divisions falling between a final consonant and an initial vowel (*eg: an ocean, an aim*) are, potentially at least, distinguishable from word divisions falling between vowel and consonant (*eg: a notion, a name*). The distinguishing features, which include greater duration and laxer articulation of the word-final consonant as against the tenser and shorter articulation of the word-initial consonant, may be treated as prosodic word markers, and set English off as prosodically different in this respect from French, where the feature of liaison in similar phonetic contexts is no respecter of grammatical word divisions.

Some further examples of the application of prosodic analysis to various languages may serve to illustrate both types of prosody that have been referred to in the preceding paragraphs. (It may be felt that these examples are mostly drawn from relatively unfamiliar and little known languages. This should not be taken as implying that prosodic analysis is more readily applicable to such languages than to more familiar ones; the choice of languages is governed by the fact that the linguists whose work is being described are, or have been, members of the staff of the School of Oriental and African Studies in the University of London, with the consequent concentration of their attention in the main on languages coming within the purview of the School. It is greatly to be hoped that the attention of linguists in Great Britain will progressively be turned to the languages that form the basis of our general educational system.) The well-known feature of Sanskrit word structure usually referred to as Cerebralization has been re-examined prosodically (Allen (3)). This feature, which concerns the relations between certain retroflex consonants in Sanskrit words, is generally expressed in such terms as these (A. A. Macdonnell, *Sanskrit Grammar*, 2nd edition, London, 1911, *p* 28): 'A preceding cerebral ṛ, r̄, r, ṣ (even though a vowel, a guttural, a labial, y, v, or Anusvāra (a nasal consonantal unit whose precise phonetic value is obscure (*cf* Allen (4), *pp* 39–46)) intervene) changes a dental n (followed by a vowel or n, m, y, v) to cerebral ṇ'. It is an unsuitable metaphor to say that one sound operates at a distance over intervening sounds to exert a force on another sound, and change it from something which in fact it never was (in the words concerned) into something else. It is indeed generally desirable that synchronic description and analysis should as far as possible avoid the use, even metaphorically, of terms and concepts more appropriate to the diachronic study of the history and development of languages and linguistic features (*cf* C. F. Hockett, 'Two Models of Grammatical Description', *Word*, 10, 1954, *pp* 210–234).

In the re-examination of retroflexion in Sanskrit, it is suggested that an R-prosody, or prosody of retroflexion, be abstracted from the words concerned as a structural feature. This prosody was no doubt marked by a retroflex articulation not only of the lingually articulated consonants but also of the intervening vowels, though the traditional treatment makes no mention of this. Such a retroflex 'colouring' of vowels in juxtaposition to retroflex consonants is certainly a feature of many Indian languages today (*cf* Allen (3), *p* 942).

The analysis proposed requires no concept of action at a distance of one sound on another, but simply posits a non-linear, non-segmental feature, retroflexion, as part of the structure of the words, or portions of the words, concerned, realized at all points where it is phonetically possible, that is where the tongue tip is one of the organs of articulation.

Mention has already been made of the relevance of prosodic abstractions in several languages to grammatical units. It is interesting in this connection to see that in more than one language what may appear at first sight as a miscellany of separate phonetic features characterizing a particular grammatical category can all be shown to be the exponents of a single prosodic feature, which thus serves as the marker of a category in the grammar of the language. Such a congruence between the different levels of analysis (*cf* Firth, 'The Technique of Semantics', *TPS*, 1935, *pp* 36–72) of a language, as it operates between speakers, is surely an important desideratum of our linguistic operations. Two examples may be cited from widely separated languages. In Bilin (Palmer (3)), a language of Eritrea, the morphology of the very complex tense system of the nine verb classes that have been set up for that language may be analysed in terms of a single set of statements involving the prosodies of centrality, frontness, backness, and openness, realized in the consonantal and vocalic articulations of the verb forms concerned. In Sundanese (Robins (2)), two types of verb root are found for nearly all verbs, and these two types are used both by themselves, roughly speaking as active and passive verbs respectively, and as bases for a very large number of derived forms involving prefixation, infixation and suffixation, with extensive functions in the language. The relation between these two verbal roots can be simply stated by showing that the active form is always characterized by an N-prosody, or prosody of nasalization, the precise realization that the N-prosody takes being determined by the phonological structure, involving other prosodic components, of each type of verb.

One may find instances, which future research is likely to multiply, of prosodic treatment bringing into the analysis phonetic features either not noted before or dismissed as phonologically (*ie*, phonemically) irrelevant. Examples of the demarcative prosodic function of some 'allophonic' features have already been given. Fixed place word stress for example, and consonantal features invariably associated with syllable initial or syllable final position, are frequently treated as differentially irrelevant since they are positionally determined, but they are, for just that reason, prosodically relevant and functional. That phonemic analysis may let slip many phonologically relevant features is illustrated from the following observation by Leonard Bloomfield, *Language*, London, 1935, *p* 84: 'Practical phoneticians sometimes acquire great virtuosity in discriminating and reproducing all manner of strange sounds. In this, to be sure, there lies some danger for linguistic work. Having learned to discriminate many kinds of sounds, the phonetician may turn to some language, new or familiar, and insist upon recording all the distinctions he has learned to discriminate, even when in this language they are non-distinctive and have no bearing whatever'. *Distinctive* in the context of phonemic analysis often means *capable of differentiating one word from another* (*cf* Bloomfield, *op cit*, *pp* 77–78, Jones in *TPS*, 1944, *pp* 127–132), the implication being that phonetic differences not serving such a purpose are functionally and phonologically irrelevant. This implication is unjustified. In addition to the examples already given we may consider the phonological status and functions of the glottal stop in Sundanese (Robins (3)). This is a frequent phonetic component of utterances in the language, and a failure to use it properly may lead to misunderstanding and would certainly mark the speaker as a foreigner; but it is not a phoneme on a par with the other phonemes that would be set up in a phonemic analysis of the language, and it would not be easy to devise a satisfactory allophonic treatment of its occurrences (though structurally the two are very different, *cf* Jones's remarks on the glottal stop in English (*Outline, pp* 138–139)). The Roman orthography currently in use in Java today for Sundanese, which comes very near to a phonemic transcription, has no symbol for the glottal stop, except in certain, mostly Arabic, loan words, where it is represented by an apostrophe. As a prosodic element, however, the Sundanese glottal stop has several functions in words other than loans, and in various contexts serves as a syntagmatic marker of the junction of syllables, morphemes, words, and clauses.

Between like vowels, syllable division, when not marked by any other consonant, is marked by the glottal stop. Between unlike vowels, not separated by any other consonant, the glottal stop is only found at points corresponding to certain morpheme boundaries within a word, whose morphological structure it thus helps to indicate. A glottal stop between a vowel and a consonant, usually in conjunction with other features, signals a clause division within the sentence.

The glottal stop in Sundanese is, in fact, an example of a phonetic feature which should be treated less as a member of a paradigm of consonants than as a marker of certain syntagmatic relations between one structure and another, at both the phonological and grammatical levels. It is the syntagmatic or structural dimension of language that phonemic analysis may be felt to neglect, or to subordinate to the paradigmatic dimension of overall contrast in identical environment, a lack of balance that prosodic theory and practice attempts to redress.

After the description and illustrations of prosodic analysis that have been given, mention should be made of some relatively recent developments in phonemic theory that partially at least seem to cover the same ground in phonology.

One of the first phonetic features of a strictly non-segmental character to be brought into phonemic analysis was that of pitch, whether in the category of intonation or in the category of tone, in the so-called tone languages (*cf* Pike, *Tone Languages*, Ann Arbor, 1948, *p* 3). In either case pitch phenomena clearly belong to the syllable as a whole, though in transcription pitch is frequently marked over the vowel letter. Pitch (or tone), stress, and sometimes length (as distinct from shortness) are now fairly generally treated (at least in America) as Suprasegmental Phonemes, a self-explanatory and self-justificatory category which would seem at first sight to apply to the same field as syllable prosodies of the first type mentioned above, where the phonetic feature treated prosodically was phonetically realized over the whole syllable (*pp* 267–269). The terms *prosodic phoneme*, and *prosodeme* are sometimes used instead of *suprasegmental phoneme*, with no difference in technical meaning.

There are, however, two differences. Firstly, in prosodic analysis any phonetic feature whose realization extended over the whole or greater part of a syllable could be eligible for treatment as a syllable prosody of this type, irrespective of the nature of its articulation. Examples have already been given of nasalization, palatalization, and glottalization, as well as pitch, stress, and length, being prosodically analysed. But suprasegmental phonemic treatment has in practice been confined to these last three phonetic features, and Pike explicitly limits the term *suprasegmental* to 'quantitative characteristics . . . some modification of a sound which does not change the basic quality or shape of its sound waves' (*Phonemics*, *p* 63; for a suggestion that other features might be treated suprasegmentally, see G. L. Trager in *Language, Culture, and Personality*, ed L. Spier, Menasha, 1941, *pp* 131–145, *ie* pitch, stress, and length and nothing else. Secondly, suprasegmental is simply non-segmental, with the implied domain of the syllable; a syllable prosody is an abstraction of a specific order in a separate dimension (the syntagmatic), taking its place in a system of prosodies intended to cover the analysis of syntagmatic relations generally, within linguistic structures.

The demarcative aspect of prosodies (see *pp* 269–272 above) is foreshadowed by the Grenzsignale of the Prague school and the Juncture Phonemes of some American linguists. It is certainly the case that the Prague discussion of these junction features (see Trubetzkoy, *Anleitung zu Phonologischen Beschreibungen*, Brno, 1935, *pp* 30–32, *Principes* (trans Cantineau), *pp* 290–314) was one of the first factors drawing the attention of linguists to the neglected syntagmatic aspect of phonology, but the Prague treatment of them, left where Trubetzkoy left it, does not fully exploit the analytic and structural potentialities of these features, and the status of the Grenzsignale, partly phonemic (phonematische) and partly non-phonemic (aphonematische), remains rather in a phonological limbo, as a sort of appendage rather than a fully integrated part of a complete theory.

Structurally similar features to those treated under the category of Grenzsignale by Trubetzkoy are analysed in terms of Juncture Phonemes. It may be said that this aspect of phonemic analysis is somewhat complicated by the involvement of two separate questions: firstly, the phonological analysis of the features and their functions in the language, and secondly, their symbolization in a unilinear transcription. Juncture phonemes, like other phonemes in current theories, are also subject to the general rule that the phonemic analysis and transcription of a phonetic element or feature at any point necessarily implies the same analysis of that feature at all other points in structures, despite the quite different relations that it may contract at different places. Alone among phonemicists, it would seem, Twaddell explicitly challenged the assumptions that phonological relations were the same throughout all places in the structures of a language, and that the needs of a full phonological analysis and those of an economical transcription could be satisfied with one and the same procedure and with the same basic elements or concepts (*On Defining the Phoneme, pp* 54–55. For this reason phonemic analysis may be considered basically 'monosystemic' (Firth (2), *pp* 127–128)).

Perhaps symptomatic of the unsettled state of juncture analysis in phonemic terms are the wholly contrasting natures of the juncture phonemes of Harris and of Hockett (*cf* Zellig S. Harris, *Methods in Structural Linguistics*, Chicago, 1951, *pp* 79–89, Charles F. Hockett, 'A Manual of Phonology', *IJAL*, 21.4, Part 1, 1955, *pp* 167–172). For Harris juncture phonemes are zero phonemes, with no phonetic realization, put into the analysis to complete the picture, and the border phenomena involved in the analysis are assigned to the allophones of the phonemes in the new environment created by the insertion of the juncture zero phonemes. For Hockett, on the other hand, juncture phonemes are bundles of all the phonetic features, of whatever nature, associated with the boundaries or borders to be analysed.

In general, juncture phonemes tend to be associated with word and morpheme boundaries in American phonemics, just as suprasegmental phonemes are generally confined to the domain of the syllable. In this way junctures have a particular relevance to current American linguistic theory, which holds that grammatical features and grammatical units cannot be used as part of the defining environment of phonemes. (The principal opponent among American linguists to this methodological attitude is Pike; see his 'Grammatical Prerequisites to Phonemic Analysis', *Word*, 3, 1947, *pp* 155–172, and 'More on Grammatical Prerequisites', *Word*, 8, 1952, *pp* 106–121.) It is, therefore, highly advantageous if convenient grammatically defined elements, such as word and morpheme, can be for the most part matched by phonemically defined juncture marked stretches of the same length, even though the correlation between the two in a language may not be complete. As has already been said, prosodic analysis sees no objection to the use of analysis at the grammatical level for the stating of contexts in analysis at the phonological level, and prosodies may be abstracted and stated of grammatical elements as well as of more purely phonological elements (*p* 270, above; *cf* Palmer (1), *pp* 548–549).

Finally mention should be made of Phonemic Long Components, which are intended as a means of stating syntagmatic relations and structural implications between successive segmental phonemes in stretches of utterance (*cf* Harris, *Methods, pp* 125–149). There are at least three differences between abstractions of this type and the prosodies of prosodic analysis: firstly, abstraction of a component from a phoneme in one environment implies its abstraction from that phoneme in all other environments (*op cit, p* 128); secondly, long components are not all associated with specific phonological or grammatical structures; thirdly, no one phonetic feature can be stated as the mark or exponent of the long component over its domain in the way that prosodies statable of a whole structure are associated with phonetic features exhibited by that structure as a whole (*op cit, p* 129).

The remarks on certain recent developments in phonemic analysis in the last few paragraphs must not be taken as a comprehensive review of contemporary phonemic theories, and still less as a disparagement of the work of other linguists. They are merely intended to help place prosodic analysis in its context of relations with current phonological doctrines and methods elsewhere.

Bibliography

The following publications have a direct bearing on prosodic analysis as treated in this article:

ALLEN, W. S.
1 'Notes on the Phonetics of an Eastern Armenian Speaker', *TPS*, 1950, 180–206.
2 'Phonetics and Comparative Linguistics', *Archivum Linguisticum*, 3, 1951, 126–136.
3 'Some Prosodic Aspects of Retroflexion and Aspiration in Sanskrit', *BSOAS*, 13, 1951, 939–946.
4 *Phonetics in Ancient India*, London 1953.
5 'Retroflexion in Sanskrit: Prosodic Technique and its Relevance to Comparative Statement', *BSOAS*, 16, 1954, 556–565.

CARNOCHAN, J.
1 'A Study of Quantity in Hausa', *BSOAS*, 13, 1951, 1032–1044.
2 'Glottalization in Hausa', *TPS*, 1952, 78–109.

FIRTH, J. P.
1 'The Semantics of Linguistic Science', *Lingua*, 1, 1948, 393–404.
2 'Sounds and Prosodies', *TPS*, 1948, 127–152. [Reprinted in this volume, *pp* 47–65. Eds.]
3 'General Linguistics and Descriptive Grammar', *TPS*, 1951, 69–87.

HENDERSON, E. J. A.
1 'Prosodies in Siamese', *Asia Minor* (new series), 1, 1949, 189–215. [Reprinted in this volume, *pp* 127–153. Eds.]
2 'The Phonology of Loanwords in some South-East Asian Languages', *TPS*, 1951, 131–158.
3 'The Main Features of Cambodian Pronunciation', *BSOAS*, 14, 1952, 149–174.

MITCHELL, T. F.
  'Particle-Noun Complexes in a Berber Dialect (Zuara)', *BSOAS*, 15,
    1953, 375–390.
PALMER, F. R.   .
  1 'The "Broken Plurals" of Tigrinya', *BSOAS*, 17, 1955, 548–566.
  2 '"Openness", in Tigre: A Problem in Prosodic Statement',
    BSOAS, 18, 1956, 561–577.
  3 'The Verb in Bilin', *BSOAS*, 19, 1957, 131–159.
ROBINS, R. H.
  1 'Notes on the Phonetics of the Georgian Word' (with Natalie
    Waterson), *BSOAS*, 14, 1952, 55–72.
  2 'The Phonology of the Nasalized Verbal Forms in Sundanese',
    BSOAS, 15, 1953, 138–145.
  3 'Formal Divisions in Sundanese', *TPS*, 1953, 109–142.
SCOTT, N. C.
  'A Phonological Analysis of the Szechuanese Monosyllable', *BSOAS*,
    18, 1956, 556–560. [Reprinted in this volume, *pp* 299–304. Eds.]
SHARP, A. E.
  'A Tonal Analysis of the Disyllabic Noun in the Machame Dialect of
    Chaga', *BSOAS*, 16, 1954, 157–169. [Reprinted in this volume,
    pp 305–319. Eds.]
SPRIGG, R. K.
  1 'Verbal Phrases in Lhasa Tibetan', *BSOAS*, 16, 1954, 134–156,
    320–350, 566–591.
  2 'The Tonal System of Tibetan (Lhasa Dialect) and the Nominal
    Phrase', *BSOAS*, 17, 1955, 134–153.
WATERSON, N.
  'Some aspects of the Phonology of the Nominal Forms of the Turkish
    Word', *BSOAS*, 18, 1956, 578–591.
At the time of writing an article by Mitchell is to be published in the
André Basset Memorial Volume, and articles by Allen, Carnochan, Firth,
Mitchell, Palmer, Robins and Sprigg will appear in *Studies in Linguistic
Analysis*, to be published by the Philological Society.
[MITCHELL, T. F. 'Some Properties of Zuara Nouns with Special Refer-
    ence to those with Consonant Initial', 1957.
FIRTH, J. R., *et al. Studies in Linguistic Analysis*, London, 1957. [Eds]

N. C. Scott

The monosyllable in Szechuanese

In *Le Maître Phonétique* for April–June, 1940, I gave some notes on the pronunciation of Mr Su Cheng,[1] a native of Fengtuhsien, Szechuan. I have recently been able to make further observations in his case, and also to study the pronunciation of Mr Chao Che Shen,[2] a native of Ipin, Szechuan, which lies some 200 miles to the west of Fengtuhsien. Their speech is similar in most respects, but there are certain important regular differences, and, as might be expected, occasional examples of a different distribution of the phonetic forms among the words, as when 或 is given as *ho*⁵ by Su and *he*⁵ by Chao. The present paper is concerned with a detailed comparison of their pronunciations and with the construction of a systematic transcription adequate for both. For these purposes, the study is restricted to the monosyllable, which is to be understood here as the phonetic form given by the speakers in reading aloud a single character.[3]

Table I gives the systematic transcription of all the syllables that were found to be kept phonetically distinct by differences other than those associated with tone. Further differentiation is made possible by the fact that most of them may be spoken on several significantly different tones.

Tones

Chao has five such distinctions:

1. A high level tone (sometimes with a slight final rise), as in Ɣ *ya*¹ (ˉjɑ).[4]
2. A low falling tone, often ending in a creak, as in 衙 *ya*² (ˏjɑ).
3. A high falling tone, with which there is an impression of more vigorous articulation, as in 啞 *ya*³ (ˋjɑ).

First published in the *Bulletin of the School of Oriental and African Studies*, Vol XII, No 1: 197–213, 1947.

4. A low rising tone, beginning with a creak, the final lengthened, as in 亞 *ya*[4] (‚jɑː).

5. A mid level tone, checked by a glottal stop, and associated with a distinctive pronunciation of the syllable as a whole, as in 鴨 *ya*[5] (-jaʔ).

Su has four distinctions of tone:

1. A high level tone (¯jɑ) corresponding to Chao 1.
2. A low level tone with a slight final rise, breathy, (‚jɑ), corresponding to Chao 2 or to Chao 5.
3. A mid falling tone (ˌjɑ), corresponding to Chao 3.
4. A mid rising tone (ˈjɑ), corresponding to Chao 4.

For convenience of reference, the tones are numbered in accordance with the numbering in the Wade system for the tones of Pekinese to which these Szechuanese tones usually correspond. The two speakers independently, however, gave the tones in the order 1, 3, 4, 2.[5]

The realization of the tones is thus very different in the two speakers, and tone 4 spoken by Chao is very like tone 2 spoken by Su. It appears, however, that the exceptions to the correspondences indicated above are very few. Any syllable marked in the systematic transcription as having the 5th tone will be read by Su as if it were marked for the 2nd tone.

Tone 5 does not occur with syllables closed by *n* or *ng*, nor with those that have a diphthongal final.[5]

The following list gives examples of the types of syllable that may have a 5th tone. It gives (1) the systematic transcriptions, (2) a phonetic transcription indicating Su's pronunciation, (3) a phonetic transcription indicating Chao's pronunciation. With the exceptions noted, (2) will also show the pronunciation for both speakers of the syllable said with tones 1–4 when these occur. Other initials may be substituted for those in the examples (see *Table* 1). When *y* appears in the systematic transcription, the alternance will be with a palatalized initial only.

systematic transcription	*Su*	*Chao*
bi[5]	‚pi[5]	-pje
si[5], *dzi*[5], *tsi*[5]	‚sz, etc	-sɛ, etc[6]
se[5]	‚sɛ	-sɛ[7]
ye[5]	‚jɛ	-je[8]
ywe[5]	‚ɥɛ	-ɥo
gwe[5]	‚kwɛ	-ko[9]
ba[5]	‚pɑ	-pa
bo[5]	‚pɔ	-po
bu[5]	‚pu	-po[10]

Clearly, if a pronunciation of Chao's type alone had been known a

Table 1
Syllabary

	i	in	e	en	ei	eu	a	an	ang	ai	au	o	u	u...
b	bi	bin	–	ben	bei	beu	ba	ban	bang	bai	bau	bo	bu	bu
p	pi	pin	–	pen	pei	peu	pa	pan	pang	pai	pau	po	pu	pu
d	di	din	de	den	–	deu	da	dan	dang	dai	dau	do	du	du
t	ti	tin	te	ten	–	teu	ta	tan	tang	tai	tau	to	tu	tu
g	–	–	ge	gen	–	geu	–	gan	gang	gai	gau	go	gu	gu
k	–	–	ke	ken	–	keu	ka	kan	kang	kai	kau	ko	ku	k
by	–	–	bye	byen	–	–	–	–	–	–	byau	–	–	
py	–	–	pye	pyen	–	–	–	–	–	–	pyau	–	–	
dy	–	–	dye	dyen	–	dyeu	–	–	–	–	dyau	–	–	
ty	–	–	tye	tyen	–	–	–	–	–	–	tyau	–	–	
gy	gyi	gyin	gye	gyen	–	gyeu	gya	–	gyang	gyai	gyau	gyo	gyu	gy
ky	kyi	kyin	kye	kyen	–	kyeu	kya	–	kyang	–	kyau	kyo	kyu	ky
gyw	gywi	gywin	gywe	gywen	–	–	–	–	–	–	–	–	–	
kyw	kywi	kywin	kywe	kywen	–	–	–	–	–	–	–	–	–	
dw	–	–	–	–	dwei	–	–	dwan	–	–	–	–	–	
tw	–	–	–	–	twei	–	–	twan	–	–	–	–	–	
gw	–	–	gwe	gwen	gwei	–	gwa	gwan	gwang	gwai	–	–	–	
kw	–	–	kwe	kwen	kwei	–	kwa	kwan	kwang	kwai	–	–	–	
m	mi	min	–	men	mei	meu	ma	man	mang	mai	mau	mo	mu	m
n	–	nin	ne	nen	–	neu	na	nan	nang	nai	nau	no	nu	
ng	–	–	nge	ngen	–	ngeu	–	ngan	ngang	ngai	ngau	ngo	–	
my	–	–	mye	myen	–	myeu	–	–	–	–	myau	–	–	
ny	nyi	–	–	nyen	–	nyeu	nya	–	nyang	–	nyau	nyo	–	
ly	lyi	–	–	lyen	–	lyeu	lya	–	lyang	–	lyau	lyo	–	
nyw	nywi	–	–	–	–	–	–	–	–	–	–	–	–	
lyw	lywi	–	–	–	–	–	–	–	–	–	–	–	–	
nw	–	–	–	–	nwei	–	–	nwan	–	–	–	–	–	
f	–	–	–	fen	fei	feu	fa	fan	fang	–	–	–	fu	
z	zi	–	ze	zen	–	zeu	–	zan	zang	–	zau	zo	zu	
s	si	–	se	sen	–	seu	sa	san	sang	sai	sau	so	su	
h	–	–	he	hen	–	heu	ha	han	hang	hai	hau	ho	–	
hy	hyi	hyin	hye	hyen	–	hyeu	hya	–	hyang	hyai	hyau	hyo	hyu	
hyw	hywi	hywin	hywe	hywen	–	–	–	–	–	–	–	–	–	
zw	–	–	–	–	zwei	–	–	zwan	–	–	–	–	–	
sw	–	–	–	swen	swei	–	swa	swan	–	swai	–	–	–	
hw	–	–	–	hwen	hwei	–	hwa	hwan	hwang	hwai	–	–	–	
dz	dzi	–	dze	dzen	–	dzeu	dza	dzan	dzang	dzai	dzau	dzo	dzu	
ts	tsi	–	tse	tsen	–	tseu	tsa	tsan	tsang	tsai	tsau	tso	tsu	
dzw	–	–	–	dzwen	dzwei	–	dzwa	dzwan	dzwang	dzwai	–	–	–	
tsw	–	–	–	tswen	tswei	–	tswa	tswan	tswang	tswai	–	–	–	
y	yi	yin	ye	yen	–	yeu	ya	–	yang	yai	yau	yo	yu	
yw	ywi	ywin	ywe	ywen	–	–	–	–	–	–	–	–	–	
w	–	–	–	wen	wei	–	wa	wan	wang	wai	–	wo	wu	

different distribution would have suggested itself. There is, however, no ambiguity in writing the syllables in this way.

It would be possible to indicate the tone of a syllable by adding a letter to the transcription as Firth has done for Hunanese, but everything goes to show that he was entirely right in saying: 'The nature and function of the so-called tones in Chinese cannot be understood or economically represented in orthography until a thorough study of types of sentences in general speech behaviour has been completed. . . .' Literal tone-marks would be very desirable if the transcriptions were to be used as a practical orthography, but as I am here concerned only with the isolated syllable, and the 'qualitative' structure of this is more readily seen from the transcription when the tone letters are absent, I use numbers to mark the tones in this paper.

The systematic transcription

The syllable is a whole, not merely a number of pieces added one to another. If Roman letters are used to represent it, it must not be taken that their space-order corresponds point for point with an order in the syllable. It is, however, possible to use the letters in a systematic fashion to build up a series of characteristic shapes, each of which will serve to denote one of the syllables that are kept phonetically distinct, and at the same time, by the application of relatively simple conventions, unambiguously indicate the pronunciation to be given to each. For this purpose it is possible to regard the syllable in the traditional manner as having an 'initial' and a 'final', and to observe, classify, and symbolize, the differences in each of these positions or 'places'. The form of the syllable does not, however, depend on the initial and final taken separately. The value of a letter, then, depends on its position in the series and on the other letters in the series. It cannot be interpreted without reference to the syllable as a whole.

Finals

The final may be considered as having one of the following forms:
1. A simple vowel; the letters *i*, *e*, *a*, *o*, and *u*, are used for writing these.
2. A simple vowel with the syllable closed by n (or, in some cases, nasalization of the vowel); *in*, *en*, *an*, are used.
3. A simple vowel with the syllable closed by ŋ; *ang* and *ung* are used.
4. A diphthong moving in the direction of i; *ei* and *ai* are used.
5. A diphthong moving in the direction of u; *eu* and *au* are used.

The forms actually occurring are shown in *Table 2*. Since the sound to be made for the vowel of the final depends, in some cases, on the presence or absence of preceding palatalization or labio-palatalization, the table also gives examples of the cases in which the final may be preceded by the semi-vowels *y*, *yw*, and *w*, for which certain initials with palatalization, labio-palatalization, or labio-velarization, as the case may be, can be substituted. Thus there is *yen*¹ 烟 (‾jɛn or ‾jɛ̃) *smoke*, in which *y* represents the palatal semi-vowel, and *dyen*¹ 顚 (‾tjɛn or ‾tjɛ̃) *top*, in which *dy* represents an initial with palatalization. Summary indications of the pronunciation of these forms by Su and by Chao are given in *Tables* 3 and 4, which are arranged on the same plan as *Table* 2.

Table 2
Finals with contexts

		-n	-ng	-i	-u
	-i	-in			
y-	yi	yin			
yw-	ywi	ywin			
	-e	-en		-ei	-eu
y-	ye	yen			yeu
yw-	ywe	ywen			
w-	-we	wen		wei	
	-a	-an	-ang	-ai	-au
y-	ya		yang	yai	yau
w-	wa	wan	wang	wai	
	-o				
y-	yo				
w-	wo				
	-u	-ung			
y-	yu	yung			
w-	wu				

NOTE: The forms of final that occur with simple initials are shown in the first row of each section, the hyphen indicating that they are not found in isolation. Those that may also occur with palatalized, labio-palatalized, or labio-velarized initials appear in the rows marked *y-*, *yw-*, and *w-* respectively, shown with the corresponding palatal, labio-palatal, or labio-velar semi-vowel.

Initials

There is no 'zero initial'; -*i*, when it has no other initial, has the palatal semi-vowel (*yi*); -*o* and -*u*, when they have no other initial, have the bilabial semi-vowel (*wo*, *wu*); -*e* and -*a*, when they have no other initial, have *ng-* (*nge*, *nga*). It is to be noted, however, that both Su and Chao give *ngo*³ for 我, and that Chao alone gives *ngo*⁵ for 惡 and 噩, for which Su uses *wo*⁵. I have found no other examples of *ng*- before *o*. While it would be possible to write *i*¹ (衣), *o*² (俄), *u*¹ (烏), *e*⁵ (額), *an*¹ (安), without ambiguity, the omission of *y*, *w*, or *ng* could not be taken to imply that there was no initial. I write them in each case with the initial.

The system of initials is shown in *Tables* 5 and 6. They may be classified as (1) plosives, (2) nasals, (3) fricatives, (4) affricates, (5) semi-vowels. These terms are used to name the classes of initials recognized in the system; they do not necessarily indicate the phonetic type of the particular sound used to represent one of the classes of initials in a particular utterance.

Plosives

1. There are three simple, unaspirated plosives, for which the letters *b*, *d*, *g*, are used.
2. The presence of palatalization gives three further terms which are written *by*, *dy*, *gy*.[11]
3. The presence of labio-palatalization gives one more term, written *gyw*.
4. The presence of labio-velarization gives two more terms, written *dw*, *gw*.

A further series, with an equal number of terms, results from the significant difference between aspirated and unaspirated plosives. The aspirated series is written as follows, parallel with the unaspirated series:

1. *p*, *t*, *k*.
2. *py*, *ty*, *ky*.
3. *kyw*.
4. *tw*, *kw*.[12]

Nasals

These are:
1. Three simple nasals, written *m*, *n*, *ng*.
2. With palatalization (*a*) fricative, *ny* alone.
   (*b*) frictionless, *ly* and *my*.
3. With labio-palatalization; *nyw* alone.
4. With labio-velarization; *nw* alone.

The distinction between nasal with fricative palatalization and nasal with frictionless palatalization is made only by Su, who uses the difference to separate words that have initial *n* with palatalization from those that, in other dialects, have *l* with palatalization. Thus he gives 年 *nyen*², and 臉 *lyen*³. He does not appear to make the distinction when the final is -*in*.

Fricatives

1. There are three simple voiceless fricatives, written *f*, *s*, *h*.
2. With palatalization, *hy* only.

3. With labio-palatalization, *hyw* only.

4. With labio-velarization, *sw* and *hw*.

To these must be added *z* and *zw*, distinguished by the presence of voice from *s* and *sw*.

Affricates

1. There is one simple unaspirated-voiced affricate, written *dz*.

2. With labio-velarization, *dzw*. To these must be added the aspirated-voiceless terms *ts* and *tsw*.

Semi-vowels

These are:

1. The palatal semi-vowel, written *y*.

2. The labio-palatal semi-vowel, written *yw*.

3. The labio-velar semi-vowel, written *w*.[13]

Table 3

Su's pronunciation of the forms in *Table 2*

	-n	*-ng*	*-i*	*-u*
	(m)i	(m)in		
y-	ji	jin		
yw-	ɥ(i)	ɥyn		
	(t)ɛ	(t)ən	(f)əi	(t)əu
y-	jɛ	jɛn		jəu
yw-	ɥɛ	ɥɛn		
w-	(k)wɛ	wən	wəi	
	(p)ɑ	(p)an	(p)ɑŋ	(p)ɑi	(p)ɑu
y-	jɑ		jɑŋ	jɑi	jɑu
w-	wɑ	wan	wɑŋ	wɑi	
	(p)ɔ			
y-	jɔ			
w-	wɔ			
	(p)u		(p)uŋ	
y-	ju		juŋ	
w-	wu		wuŋ	

NOTE: The hyphens of *Table 2* are here replaced by examples of simple initials in round brackets.

Table 4

Chao's pronunciation of the forms in *Table* 2

		-n	-ng	-i	-u
	(m)i, (m)je⁵	(m)in			
y-	ji, je⁵	jin			
yw-	y	ɥin			
	[(s)əi], (s)ɛ⁵	(t)ən		(f)əi	
y-	[ji, je⁵]	jɛ̃			j(ə)u
yw-	[jo⁵]	ɥɛ̃			
w-	[(k)o⁵]	wən		w(ə)i	
	(p)ɑ, (p)a⁵	(p)æ̃	(p)ɑŋ	(p)ai	(p)au
y-	jɑ, ja⁵		jaŋ	[ŋgai]	jau
w-	wɑ, wa⁵	wæ̃	wɑŋ	wai	
	(p)ɔ				
y-	[jo⁵]				
w-	wɔ, wo⁵				
	(p)u		(p)uŋ		
y-	jo⁵		juŋ		
w-	wu		wuŋ		

NOTE: The hyphens of *Table* 2 are here replaced by examples of simple initials in round brackets. Square brackets are placed round the forms used by Chao where he lacks the form used by Su. Tone-numbers are given only for the 5th-tone forms.

Phonetic interpretation of the transcription
Finals

In the following account of the pronunciations of Su and Chao, the finals are dealt with first, each in its possible contexts. If no indication is given to the contrary, it may be taken that the two pronunciations do not noticeably differ in the feature concerned.

i

i in *eg: bi*¹ represents a close front vowel (i, Cardinal vowel No 1). The closing may, however, go beyond the vowel limit, so that friction of a palatal type is produced. This appears to happen most frequently and most markedly for Su with tone 2. Voiceless friction of a palatal type is heard during the aspiration in *pi*. When n precedes, there is for Su, but not for Chao, a significant difference between *i* with friction and *i* without. Su pronounces *nyi*³ 你 *you* as ˏnji with friction, and *lyi*³ 里 *mile* as ˏni without friction. He uses the latter form for words in which other dialects have initial *l*.

When syllables of the type of *bi* have the 5th tone, Chao realizes the *i* as je, a frictionless palatal semi-vowel followed by a short front, or nearly front, half-close vowel checked by a glottal stop. Thus for 筆 *bi*⁵ *pencil* he gives -pjɛ.

Special phonetic interpretations are to be given to *si*, *dzi*, *tsi*, and *zi*. In the pronunciation of *si*, the s is followed by a voiced sound made with the tip and blade of the tongue in approximately the position for z, little or no friction being produced. The sound has some resemblance to a retracted i. In *dzi*, the s is replaced by the voiced, and in *tsi*, by the voiceless, affricate.[14] Words with the 5th tone given by Su with the pronunciation ˏsz, ˏtsz, ˏtshz, are given by Chao as -sɛ (*eg: si*⁵ 石 *stone*), -tsɛ (*dzi*⁵ 直 *straight*), -tshɛ (*tsi*⁵ 尺 *measure*).[15] *zi* as a whole represents a kind of retroflex retracted æ.[16] The character 日 alone is spoken by Su as ˏz. Chao gives it as -zɛ. This might be *ze*⁵, but Su has ˏzɛ (*ze*⁵) 熱 *hot*, and as Chao's -zɛ also falls into line with the type of syllable he gives for *si*⁵, *dzi*⁵, and *tsi*⁵, it seems appropriate to write ˏz as *zi*⁵, even if this is the only case in which Su uses a different phonetic form for the 5th tone.[17]

in represents for both speakers i followed by n. The i is usually frictionless, but friction is to be heard in *yin*, most noticeably with the second tone for Su.

ywi represents a nearly front rounded vowel, somewhat lowered from the close position (y). It is sometimes accompanied by friction of a pre-palatal type; there may also be bilabial friction. Su has a tendency to relax the lip-rounding before the end of the vowel, giving an effect of yi. He makes the same kind of difference between *nywi* and *lywi* as between *nyi* and *lyi*, the vowel having friction in the first, as in *nywi*³, 女, and being frictionless in the second, as in *lywi*³ 旅.

ywin pronounced by Su has a vowel of the type just described, but with lip-rounding maintained throughout, followed by n. Chao, on the other hand, regularly unrounds before the end of the vowel, giving ɥin.

e

For Su, *e* preceded by a simple consonant represents a front vowel rather than Cardinal No 3, ɛ. The syllables of this type that have a 5th tone are pronounced by Chao with this vowel, *eg: se*⁵ 色 -sɛ *colour*, but those that have tones 1–4 he gives with ei, *eg: se*² 蛇 *snake*, Su ˏsɛ, Chao ˏsəi. See below.

Preceded by a simple consonant, *en* is given by both speakers as a somewhat advanced central vowel, between half-open and half-close, followed by n, ən.

With preceding palatalization, Su makes *e* as a vowel slightly closer than the one described under *e* above. Chao treats syllables of this kind as belonging to the *i* set. Thus 夜 *ye⁴ night* is given by Su as ′jɛ, by Chao as ˌji; 葉 *ye⁵ leaf* is given by Su as ˌjɛ, by Chao as -je.

In the group *yen*, the *en* represents for Su a vowel of the kind just described followed by n. The vowel is, however, usually nasalized, at least in part, and the contact for the n may not be complete. Chao regularly makes a nasal vowel (front, between half-close and half-open), with no n. Thus *yen¹* is ⁻jɛn for Su, ⁻jɛ̃ for Chao.

For Su, *ywe* represents a vowel of the type described under *ye* with preceding labio-palatalization. Chao has no syllables of this kind; for most of the words in which Su has *ywe*, he uses *yo*, eg 越, Su *ywe⁵*, Chao *yo⁵*; 絕 Su *gywe⁵*, Chao *gyo⁵*. Exceptionally, I have found 靴 Su *hywe¹*, Chao *hywi¹*, and 血 Su *hywe⁵*, Chao *hyi⁵*. Su gives *ywe⁵* as ˌɥɛ; for *yo⁵* see below.

ywen has the same relation to *ywe* as *yen* has to *ye*. Su uses ɥɛn, Chao ɥɛ̃.

we, for Su only, represents *e* preceded by labio-velarization. It occurs only in the syllables 國 *gwe⁵ country* and 闊 *kwe⁵ well-to-do*. For these Chao gives *go⁵* and *ko⁵*. See the note on *yo*. Su says ˌkwɛ and ˌkhwɛ.

With preceding labio-velarization, *en* represents a short central vowel, between half-open and half-close followed by n. The w tends to be more prominent than the ə, but this effect is less marked when the syllable is spoken with tone 2 for Su.

Preceded by a simple consonant, *ei* represents a diphthong having as its starting-point a rather advanced central vowel, between half-open and half-close, and moving in the direction of i. As was mentioned above, Chao uses this final whenever Su has *e* preceded by a simple consonant in a syllable with a tone other than the 5th. It will be seen from *Table* I (the systematic transcription being based, in this instance, on Su's pronunciation), that, for Su, *ei* does not occur after any initial that is found before *e*, and that *e* does not occur after any initial found before *ei*.[18] It would be possible to write *ei* for *e* in all cases after a simple consonant with the convention that Su pronounces əi after *b, p, m, f,* and ɛ after other simple initials; while Chao pronounces əi in all cases for tones 1–4, ɛ for tone 5. The rule as it stands is simpler.

With preceding labio-velarization, the ə element in the diphthong described above tends to be less prominent than the i, and especially in Chao's pronunciation *wei* sounds almost like wi. This tendency is less marked in syllables bearing the 4th tone.

Preceded by a simple consonant, *eu* represents a diphthong having as its starting point a slightly rounded central vowel and moving in the direction of u, əu.[19]

In saying *yeu*, the ə element of the diphthong tends to be less prominent than the u, and in Chao's case especially the effect is almost ju; less markedly so in syllables with the 4th tone.

a

In -*a*, *ya*, and *wa*, the *a* is spoken as an open vowel with the raising of the tongue rather nearer the back than the front. When a syllable of this type bears the 5th tone it is pronounced by Chao with an open front vowel, *eg* 疤 *scar* ⁻pɑ, 八 *eight* -pa; 丫 *fork* ⁻jɑ, 鴨 *duck* -ja; 花 *flower* ⁻xwɑ, 滑 *smooth* -xwa.

In -*an* and *wan*, Su makes an open front vowel, which may be nasalized, followed by n. Chao uses a front nasal vowel between open and half-open with no following n, *eg: ban* pæ̃.

In -*ang*, *yang*, and *wang*, both speakers use an open vowel, made nearer the back than the front, followed by a velar nasal. There are thus at least two phonetic features in the distinction of *eg: wan* and *wang*, the quality of the vowel, and the type of closing nasality.

For *ai* in -*ai* and *wai* both speakers make a diphthong having as its starting-point an open vowel between front and back, and moving in the direction of i. Su alone has this diphthong with preceding palatalization. For Su's *yai*⁴, Chao gives *ngai*⁴ (捱 *delay*); for Su's *gyai*¹ (皆 *all*), he gives *gai*¹. Su has few syllables of this type. I have found 捱 *yai*⁴, 孩 *hyai*², 蟹 and 懈 *hyai*⁴, 皆 *gyai*¹, 解 *gyai*³, 界 *gyai*⁴.[20] For 崖 and 捱, both give *ngai*²; for 涯, both give *ya*².

The diphthong in -*au* and *yau* has as its starting-point an open vowel, nearer the back for -*au* than for *yau*, and moving in the direction of u.

o

Preceded by a simple consonant, or with preceding labio-velarization, in -*o* or *wo*, the vowel is sounded as a rounded back vowel, a little closer than Cardinal No 6, ɔ. Su also uses this vowel with preceding palatalization, *yo*. *yo* is found only in syllables given with the 5th tone by Chao,[21] who uses a short vowel in the neighbourhood of Cardinal No 7, perhaps somewhat advanced, checked by a glottal stop. He uses this vowel also for -*o* and *wo* with the 5th tone.

u

The *u* preceded by a simple consonant and in *yu* and *wu* is sounded as a close back vowel, not far from Cardinal No 8. When syllables written with *u* are marked for the 5th tone, Chao uses the same vowel sound as he uses for syllables written with *o* for the 5th tone. Thus 屋, which Su gives as ˌwu, and 鵝, which he gives as ˌwɔ, are both given as -wo by Chao.

yu occurs only with the 5th tone, *eg* 速 *hyu*⁵, 足 *gyu*⁵, 曲 *kyu*⁵. It would be possible, without ambiguity, to write these as *hywi*⁵, *gywi*⁵, *kywi*⁵.[22] Their phonetic form does not rule this out – the palatalization which pervades the whole syllable in *hywi* (ɕy) is restricted to the initial in *hyu* (ɕju).

The investigation of the systems of other Szechuanese speakers may, however, throw further light on the matter.

Initials

Plosives

b, *d*, *g*, are unaspirated bilabial, dental, and velar plosives. Voice is not normally present. *p*, *t*, *k*, are the corresponding fairly strongly aspirated voiceless consonants. Preceding *i*, there is fairly strong palatal friction in the aspiration of *p*, and, to a less extent, in that of *t*.

With palatalization, the *b*, *p*, *d*, *t*, are followed by a rather prominent j before the vowel of the final. *gy* represents an unaspirated alveolo-palatal affricate with a fairly prominent j before the vowel of the final. The stop is voiceless, but voice may start in the fricative element. *ky* represents the corresponding voiceless aspirated affricate. The passage seems to be enlarged before the beginning of the voice in j.[23]

Table 5
Initials 1. Plosives and nasals

PLOSIVES	bilabial unasp.	bilabial asp.	dental unasp.	dental asp.	alveolo-palatal unasp.	alveolo-palatal asp.	velar unasp.	velar asp.
1. simple	*b*	*p*	*d*	*t*			*g*	*k*
2. -*y*	*by*	*py*	*dy*	*ty*	*gy*	*ky*		
3. -*yw*					*gyw*	*kyw*		
4. -*w*			*dw*	*tw*			*gw*	*kw*
NASALS								
1. simple	*m*		*n*				*ng*	
2. -*y*								
(*a*) fric.			*ny*					
(*b*) non-fric.	*my*		*ly*					
3. -*yw*			*nyw*					
4. -*w*			*nw*					

NOTE: The rows marked -*y*, -*yw*, and -*w*, show initials with palatalization, labio-palatalization, and labio-velarization respectively.

Only *g* and *k* occur with labio-palatalization. In pronouncing syllables with *gyw* and *kyw*, the affricates described above are made with fairly strong lip-rounding. When *i* follows, the vowel also is rounded; when *e* and *en* follow, there is a rather prominent ɥ before the vowel.

For *dw* and *gw*, the sounds described for *d* and *g* are made with fairly strong lip-rounding, and are followed by a rather prominent w before the vowel. *tw* and *kw* are made as the corresponding voiceless aspirated consonants followed by a similar w.

The pronunciation of syllables with plosive initials is indicated in the following examples, in which the tones and finals are noted as they would be said by Su:

*ba*¹⁻pɑ, *pa*⁴′pha, *do*¹ ⁻tɔ, *to*¹ ⁻thɔ, *gu*¹ ⁻ku, *ku*¹⁻khu, *byau*¹ ⁻pjau, *pyau*¹ ⁻pçjau, *dyau*¹ ⁻tjau, *tyau*¹ ⁻tçjau, *gyang*¹ ⁻tçjɑŋ, *kyang*¹ ⁻tçhjɑŋ, *gywi*³ ˌtçy, *kywin*¹ ⁻tçhyn, *gywen*¹ ⁻tçyɛn, *kywen*¹ ⁻tçhyɛn, *dwan*¹ ⁻twan, *twan*² ˌthwan, *gwang*¹ ⁻kwɑŋ, *kwang*¹ ⁻khwɑŋ.

Nasals

The bilabial, dental, and velar nasal consonants are followed, markedly in the case of Chao, less so in the case of Su, by the corresponding voiced plosive. Thus *ma*¹ is pronounced as ⁻mbɑ, *na*¹ as ⁻ndɑ, *nge*⁵ as ˌŋgɛ. They might, indeed, be classified as plosives with nasalization.[24]

Table 6
Initials 2. Fricatives and affricates

FRICATIVES	bilabial		alveolar		alveolo-palatal		velar	
	voiced	voiceless	voiced	voiceless	voiced	voiceless	voiced	voiceless
1. simple	*f*		*z*	*s*				*h*
2. -*y*						*hy*		
3. -*yw*						*hyw*		
4. -*w*			*zw*	*sw*				*hw*
AFFRICATES								
1. simple			*dz*	*ts*				
2. -*w*			*dzw*	*tsw*				

NOTE: The rows marked -*y*, -*yw*, and -*w*, show initials with palatalization, labio-palatalization, and labio-velarization respectively.

Reference has already been made to Su's distinction of n with fricative palatalization from n with non-fricative palatalization. In the former case, n is followed by voiced alveolo-palatal friction, *eg* ˌnzjɛn *nyen*²; in the latter, by a lowered variety of ɨ, *eg:* ˌnɨɛn. These differences are not made by Chao, who uses, in both cases, n followed by j before the vowel.

Labio-palatalization occurs only before *i*, and the effect has been described under that final.

With labio-velarization, the n is rounded and followed by a rather prominent w before the vowel.

Fricatives

The labio-dental fricative occurs only voiceless, f. *z* represents a voiced fricative made at the hinder part of the teeth-ridge, with apparently a fairly narrow channel for the air. *s* represents a voiceless alveolar fricative. Labio-velarized *z* and *s* (*zw*, *sw*) are pronounced with lip-rounding, and are followed by a prominent w.

h as a simple initial is made with fairly strong velar friction, *eg* ⁻xan *han*¹. With palatalization, it is spoken as a voiceless alveolo-palatal fricative, ɕ, with a prominent j, *eg* ⁻ɕjɛn *hyen*¹. For labio-palatalized *h* (*hyw*) a similar articulation is made with lip-rounding, which in *hywi* persists throughout the vowel, or may, in Su's case, be relaxed before the end of the vowel, *eg* ⁻ɕy *hywi*¹. In *hywin*¹ (⁻ɕyn or ⁻ɕɥin), it is Chao who relaxes the rounding before the end of the vowel.[25] In *hw*, fairly strong velar friction is followed by a prominent w, *eg* ⁻xwan *hwan*¹.

Affricates

dz represents an alveolar affricate. There is normally no voice during the stop, but it may start towards the end of the fricative element. *ts* is made unvoiced and with aspiration. With labio-velarization, these sounds are made with lip-rounding and are followed by w before the vowel of the final. Examples are *dzu*¹ ⁻tsu, *tsu*¹ ⁻tshu; *dzwan*¹ ⁻tswan, *tswan*¹ ⁻tshwan.

Semi-vowels

The palatal semi-vowel, *y*, before vowels other than *i* is a fairly prominent j. In *yo*⁵ spoken by Chao it is rounded, -ɥo. With *i* it may be manifested as palatal friction running through the whole syllable, but it is sometimes inaudible.

The labio-palatal semi-vowel, *yw* with *i* is realized in the rounding of the vowel; there may also be alveolo-palatal friction running through the syllable. It precedes other vowels as a fairly prominent ɥ.

The labio-velar semi-vowel, *w*, with *o*, is not prominent, and is sometimes inaudible. With *u* it appears as bilabial friction. Sometimes there is labio-dental friction. I have observed this most consistently in the pronunciation of 五 *five* (*wu*³ ˎvu), but it is doubtful whether there is any significant difference here.

The differences between the speakers

Apart from those directly and obviously linked with one tone in a series, Su has more 'qualitative' differences than Chao; but some of these are also, it would seem, connected with tone. Su's *yu* and *yo* for which Chao has only -jo, occur only where Chao gives the 5th tone, and, as was pointed out above, it may be possible to consider *yu* as the 5th tone of *ywi*. *we* occurs only where Chao gives a 5th tone syllable, and, with very few exceptions, this is true for *ywe* also. It is perhaps significant, in view of the fact that Chao uses i with tones 1–4, and je with tone 5 for *yi* as well as for *ye*, that his -je is not unlike the pronunciation Su gives for *ye* with tone 5 as with tones 1–4.

It may be observed with regard to *yai* that the difference in usage is essentially lack of palatalization in Chao's case; *ngai* is the form that would be expected if there were no other consonant, so that the *ngai*[4] that Chao gives for Su's *yai*[4] is, in a certain sense, *yai* minus the palatalization.

In connection with the *e* and *ei* sets, the relation of which is peculiar, it may be mentioned that *ge*, *ke*, *de*, *te*, and *ne* occur only with the 5th tone. Only Su has *ne*[5] (列); Chao gives -nje, which could be written *ni*[5] for him, Su having no *nye*. On the other hand, for 麥 Su gives ˌmjɛ (*mye*[5]) and Chao -mɛ (*me*[5]).

List of characters to illustrate the distribution of the syllables in *Table* 1

The order is that of *Table* 1, starting on the left and reading down the columns. Where possible, at least one character is given for each of the syllables to show its use with one of the five tones. The Wade romanization for Pekinese is given on the right of the character.

bi[3]	比	*pi*[3]		*si*[1]	思	*ssu*[1]	
bi[5]	筆	*pi*[3]		*si*[5]	石	*shih*[2]	
pi[2]	皮	*p'i*[2]		*hyi*[1]	西	*hsi*[1]	
di[1]	低	*ti*[1]		*hywi*[1]	虛	*hsü*[1]	
ti[2]	提	*t'i*[2]		*dzi*[1]	知	*chih*[1]	
gyi[1]	雞	*chi*[1]		*tsi*[2]	遲	*ch'ih*[2]	
kyi[1]	欺	*ch'i*[1]		*yi*[1]	衣	*i*[1]	
gywi[3]	舉	*chü*[3]		*ywi*[1]	迂	*yü*[1]	
kywi[3]	取	*ch'ü*[3]		*bin*[1]	兵	*ping*[1]	
mi[3]	米	*mi*[3]		*pin*[1]	拼	*p'in*[1]	
nyi[3]	你	*ni*[3]		*din*[1]	釘	*ting*[1]	
lyi[3]	里	*li*[3]		*tin*[1]	廳	*t'ing*[1]	
nywi[3]	女	*nü*[3]		*gyin*[1]	金	*chin*[1]	
lywi[3]	旅	*lü*[3]		*kyin*[3]	請	*ch'ing*[3]	
zi[2]	兒	*êrh*[2]		*gywin*[1]	君	*chün*[1]	
zi[5]	日	*jih*[4]		*kywin*[2]	群	*ch'ün*[2]	

min³	敏	min³	byen¹	邊	pien¹
nin²	林	lin²	pyen⁴	騙	p'ien⁴
hyin¹	心	hsin¹	dyen¹	顛	tien¹
hywin¹	熏	hsün¹	tyen¹	天	t'ien¹
yin¹	音	yin¹	gyen⁴	見	chien⁴
ywin³	允	yün³	kyen¹	千	ch'ien¹
de⁵	得	té²	gywen¹	捐	chüan¹
te⁵	特	t'ê⁴	kywen¹	圈	ch'üan¹
ge²	格	kê, ko²	gwen³	滾	kun³
ke⁵	客	k'o, k'ê⁴	kwen¹	坤	k'un¹
bye⁵	別	pieh²	men¹	們	mên¹(27)
pye⁵	拍	p'ai¹	nen³	冷	lêng³
dye¹	爹	tieh¹	ngen¹	恩	ên¹
tye⁵	貼	t'ieh¹	myen³	免	mien³
gye³	姐	chieh³	nyen²	年	nien²
kye⁵	切	ch'ieh¹	lyen³	臉	lien³
gywe⁵	絕	chüeh²	fen¹	分	fên¹
kywe⁵	缺	ch'üeh¹	zen³	忍	jên³
gwe⁵	國	kuo²	sen¹	生	shêng¹
kwe⁵	闊	k'uo⁴	hen³	很	hên³
ne⁵	列	lieh⁴	hyen¹	先	hsien¹
nge⁵	額	o²	hywen¹	宣	hsüan¹
mye⁵	滅	mieh⁴	swen⁴	順	shun⁴
ze³	惹	jê³	hwen¹	昏	hun¹
se³	捨	shê³	dzen¹	眞	chên¹
he⁵	黑	hei¹	tsen¹	秤	ch'êng¹
hye³	寫	hsieh³	dzwen¹	諄	chun¹
hywe¹	靴	hsüeh¹(26)	tswen¹	春	ch'un¹
dze¹	遮	chê¹	yen¹	烟	yen¹
tse¹	車	ch'ê¹	ywen¹	冤	yüan¹
ye⁴	夜	yeh⁴	wen¹	溫	wên¹
ywe⁵	越	yüeh⁴	bei¹	碑	pei¹
ben¹	崩	pêng¹	pei¹	披	p'ei¹
pen²	盆	p'ên²	dwei¹	堆	tui¹
den¹	登	têng¹	twei¹	推	t'ui¹
ten¹	吞	t'un¹	gwei¹	龜	kuei¹
gen¹	根	kên¹	kwei¹	盔	k'uei¹
ken¹	坑	k'êng¹	mei³	美	mei³

nwei^2	雷	lei^2	gwa^1	瓜	kua^1
fei^1	飛	fei^1	kwa^1	誇	k'ua^1
zwei^4	銳	jui^4	ma^3	馬	ma^3
swei^3	水	shui^3	na^2	拿	na^2
hwei^1	灰	hui^1	nya^1	粘	nien^2[30]
dzwei^1	追	chui^1	lya^1		[31]
tswei^1	吹	ch'ui^1	fa^5	發	fa^1
wei^1	威	wei^1	sa^5	殺	sha^1
beu^1	褒	pao^1	ha^1	哈	ha^1
peu^3	剖	p'ou^3	hya^4	夏	hsia^4
deu^4	豆	tou^4	swa^3	要	shua^3
teu^2	頭	t'ou^2	hwa^1	花	hua^1
geu^1	勾	kou^1	dza^5	渣	cha^1
keu^3	口	k'ou^3	tsa^5	擦	ts'a^1
dyeu^1	丟	tiu^1	dzwa^1	抓	chua^1
gyeu^3	酒	chiu^3	tswa^1		[32]
kyeu^1	秋	ch'iu^1	ya^1	丫	ya^1
meu^3	某	mou^3[28]	wa^1	挖	wa^1
neu^2	樓	lou^2	ban^1	搬	pan^1
ngeu^1	毆	ou^1	pan^1	攀	p'an^1
myeu^4	謬	miu^4	dan^1	單	tan^1
nyeu^2	牛	niu^2	tan^1	貪	t'an^1
lyeu^2	流	liu^2	gan^1	乾	kan^1
feu^2	浮	fou^2	kan^1	看	k'an^1
zeu^2	揉	jou^2	dwan^1	端	tuan^1
seu^3	手	shou^3	twan^2	團	t'uan^2
heu^4	後	hou^4	gwan^1	官	kuan^1
hyeu^1	休	hsiu^1	kwan^1	寬	k'uan^1
dzeu^1	舟	chou^1	man^3	滿	man^3
tseu^1	抽	ch'ou^1	nan^2	南	nan^2
yeu^3	有	yu^3	ngan^1	安	an^1
ba^1	疤	pa^1	nwan^3	暖	nuan^3
pa^4	怕	p'a^4	fan^4	飯	fan^4
da^3	打	ta^3	zan^3	染	jan^3
ta^1	他	t'a^1	san^1	山	shan^1
ka^1	卡	k'a^1	han^2	合	han^2
gya^1	家	chia^1	zwan^3	輓	juan^3
kya^5[29]	宅	chai^2	swan^1	酸	suan^1

hwan¹	歡	huan¹	kai¹	開	k'ai¹
dzan⁴	站	chan⁴	gyai¹	皆	chieh¹⁽³³⁾
tsan²	甕	ts'an²	gwai⁴	怪	kuai⁴
dzwan⁴	磚	chuan¹	kwai⁴	快	k'uai⁴
tswan¹	穿	ch'uan¹	mai³	買	mai³
wan¹	彎	wan¹	nai²	來	lai²
bang¹	幫	pang¹	ngai¹	哀	ai¹
pang²	旁	p'ang²	sai¹	篩	shai¹
dang¹	當	tang¹	hai³	海	hai³
tang¹	湯	t'ang¹	hyai⁴	蟹	hsieh⁴
gang¹	缸	kang¹	swai¹	衰	shuai¹
kang¹	康	k'ang¹	hwai⁴	壞	huai⁴
gyang¹	薑	chiang¹	dzai¹	栽	tsai¹
kyang¹	鎗	ch'iang¹	tsai¹	猜	ts'ai¹
gwang¹	光	kuang¹	dzwai³⁽³⁴⁾		
kwang²	狂	k'uang²	tswai³	喘	ch'uan³
mang²	忙	mang²	yai²	摧	yai²
nang³	朗	lang³	wai¹	歪	wai¹
ngang¹	腌	ang¹	bau¹	包	pao¹
nyang²	娘	niang²	pau³	跑	p'ao³
lyang⁴	亮	liang⁴	dau¹	刀	tao³
fang¹	方	fang¹	tau³	討	t'ao³
zang⁴	讓	jang⁴	gau¹	高	kao¹
sang¹	傷	shang¹	kau³	攷	k'ao³
hang²	航	hang²	byau³	表	piao³
hyang¹	香	hsiang¹	pyau³	飄	p'iao¹
hwang¹	荒	huang¹	dyau³	雕	tiao¹
dzang⁴	丈	chang⁴	tyau¹	挑	t'iao¹
tsang¹	蒼	ts'ang¹	gyau¹	膠	chiao¹
dzwang¹	裝	chuang¹	kyau³	巧	ch'iao³
tswang²	床	ch'uang²	mau²	毛	mao²
yang¹	秧	yang¹	nau³	老	lao³
wang¹	汪	wang¹	ngau²	敖	ao²
bai⁴	拜	pai⁴	myau³	廟	miao⁴
pai⁴	派	p'ai⁴	nyau³	鳥	niao³
dai¹	呆	tai¹	lyau³	了	liao³
tai⁴	太	t'ai⁴	zau³	繞	jao⁴
gai⁴	蓋	kai⁴	sau¹	燒	shao¹

hau^3	好	hao^3	gu^1	姑	ku^1
hyau^3	小	hsiao^3	ku^3	苦	k'u^3
dzau^3	早	tsao^3	gyu^5	足	tsu^2
tsau^1	抄	ch'ao^1	kyu^5	曲	ch'ü^1
yau^4	要	yao^4	mu^3	母	mu^3
bo^1	波	po^1	nu^4	怒	nu^4
po^1	坡	p'o^1	fu^1	夫	fu^1
do^1	多	to^1	zu^3	乳	ju^3
to^1	拖	t'o^1	su^1	書	shu^1
go^1	哥	ko^1	hyu^5	速	su^2
ko^3	可	k'o^3	dzu^1	猪	chu^1
gyo^5	脚	chiao^3, chüeh^2	tsu^5	出	ch'u^1
			yu^5	育	yü^4
kyo^5	雀	ch'iao^3, ch'üeh^4	wu^3	武	wu^3
			bung^1	弼	pêng^1
mo^2	磨	mo^2	pung^3	捧	p'êng^3
no^3	裸	lo^3	dung^1	東	tung^1
ngo^3	我	wo^3	tung^4	痛	t'ung^4
nyo^5	虐	nüeh^4(35)	gung^1	工	kung^1
lyo^5	掠	lüeh^4, liao^4	kung^1	空	k'ung^1
			gyung^3	窘	chiung^3
zo^5	弱	jo^4	kyung^2	窮	ch'iung^2
so^3	鎮	so^3	mung^4	孟	mêng^4
ho^2	河	ho^2	nung^2	農	nung^2
hyo^5	學	hsüeh^2	fung^1	風	fêng^1
dzo^3	左	tso^3	zung^3	冗	jung^3
tso^4	錯	ts'o^4	sung^1	松	sung^1
yo^5	約	yo^5	hung^2	紅	hung^2
wo^1	窩	wo^1	hyung^1	兄	hsiung^1
bu^3	補	pu^3	dzung^1	中	chung^1
pu^3	普	p'u^3	tsung^2	蟲	ch'ung^2
du^1	都	tu^1	yung^4	用	yung^4
tu^2	圖	t'u^2	wung^1	翁	wêng^1

Notes

[1] Referred to henceforth as Su.
[2] Referred to henceforth as Chao.

[3] See J. R. Firth and B. B. Rogers, 'The Structure of the Chinese Monosyllable in a Hunanese Dialect (Changsha),' *BSOAS*, VIII, 1055–1074. Their technique is used here.

[4] The systematic transcription is given in italic, the phonetic transcription in IPA symbols.

[5] This would not be true for Chao's pronunciation taken by itself. Where Su has ε^{1-5}, he has ∂i^{1-4}, ε^5. For the syllables in which both use ∂i^{1-4}, however, there is no tone 5. See *Table* 1 and the section on the phonetic interpretation of the systematic transcription.

[6] For zi^5, Su ₍z, Chao ₋zɛ, see Phonetic interpretation below.

[7] Chao $s\partial i^{1-4}$.

[8] Chao gives ji with tones 1–4.

[9] Only gwe^5 國, and kwe^5 閼.

[10] For *yo* and *yu*, which are found with tone 5 only, see Phonetic interpretation below.

[11] See J. R. Firth, 'Alphabets and Phonology in India and Burma,' *BSOAS*, VIII, *pp* 532–533.

[12] It would be convenient and permissible to refer to 'y-initials', 'yw-initials', and 'w-initials'; and, indeed, to 'y-syllables', 'yw-syllables', and 'w-syllables'.

[13] The letters *y*, *yw*, and *w* are in these cases used to stand for initials.

[14] The allocation of these syllables to the *i* set seems to be supported by the history of *eg* the word, 絲, given by Karlgren, *Grammata Serica*, No 974 in the dictionary, as $*s\underset{.}{i}\partial g/si/s\ddot{i}$.

[15] While Su gives 四 as si^4, Chao gives it as si^5 (-sɛ). *Cf* Karlgren, *op cit*, No 518, $*s\underset{.}{i}\partial d/si/s\ddot{i}$, and the remark, 'Tsiyün mentions a dialectal reading $s\underset{.}{i}\ddot{e}t$ in Shensi.'

[16] *Cf* Karlgren, *op cit*, No 981, 耳 $*\acute{n}\underset{.}{i}\partial g/\acute{n}\acute{z}i/er$ ⟨zi^3⟩.

[17] See, however, under *yo* and *yu* below.

[18] Su has *nge* with 5th tone only, 額 *forehead*. Chao also gives this as nge^5. He has also given me $ngei^1$, meaning something like *snuggle*, for which he knows no character.

[19] For Su's *meu*, which occurs with tones 2, 3, and 4, Chao gives *mung* with the corresponding tones.

[20] These are the only cases in which 'palatalization' occurs twice in the syllable.

[21] *eg* 約 yo^5, 學 hyo^5, 脚 gyo^5, 雀 kyo^5, 掠 lyo^5, (虐 and 謔 are given as nyo^5 by Su, yo^5 by Chao). It is interesting to note that, but for the fact that Su has both ₍jɔ and ₍ɥɛ (corresponding to Chao's single -ɥo), and both ₍kwɛ and ₍kɔ (corresponding to Chao's single -ko), it would be possible to dispense with *o* in the systematic transcription without introducing any ambiguity. But for these few syllables, it would be possible to regard ɔ as the realization of *e* with preceding labio-velarization, and write *po* as *pwe*, *do* as *dwe*, etc. The investigation of the systems of other Szechuanese speakers may throw further light on the matter. It will be noticed that the elimination of *o* would make *Table* 2 much more nearly symmetrical.

[22] Compare Karlgren, *Gram. Ser.* 1213 曲 $*k'\underset{.}{i}uk/k'\underset{.}{i}wok/k'\ddot{u}$. Note also 1219 足 $*ts\underset{.}{i}uk/ts\underset{.}{i}wok/tsu$ ... for $*ts\underset{.}{i}ug/ts\underset{.}{i}u/ts\ddot{u}$.

[23] It would have been possible to assign *gy* and *ky* to the affricates and regard them as *dz*, *ts*, with palatalization, writing *dzy*, *tsy*. Similarly, *gyw* and *kyw* might have been regarded as *dz* and *ts* with labio-palatalization and written *dzyw*, *tsyw*. Note, however, that Chao has gai^1 for Su's $gyai^1$. It is not surprising to find that tɕ is derived in some cases from ancient *k*, and in others from ancient *ts*. See Karlgren, *op cit*, *pp* 46, 48.

[24] The list of derivatives of *d*, for example, would then be *dy*, *dw*, *nd*, *ndy*, *ndyw*, *ndw*.

[25] It would have been possible to assign *hy* and *hyw* to the fricatives and regard them as *s* with palatalization (*sy*) and labio-palatalization (*syw*). ɕ appears to be derived in some cases from ancient χ, and in others from ancient *s*. See Karlgren, *op cit, pp* 46, 48.

[26] Chao uses *hywi*[1].

[27] Chao *men*[2].

[28] Chao uses *mung*[3].

[29] Chao gives *tse*[5].

[30] Given as used colloquially for *nyen*[1].

[31] Given as a colloquial word, 'sweet' (of *eg* a child).

[32] Given by Chao as 'tear off (wrappings)'; no character. He gives *hyin*[1] for 扺.

[33] Chao gives *gai*[1].

[34] Given as 'haughty'; no character.

[35] Chao gives *yo*[5].

N. C. Scott

A phonological analysis of the Szechuanese monosyllable

A reconsideration of the material used for my article 'The monosyllable in Szechuanese'[1] in the light of the technique of prosodic analysis being developed in the Department of Phonetics of the School of Oriental and African Studies[2] has led me to believe that it is susceptible of a more rigorous and satisfying treatment, in which some of the apparently eccentric features take a normal place.

The material consists of the spoken forms of all the isolated monosyllables of their native language known to two speakers referred to as Su (a native of Fengtuhsien) and Chao (a native of Iping), whose pronunciations differ in certain respects. The monosyllables will be sufficiently well identified for the purposes of this paper by the 'systematic transcription' used in the previous article, to which reference may be made for its phonetic interpretation.

In the present analysis, the structure of any monosyllable is considered to be either CVπ or Vπ. The phonological description of a monosyllable requires, for one of the first category, the statement of a member of the consonant system, and for those of both categories, the statement of a member of the vowel system and of a number of features referred to as prosodies. I find it necessary to recognize (a) prosodies of the syllable as a whole, (b) prosodies of syllable-initial, (c) prosodies of the syllable-final. These may be referred to as syllable-prosodies, initial-prosodies, and final-prosodies. The words 'initial' and 'final' are used here as phonological terms, and not as they are traditionally used by sinologists.

First published in *Bulletin of the School of Oriental and African Studies*, Vol XVIII, No 3: 556–560, 1956.

1. *Consonants*
Two systems of consonants are recognized.
  (a) Three occlusives, *P, T, K*. The only phonetic implications of these
  taken by themselves are bilabial, dental to alveolo-palatal, and velar
  plosion respectively.
  (b) Three fricatives, *F, S, H*. The only phonetic implications of these
  taken by themselves are labio-dental, alveolar to alveolo-palatal,
  and velar friction respectively.

2. *Vowels*
Three vowels are recognized, ι, ϵ, α. The phonetic implications of these
are grades of openness: ι, grade 1, close; ϵ, grade 2, between close and
open; and α, grade 3, open.

3. *Prosodies of the syllable as a whole*
  (a) Tone. For a phonetic description of the tonal features, see 'MS'.
  Syllables marked there as having tone 5 are those considered here
  as having a final-prosody of glottalization (see below). It is possible
  to assign them to tone 2[3] and to regard each syllable as having one
  of four tonal prosodies. I do not propose to deal further with tone in
  the present paper, and the mark for the tonal prosody will be
  omitted from the phonological formulae.
  (b) Every syllable as a whole is considered to have the prosodic feature
  of either frontness (*y*) or backness (*w*). For typographical convenience, the symbols for these will be shown on the line in the first
  place of the phonological formula.
In the pronunciation of syllables with frontness-prosody, the articulation is of a dominantly front type. They will be referred to as *y*-syllables.
In the pronunciation of syllables with backness-prosody, the articulation
is of a dominantly back type. They will be referred to as *w*-syllables. In
the pronunciation of both *y*- and *w*-syllables, there is absence of lip-
rounding unless the syllable has labio-palatalization or labio-velarization
as an initial prosody or as a final prosody or as both. In the last case, there
is lip-rounding throughout the utterance. The vowel-sound in the pronunciation of *y*-syllables with grade 2 vowel is of a fully front type when
the syllable has *y* or ψ initial prosody, and also when (except for glottalization) 'absence' is the feature in the prosodies of syllable final. See below.
Although in pronunciation the front or back quality is most obvious in
the vowel-sound, it is not confined to it. See under final-nasalization
below.
    Examples[4] of *y*-syllables are $y^y P\iota^y$ (*bi*), $y^h S\epsilon$ (*se*), $y^h H\epsilon^n$ (*hen*), $yP\alpha^n$
(*ban*), $y^{hw}K\alpha^n$ (*kwan*).
    Examples of *w*-syllables are $w^w P\iota^w$ (*bu*), $w^{hw}T\epsilon^w$ (*to*), $wP\alpha^n$ (*bang*),
$w^w K\alpha$ (*gwa*).

4. *Prosodies of the syllable-initial*

The following prosodic features are considered to be operative for the syllable-initial. In the phonological formulae, the symbols for these will be shown in superior position after the symbol for the prosody of the syllable as a whole.

(*a*) Aspiration (*h*) or its absence (unmarked),
(*b*) Palatalization (*y*), labio-palatalization (*ɥ*), labio-velarization (*w*), or the absence of all three (unmarked),
(*c*) Nasalization (*n*), or its absence (unmarked),
(*d*) Affrication (*s*), or its absence (unmarked).

(*a*) In the pronunciation of syllables having initial-aspiration, there is necessarily absence of voicing during the stop or constriction, voice beginning only after the opener position is reached. Examples are $w^hT\alpha$ (*ta*), $w^{hw}S\iota^w$ (*su*), $y^{hys}T\iota^y$ (*kyi*).

In the pronunciation of syllables without initial-aspiration, there is voicing from the start, except in the case of those with occlusive consonant and absence of initial-nasalization, in which voice is usually absent during the stop, beginning with the release. Examples are $wT\alpha$ (*da*), $w^wS\iota^w$ (*zu*), $y^{ys}T\iota^y$ (*gyi*), $y^{yn}P\iota^y$ (*mi*).

(*b*) In the pronunciation of a syllable with initial-palatalization, there is a close front element throughout the earlier part of the utterance, the lips being unrounded. When the syllable has also initial-affrication, the closure and following constriction are in the alveolo-palatal region. When the consonant is *S*, the friction is of alveolo-palatal type. Examples are $y^y\iota^y$ (*yi*), $y^{ys}T\epsilon^w$ (*gyeu*), $w^{hy}S\alpha^n$ (*hyang*), $w^{hy}P\alpha^w$ (*pyau*).

In the pronunciation of a syllable with initial-labio-palatalization, there is a close front element throughout the earlier part of the syllable with lip-rounding either from the start or increasing. When there is also initial-affrication, the closure and following constriction, and when the consonant is *S*, the constriction, are in the alveolo-palatal region. Examples are $y^{ɥ}\iota^{ɥ}$ (*ywi*), $y^{ɥs}T\epsilon$ (*gywe*), $w^{ɥs}T\iota^{wn}$ (*gyung*).

In the pronunciation of syllables with initial-labio-velarization, there is a close back element with lip-rounding throughout the earlier part of the utterance. Examples are $w^wK\iota^w$ (*gu*), $y^wK\epsilon^y$ (*gwei*), $y^wT\alpha^n$ (*dwan*), $w^{hw}K\alpha^n$ (*kwang*).

All *y*-syllables with grade 1 vowel are considered to have either *y*- or *ɥ*- initial prosody, which, in pronunciation, is *eg* reflected in the articulation of the stop of $y^{hy}T\iota^y$ (*ti*) as compared with that of $y^hT\alpha^n$ (*tan*), a syllable that has none of the initial features *y*, *ɥ*, or *w*. All *w*-syllables with grade 1 vowel are considered to have *w*-initial prosody. The pronunciation of $w^{hw}T\iota^w$ (*tu*) has lip-rounding and depression of the front of the tongue from the start.

(*c*) In the pronunciation of syllables with initial-nasalization, there is a bilabial, dental, or velar nasal followed by the homorganic plosive, according as the consonant of the syllable is P, T, or K. There is no nasality following the stop unless the syllable is one with the final prosody of nasalization. Examples are $y^{yn}P\iota^y$ (*mi*), $y^{yn}T\epsilon^n$ (*lyen*), $w^nK\alpha^w$ (*ngau*).

(*d*) In the pronunciation of syllables with initial-affrication, which is restricted to syllables with consonant T, the plosion is followed by homorganic friction. When the syllable has *y*- or *ɥ*- initial prosody, the closure and following constriction are in the alveolo-palatal region; for other types of syllable-initial, they are in the alveolar region. Examples are $y^{hys}T\iota^y$ (*kyi*), $y^{ɥs}T\iota^ɥ$ (*gywi*), $y^sT\epsilon$ (*dze*), $w^{ws}T\epsilon^w$ (*dzo*).

In 'MS', attention was drawn to the fact that Su pronounced syllables written with *ny*- in the 'systematic transcription' with friction and syllables written with *ly*- without friction. In the present analysis, syllables of the former type are considered to have initial-affrication, which is absent from syllables of the latter type. Thus, $y^{yns}T\epsilon^n$ (*nyen*), and $y^{yn}T\epsilon^n$ (*lyen*). For Chao, initial-affrication excludes initial-nasalization.

5. *Prosodies of the syllable-final*

The following prosodic features are considered to be operative for the syllable-final. In the phonological formulae, the symbols for these will be shown in superior position following the vowel-symbol.

(*a*) Palatalization (*y*), labio-palatalization (*ɥ*), labio-velarization (*w*), or the absence of all of these (unmarked),

(*b*) Nasalization (*n*) or its absence (unmarked),

(*c*) Retroflexion (*r*) or its absence (unmarked),

(*d*) Glottalization (*q*) or its absence (unmarked).

(*a*) In the pronunciation of syllables with final-palatalization, there is a close front element with absence of lip-rounding in the latter part of utterance; in that of syllables with final-labio-palatalization, a close front element with lip-rounding; and in that of syllables with final-labio-velarization, a close back element with lip-rounding. It is to be noted that *y*-syllables with grade 1 vowel and *ɥ*-initial may have either *y*- or *ɥ*-final. The phonological formula for the syllable written as *gywi* in 'MS' is $y^{ɥs}T\iota^y$ for Su; for Chao, it is $y^{ɥs}T\iota^ɥ$. Other *y*-syllables with grade 1 vowel have *y*-final, and *w*-syllables with grade 1 vowel have *w*-final. Examples of syllables with y-final are $y^yP\iota^y$ (bi), $y^wK\epsilon^y$ ($gwei$), $y^hK\alpha^y$ (kai). Examples of syllables with w-final are $w^wT\iota^w$ (du), $yK\epsilon^w$ (geu), $w^yP\alpha^w$ ($byau$).

(b) In the pronunciation of y-syllables having final-nasalization, there is nasality in the latter part of the utterance, and if there is oral occlusion (see 'MS') it will be dental. In the pronunciation of w-syllables having final-nasalization, the utterance ends in a velar nasal. w-syllables with grade 1 vowel having final-nasalization have also final-labio-velarization; y-syllables with grade 1 vowel and final-nasalization have also final-palatalization, unless they have $\mathfrak{y}$-initial, in which case they may have either y- or $\mathfrak{y}$-final. For Chao, the syllable written in 'MS' as $gywin$ is to be considered as $y^{\mathfrak{y}s}T\iota^{yn}$, for Su it is to be considered as $y^{\mathfrak{y}s}T\iota^{\mathfrak{y}n}$. Examples of y-syllables with final-nasalization are $y^yT\iota^{yn}$ (din), $y^yT\epsilon^n$ ($dyen$), $y^hP\alpha^n$ (pan). Examples of w-syllables with final-nasalization are $w^wT\iota^{wn}$ ($dung$), $wK\alpha^n$ ($gang$).

(c) The syllables identified in 'MS' as si^{1-4} (Wade $s\breve{u}$) are here considered to have a final-prosody of retroflexion. In pronunciation, the raising of the tongue-tip is maintained after the alveolar constriction. They are analysed as $y^hS\iota^r$, with tones 1–4. The syllable identified in 'MS' as zi^5 is here analysed as $yS\iota^r$ with tone 2. The syllables identified in 'MS' as zi^{1-4} (pronounced as a half-open front vowel with retroflexion) are here analysed as $y\epsilon^r$ with tones 1–4.

(d) Pronounced by Chao, syllables with final-glottalization end with a glottal stop and have mid-level pitch. They are here assigned to tone 2. Su makes no difference in pronunciation between such syllables and syllables without final-glottalization having tone 2. Examples are $y^hS\epsilon^q$ (se^5), $w^{\mathfrak{y}}\epsilon^{wq}$ (yo^5), $yP\alpha^q$ (ba^5), $y^{hys}T\epsilon^q$ (kye^5).

In 'MS', whenever it was possible without ambiguity, a single formula was given to cover the reading of the same single character by the two speakers. Thus sei was not shown in $Table$ 1, the syllabary, though this would have been appropriate for Chao and it was necessary to make the rule that se with tones 1–4 would be pronounced by him as if written sei. The present analysis makes it possible to deal with the two speakers separately within the systems established, and the formulae make clear the nature and extent of the likeness and difference of the forms. Thus, for the syllables just mentioned, the analysis for Su would give $y^hS\epsilon$ and for Chao $y^hS\epsilon^y$. On the other hand, it was necessary in 'MS' (p 287) to identify the forms used in reading a particular character as gwe for Su and go for Chao. The formulae in terms of the systems established here are $y^wK\epsilon$ and $w^wK\epsilon^{wq}$, which indicate the relation of the forms while still making clear the differences.

Notes

[1] *BSOAS*, XII, I, 1947, 197–213 (hereafter referred to as 'MS'). [Reprinted in this volume, *pp* 278–298. Eds.]

[2] See J. R. Firth, 'Sounds and Prosodies', *TPS*, 1948, 127–152.

[3] The speaker referred to tone 5 as 'upper 2'.

[4] In the examples, the phonological formula is given first, followed in brackets by the 'systematic transcription' used in 'MS'.

A. E. Sharp

A tonal analysis of the disyllabic noun in the Machame dialect of Chaga

This paper deals with certain features of the Bantu dialect spoken at Machame on the western slopes of Mt Kilimanjaro in Tanganyika Territory. It arises very largely as the result of work done in London with the help of Mr S. J. Nitro, whose home is in Machame, but in part from observations made in the field during study-leave in Africa. The subject-matter of what follows is narrowly circumscribed, but the treatment is relevant to problems of more general interest in linguistic analysis, especially those involved in the analysis of so-called 'tone languages'.

The material to be considered consists of disyllabic[1] words of which the syntactical function is identical except in so far as they are sub-categorized by features of grammatical concord: it is by reference to this function that these words are here called 'nouns'. They are all equally analysable in terms of a single prefix and a stem.[2] Where the same stem is found with various prefixes, forms which are (where lexically feasible) in complementary distribution with regard to -mwi 'one' and -vii 'two' are considered to be the same word: forms not in such complementary distribution are considered separate words. Thus kilwa 'frog', filwa 'frogs' are counted together, whereas ukwa 'yam', kikwa 'small yam' are counted separately. Some of the words under review stand in the relationship specified above to words of one syllable or of three syllables, as ukwa 'yam' to ŋgwa 'yams' and mbivi 'spiders' to uvivi 'spider'.

The material may be further subdivided into those words of which the first syllable may be regarded as the exponent of the prefix only (eg kilwa 'frog'); those of which the first syllable may be regarded as the cumulate exponent of the prefix and the initiation of the stem, and the second as

First published in *Bulletin of the School of Oriental and African Studies*, Vol XVI, No 1: 157–169, 1954.

assignable exclusively to the stem (*eg* kyoo 'dirt'); and those where the assignment of the syllables to prefix or stem is more difficult (*eg* kkyo 'night'). There appears to be only a very limited correlation between tonal behaviour and syntactical sub-class,[3] and probably none at all between tonal behaviour and shape of prefix; it is therefore found convenient to treat the material as homogeneous from the standpoint of this paper.

The forms in question are 'minimal free forms', although they seldom constitute complete utterances. They can, however, be used 'in isolation' with, for example, the intonation appropriate to a surprised or sarcastic echo of part of another speaker's utterance or, in a few cases, as a call to attract attention. They would occur frequently bounded by spaces in any feasible system of orthography for the language, and are abstractions suitable for listing in one type of dictionary. As such they are held to form an appropriate unit for tonal analysis leading to a method of lexical classification, and it is with an analysis of this kind that this paper is concerned.

The analysis was carried out by the use of a large number of 'frames' as dialytics or filters, with the words under review as *inserenda*. Ten such frames are given here: they have been chosen to show the nouns in initial, medial, and final position in the utterance, and also to exemplify 'affirmation', 'interrogation', 'negation', and 'command' (terms which must here remain undefined). They may be translated as follows:

A: kapa.....!   A: (Beat) ......!
B: lola .....!   B: (Look at) ......!
C: ʃallola   C: I have (looked at) ....
D: ʃilelola ......   D: I (looked at) ....
E: kulelola ....?   E: Did you (look at) ......?
F: kulalole ...... fo! F: Do not (look at) ......!
G: nʃilelola ...... fo G: I did not (look at) ....
H: kulelola ...... ndesa? H: Did you (look at) ......, pray?
I: ...... -aŋxeka   I: ...... has (got lost).
J: ...... -kaʃa -aŋxeka J: The (bad) ...... has (got lost).

As an insurance that the insertion of a particular noun into any frame makes collocational as well as grammatical sense, those elements in the frames that have been underlined and of which the translation has been enclosed in brackets may be replaced, without prejudice to the analysis, by other elements which have been found by exhaustive tests to have the same tonal classification as the given elements. Thus, for example, -kap- 'beat' and -lol- 'look at' are typical examples of the two tonal categories into which fall the great majority of verbal radicals of the shape CVC. For -kap- may be substituted, *eg* -fiʃ- 'break', -xik- 'send', -loʃ- 'teach', and for -lol- may be substituted, *eg* -ur- 'buy' or -kumb- 'sell'. For -kaʃa 'bad' in Frame J we may substitute, *eg* -kuu 'old' or -ovi 'sharp', and for

-xek- 'get lost' we may substitute, *eg* -fik- 'get broken', -wuy- 'return', etc.

FRAME A	kapa	———	noun categories with which pattern is associated
contonation pattern a^1			1
,, a^2			2, 6, 9
,, a^3			3
,, a^4			4
,, a^5			5
,, a^6			7
,, a^7			8

FRAME B	lola	———	noun categories with which pattern is associated
contonation pattern b^1			1
,, b^2			2, 7
,, b^3			3, 4
,, b^4			5
,, b^5			6, 9
,, b^6			8

FRAME C	ʃal<u>lo</u>la	———	noun categories with which pattern is associated
contonation pattern c^1	- ‾ - -	- \	1
,, c^2	‾ - - -	- \	2
,, c^3	‾ - - -	-	3
,, c^4	‾ - - -	- -	4
,, c^5	‾ - - -	\	5
,, c^6	‾ - - -	- \	6, 9
,, c^7	‾ - - - -	-	7
,, c^8	‾ - - -	- \	8

FRAME D	ʃile<u>lo</u>la	———	noun categories with which pattern is associated
contonation pattern d^1	- - - -	- \	1
,, d^2	- - - -	- \	2
,, d^3	- - - -	- \	3, 5
,, d^4	- - - -	- \	4, 8
,, d^5	- - - -	- \	6, 9
,, d^6	- - - -	- -	7

FRAME E	kulel<u>o</u>la	—————— ?	noun categories with which pattern is associated
contonation pattern e^1	- - - - -	- ‾	1, 4, 8
,, e^2	- - - - -	- \	2
,, e^3	- - - - -	/	3, 5
,, e^4	- - - -	- \	6, 9
,, e^5	- - - -	- -	7

FRAME F	kula<u>lo</u>le	———— : fo	noun categories with which pattern is associated
contonation pattern f^1	- - -	- - \	1, 6
,, f^2	- - -	- - \	2
,, f^3	- - -	- - \	3, 4
,, f^4	- - -	- \	5, 7, 9
,, f^5	- - -	- - \	8

FRAME G	nʃilelola	——	fo	noun categories with which pattern is associated
contonation pattern g^1			\	1
,, g^2			\	2
,, g^3			\	3
,, g^4			\	4
,, g^5			\	5, 7
,, g^6			\	6
,, g^7			\	8
,, g^8			\	9

FRAME H	kulelola	——	ndesa	noun categories with which pattern is associated
contonation pattern h^1				1, 6
,, h^2				2
,, h^3				3, 5, 7
,, h^4				4, 8
,, h^5				9

FRAME I	——	-aŋxeka	noun categories with which pattern is associated
contonation pattern i^1			I
,, i^2			2, 6
,, i^3			3, 5, 7
,, i^4			4
,, i^5			8
,, i^6			9

FRAME J	——	-kaʃa -aŋxeka	noun categories with which pattern is associated
contonation pattern j^1			1, 6
,, j^2			2
,, j^3			3, 5, 7
,, j^4			4, 8, 9

The nouns were inserted in turn into a given frame at the point indicated by the line,[4] and the informant was asked to utter the resultant complexes. The tonal features of these utterances were recorded impressionistically between parallel lines by means of one mark per syllable indicating the approximate relative pitch of that syllable. For any given frame, every different sequence of such marks may be said to form a 'pattern'. It will be seen that a number of such patterns is given under each frame: no other patterns were recorded for that frame. The patterns are referred to by a combination of the lower-case letter corresponding to the lettering of the frame with a superscript figure to indicate the individual pattern (thus a^3 indicates the third pattern given under Frame A): they have been called 'contonation patterns'.

The term 'contonation'[5] is here found appropriate for two main reasons. In the first place, it serves to emphasize the interdependence of frame and *inserendum*. In this connection numerous instances will be observed where it is on the pitch of a frame-syllable rather than on any pitch-feature of the noun itself that the differentiation of one pattern from another depends (compare, *eg*: f^3 with f^4 or i^1 with i^5).[6] Secondly, we are left free to reserve the term 'intonation' for other uses (see, in addition, note 10 below).

The number of contonation patterns recorded for the frames given varies from eight (Frames C and G) to four (Frame J). That is to say, if on hearing the informant utter the complexes constituted by a particular frame and our *inserenda* we group together all the nouns that elicit a particular pattern, the number of such groupings is never greater than eight. For the purposes of lexical classification, however, we have to set up nine categories of nouns on the basis of their association not with one individual pattern, but with a number of such patterns taken from a variety of frames. We arrive at this result by linking together the numbers of any contonation patterns – one from each frame – that are associated in common with any given noun, and counting the different chains that are formed by this process. This gives us:

Chain $1 = a^1 \ b^1 \ c^1 \ d^1 \ e^1 \ f^1 \ g^1 \ h^1 \ i^1 \ j^1$
Chain $2 = a^2 \ b^2 \ c^2 \ d^2 \ e^2 \ f^2 \ g^2 \ h^2 \ i^2 \ j^2$
Chain $3 = a^3 \ b^3 \ c^3 \ d^3 \ e^3 \ f^3 \ g^3 \ h^3 \ i^3 \ j^3$
Chain $4 = a^4 \ b^3 \ c^4 \ d^4 \ e^1 \ f^3 \ g^4 \ h^4 \ i^4 \ j^4$
Chain $5 = a^5 \ b^4 \ c^5 \ d^3 \ e^3 \ f^4 \ g^5 \ h^3 \ i^3 \ j^3$
Chain $6 = a^2 \ b^5 \ c^6 \ d^5 \ e^4 \ f^1 \ g^6 \ h^1 \ i^2 \ j^1$
Chain $7 = a^6 \ b^2 \ c^7 \ d^6 \ e^5 \ f^4 \ g^5 \ h^3 \ i^3 \ j^3$
Chain $8 = a^7 \ b^6 \ c^8 \ d^4 \ e^1 \ f^5 \ g^7 \ h^4 \ i^5 \ j^4$
Chain $9 = a^2 \ b^5 \ c^6 \ d^5 \ e^4 \ f^4 \ g^8 \ h^5 \ i^6 \ j^4$

Thus, *eg*, the first contonation pattern of the frames is in every case associated with mwana, the third similarly with kilwa, and from these associations we derive Chains 1 and 3 respectively, whereas it is the first pattern of Frame E, the third of Frames B and F, and the fourth of the remaining frames that are associated with ŋguku and together form Chain 4.

The chains may be indefinitely lengthened by the examination for further frames, but no new chains appear. The process is similar to that used by comparative philologists for the setting up of starred forms. Alternatively, we may first divide our nouns into groups according to the patterns they elicit from the informant in one frame, and then subdivide these groups wherever their members do not all elicit the same pattern in other frames: when no further subdivisions are necessary, we find that we have allotted the nouns to nine categories on the basis of their association with the nine chains of contonation patterns given above.

The figures 1 to 9 which summarize these chains may now be applied to the nouns themselves, and we may set up a nine-term commutation [7] system of word-prosodies statable for the disyllabic noun at the lexical level of abstraction. Every such noun can be allotted to one of nine categories – here termed 'contonational categories' – by reference to this system, and without such reference the form of a disyllabic noun is incompletely stated. Thus since mwana elicits the patterns of Chain 1, kilwa those of Chain 3, and ŋguku those of Chain 4, we may now write mwana[1], kilwa[3], ŋguku[4], and so on.

The contonational categories thus comprise words which exhibit certain common features of pitch behaviour in identical frames *when considered in conjunction with those frames*. The figures 1 to 9 which indicate the word-prosodies are at once expressions of the limitations on the random occurrence of relative pitches, and monosymbolic formulæ from which a contextual scatter may be deduced by the application of certain conventions. They summarize, however, not so much the scatter of the tonal forms of the noun itself as the scatter of various tonal features of the utterances as wholes that are the exponents of the complexes of the noun with its frames.

The material is unevenly distributed amongst the nine categories, the great majority of the nouns falling into five categories and only a very few into the remaining four. One category (6) appears – at least as far as my research goes – to have only one member, and as the latter is comparatively limited in its collocational possibilities, it is tempting to regard it as outside the *corpus inscriptionum*. Its inclusion in the material serves, however, to underline an important principle.[8]

Of a total of 372 nouns computed as indicated above, there are:

89 in Category 1
100 ,, ,, 2
85 ,, ,, 3
58 ,, ,, 4
24 ,, ,, 5
1 ,, ,, 6
6 ,, ,, 7
5 ,, ,, 8
4 ,, ,, 9

Examples will be given for the first five categories, and the remaining four categories will be given in full.

Category 1 : mwana 'child', ʃoka 'snake', mmbwa 'rain', nsu 'smoke', munyi 'handle', muxo 'fire'

Category 2 : ɲumbe 'cow', ʃofu 'elephant', mmbwa 'nose', nsu 'messenger', nyama 'meat', kindo 'thing'

Category 3: kilwa 'frog', kixi 'chair', mmba 'house', nuŋgu 'pot',
       ndeye 'bird', mfu 'dead person'
Category 4: ŋguku 'chicken', mbeu 'seed', mbuŋgu 'gourd', mmwa
       'cousin'
Category 5: ukwi 'stick of firewood', ukwa 'yam', ndeu 'stomach',
       ifu 'ashes', woi 'palm of the hand'
Category 6: mfu 'married sister'
Category 7: ŋunde 'fist', muŋgo 'back', kkyo 'night', poo 'com-
       pound', ire 'blade of grass', udu 'infancy'
Category 8: ŋgaʃe 'calf of a cow', lakwa 'virgin honey', mbeʃe 'grain-
       store', mbora 'swamp', ŋgyonwa 'banana-tips'
Category 9: dede 'truth', waa 'whiteness', umwi 'unity', saa 'grand-
       father'

There is an almost complete lack of correlation between either the
phonematic or the non-tonally prosodic structure of a noun and its contonational category. It is interesting to note, however, that approximately
one-third of the words in Category 5 have labio-velarization as a feature of
the second syllable, eg ukwa 'yam', ukwi 'stick of firewood', and that this
occurs only rarely in the remaining categories. An examination of the incidence of the various prefixes and their shapes proved equally inconclusive,
though here we note that all members of Category 8 belong to a single syntactical subclass (Meinhof 9).

Twenty-two loan-words from Swahili and English which were studied
in addition to the 372 above are equally divided between Categories 1 and
2, eg

Category 1: tai 'tie', supu 'soup', tupa 'file' < Sw. 'tupa'
Category 2: piʃa 'picture', ŋgasi 'ladder' < Sw. 'ngazi', pana Sw.
       'bwana'.

We have stated that a contextual scatter may be deduced from our
formulæ 'by the application of certain conventions'. These conventions
have reference to the 'context' in the widest non-situational sense of the
word. We can, for instance, establish as one type of context intonational
prosodies of various kinds that may be set up as key-signatures for the
sentence or the piece as a whole, the resources of punctuation being
adapted and augmented for their notation. A full analysis of the intonational characteristics of the Machame dialect is outside the scope of this
paper, but we may point out that the question-mark actually used in the
heading of Frame E is quite adequate for the representation of the difference between that frame and Frame D (which is not implied by the lexical
or grammatical structure);[9] and similarly the notation ? ! might be used
for surprised echo – eg mwana[1] ? ! (of which the tonal features may be

transcribed ↑ - ‾[10]), where the superscript figure indicates, as above, the contonational category of the noun, and the 'extra' features of higher general voice-level, special voice-quality, etc, are indicated by !. An interesting type of context is illustrated by a comparison of Frame C with Frame D. Both frames exemplify 'affirmation', but it is found that there is a distinction in the phonetic forms of certain of the contonational categories in final position (compare particularly c^3 and c^4 with d^3 and d^4 in association with Categories 3 and 4) which correlates with the particular tense-formative of the verb (eg -al- -a in C and -le- -a in D), more or less independently of the number of words, if any, standing between the verb and the noun. The following is a more extended example utilizing ŋguku⁴ as the noun:

ʃallola fivana fyaŋguku (I have looked at the chicks)

but

ʃilelola fivana fyaŋguku (I looked at the chicks)

It is instructive to compare the present approach with that of 'tonemics', which derives much of its technique from the assumption that a 'tone language' is 'a language having lexically significant, contrastive, but relative pitch *on each syllable*' (my italics).[11] By a monosystemic method, tonemics, which takes the syllable as the essential recurrent element of all utterances and treats all syllables as equipollent for the purposes of tonal analysis, achieves (as does its sister methodology 'phonemics') what is essentially an overall reading transcription best adapted for the recording of individual utterances or individual texts.[12] We have referred to it here in order to emphasize that the problems which it is designed to handle are quite other than those with which we are concerned in this paper, and that neither its assumptions nor its findings must be held to have cogency outside their own legitimate sphere. Outside the essentially practical field of textual transcription, such a monosystemic syllable-by-syllable method is unsatisfactory for various reasons. One of these is that for any syllabic there is assumed to be a commutation system congruent with that of every other syllabic, so that the whole statement comes to be based on the commutation system with the greatest number of terms,[13] and takes no account of the different meaning[14] of homomorphous terms in incongruent systems. Another disadvantage which touches us more closely in this paper is the widely divergent phonological forms corresponding to single grammatical abstractions. If we attempt to 'tonemicize' the Chaga material above,[15] the nouns will vary in tonemic shape from context to context, and if we require a single lexical entry we shall be faced with the problem of selection.[16]

A polysystemic approach to linguistic analysis,[17] on the other hand, does not attempt to measure everything by the same yardstick. It assumes *inter alia* that such grammatically recurrent elements as the morpheme or word may just as profitably be subjected to systemic analysis as such phonologically recurrent elements as the syllable; and that just as at the phonological level the characteristics of any given place in an utterance or part of an utterance should preferably be stated in terms of an analysis peculiar to that place, so at the grammatical level at least the major syntactical categories, such as the nouns of the present study, should be subjected to individual analyses leading to the setting up of commutation systems applicable to those categories alone. A polysystemic analysis must not be beholden to a monosystemic one, however necessary the latter for practical purposes. We have been able to classify our material without recourse to tonemic analysis as a prerequisite: we have worked directly on our phonic material and made a separate analysis at a different level of abstraction. It is neither necessary nor in general practicable to be so limited by the findings of tonemics that we must search around for the tonemic marking of a word as it occurs under certain stated conditions in order to set up that form as the 'real' or 'basic' tonal analysis of the word in question. To speak, *at the tonemic level*, of the 'basic' tones of a word is, we submit, as much a solecism as to speak of the 'principal member' or 'norm' of a phoneme. It follows from this that there are for us no 'tonemic perturbations',[18] no 'shifted tones'[19] or the like: our formulæ are invariants like Pāṇini's 'sthānin'[20] forms.

It seems that all too little attention has hitherto been paid to the tonal analysis as wholes of recurrent elements of utterances other than the sentence and the syllable. Yet words and morphemes have an equal claim to prosodic analysis, and it is no less a part of the lexicographer's responsibility to summarize the full range of their prosodic potentialities than it is to summarize their syntactical potentialities by labelling them as particular 'parts of speech'. Conversely, it is just as much an abnegation of that duty to indicate in a dictionary some one prosodic realization of a word (such as the 'isolate' form)[21] as it would be to replace its grammatical classification by a single citation exemplifying a particular collocation. If, furthermore, we can once be freed from the shackles of the syllable-by-syllable approach, two notable advantages accrue. In the first place we are free to equate the prosodic patterns of related forms of which the essential unity is masked by the hazard of syllabic disparity;[22] and secondly, we are spared the embarrassment of choosing one side or other of the thin partition that maintains the uneasy dichotomy of 'tone' languages and 'non-tone'[23] languages. In general, it will frequently be found more appropriate to think in terms of prosodic patterns that are features of the word as a whole, and such an approach seems capable of wide application in the analysis of languages of diverse prosodic types.

Notes

[1] Brief reading conventions are as follows:
  i, e are front spread vowels, close and mid respectively; u, o are back rounded vowels, close and mid respectively; a is an open vowel midway between front and back. Geminated vowels count as disyllabic for purposes of tonal analysis.
  The voiceless plosives p, t, k are unaspirated, and t is dental; d and l are alveolar; v is a weak voiced bilabial fricative; x is a voiceless uvular fricative-trill; ʃ is a voiceless palato-alveolar sibilant fricative; ny is a palatal nasal; intervocalic m, n, ŋ are bilabial, alveolar, and velar nasals respectively.
  All 'sequences of consonants' ('consonant' here means anything except a, e, i, o, u) are, like all simple consonants, homosyllabic with the following vowel, except that (a) the first consonant of a gemination is syllabic, eg ʃa-l-lo-la, k-kyo, m-mwa, and (b) nasals are syllabic before voiceless consonants, with which they are then homorganic, eg n-su, m-fu, a-ŋ-xe-ka. All homosyllabic 'sequences' arise from the linear representation of the prosodies of nasalization, labio-velarization, and yotization: this 'orthographic' transcription has been adopted here in order that attention may be more readily concentrated on the subject of the paper. Thus, u-k̲w̲i, m-m̲b̲w̲a, ŋgyo-n̲w̲a, ŋu-n̲d̲e, etc, where the underlined 'sequences' all function as C in a syllable-structure CV.

[2] For some account of the operation of grammatical concord in Bantu languages see Malcolm Guthrie, 'Gender, Number and Person in Bantu Languages', *BSOAS*, xii, *pp* 847–856; and for the prefixes of the Machame noun see Meinhof's introduction to Pfarrer Emil Müller's *Wörterbuch der Djaga-Sprache (Madjame-Mundart)*, Hamburg, 1947, especially *p* 39*.

[3] This correlation is observable only where a noun occurs in conjunction with certain kinds of concordial elements, and must be considered at least as much a feature of those elements, which form part of other words, as of the noun itself. Within these limitations, Meinhof classes 1, 4, and 9 in some cases, class 1 alone in others, stand in opposition to the remaining classes.

[4] In Frames I and J the concordial prefixes of the words of the frames themselves are similarly left unindicated, as their form naturally depends on the grammatical subcategory of the particular noun inserted into the frames.
Thus for Frame J we have, eg
          mwana ŋkaʃa aŋxeka
          ŋumbe ʃikaʃa yaŋxeka, etc
As far as the frames are concerned, this alternation of concordial prefixes is entirely without consequence for the tonal analysis.

[5] The terms *contonation* and *contonational* were first used by Professor J. R. Firth in the Staff seminar of the Department of Phonetics and Linguistics at the School during discussions on pitch, tone, and intonation. Professor Firth has sent me the following amplificatory note. 'In pursuance of my theory of levels of analysis first outlined in "The Technique of Semantics", *TPS*, 1935 (see especially *p* 52 for intonation), I suggest that the general word "intonation" be used as at present to refer to the "tunes", "contours", or relative pitch patterns considered as some sort of "music" or speech melody to which pieces or sentences are, so to speak, "sung". D. Jones, Ida Ward and others use such expressions as "falling intonation", "rising intonation", "Tune 1" and "Tune 2". These "tunes" have sometimes been loosely associated with other classifications of the text, such as emphatic and unemphatic, interrogation and affirmation. In accordance with

this view, attempts have been made from time to time to relate "sentence intonation" to syllable tones, word tones, "basic" tones, "inherent" tones, and other types of lexical tone pattern. The terms "contonation" and "contonational" are intended to refer to "intonational" and prosodic patterns abstracted from and correlated closely with formally established grammatical structures, colligations, and collocations.'

[6] Contrast the technique of Robert F. Longacre, who states in 'Five Phonemic Pitch Levels in Trique' (§ 2.1, *p* 67) in *Acta Linguistica*, Vol VII, Fasc 1–2, 1952: 'Tonemic contrasts may be established among the pitches of items of a given substitution list relative to the pitches of the frame syllables, if it can be shown that (*a*) the tones of the frame itself remain unchanged regardless of which item of that substitution list is employed; . . .'

[7] See R. H. Robins, 'Phonology of the Nasalized Verbal Forms in Sundanese', *BSOAS*, xv, *p* 140, footnote 3.

[8] See note 16.

[9] The change from 1st to 2nd person singular in the verb has no tonal significance.

[10] ↑ is used here at the phonetic level to indicate a high voice-register.

[11] See Kenneth L. Pike, *Tone Languages*, University of Michigan Press, 1948, *p* 3.

[12] And less well adapted than is generally supposed for use as an orthography.

[13] See Longacre, *loc cit*, § 3, for the asymmetrical nature of the tonal 'system' of Trique.

[14] See J. R. Firth, 'General Linguistics and Descriptive Grammar', *TPS*, 1951, *p* 85.

[15] No such attempt will be made here, but it may be of interest to note the serious disequilibrium between the tonal possibilities in utterance-final position and those in other positions (see, *eg*, Frame B). Reference to what was said earlier about the cases where the differentiation of patterns depended on a difference in the pitch of a frame-syllable, and also to those cases where the pitch-indication of the first syllable of a noun is constant throughout a frame (*eg* Frames B and F) suggests that this disequilibrium may be resolvable by regarding the tonal features of final syllables as the cumulate exponents of two tonal abstractions. Compare in this connection the phenomena described for Kikuyu by Lyndon Harries ('Some Tonal Principles of the Kikuyu Language', *Word*, Vol VIII, No 2, 1952), who states (§ 3), 'the tone actually heard on a syllable (the speech tone) may be the shifted basic tone of the preceding syllable' – and see note 19.

[16] It may be objected that all that is required to select a tonemic form from which all the others are predictable. It not infrequently happens, however, that no tonemic variant whatever will serve as a basis for prediction.
The retention of Category 6 in our material helps to illustrate this state of affairs: for although the forms of Frame C would serve as bases for prediction for all the contonational categories other than 6 and 9, these latter would still have to be differentiated by other means.

[17] See J. R. Firth, 'Sounds and Prosodies', *TPS*, 1948. [Reprinted in this volume, *pp* 47-65. Eds.]

[18] See Pike, *op cit*, *p* 25.

[19] See note 15. We do not need the device of 'shifted tones' because our contonational formulae need have no more implication of linear extension in time than we care to give them.

[20] For a reference to these, see H. E. Buiskool, *The Tripādī, Being an abridged English recast of Pūrvatrāsiddham (An analytical-synthetical inquiry into the*

system of the last three chapters of Pāṇini's Aṣṭādhyāyī), Leiden, 1939, Chap
1, § 3, A. I am indebted for this reference to my colleague, Dr W. S. Allen.

[21] See note 16 and also the discussion of the difficulties experienced by
lexicographers when marking the stress features of English words in K. L.
Pike, *The Intonation of American English*, Univ. of Michigan Press, 1946, *p*
84. The parallel with English stress patterns is instructive throughout.

[22] There is an obvious parallel here with the variable domain of intonational
sentence-prosodies. For the particular relevance of the point at issue to the
present material, see what was said earlier about the related forms ukwa/
ŋgwa, mbivi/uvivi. In all such cases, the contonational category of either
member of the correlative pair is predictable from that of the other.

[23] *cf* D. M. Beach ('The Science of Tonetics and Bantu Languages', *Bantu
Studies*, Vol II (1923–6), *p* 104, § 48), 'But in view of the great importance of
tone in all languages, the term *tone-language* is peculiarly inappropriate and
should be replaced by some other term . . .' His suggested alternative –
'semantic tone language' – is, however, scarcely less inappropriate.

J. L. M. Trim

Major and minor tone-groups in English

'siŋgl | ən'dʌbl | ˇbaː‚maːks | həv 'lɔŋ bin'juːzd | təˈrepri'zent
ðə'limits | əvˇsens‚gruːps | ənˇbreθ‚gruːps | ri‚spektivli ‖ it‚mei
biˋkwestʃnd | hau‚evə ‖ weðə 'sʌtʃ‚gruːps | hæv 'eni li'dʒitimət
ˎpleis | inəsisti'mætik fə'netik nou‚teiʃn ‖ ðəˇfɔːst ‚kənsept |
iz'pjuəli si‚mæntik | ðə'sekənd | 'pjuəli fiziəˎlədʒikl ‖ ðɛə‚siːmz
'nou 'koudʒnt ‚riːzn | wai ‚sʌtʃ dis'pærət 'gruːps ʃədˈfɔːm
ə‚haiəraːki | nɔːr 'eni təsə'pouz | ðətðɛə'baundəriz ʃədbi'maːkt |
bai'fɔːml liŋ'gwistik ˎfiːtʃəz ‖
inˇfækt | 'ðiːz di‚viʒnz | ə'rɛəli ˎmaːkt tə‚dei ‖ inˇsted |
əpʌŋktju'eiʃn | ə'proupriət tuɔːˋθəgrəfi | izim‚pləid ‖ ‚witʃ ‚mei |
bətənði'ʌðəhænd 'mei ˋnət | ‚hæv prou'sədik impli‚keiʃnz ‖
ðəpə'ziʃn | iz'similə tə'ðæt əvðə‚wəːd ‖ ðədis'kʌvəri bai‚dʒounz |
ðət‚wəːddiviʒn | di'təːmind ðədistri'bjuːʃn əv‚æləfounz ‖ wəz'laːdʒli
'djuː | tuizəbzə'veiʃn əvæmbi'gjuːitiz | in"teksts | witʃ‚ʃoud 'nou
in'təːnl 'baundəriz wiðin‚breθgruːps ‖ ðədis‚kʌvəri ˇled hau‚evə |
tuə'simpl ri'vəːʃn | tu'ɔːθəˋgræfikli di‚təːmind ‚wəːddiviʒn ‖
ik‚septinə 'hændfuləv ˇfleigrənt‚keisiz laik ə‚təːl ‖ 'ðisdi‚siʒn |
ə'laud ðə'prɒbləm witʃədbin‚reizd | təbi'dʒentli 'leid tə‚restəgen ‖
wiər‚ʌndə 'nou əbli'geiʃn təˇdʒʌstifai ðədi‚viʒnz wiːi‚stæbliʃ |
əndəzəri'zʌlt | wiːhəv'skɛəsli prə'grest | "eni ‚fɔːðə | tə‚wəːdz
ðə‚sistimətai'zeiʃn əv‚founou'lədʒikl ˎbaundəriz ‖
ˇsimiləli | ðə'juːs | əv‚ɔːθou'græfik pʌŋktju'eiʃn | ri'liːvzəs
əvðə'niːd tui'stæbliʃ ˇfɔːməli | ðə'haiəraːki əv‚founou'lədʒikl |
'juːnits | inə'givn kən'tinjuəs ‚tekst | in‚diːd | 'evri mi'kænikl
'trænsfəːr | əv'ɔːθou'græfik 'fiːtʃəz | tuəfə'netik ‚tekst | 'indikeits
auə‚feiljə tui‚stæbliʃ 'ædikwət kraiˊtiəriə | prə'siːdʒəz | ən‚simblz |
əvauər‚oun ‖

First published in *Le Maître Phonétique*, 3rd series, No 112:26–29, 1959.

itizˇpɔsibl əvˌkɔːs | tuimˇplɔi pʌŋktjuˌeiʃn maːks | wiðkən'venʃnl
ˌvæljuːz | əzmeniəvauərəˌmerikən ˌkəliːgz ˌduː ‖ ˌðʌs | 'wətə 'lətəv
'nɔiz!' | kədˌmiːn | ðə'laːstˌgruːp | witʃ'endz ˌhiə | hæzə'hai 'fɔːl |
ɔnðə'laːst 'siləbl | wið'ful ˌstres ‖ ðisizəˇfiːzibl səˌluːʃn |
wɛərə'smɔːl 'nʌmbər əv''endˌkəntuəz | 'kərileits ˇhaili |
wiððiəˌkʌrəns əv'sɔːtn ˌpʌŋktju'eiʃnz inˌɔːθou'græfik ˌteksts ‖
itˌsiːmz 'dʒenərəli ˇprefərəbl hauˌevə | tə'sepəreit ðəˌfʌŋkʃnz |
əv kærəktəraiˌzeiʃn | ənddilimiˌteiʃn ‖ 'giviŋ infə'meiʃn | ət
ðə'pɔint wɛər 'ækʃn izri'kwaːəd | 'raːðəðən'wɛər itizˌnou ˌləŋgə
riˌkwaiəd ‖ 'ðisizˌdʌn | inðəˌsistəməv tou'netik ˇstres maːks |
diˌveləpt bai ˇpaːmər ən''kiŋdən | witʃizˌnau in'dʒenərəl 'juːs
bai'iŋgliʃ founiˌtiʃnz ‖ 'ðis ˌsistəm | səb'sjuːmz ən sjuːpəˌsiːdz |
ðə'fɔːmə ˌstresˌmaːkiŋ əvtrænˌskripʃnz | fəˌwitʃ itiz'difiklt təfɔː'siː
''eni'fjuːtʃə ˌjuːs ‖ ðɛərindiˇtəːminəsi | ənd 'hevi ri'laiəns
ɔnpʌŋktjuˌeiʃn | ə'laːdʒli ouvəˌkʌm ‖
    'nʌθiŋ ˌfɔːðə | ʃədˌnau biˌhaːd ˇaiðər | əvðəˌsensˌgruːp ‖
itiz'simpli əmisˌnoumə | fərənin'tjuitivli pə'siːvd 'toun kʌm
ˌriðmˌgruːp ‖ ðə'siŋgl ˇbaːˌmaːk | iznau in'waidˌjuːs | tu
i'stæbliʃ ðə'baundəri | bitwiːn 'tuː əd'dʒeisnt ˌtoungruːps
wiððiə'proupriət 'fɔːml kærəktəˌristiks ‖ ðou ˇsevərəlˌraitəz |
mi'steikənli inˌmaivjuː | imˌplɔiit 'ounli inði'æbsəns
əvəpʌŋktjuˌeiʃn ‖ ðəˇdʌblˌbaː | ˌsiːmz tuəvˌfɔːlən 'laːdʒli
intədisˌjuːs ‖ 'iːtʃ sək'sesiv ˌtoungruːp | izˌtriːtid əzən'indi'pendənt
ˌentiti ‖ 'ifitkədbiˌʃoun | ðət'sʌm ˇsiːkwənsiz əvˌtoungruːps |
ˌkənstitjuːtid ˇmeidʒə ˌjuːnits | intəˌwitʃ ðəkən'stitjuənt
'toungruːps wər'intigreitid | bai 'sʌm 'fɔːml di'vais ɔːdiˌvaisiz |
ðə'dʌbl'baː | wudə'gen biˌjuːsfl ‖ ˇbreθˌgruːp | wudˌpruːv
ə''nʌðə misˌnoumə | fərə'vælid | in'tjuitivli pə'siːvd prə'sədik ˌjuːnit ‖
ðə'siŋglˌbaː | wud'ðen 'maːk | ði'end əvə'toungruːp | 'fɔːməli
'kærəktəraizd əzdiˌpendənt | 'nən ˌfainl | əˌmainə ˌtoungruːp ‖
ˌwailst ðə'dʌblˌbaː | wudˌsignl ðə'kænsə'leiʃn əv'ɔːlinˌstrʌkʃnz |
ətə'baundəri | biˌtwiːn sək'sesiv ˌʌnriˌleitid | 'indiˌpendənt
ˌtoungruːps | ˌmeidʒə ˌtoungruːps ‖
    ðɛəriz'plenti əvˌevidəns | ðətðisizin'fækt ðəˌkeis ‖ inhɔː'riːsnt
ˌbuk | ˌmis'ʃuːbigə | həz ʃoun ðətin'kəmpleks 'sentənsiz |
'toungruːp 'siːkwənsiz | ə'nət ˌfriː | ðeiə 'strəŋli kə'nektid | wið
grə'mætikl ˌsentənsˌstrʌktʃə | ən''sɔːtn ˌtoungruːps | əˌpiə
təbi'njuːkliə ‖ 'ðætiztəˌsei | 'ðɛə ˌnjuːkliəs | ˌkærəktəraiziz 'nət
sou'mʌtʃ ðə'gruːp in'witʃitəˌkəːz | əzðə'siːkwəns əzə'houl ‖
wɛəˌræz ðə'njuːkliai əv''ʌðəˌgruːps | 'miəli 'kærəktəraiz
ðɛə'rileiʃn | tu'ʌðə'gruːps inðəˌsiːkwəns ‖
    'wʌn kən'səlideitiŋ 'fiːtʃərəv 'meidʒə ˌtoungruːps | iztəbiˌfaund
inðəˌwei ðətðə'hedz | əvsək'sesiv 'mainə ˌtoungruːps | 'stepˌdaun |
laik 'prəminənt 'siləblz inðə'bədi əvəˌsiŋgl ˌtoungruːp ‖ ðɛəmei

'siməli bi'breiks | ɔːr'ʌpwəd di‚flekʃnz | tuə‚pitʃ 'haiə | ðənðə'hed
əvðə‚priːviəs ᵛmainə ‚toungruːp | bət'louə | ðənðə‚hedəvðə‚fɔːst ‖
'ðiːz kənbi'ʃoun bai‚pleisiŋ ə‚breik sain | bifɔː ðə'hed
əvðə‚mainə 'toungruːp kən‚səːnd ‖
   əᵛfəːðə 'fiːtʃə | witʃ mei kən‚səlideit ə‚siːkwəns əv‚mainə
‚toungruːps | izðə'fjuːʒn | əvðə'teil əvðə‚fəːst | wiððə'priːhed
əvðə‚sekənd ‖ ðisiz'veri ‚kəmən | wen ə'hai‚fɔːl | izpri‚siːdid
baiə'lou ‚raiz | ɔːrə‚fɔːl‚raiz ‖ ðə'hait | tə‚witʃ ðə'teil əvðə'fəːst
gruːp ə‚sendz | ən‚frəmwitʃ | ðə'priːhed əvðə'sekənd ‚raiziz | aː
'nət indiᵛpendəntli di‚təːmind | bətəd'dʒʌstid ‚souəztə'fɔːm |
ə'smuːð kən'tinjuəs ‚siːkwəns ‖ ‚ðʌs in | if'dʒən əd‚sentittuər
iːdəv'siːn ʃiː‚gətit ‖ ðɛərizə 'regjuːlər ə'sent frəm ‚sent tə 'siːn |
wið 'nou 'tʃeindʒ əv'greidiənt ətðə'gruːp ‚baundəri ‖ ‚iːvn if
ðə‚fəːst gruːp hæz 'nou ‚teil | ðəᵛnjuːkliəs | 'mei teikðə'fɔːm
'faund bi‚fɔːrə‚teil ‖ ‚ðʌs ‚ifwiripleis ‚sentittuə | bai ‚gən | ‚gən
wilbi‚sed ənə'lou ‚levl‚pitʃ | wiðə'raiz ən‚iːdəv | ‚kʌvəriŋ ðə'seim
'reindʒ əz 'ittuər iːdəv inðə‚fəːst ig‚zaːmpl ‖ ðəᵛlaiklihud əv‚sʌtʃ
‚fjuːʒnz | izᵛgreitist | ‚æz wʌn wud ikᵛspekt | in'ræpid fə‚miliə
‚stail | əndin'set kəmbi‚neiʃnz | laik‚ðæt əv 'fɔːl'raiz ənd 'fɔːl
in'dʌbl ‚kəntraːsts ‖ ‚iː‚dʒiː | ᵛaid | veri mʌtʃ 'laiktuː | bət'fuːðə |
wount 'hiərəvit ‖
   itizᵛpəsibl | əndaiwudsə‚dʒest inmeni‚weiz ᵛprefərəbl | tə'triːt
'keisizəv 'priː'njuːkliə ‚glaidz | di'vaidid 'fɔːl‚raiz ət‚setrə |
əz'meidʒə ‚toungruːps | kəm‚pouzd əvə'nʌmber əvᵛmainə
‚toungruːps | 'iːtʃ kən'teiniŋ | ətᵛmoust | 'wʌn ki'netik ‚toun ‖
   ðɛər ə'piə təbi'səːtn 'kaindz əv‚gruːp | witʃ kənə‚kəːr 'ounli in
kəmbi‚neiʃn | ‚ai ‚iː 'ɔːlweiz əz‚mainə‚gruːps | 'wʌn 'taip witʃ dəz
ᵛnətə‚kəː ‚fainəli | ‚hæz ə'nən'lou 'levl ‚njuːkliəs ‖ 'tuː 'tuːz
ə-fɔːr | ən'siks iz‚ten ‖ ðisiz'kliəli dis'tiŋgwiʃt | frəm 'tuː 'tuːz
ə'fɔːr ən ⁿ⁽ᵗ⁾'siks iz‚ten | baiðə'lou 'pitʃ əv ‚ən | witʃ i'stæbliʃizit
əzə‚priːhed | itᵛmei‚biː | ðət‚meni ə‚ledʒd ‚breiks | ərəv‚ðis‚səːt |
məː'rouvə | 'wʌns 'ðis 'taipəv'gruːp iziᵛstæbliʃt | 'ɔːl ‚breiks
wi‚ðin ‚toungruːps | kən bi‚triːtid əzðə'hedz əv'njuː 'mainə‚gruːps
'wið ɔːwi'ðaut 'priːhed ‚fjuːʒn | əndðə'niːd | fəðɛə 'sepərət
‚reprizen'teiʃn 'disə‚piəz ‖
   itiz'nət 'iːzi tə‚pleis ðis‚taip əv‚nən‚fainl‚gruːp | 'hæzit
ə‚njuːkliəs ‖ 'if‚sou | 'izit ə'njuːkliəs inits'oun‚rait |
ɔːr‚izitən'æloutoun | əkən'tekstjuəl | ɔːpə‚hæps stai'listik ‚vɛəriənt |
əv 'sʌm 'njuːkliəs | ðə'lou ɔː'haiᵛraiz | fərig‚zaːmpl | ɔːl'redi
'faund els‚wɛə ‖ in'aiðə ‚keis | ðə'juːʒuəl defi'niʃn əvðə'njuːkliəs
inkaiᵛnetik 'təːmz | wud 'hæftəbi ə‚bændənd | 'ðis'step iz‚djuː |
ðədefi‚niʃn 'dʌznt 'wəːk | ‚veri‚wel | ik‚sept fə‚fainl ‚siləblz ‖
əndiz‚sʌbdʒikt təðə‚məːfʌndəᵛmentl əb‚dʒekʃn | ðət'it'tuː |
iz'nənliŋ‚gwistik in‚kærəktə ‖ ai'hæv in'fækt di'saidid | tə'triːt

ðiːz'gruːps əz'eiˌnjuːkliə ‖ kənˌteiniŋ ˌsimpli 'wʌnɔːmɔː
'prɔminənt ˌsiləblz ‖ ðənou'teiʃn iztəˌhænd | əndðəˈkwestʃn əv
tou'niːmik aidentifi'keiʃn | mei bi pəsˈpound fərəˋdʒenərəl
kənsidəˌreiʃn ‖ ən'ei'njuːkliə 'gruːp ˌsiːmz əˌnɔmələs ‖ bət
inˇfækt | ðɛəriz 'mʌtʃ təbi'sed | fəˌtriːtiŋ 'sɔːtn eŋ'klitik
ˌriðmˌgruːps | ˌɔːlsou | inˌðisˌwei ‖ ai 'wʌndə huː ˌðisizˌfrəm |
sedˌmisiz ˌbrændən | ˌteikiŋ əˌletər ətˌrændəm | ˌautəvðəˌpail ðət
ˌlei baihɔːˌpleit | əndˌhouldiŋit ətˌɑːmzˌleŋθ | ˌʌpsaidˌdaun ‖ 'ðis
'sentəns | ˌʃouz 'riðmikˌfiːtʃəz | vɛəriˌeiʃn inðəˌreit əvrepiˌtiʃn
əvˌstrest ˌsiləblz | ˌænəˌkruːsis ː ˌsiləblˌleŋθ | ətˌsetrə | witʃ ə'best
'ʃoun baidi'viʒnz əv'ðisˌsɔːt ‖ ˌin | 'wɔt əvjuːbimˌduːiŋ ɔːlðəˌsʌmə
ˌgreis ɑːskt ˌhjuː ‖ ðə 'sʌbdʒikt əvˌɑːskt | iz ai'dentifaid |
baiə'riðmˌgruːp 'baundəri | bi'fɔːr ɔːr'ɑːftəˌgreis ‖ it 'mei bi
əbˌdʒektid | ðət'riðmˌgruːps ə'nɔttəbi ai'dentifaid wiðˌtounˌgruːps |
ɔnðiˇʌðəˌhænd it 'hæz 'sou 'fɑː 'pruːvd ˇpɔsibl | ənd'juːsfl |
təˌrepriˌzent 'bouθ 'klousli ri'leitidˌsistəmz | baiə'siŋgl
nouˌteiʃn ‖ 'wʌns ðə'juːs əvə'mɑːk | fə 'strest 'nɔn'prɔminənt
ˋsiləblz | izədˌmitid | ðɛəriz ˌʃuəli 'nou 'riːzn | wai 'ei'tounl
'riðmˌgruːps ʃud'nɔt bi'mɑːkt əz 'mainə ˌtounˌgruːps ‖
    in'ʃɔːt | ðɛə ˌsiːmz 'æmpl dʒʌstifi'keiʃn | fə riˋteiniŋ | ðəˌdʌblˌbɑː
tərepriˌzent 'nɔt əriˇspirətri ˌjuːnit | bətə'juːnit inðiintəˇneiʃənl
ˌsistəm | kəmˌpouzd əvən'intigreitid 'siːkwəns | əv'liŋkt
ˌtoungruːps ‖ 'givn | dis'kriːt ˌletəz | ˇwəːdspeis | ˊsiŋglbɑːr |
ən'dʌblbɑː | tə di'limit 'juːnits əv'iŋkriːsiŋ ˌmægnitjuːd ‖ wið
'letəˌʃeips | ən tou'netik 'stresmɑːks əzˌkæriktəraizəz | wiː
ʃədəˋbændən | 'ɔːθəˇgræfik ˌwəːd speis | əndpʌŋktjuˌeiʃn ‖
implɔiiŋ 'ounli auər'oun riˌzɔːsiz ‖ ai həvə'temptid
tətræn'skraib ðis'ɑːtikl əˌkɔːdiŋli | inðə'houp ðətitsin'ædikwəsiz |
wilˌliːd tu ə ri'fainmənt əvðə'kənvenʃnz riˌkwaiəd ‖

Elizabeth Uldall

Attitudinal meanings conveyed by intonation contours

This paper[1] describes experiments in which Osgood's *semantic differential* was used to measure the attitude of listeners to a variety of intonation patterns. Sixteen pitch contours were applied by synthesis to recordings of four sentences and listeners were asked to rate the patterns with respect to ten scales of the type BORED/INTERESTED, POLITE/ RUDE. From the results it was possible to draw some conclusions about some general features of the intonation patterns which had particular weight with respect to three factors: pleasant/unpleasant, interest/lack of interest and authoritative/submissive.

It is clear that some kind of meaning is conveyed by the intonation of connected speech in both tone-languages (Chang, 1958) and non-tone-languages. There is little agreement about the terms in which this meaning is to be described; every writer on the subject employs an open-ended supply of terms for this purpose. One kind of meaning conveyed is, however, clearly social and emotional rather than referential. Intonation can express social attitudes: speaker to listener – 'It wasn't what she said, it was the way she said it!'; to subject matter – 'Well, don't get in a temper with me; *I'm* not the Income Tax collector'; to the world in general – 'He sounds so arrogant', 'Don't whine!' (Allport and Cantril, 1934).

Attitude measurement (Thurston and Chave, 1929; Krech and Crutchfield, 1948) seemed a promising technique by which to attempt to find out whether a group of subjects from the same linguistic community would in fact agree on the 'meanings' of intonations, and whether some few very general 'dimensions of meaning' in the emotional area could be extracted. Osgood's *semantic differential* (Osgood *et al*, 1957) was the attitude-measuring technique used in the experiment which will be described here.

First published in *Language and Speech*, Vol III, Pt 4: 223–234, 1960.

The part or aspect of meaning with which the semantic differential can and does deal is precisely the emotional one.

Stated briefly, the experiment to be described here consisted in presenting the same sentence, with differing intonation contours imposed upon it synthetically, to a set of subjects, who rated each sentence-plus-intonation as to whether it conveyed the impression that the speaker was bored or interested, rude or polite, agreeable or disagreeable, and so on down a list of ten paired opposites, the 'scales'.

Synthesized speech was essential in order to be quite sure that all features except the intonation remained the same while the intonation varied. A human speaker making such an array of intonations on the same sentence would at the same time make changes in length, stress and tempo. Since these features appear to convey the same kind of emotional information as intonation (Chang, 1958; Fairbanks and Hoaglin, 1941; Fairbanks and Pronovost, 1939), it was essential to exclude variations in them.

Four sentences were used, to each of which the various contours were applied in turn. The sentences were:

A: He expects to be here on Friday. (statement)
B: Did all of them come in the morning? (yes-or-no question)
C: What time did they leave for Boston? (question-word question)
D: Turn right at the next corner. (command)

The sentences were intended to be as colourless as possible so as to allow the intonation to add as much as possible to their meaning, and so that they would fit into as many situations as possible when combined with different intonations. In the conduct of the experiment no attempt was made to provide a context of situation for any of the sentences; possibly it would be better to provide a context or set of contexts, but sound film would be necessary to ensure that all subjects were offered the same context as nearly as possible.

Objection was made by some subjects at the end of the experiment that the command was in fact one which was limited to a smaller range of social situations than the other sentences were. This may be the case with commands in general.

Sentences were chosen consisting of alternations of strong and weak syllables, in order that contours whose effects depend on different treatments of strong and weak could be applied to them. Each contained at least three strong syllables and ended in a strong-weak combination – 'Friday', 'morning', 'Boston', 'corner'.

These sentences were recorded as spoken by Dr Alvin Liberman of the Haskins Laboratories. All were spoken on a steadily falling intonation of rather narrow range.

Sixteen intonation contours were synthesized and applied in turn to the four sentences by means of the Intonator, a component of the Voback synthesizer at the Haskins Laboratories (Borst and Cooper, 1957); this removed the original intonation and allowed another to be combined with the spoken material by painting patterns on a pitch-control tape. The pitch range chosen was 75 cps to 250 cps. 250 cps is perhaps rather a high limit for a man's voice, but a wide range was desired partly for the purpose of making some 'extreme' contours and partly to make it possible to synthesize contours of the same 'shape' but placed in distinctively different parts of the range.

All but four of the contours (see *Fig* 1) were perfectly 'smooth', that is, the changes in pitch took place at a regular rate in time whatever the sounds, voiced or voiceless, of which the sentence consisted. It was thought that this treatment would make the various sentences on the same contour more readily comparable. These 'smooth' contours in fact sound fairly natural. The remaining four contours, shown in a dot-and-dash notation in *Fig* 1, nos 13–16, are contours with 'perturbed' weak syllables. These syllables are either, as in contours 15 and 16, on a *higher* pitch than the course of the nearby strong syllables, or, as in contours 13 and 14, on a *lower* pitch. The number of weak syllables between the strong ones is not exactly the same in all the sentences; the notations in the figure are symbolic of the treatment of weak syllables, not exact maps of any sentence.

The following kinds of difference were incorporated in the contours:

1. Range used: compare contours 1, 2 and 3; 4, 5, and 6; 7 and 8; 9 and 10; 11 and 12.
2. Direction at end: compare contours 13 and 14; 15 and 16.
3. Shape: unidirectional or with a change of direction. Compare contours 5 and 10; 2 and 8.
4. Treatment of weak syllables:
   (*a*) Continuing the line of strong syllables; all contours except 13, 14, 15 and 16.
   (*b*) Dropping below the line of strong syllables; 13 and 14.
   (*c*) Rising above the line of strong syllables; 15 and 16.

In all the 'smooth' contours in which a change of direction took place, the 'turn' was always on the same syllable, the last strong one, so as to reduce the effects of 'stress' being differently placed in the different contours. In the contours with 'perturbed' weak syllables there was some difference of opinion among listeners as to where the main 'stress' fell, though they were intended to give the impression of the main 'stress' on the last strong syllable, as in the other patterns.

The 'scales' on which the contours were rated consisted of pairs of opposed adjectives. These were chosen after inspecting the results from a pilot experiment using intonations synthesized on the speech synthesizer PAT in the Phonetics Department of the University of Edinburgh

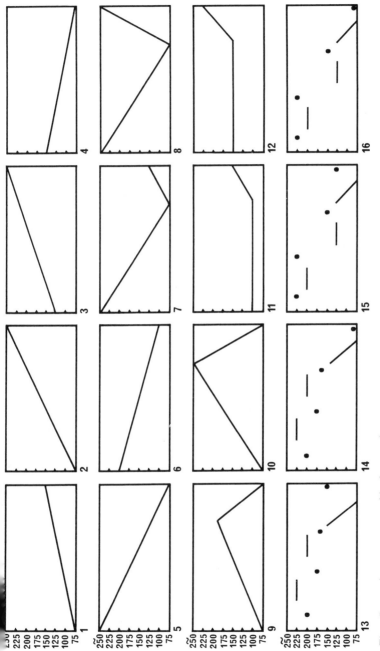

Fig 1 : Intonation contours used in the experiment

(Strevens, 1959). The page to be marked by the subjects for each contour
on each sentence was as follows:

BORED – – – – – – – INTERESTED
POLITE – – – – – – – RUDE
TIMID – – – – – – – CONFIDENT
SINCERE – – – – – – – INSINCERE
TENSE – – – – – – – RELAXED
DISAPPROVING – – – – – – – APPROVING
DEFERENTIAL – – – – – – – ARROGANT
IMPATIENT – – – – – – – PATIENT
EMPHATIC – – – – – – – UNEMPHATIC
AGREEABLE – – – – – – – DISAGREEABLE

The terms were arranged with seven places between them; the subjects
were instructed that the places next to the terms should be checked to indicate 'extremely' (bored or interested, etc), the two places a little farther
in from the terms to indicate 'quite' (bored or interested, etc), the two
places flanking the middle to indicate 'slightly' (bored or interested, etc),
and the middle space to indicate 'neutral' or 'neither' in relation to the
scale under consideration.

The assumption made in choosing the 'scales', the pairs of adjectives,
was that there are three main kinds of attitude conveyed in intonation:
(1) amount or strength of feeling or interest, 'emphasis', (2) pleasantness
or unpleasantness of personal relations, (3) a 'power' relationship between speaker and listener, authority versus submission.

The twelve subjects in the experiment were seven men and five women,
two thirds of them eastern Americans, the rest Americans rather mixed as
to education and residence; they were mostly in their late twenties or
thirties. Twelve is rather a small number of subjects for an experiment of
this sort, but the subjects gave a satisfactory spread of ratings over most
of the scales. This and the high correlations between some of the scales
makes it likely that the results have some validity.

The conduct of the experiment was as follows: the subjects first under-
went a training period in which they heard one of the sentences (the statement) on all its contours without being asked to write anything. It was
thought desirable that they should hear the whole range of variation before being asked to rate any one contour on the scales. For the test itself,
which was taken in four parts on four different days, one for each sentence,
each intonation contour, on a loop of tape, was played repeatedly while
the subjects rated it on a mark sheet as shown above. Ten to fifteen repeti-
tions were generally required before all subjects had given the contour a
rating on all of the ten scales. On a signal that all subjects had completed
the page referring to that contour, the next contour was played and rated
on another page, and so on. The arrangement of the contours was random;

half the subjects were given the test in the original randomized order, the other half in the reverse order.

The seven spaces for scoring, *eg* from 'extremely bored' through 'quite bored', 'slightly bored', 'neutral', 'slightly interested', 'quite interested', to 'extremely interested', were given values, 1 to 7. The scores given by the subjects to the various contours on the various scales were averaged; each contour thus received an average score on each scale. In discussing the results of the experiment any numbers given will be scores of this kind. Thus a score of 2·8 for one contour on the 'bored/interested' scale indicates that the average of the scores places it between 'quite bored' and 'slightly bored', a little closer to the latter.

Quite a wide scatter of scores over the scales was obtained for the various contours. The subjects obviously found some of the scales easier to use than others in relation to intonation contours. *Table* 1 shows the range of

Table 1(*a*)

A: He expects to be here on Friday.

	1	2	3	4	5	6	7
BORED/INTERESTED	1·5————————————5·5
TENSE/RELAXED	3·0————————5·8
AGREEABLE/DISAGREEABLE	2·9————————5·7
POLITE/RUDE	2·7————————5·4
SINCERE/INSINCERE	2·0————4·5
DISAPPROVING/APPROVING	2·7————5·0
EMPHATIC/UNEMPHATIC	2·5————4·8
TIMID/CONFIDENT	3·7————5·6
DEFERENTIAL/ARROGANT	3·5—4·8
IMPATIENT/PATIENT	3·3—4·4

B: Did all of them come in the morning?

	1	2	3	4	5	6	7
BORED/INTERESTED	1·2————————————5·5
POLITE/RUDE	2·4————————5·5
AGREEABLE/DISAGREEABLE	2·5————————5·6
DISAPPROVING/APPROVING	2·3————————5·1
TENSE/RELAXED	3·5————————6·1
SINCERE/INSINCERE	2·5————5·0
EMPHATIC/UNEMPHATIC	2·8————4·9
TIMID/CONFIDENT	3·5—5·2
DEFERENTIAL/ARROGANT	3·1—4·7
IMPATIENT/PATIENT	3·2—4·7

Range of the means of 16 contours on the 10 scales. For each sentence, the scales are ordered with respect to the amount of the scale covered by the mean scores.

Table 1(*b*)

c: What time did they leave for Boston?

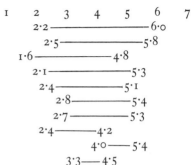

	1	2	3	4	5	6	7
BORED/INTERESTED		2·2 ————————— 6·0					
DISAPPROVING/APPROVING		2·5 ———————— 5·8					
POLITE/RUDE	1·6 ———————— 4·8						
AGREEABLE/DISAGREEABLE		2·1 ——————————— 5·3					
SINCERE/INSINCERE		2·4 —————————— 5·1					
TENSE/RELAXED			2·8 —————— 5·4				
IMPATIENT/PATIENT			2·7 ——————— 5·3				
EMPHATIC/UNEMPHATIC			2·4 —— 4·2				
TIMID/CONFIDENT					4·0 —— 5·4		
DEFERENTIAL/ARROGANT			3·3 — 4·5				

d: Turn right at the next corner.

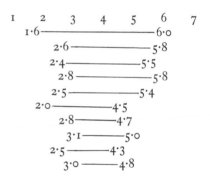

	1	2	3	4	5	6	7
BORED/INTERESTED	1·6 ———————— 6·0						
TENSE/RELAXED		2·6 ——————— 5·8					
POLITE/RUDE		2·4 —————— 5·5					
TIMID/CONFIDENT			2·8 —————— 5·8				
AGREEABLE/DISAGREEABLE		2·5 —————— 5·4					
SINCERE/INSINCERE	2·0 ————— 4·5						
DISAPPROVING/APPROVING			2·8 ——— 4·7				
IMPATIENT/PATIENT			3·1 —— 5·0				
EMPHATIC/UNEMPHATIC		2·5 —— 4·3					
DEFERENTIAL/ARROGANT			3·0 —— 4·8				

Range of the means for 16 contours on the 10 scales. For each sentence, the scales are ordered with respect to the amount of the scale covered by the mean scores.

mean scores for different contours over the various scales. 'Bored/ interested' in the case of all four sentences was the scale on which the contours varied the most. 'Deferential/arrogant', on the other hand, was clearly a less convincing concept in this connection.

The contours were then arranged in the order of their mean scores on each scale, *eg*, from the 'most bored' to the 'most interested'. Spearman rank-correlations between these orders were calculated, with corrections for tied ranks. *Table* 2 shows the correlations between the various word scales for each sentence. *Table* 3 shows the correlations between the various sentences.

From *Table* 2 it will be seen that scales 1, 3, 6 and 8 produced predominantly negative correlations. These scales were therefore reflected, *ie*, the positions of the defining scale terms were treated as reversed. As a result, *ie*, the terms 'interested' 'confident', 'approving' and 'patient' are aligned with the first term in each of the other pairs, and are associated with them in respect of the factor loadings mentioned below.

On the basis of these correlations a factor analysis was made with the object of extracting what may be described as the dimensions of emotional meaning contained in the scales used. The hypothesis in choosing the scales was that an 'emphasis' or 'interest' dimension would be the first and largest factor to emerge; however, as in Osgood's experiments, the 'evaluative' or 'pleasant/unpleasant' factor is by far the strongest, accounting for more than 50 per cent of the variance, followed by a much less prominent 'interest' or 'emphasis' factor, about 20 per cent, and 'authority/submission' 8–13 per cent. It seems reasonable to equate Factor II in this material with Osgood's second factor which he calls 'activity', and Factor III with his third factor which he calls 'potency'.

Table 4 shows the results of inspecting the contours, arranged under each word-scale according to mean score, and picking out the tonal-factors common to the most strongly rated contours at each end of the scales, in order to relate them to the meaning-factors extracted by the factor analysis.

Table 2(a)

A: He expects to be here on Friday.

	BOR-INT	POL-RUD	TIM-CON	SIN-INS	TEN-REL	DIS-APP	DEF-ARR	IMP-PAT	EMPH-UN	AGR-DIS
BOR-INT		−0·52	0·09	−0·17	−0·68	0·42	−0·36	−0·12	0·37	−0·33
POL-RUD	−0·52		−0·57	0·91	0·18	−0·88	0·40	−0·40	0·72	0·83
TIM-CON	0·09	−0·57		−0·71	0·20	0·69	0·16	0·37	−0·53	−0·62
SIN-INS	−0·17	0·91	−0·71		0·19	−0·86	0·25	−0·34	0·80	0·87
TEN-REL	−0·68	0·18	0·20	0·19		0·06	0·17	0·20	0·16	−0·03
DIS-APP	0·42	−0·88	0·69	−0·86	0·06		−0·30	0·48	−0·68	−0·83
DEF-ARR	−0·36	0·40	0·16	0·25	0·17	−0·30		−0·12	0·01	0·34
IMP-PAT	−0·12	−0·40	0·37	−0·34	0·20	0·48	−0·12		−0·05	−0·30
EMPH-UN	−0·37	0·72	−0·53	0·80	0·16	−0·68	0·01	−0·05		0·59
AGR-DIS	−0·33	0·83	−0·62	0·87	−0·03	−0·83	0·34	−0·30	0·59	

B: Did all of them come in the morning?

	BOR-INT	POL-RUD	TIM-CON	SIN-INS	TEN-REL	DIS-APP	DEF-ARR	IMP-PAT	EMPH-UN	AGR-DIS
BOR-INT		−0·63	0·23	−0·56	−0·65	0·83	−0·53	0·46	−0·55	−0·71
POL-RUD	−0·63		−0·23	0·72	0·59	−0·68	0·25	−0·59	0·53	0·77
TIM-CON	0·23	−0·23		−0·37	0·27	0·45	0·17	0·30	−0·65	−0·58
SIN-INS	−0·56	0·72	−0·37		0·36	−0·63	0·17	−0·49	0·66	0·72
TEN-REL	−0·65	0·59	0·27	0·36		−0·39	0·37	−0·05	0·31	0·37
DIS-APP	0·83	−0·68	0·45	−0·63	−0·39		−0·50	0·70	−0·50	−0·87
DEF-ARR	−0·53	0·25	0·17	0·17	0·37	−0·50		−0·41	0·03	0·33
IMP-PAT	0·46	−0·59	0·30	−0·49	−0·05	0·70	−0·41		−0·10	−0·56
EMPH-UN	−0·55	0·53	−0·65	0·66	0·31	−0·50	0·03	−0·10		0·76
AGR-DIS	−0·71	0·77	−0·58	0·72	0·37	−0·87	0·33	−0·56	0·76	

Spearman rank-correlation coefficients between the various scales for each sentence.

Table 2(b)

C: What time did they leave for Boston?

	BOR-INT	POL-RUD	TIM-CON	SIN-INS	TEN-REL	DIS-APP	DEF-ARR	IMP-PAT	EMPH-UN	AGR-DIS
BOR-INT		−0·55	0·49	−0·81	−0·60	0·64	−0·61	0·38	−0·83	−0·69
POL-RUD	−0·55		−0·07	0·65	0·10	−0·78	0·85	−0·77	0·56	0·87
TIM-CON	0·49	−0·07		−0·37	−0·06	0·30	0·03	0·09	−0·45	−0·24
SIN-INS	−0·81	0·65	−0·37		0·56	−0·65	0·53	−0·47	0·84	0·73
TEN-REL	−0·60	0·10	−0·06	0·56		−0·12	0·11	0·07	0·59	0·23
DIS-APP	0·64	−0·78	0·30	−0·65	−0·12		−0·58	0·68	−0·68	−0·89
DEF-ARR	−0·61	0·85	0·03	0·53	0·11	−0·58		−0·67	0·37	0·69
IMP-PAT	0·38	−0·77	0·09	−0·47	0·07	0·68	−0·67		−0·19	−0·67
EMPH-UN	−0·83	0·56	−0·45	0·84	0·59	−0·68	0·37	−0·19		0·74
AGR-DIS	−0·69	0·87	−0·24	0·73	0·23	−0·89	0·69	−0·67	0·74	

D: Turn right at the next corner.

	BOR-INT	POL-RUD	TIM-CON	SIN-INS	TEN-REL	DIS-APP	DEF-ARR	IMP-PAT	EMPH-UN	AGR-DIS
BOR-INT		−0·83	0·15	−0·54	−0·73	0·44	−0·55	0·23	−0·73	−0·65
POL-RUD	0·83		−0·33	0·84	0·50	−0·73	0·64	−0·51	0·73	0·49
TIM-CON	0·15	−0·33		−0·41	0·37	0·51	0·24	0·19	−0·43	−0·38
SIN-INS	−0·54	0·84	−0·41		0·22	−0·94	0·55	−0·76	0·61	0·80
TEN-REL	−0·73	0·50	0·37	0·22		−0·10	0·68	−0·05	0·42	0·35
DIS-APP	0·44	−0·73	0·51	−0·94	−0·10		−0·51	0·78	−0·52	−0·72
DEF-ARR	−0·55	0·64	0·24	0·55	0·68	−0·51		−0·52	0·36	0·52
IMP-PAT	0·23	−0·51	0·19	−0·76	−0·05	0·78	−0·52		−0·20	−0·52
EMPH-UN	−0·73	0·73	−0·43	0·61	0·42	−0·52	0·36	−0·20		0·59
AGR-DIS	−0·65	0·89	−0·38	0·80	0·35	−0·72	0·52	−0·52	0·59	

Spearman rank-correlation coefficients between the various scales for each sentence.

I have attempted to get at a possible 'conventional neutral' associated with each of the sentence-types by looking for those contours which in each case scored the smallest total difference from the 'neutral' score of 4 on all the scales. This procedure does not point out any particular type of contour for each sentence as conveying 'least feeling', but suggests only that, on the whole, contours of small range or small change of direction at the end are rated less strongly than those with more 'lively' tonal behaviour.

It is possible that with a larger number of subjects and a treatment of the *modal* score rather than the *mean*, something more like a 'conventional neutral' contour for each sentence might emerge.

A study of the results for each of the 16 contours when the scales are grouped in the three categories, pleasant/unpleasant, interest/lack of interest, authoritative/submissive, shows that certain contours carry particular weight with respect to these factors. No 6, the narrow-range fall from 200 cps to 100 cps, was, for instance, the most disliked, and is frequently found rated most strongly unpleasant, on all four sentences. The low narrow-range fall, no 4, 150 cps to 75 cps, is often found with it.

Narrow range is generally disliked, and 'smooth' contours proceeding steadily in one direction (particularly downward) are found less pleasant than 'broken' contours with a change of direction or movement up and down of strong and weak syllables. Weak syllables rising above the surrounding strong ones are on the whole 'unpleasant' when followed by a final fall.

It is clear that the various kinds of tonal difference which were incorporated in the sixteen contours convey different meanings on the different sentence types. I had supposed that the emotional effect of a given contour would be more nearly the same on the different sentences than was in fact the case.

In the case of 'pleasant' vs 'unpleasant', the value of final rise or fall is different on the statement from what it is on the other sentence types: statements can be 'pleasant' while either falling or rising at the end, while on the questions and the command contours with final rises tend to be the 'pleasant' ones.

When we look at the factor of 'interest' vs 'lack of interest', it is the yes-or-no question which is indifferent as to whether the contour is rising or falling finally.

Table 3

		BOR-INT	POL-RUD	TIM-CON	SIN-INS	TEN-REL	DIS APP	DEF-ARR	IMP-PAT	EMPH-UN	AGR-DIS
SENTENCES	A-B	0·76	0·38	0·17	0·18	0·51	0·15	0·36	−0·18	0·24	0·35
	A-C	0·86	0·45	0·39	0·56	0·78	0·73	0·51	−0·11	0·58	0·56
	A-D	0·87	0·26	0·69	0·22	0·89	0·40	0·36	0·09	0·33	0·09
	B-C	0·68	0·52	0·31	0·49	0·69	0·52	0·14	0·34	0·40	0·58
	B-D	0·75	0·81	0·56	0·56	0·66	0·56	0·44	0·51	0·66	0·74
	C-D	0·78	0·40	0·46	0·34	0·81	0·60	0·21	0·45	0·47	0·41

Spearman rank-correlation coefficients between sentences for each scale.

The third factor is perhaps too small to discuss profitably, but again a final fall or rise does not seem important in distinguishing the 'authoritative' and 'submissive' contours; range takes first place, as it does in the 'interest' factor in yes-or-no questions.

The behaviour of unstressed syllables appears to have different values on different sentence types. Rising unstressed syllables are unpleasant on the statement and the question-word question, but acceptable on the yes-or-no question if the contour ends in a rise.

These differences must be related to conventional 'neutral' or 'carrier' tunes for the sentence types in a given speech community.

Further work with larger groups of subjects and other sentences will be necessary to determine whether the differing values of the contours on different sentence types are consistently true of them as types.

It will also be interesting to try similar experiments on groups of

Table 4

	A: statement contours	B: yes-or-no question contours	C: question-word question contours	D: command contours
I **PLEASANT**	10, 4 tendency to wide range; 13, 9 change of direction; 14, 8 lowered weak syllables; 15 tendency to narrow range	13, 10 tendency to wide range; 15, 9 final rise; 2, 14 fall with change of direction; 8, 3	8, 14 wide range / final rise; 2, 9 fall with change of direction; 10, 3 of direction; 13, 1 lowered weak syllables	8, 1 tendency to wide range; 10, 12 final rise; 9, 11 final fall with change of direction; 2, 15
UNPLEAS- **ANT**	6, 12 little or no change of direction; 16, 5 raised weak syllables	4, 7 final fall, especially with narrow range; 6, 16 fall with raised weak syllables; 5	16, 5 narrow range / final fall; 15, 6 raised weak syllables; 4	4, 16 final fall, especially without change of direction; 6, 14 direction; 5, 7
II **INTEREST**	2, 12 final rise; 3, 13 lowered weak syllables; 1, 10 tendency to narrow range; 8	10, 9 tendency to wide range; 5, 8 change of direction; 7	8, 1 tendency to wide range; 2, 11 final rise; 3, 14 lowered weak syllables; 10, 13	10, 8 final rise; 1, 3 final fall with change of direction; 11, 2; 9, 12
LACK OF **INTEREST**	6, 15 narrow range; 5, 7 tendency to final fall; 4, 9 raised weak syllables; 16	4, 6 narrow range, little or no change of direction; 3, 9	6, 15 narrow range; 4, 5 tendency to final fall; 16 raised weak syllables	4, 16 tendency to final fall, especially without change of direction; 6, 5; 14
III **AUTHORI-** **TATIVE**	5, 12 tendency to wide range; 2, 8; 10, 9; 3 tendency to narrow range	4, 6 final fall; 14	*no discernible tendencies*	4, 6 tendency to final fall; 7 no perturbed weak syllables
SUBMISSIVE	6, 9 narrow range, perturbed weak syllables; 7	1, 2 final rise; 15		3, 12 final rise; 15 perturbed weak syllables

speakers of other kinds of English, *eg* RP and Scots. Presumably the most nearly usual contours on given sentence types will receive 'pleasant' or at least 'neutral' ratings; almost certainly the various contours will be differently ordered by the different speech communities, depending on their own norms.

For instance, the fall-plus-low-rise contour, no 7, was rated by the American group in this experiment, on the yes-or-no question, as 'bored, polite, confident, insincere, relaxed, disapproving, arrogant, impatient, emphatic, agreeable', whereas one would expect it to be rated as more pleasant by speakers of an accent such as RP in which it is described as the typical contour for this kind of question.

Note

[1] The work described here was carried out with the benefit of research funds from the Haskins Laboratories, New York, in connection with a grant from the Carnegie Corporation of New York. It is a pleasure to acknowledge my debt to both organizations.

The factor analysis mentioned in the text was carried out by Dr Boris Semeonoff of the Department of Psychology of Edinburgh University, who also supervised the calculation of rank difference correlations. I am very grateful for his help and advice.

My colleagues in the Phonetics Department at Edinburgh have been kind enough to discuss this project with me at length, which has clarified the assumptions underlying the experiment; they have also made helpful suggestions regarding further experiments of this kind.

Bibliography

ALLPORT, G. W. and CANTRIL, H. 'Judging personality from voice', *J. Soc. Psychol*, 5, 1934, 37.

BORST, J. M. and COOPER, F. S. 'Speech research devices based on a channel Vocoder', *J. Acoust. Soc. Amer.*, 29, 1957, 777.

CHANG, N-C. T. 'Tone and intonation in the Chengtu dialect (Szechuan, China)', *Phonetica*, 2, 1958, 59.

FAIRBANKS, G. and HOAGLIN, L. W. 'An experimental study of the durational characteristics of the voice during the expression of emotion', *Speech Mono.*, 8, 1941, 85.

FAIRBANKS, G. and PRONOVOST, W. 'An experimental study of the pitch characteristics of the voice during the expression of emotion', *Speech Mono.*, 6, 1939, 87.

KRECH, D. and CRUTCHFIELD, R. S. *Theory and Problems of Social Psychology*, New York, 1948.

OSGOOD, C. E., SUCI, G. J. and TANNENBAUM, P. H. *The Measurement of Meaning*, Urbana, Illinois, 1957.

STREVENS, P. 'The performance of PAT', *Revista do Laboratorio de Fonetica Experimental, Universidade de Coimbra*, 4, 1959, 5.

THURSTON, L. L. and CHAVE, E. J. *The Measurement of Attitude*, Chicago, 1929.

Index